# P

## The
## henomenology
## of Merleau-Ponty

*A Search for the Limits
of Consciousness*

# The
# Phenomenology
# of Merleau-Ponty

## by GARY BRENT MADISON
Docteur en Philosophie de l'Universite de Paris

*Foreword by PAUL RICOEUR
translated from the French by the Author*

 *Ohio University Press*
ATHENS, OHIO

Originally published as:
*La phenomenologie de Merleau-Ponty:*
*une recherche des limites de la conscience*
© Editions Klincksieck, 1973

Madison, Gary Brent.
  The phenomenology of Merleau-Ponty.

  (Series in Continental Thought: V.3)
  Translation of: La phenoménologie de Merleau-Ponty.
  Bibliography: p.
  1. Merleau-Ponty, Maurice, 1908–1961.
2. Phenomenology.  I. Title.    II. Series.
B2430.M3764M3213      194        81–4026
ISBN 0-8214-0448-2                AACR2
ISBN 0-8214-0644-2 (pbk.)

*Ψυχῆς πείρατα ἰὼν οὐχ ἀν ἐξεύροιο, πᾶσαν*
*ἐπιπορευόμενος ὁδόν · οὕτω βαθὸν λόγον ἔχει.*

You would not find out the limits of the psyche, even though
you should travel every road: so deep a logos does it have.

HERACLITUS

# Contents

# List of Abbreviations

## English

| | |
|---|---|
| AD | *Adventures of the Dialectic,* trans. Joseph Bien (Evanston: Northwestern University Press, 1973) |
| CAL | *Consciousness and the Acquisition of Language,* trans. Hugh J. Silverman (Evanston: Northwestern University Press, 1973) |
| HT | *Humanism and Terror,* trans. John O'Neill (Boston: Beacon Press, 1969) |
| IPP | *In Praise of Philosophy,* trans. John Wild and James M. Edie (Evanston: Northwestern University Press, 1963) |
| PhP | *Phenomenology of Perception,* trans. Colin Smith (London: Routledge and Kegan Paul, 1962) |
| PriP | *The Primacy of Perception,* trans. James M. Edie (Evanston: Northwestern University Press, 1964) |
| S | *Signs,* trans. Richard C. McCleary (Evanston: Northwestern University Press, 1964) |
| SB | *The Structure of Behavior,* trans. Alden L. Fisher (Boston: Beacon Press, 1963) |

SNS         *Sense and Non-Sense,* trans. Hubert L. Dreyfus and Patricia Allen
            Dreyfus (Evanston: Northwestern University Press, 1964)
TFL         *Themes from the Lectures at the Collège de France 1952–1960,*
            trans. John O'Neill (Evanston: Northwestern University Press, 1970)
VI          *The Visible and the Invisible,* trans. Alphonso Lingis (Evanston:
            Northwestern University Press, 1968)

## French

AD          *Les Aventures de la dialectique* (Paris: Gallimard, 1955)
BP          *Bulletin de psychologie,* Maurice Merleau-Ponty à la Sorbonne,
            xviii, 236 (Nov. 1964)
EP          *Eloge de la philosophie* (Paris: Gallimard, 1953)
HT          *Humanisme et terreur* (Paris: Gallimard, 1947)
Inédit      "Un inédit de Merleau-Ponty," *Revue de Métaphysique et de
            morale,* no. 4 (Oct.–Dec. 1962)
OE          *L'Oeil et l'esprit* (Paris: Gallimard, 1964)
PP          *Phénoménologie de la perception* (Paris: Gallimard, 1945)
RC          *Résumés de cours, Collège de France 1952–1960* (Paris: Gallimard,
            1968)
S           *Signes* (Paris: Gallimard, 1960)
SC          *La Structure du comportement* (Paris: Presses Universitaires de
            France, 1942)
SHP         *Les Sciences de l'homme et la phénoménologie* (Paris: Centre de
            documentation universitaire, 1953)
SNS         *Sens et non-sens* (Paris: Éditions Nagel, 1948; 4th ed. 1963)
VI          *Le Visible et l'invisible* (Paris: Gallimard, 1964)

# Foreword

This work by Gary Madison is to be recommended because of the deliberate choice which throughout guides his analyses: that of an "ontological" reading of Merleau-Ponty's entire work. The focal point is thus shifted from the *Phenomenology of Perception* towards *The Visible and the Invisible* and those other finished and published texts—"Eye and Mind" in particular—which, more than merely announcing the final shift (in Merleau-Ponty's philosophy), actually accomplished it although only in part.

This methodological option is fruitful; it allows the author to release Merleau-Ponty's first two works, *The Structure of Behavior* and the *Phenomenology of Perception,* from their immediate horizon and thus withdraw them from the double polemic that exhausts a good part of Merleau-Ponty's energy: on the one hand the polemic against naturalism and the psychology of behavior, and on the other the polemic against the intellectualism of neo-Kantianism and the reflective conception of Husserl's phenomenological philosophy in the *Ideas* and the *Cartesian Meditations.* I might add that this same concern for rereading the first works in the light of the final ontology discourages us from subjecting Merleau-Ponty's thought to a measurement in terms of doctrines which have occupied the scene since his death, whether they have sprung from Structuralism or Freudianism; indeed, to do so would be to withdraw the reading of his first works from a concern with an old polemic which limited the author's horizon only to subject the reading to one which limits our own.

To assess the early work, which has at least the merit of existing, in terms of a project whose full realization was interrupted by death is also to raise another set of difficulties. Does one not run the risk of projecting back into the early work problems which did not exist when it was conceived? Worse still: does one not run the risk of weakening the finished work by placing it under the critical gaze of the unfinished work? In particular, does one not run the risk, in drawing one's argument from the kind of self-criticism that the final ontology exercises in regard to the initial phenomenological positivism, of justifying and reinforcing criticisms directed to his work from the outside and which today tend to minimize its importance?

The author has lucidly run these various risks in a way which seems to me to render complete justice to Merleau-Ponty's entire work. Indeed, the sort of relation he perceives between the *Phenomenology of Perception* on the one hand and *The Visible and the Invisible* on the other is neither a developmental relation of the implicit to the explicit, nor one of a denial of the explicit in the name of a new implicit which would not itself have attained the maturity of a developed expression; it is rather a relation which is explicitly suggested by Merleau-Ponty himself and which conforms to his own conception of philosophy, namely, the relation of "reappropriation" (*reprise*). The text quoted in the Introduction to this study expresses it admirably: "We cannot define a philospher's thought solely in terms of what he has achieved. We have to take account of what at the very end still he was struggling to think. Naturally, this unthought thought [*impensé*] must be shown to be present through the words which circumscribe and delimit it. But then these words must be understood through their lateral implications as much as through their manifest or frontal significance." Applying to Merleau-Ponty this concept of an unthought thought, the author can consider that "there emerges from the various texts, in their mutual referrings back and forth, a meaning which is nowhere fully expressed but which is present everywhere and which makes all the writings spread out over the course of the author's history belong to a single development effected through many changes of direction. This path winds through Merleau-Ponty's various writings, binding them together; and it is nothing other than this invisible bond that we are going to attempt to bring out and pursue."

In short, Gary Madison intends to read Merleau-Ponty as the latter read Husserl when he said: "We should like to try to evoke this unthought thought in Husserl". (S, 160; S, 202)

Hence it is indeed *The Structure of Behavior* and the *Phenomenology of Perception* that we read along with Gary Madison, but from the point of view of the excess of the signified over the signifying. In addition to not lingering in the polemics referred to above, we go directly to the theme which has the greatest strength, and I mean not only the greatest force but also the greatest resource: the circularity between the symbolism of the body and the play of intersignification which runs throughout the various profiles of the perceived—the emergence of a transforming and creative existence which impresses a movement of transcendence or verticality onto the horizontal relation of the body to the world—the rootedness or inherence of the *Cogito* in the body and the world at the level of opinion, of the primordial faith from which all our knowledge arises.

Having thus mastered the major problematic freed from its circumstantial polemics, the author can discern, certainly not the last philosophy, but its hollowed-out place in the difficulties of the first phenomenology. Indeed, what exactly is this "ground of inhuman nature" into which the circular play between the perceiving body and the perceived vanishes? What is this intentionality which would like to protect itself from the idealistic implications of Husserlian phenomenology and which nonetheless remains dependent on a philosophy of consciousness and of the subject? What is this world which we do not constitute as reflective consciousness but which we indeed seem to project as a tacit or bodily *Cogito*? Are we still in a philosophy of reflection or are we in a philosophy which, in order to take account of the unreflected, is beginning to break up the vocabulary of noesis and noema, subjectivity, and the *Cogito*, but without shifting elsewhere its originating source?

Gary Madison can indeed speak in Merleau-Ponty's own voice when he characterizes as "bad" the ambiguity attributed to this philosophy.

The first movement—by way of painting—is perhaps the most successful. In the first place, the author seeks to find in the sequence of the three writings—"Cézanne's Doubt," "Indirect Language and the Voices of Silence," "Eye and Mind"—the very model for all the other transformations: In 'Cézanne's Doubt' (1945) the author's attention is fixed essentially on the attempt of the *painter* to express being, to capture it alive on his canvas. 'Indirect Language and the Voices of Silence' (1952) appears as a transition between this phenomenological approach and a more intensive interrogation; it sets out in fact the first elements of an *ontology* of painting. Finally, in 'Eye and Mind' (1960) a sort of "reversal" becomes manifest in that now painting is envisaged rather as an ontological function, as a demand, it would seem, that Being places on man. The painter's operation is here viewed as an operation of Being, as the primordial and privileged instance where Being *manifests and sees itself.*

In addition, the author shows the decisive importance of a meditation on painting for the constitution of the central theme of visibility; art, Merleau-Ponty could have said with Klee, "does not reproduce the visible; it makes things be visible." It neither imitates nor constructs; it expresses that which in some way was waiting to be said. Thus the theme of expression—in the double sense of expression *of* Being and expression *by* the artist—tears us in one stroke away from the philosophy of the subject and the object.

Above all, however, the passage by way of Merleau-Ponty's writings on painting brings out the special importance of the third essay, "Eye and Mind," which is on a level with *The Visible and the Invisible* itself; it is here, indeed, that new expressions make their appearance: "It is, therefore, mute Being which itself comes to show forth its own meaning." A Transcendence becomes visible which "no longer hangs over man: he becomes, strangely, its privileged bearer." Being wants to see itself, wants to express itself. Painting testifies to this better than language, precisely because it is mute and reveals universal Being without the aid of concepts.

A philosophical reversal has thus been taken: perception is called vision, the body becomes the flesh, Being is given a capital; these terminological changes indicate that everything has "shifted." Gary Madison expresses it well: the key word is the word "flesh"; it points to the essential: a visible-seeing body which is no longer a view on the world but a vision occurring in the world, an invisible which is the other side of its seeing power, a vision which is the visible itself seeing itself.

At the same time, the chapter on language which, by itself, might appear weak, not only in Gary Madison but in Merleau-Ponty himself, is reinforced by this powerful subversion which moves perception towards vision and the body towards the flesh. Gary Madison seems to me to have hit the nail on the head in his assessment of the chapter on language in the *Phenomenology of Perception.* It is above all here that Merleau-Ponty the philosopher remained a prisoner of his fight against intellectualism and reflective philosophy, whence his concern to bring language down to its perceptual and bodily foundation rather than guide it towards its proper field of actualization. But Gary Madison also seems to me to be fully justified when he makes use of the texts on painting in order to discern the unthought thought of the philosophy of expression, which is Merleau-Ponty's real philosophy of language. Everything which is said about the excess of the signified in relation to the signifying, about the open and indefinite power of the signified, takes on a consistency when one relates it to what is said elsewhere about the inauguration of the world's visibility by means of painting. At the same time, the resistances put up by a philosophy of consciousness and the subject, entrenched in a theory of speaking speech (*la parole parlante*), appear even more eloquent, even though the philosopher did not fail to note the ontological implications of his own remarks on the "instructive spontaneity" which refer to a power of speaking which is neither a constituting consciousness nor a perceptual consciousness but something like a "cultural logos."

As to the third path, the one which goes by way of a reflection on philosophy itself, of particular interest to the reader will be the conflict which he sees take place between several possible philosophical projects: a deliberately criticist project, in *The Structure of Behavior* and even still in the *Phenomenology of Perception* (equaling reflection to the unreflected); an existential philosophy close to the late Husserl whose "genetic" program inclines it towards an "archeology" of meaning; a philosophy of the ascent of meaning whose "teleology" brings it into the vicinity of Hegel but whose keen sense of contingency prevents it from finding fulfillment in a total reflection and assigns to it the destiny of the unhappy consciousness; finally, a philosophy of originating being which would ally it with Heidegger were it not for the rejection of any notion of a difference and a leap between being and beings. This in the last resort throws the philosopher over and over again onto the side of Husserl's unthought thought: better to do battle with the self-consciousness of modern philosophy than attempt to take the short cut by way of the Presocratics; ontology will therefore never be "direct" but always "indirect."

And thus this play of affinities and aversions allows us to see something of the difficulty that the philosopher must have experienced in discovering the "locus" of his philosophy and the meaning of the philosophical act itself. Does he not invoke more than once, as though despairing of his case, "the barbarous principle Schelling spoke of"?

It is thus in a triple way that Gary Madison prepares his reader for the difficult deciphering of *The Visible and the Invisible.* The tone of the reading is correct: it is at once an "introduction to a non-existent thought" and the painstaking explicitation of a thought which "is beginning to make itself explicit." The relation to the earlier work is now treated in its own right. It is a matter in the first instance of a radical calling into question, as this text indicates: "The tacit Cogito does not, of course, solve these problems. In disclosing it as I did in *Ph.P.* [*Phenomenology of Perception*] I did not arrive at a solution (my chapter on the Cogito is not connected with the chapter on speech): on the contrary I posed a problem. The tacit Cogito should make understood how language is not impossible, but cannot make understood how it is possible——There remains the problem of the passage from the perceptual meaning to the language meaning, from behavior to thematization. Moreover the thematization itself must be understood as a behavior of a higher degree——the relation between the thematization and the behavior is a dialectical relation: language realizes, by breaking the silence, what the silence wished and did not obtain." (VI, 175–6; *VI*, 229–30) All the former concepts are subjected to the same shift in meaning that one can see as well in the difficulties of the first philosophy as in the excess of its meaning in relation to its own expression. What struck me as convincing in this estimation of *The Visible and the Invisible* is the author's concern to make his reader participate in the invention of a new vocabulary—*flesh, intertwining, chiasm,* etc.—under the pressure of a not yet worked out experience. It then becomes possible to measure the distance between the tacit *Cogito* of a philosophy which remained a philosophy of consciousness and the flesh, which has become an attribute of Being. At the same time is gathered together everything which had been anticipated in a philosophy of painting, for which the hollow of the visible, that is, the invisible, was vision itself, for which, consequently, the invisible of vision was the very power of the visible; *The Visible and the Invisible* speaks in an identical way of this "logos which is silently pronounced in every sensible thing."

The reader will be thankful to Gary Madison for not having tried to *write The Visible and the Invisible* in attempting to *read* it. The enigmas are only more enigmatic: what is a negative philosophy which remains a philosophy of the visible (or of the invisible of the visible)? How does nothingness remain a "methodology" if it is not to be set up in a noctural transcendence? In what sense is Being—or is it not—the opening of the world or the dynamism of nature? Do we, however, still understand these words after *The Visible and the Invisible?*

In what sense can undivided Being be said to call for the "deflagration," the "fission," which bears the task of consciousness and the *Cogito?*

More than anything, the most penetrating view which Gary Madison proposes of Merleau-Ponty's final ontology concerns the paradox of contingency; this paradox emerges from the first philosophy, is then sharpened by Merleau-Ponty's meditation on Christianity, Pascal, and Malebranche. The author is perhaps right in seeing here the heart of the late philosophy: existential contingency is now taken up by a movement of coming to light of Being itself which is no longer in any way an "accident." If this is the way it is, is it not to Schelling, who moreover is referred to, and to the philosophies of an absolute genesis of the finite, that one would have to relate Merleau-Ponty rather than to Heidegger and Husserl? Or would it not rather be necessary to say that Husserl's unthought thought is the one which Fink enunciated in his famous article in *Kant-Studien* (1934), when he asserted that the last (or first) question of phenomenology is that of the origin of the world?

Paul Ricoeur

# Translator's Preface

Translation is never an easy task. It is difficult because it calls for skill and technical competence. It demands a mastery of the syntactical rules of two different languages as well as a knowledge of how the rules are interrelated. It also requires an extensive knowledge of semantical equivalences, of the "meanings" of the words of one language in the other. And translation is difficult for still other, more serious, reasons.

For translation, as Heidegger has said, is interpretation. This means that it requires, in addition to technical skill, the specifically human ability to emphathetically and understandingly penetrate into what is humanly other. Translation—in the case at least of literature and philosophy, if not of science and technology—is applied hermeneutics. It is therefore not a science or a technical skill which could be done by a machine or programed into a computer, but an *art* which only humans, qua humans, are capable of performing properly. As an instance of hermeneutics, translation is the attempt to make what is distant and alien close and familiar. To interpret an ancient text is difficult enough in itself, but when the distance to be overcome is not only temporal but cultural and linguistic as well, the difficulties are compounded. They are doubly compounded when, as in the present instance, the task is that of translating, not just another author, but a second author's interpretation of that author.

No doubt, these difficulties are attenuated to some extent when the author to be translated is oneself. Attenuated perhaps, but not eli.ıinated. To be sure, I have better access than would another to w .at was going on in my—the author's—mind when I originally wrote this book in French. Nevertheless, the meaning of a text cannot be purely and simply equated with the author's intended meaning.[1] A text is something which exists in its own right and which must be taken on its own terms. After all, it is the text one translates, not the author. And because to translate is to interpret, a translation is never "the same" as the original.

Interpretation, one should therefore add, is distortion. To *translate* a meaning is to *transfer* it into another context (*translatio = transferre*), and in this carrying over something of the original is always lost in the process. This is in fact why I had originally decided to write this book in French. Working with the standard English translations of Merleau-Ponty would, it seemed to me, have meant working with something which was *not quite* Merleau-Ponty himself. I would then have been interpreting, not Merleau-Ponty, but a translation-interpretation of Merleau-Ponty. I could, of course, have done my own translations of the original writings but this too would have been an interpretation, even if my own, and it would have made of the book too much a monologue and not enough a dialogue. Moreover, how could I properly translate Merleau-Ponty when to do so is to interpret him, and I had not yet worked out my interpretation because it required an understanding of the texts themselves? Alternatively, I could have quoted Merleau-Ponty in French while commenting on him in English. This, though, would have made for an awkward text which only bilingual persons could read. All in all, it seemed to me far simpler to learn how to express myself directly in French. This was not easy; it took time and necessitated a thoroughgoing *dépaysement*, both physical and mental, but it did enable me to avoid an additional layer of interpretive difficulties.

The difficulties I circumvented qua author, however, return to haunt me qua translator. As a means of coping with them, I have adopted and attempted to follow what could be called the "principle of the middle way." That is, while I have attempted to render the meaning of the French original (both mine and Merleau-Ponty's) intelligible in grammatically correct English, I have not attempted to make the text appear as though it had been composed in English. This is, in my opinion, what a correct hermeneutical theory demands. Interpretation is making the distant and alien close and familiar—so that one may *understand* it. It is, though, *something other* that is being understood. Thus one understands it properly only so long as one recognizes that it is indeed something other that one is understanding. A translation which would be so "free" that it completely obliterated the stylistic peculiarities of the original would, it seems, constitute *too* great a distortion of the meaning of the original. When we read Merleau-Ponty, we are not reading an Anglo-Saxon author. It is a fact that Merleau-Ponty wrote in French and not in English, and, as a general rule, one does not write philosophy in French the same way one does in English (nor would I have written this book in the same way had I written it in English). Translation should not make us forget this fact. A good translation of Merleau-Ponty should not do away with what, from the point of view of English-speaking philosophy, will appear as something of an oddity. For oddity here is part of the very meaning of the original; that is, it is due to the linguistic alienness of the original (which is, as far as we are concerned, an objective characteristic of the text). While bringing the alien closer, interpretation must not suppress distance altogether. Moreover, as Merleau-Ponty himself so much insisted, peculiarity of style is precisely what constitutes specificity of meaning. *How one says something* is not irrelevant to *what* one says.[2]

The following example can serve to illustrate my meaning. One of Merleau-Ponty's favorite expressions is *le fondemental*. This is translated by one of his official translators (John O'Neill in *Themes from the Lectures*) as "what is fundamental." I have consistently translated *le fondemental* as "the fundamental." "What is fundamental" is perhaps better English than "the fundamental," but is not at all the same thing as *le fondemental;* it is more of a paraphrase than a translation. French uses the definite article much more than English does; and when, in a case such as this, it was possible to use the definite article in English, I did so. For the definite article indicates that one is dealing with a very definite philosophical concept. (The relation between French and English in this regard is not altogether unlike that which exists between Greek and Latin. To a great extent it was, as Bruno Snell pointed out in his now classic *The Discovery of the Mind*, because Greek, unlike Latin, possessed the definite article that it was able, by affixing a definite article to an adjective (e.g., "the good"), to transform common words into abstract concepts ("the good" is not at all the same thing as "goodness"). In other words, the stylistic peculiarity of the Greek language is what gave rise to philosophy in the first place.)

All things considered, the actual work of translation can teach one that there is a residual but nonetheless insurpassable futility in attempting to understand the other (and, as well, in attempting to understand ourselves, for, as Merleau-Ponty remarked, we are in some respects for ourselves an other). The work of translation reminds one that although we can always overcome obstacles and communicate, if we so will, we can never hope to overcome definitively our mutual misunderstandings. We simply have to live with them.

A few remarks on specifics follow.

When quoting Merleau-Ponty, I used the existing standard English translations. But I freely altered them when it has appeared desirable to do so. I did so for one or more of the following reasons: to adhere to my "principle of the middle way"; to preserve uniformity in terminology; to better bring out what I take to be the meaning of the French; to correct a faulty translation.

Since I have altered translations quite often and often in minor ways, I have not bothered to indicate when I have done so. My reference to the standard English translations is, in any event, meant only as a convenience to the reader; in all cases I have based my interpretation, not on the English, but solely on the French. This is why I have always cited the French pagination along with the English (English first, French second, e.g., PhP, 100; *PP*, 110); the reader who so desires can verify the translation for himself. (If only a French reference is given, it is because the word or phrase quoted is not to be found, as I have translated it, in the standard English translation.)

All translations from works cited in French (e.g., Hyppolite's *Etudes sur Marx et Hegel*) are always my own.

My use of punctuation, especially for quotations, does not follow standard American practice. I have adopted features common to both French and British punctuation, which seem to me more logical and more economical than the corresponding American features. Since I often quote only segments of sentences, I would be obliged in American practice to add ellipsis points at the beginning and/or the end of the segment. This proliferation of dots would have given the printed page an unsightly appearance. Thus, for instance, if a period *follows* end of quotation marks, instead of preceding them, this indicates that I have not quoted the sentence in its entirety and that a period does not follow the word in the French.

As translator I have taken the liberty of adding two appendices to this book. The first, "Concerning Merleau-Ponty: Two Readings of His Work," deals with problems of interpretation and is the record of a public discussion between Th. F. Geraets and me of our respective readings of Merleau-Ponty. The second, "Merleau-Ponty and the Counter-Tradition," pursues the comparison of Merleau-Ponty with Husserl and Heidegger to be found in appendix I and, in addition, situates him within the overall history of philosophy. It also fills a lack in my book in that it sets out Merleau-Ponty's position in regard to political philosophy.

Speaking both as author and translator, I would like to express my gratitude to Paul Ricoeur for his help in bringing the original manuscript into being, to my parents for their encouragement in this endeavor, to Jean-Pierre Tafforeau for his assistance in eliminating many of the grammatical and stylistic imperfections from the first draft of the original, to Robert Lechner for his concern in seeing an English translation of the book appear, and to Patricia Elisar and Helen of Ohio University Press for their help throughout the time of translation and publication.

G.B.M.
*McMaster University*
*August-September 1979*

# Introduction

Maurice Merleau-Ponty died on May 3, 1961, at the age of fifty-three at the moment when he had barely begun a new and important stage in the working out of his philosophy. Thus this thought which has been referred to as "arduous and disconcerting," which has been called a philosophy of ambiguity, terminates in incompletion and in ambiguity. Under the impact of feelings aroused by this unexpected and tragic death, Paul Ricoeur gave expression to a widespread feeling in saying that the incompletion of a philosophy of incompleteness is doubly disconcerting. And he went to the bottom of things when he remarked that what was tragic in this death, in this interruption of a thought, "is that the philosophical basis of the major book of 1945—the *Phenomenology of Perception*—had for a long time been called into question." Indeed, the intention of the philosopher's last, unfinished manuscript, *The Visible and the Invisible,* was to take up, deepen, and correct his entire philosophy as he had previously formulated it.

This is to say that before his death Merleau-Ponty had become aware of the insufficiencies of the argument in the *Phenomenology of*

*Perception.* What he had at that time looked upon as the "fundamental philosophical problem," that of rationality, he had also thought he could resolve in a satisfactory way by postulating, as the ultimate ground of *reason,* an absolutely contingent *fact* which was itself without reason: our bodily insertion in the world. It is however doubtful if a philosophy such as this—a like mixture of realist and idealist themes—can genuinely be defended; and, in any event, Merleau-Ponty himself recognized afterwards that what the *Phenomenology* teaches is a "bad ambiguity." We can thus observe a development in his thought: we see him, in his late writings, returning to this question of the ground, the ἀρχή, of rationality, and we see him in the process of taking the question up again in a new spirit. It is this deepening development of his thought—a development which, starting out from a "phenomenological positivism," veers afterwards towards a "negative ontology"—that we propose to follow more closely in this study. What interests us is the *meaning (sens)* of his philosophy, the *direction (sens)* of his thought.

Our analysis will therefore be essentially chronological and will attempt to intercept and follow the genesis of Merleau-Ponty's ontology, the development of this phenomenology, this philosophy of consciousness, which resolutely sets out to discover the limits of consciousness. Thus our first chapter will be concerned with the two major works which form in a way the basis or starting point of his philosophy: *The Structure of Behavior* and the *Phenomenology of Perception.* In the three following chapters which treat, respectively, of painting, language, and philosophy, our analysis will unfold in a series of progressive approximations; thus these chapters will not make up so many stages on the road traversed by the philosopher's thought, but rather each chapter will follow, in regard to a specific question, the entire road which leads from phenomenology up to ontology. Basically, therefore, it will be the same theme that each of these three chapters (2, 3 and 4) will develop, but each one will do so in its own way and will progressively clarify the meaning and the direction of Merleau-Ponty's thought as it takes shape. Finally, in chapter 5, we will attempt to grasp the final meaning of this thought and to "close the gap" by insisting on its inner circularity: if Merleau-Ponty's last philosophy (his ontology) is to all appearances a follow-up to his earlier thought (his phenomenology) and is erected on it, this basis itself (phenomenology) is in the last analysis understandable only through the (ontological) transformations that his later thought imposes on it.

However, before taking up this reading we should specify just what we understand by a "reading." To assert that this essay will be an exposition of Merleau-Ponty's philosophy is to assert that we are assigning ourselves the task of saying what Merleau-Ponty meant to say. But what, precisely, is the relation between our saying and the saying of the philosopher? The following questions arise: how can one *remain* faithful to a thought when one's exposition of it is already a *reappropriation* of it? How can there be exactitude in difference? For, indeed, no matter how exact it be, by its very nature a commentary differs from that which it comments on.

It seems to us that this question can be resolved if we direct our attention to the *work* in question rather than lose ourselves in speculations as to what the man who wrote it might have been thinking in his inner life (a temptation which is all the greater because Merleau-Ponty's work was interrupted by his unexpected death). The fact is that a work has two sides to it. As others have already pointed out, the writer writes in order to know what it is he has to say. For him the meaning of his writings does not lie in these writings, behind him in what he has done; it lies rather beyond him in what he has not yet done, and his entire work is the attempt to realize and win possession of his intentions. In this sense, the writer writes precisely in order to know what he *has* written. Whereas for the writer the meaning of what he has written resides in what he is going to write and has not yet written, for the reader the meaning of the work is located in the work itself, in what has, as a matter of fact, been written. He thus looks to what the writer has actually said in order to discover his meaning. When a writer is still alive, the reader can always defer his judgment and await further clarifications from the author. But when an author dies, the work itself is affected. Henceforth it has only one side, the one it presents to the reader. The ultimate meaning of the work is no longer suspended beyond it in what the author is going to say; it is entirely within the work. The work forever ceases to be the living instrument of a life in search of itself and definitively becomes a kind of thing. It is a cultural acquisition and possesses only that which is available in it. At the moment of its author's death, the work no longer lives except outside of itself, in us, its readers. Hence the question arises: how must it be *read*?

Now, what is unique about Merleau-Ponty's work is that it it-self teaches us the way in which to read it. This happens because Merleau-Ponty always found his own style of thinking and always came back to himself after starting from a reading of others; and he often reflected on what reading should be. We have therefore only to recall what he has said on this subject and follow his own requirements when we read his works.

What must first of all be emphasized is that if a reading, as we learn from Merleau-Ponty, abstracts from the author's intentions which are unfilled because of death and takes as its object the work alone, the work itself is not for all that the mere addition of the words and sentences which to all appearances constitute it. As a cultural acquisition, the property of everyone and no one, the work contains, in addition to what it explicitly says, what it says only in a lateral way: "We cannot define a philosopher's thought solely in terms of what he has achieved. We have to take account of what at the very end still he was struggling to think. Naturally, this unthought thought must be shown to be present through the words which circumscribe and delimit it. But then these words must be understood through their lateral implications as much as through their manifest or frontal signi-ficance." (TFL, 114; *RC,* 160) Behind the *visibilia* of a work there is an invisible which is equally essential to it and equally its own, and which in fact guarantees the cohesion and the meaning of what is visible. This is what Merleau-Ponty calls the work's "unthought thought" (*impensé*). There emerges from the various texts, in their mutual referrings back and forth, a meaning which is nowhere fully expressed, but which is present everywhere and which makes all the writings spread out over the course of the author's history belong to a single development effected through many changes of direction. This path winds through Merleau-Ponty's various writings, binding them together; and it is nothing other than this invisible bond that we are going to attempt to bring out and pursue.

In doing so, moreover, we are but taking up on our own account Merleau-Ponty's own project in regard to Husserl. As he wrote in 1959: "Just as the perceived world endures only through the reflections, shadows, levels, and horizons between things (which are not things and are not nothing, but on the contrary mark out by themselves the fields of possible variation in the same thing and the same world), so the works and thought of a philosopher are also made of certain articulations between things said. There is no dilemma of objective interpretation or arbitrariness with respect to these articulations, since they are not *objects* of thought, since (like shadow and reflection) they would be destroyed by being subjected to analytic observation or taken out of context, and since we can be faithful to and find them only by thinking afresh." And he added, "We should like to try to evoke this unthought thought ["*impensé*"] of Husserl's." (S, 160; *S*, 202) This "unthought thought" is what could also be called style or inner meaning or, as Merleau-Ponty referred to it in one of his courses at the Sorbonne, the work's "intention." To the students of the Sorbonne he said that the "history of philosophy can never be the simple transcription of what the philosophers have said or written.... As a matter of fact, as soon as one approaches two texts, and opposes to them a third, one begins to interpret and to distinguish what is really proper to the thought of Descartes, let us say, and, on the contrary, what is only accidental. Thus in Cartesianism, as it is defined by the texts, one begins to see an intention that the historian has taken the initiative in singling out, and this choice evidently depends on his own way of encountering the problems of philosophy. This history of philosophy cannot be separated from philosophy." (PriP, 46; *SHP*, 4)

This text says just about everything: (1) there is a never fully expressed central intention at work in the texts themselves which ties them together; (2) it is up to *us,* the readers of the work, to reveal this intention, it is we who must "single it out", who must think it "afresh"; (3) this intention is in the last analysis the intention of the work as a whole. This last remark calls for a few words of clarification.

As historians it is our intention to disengage the meaning of the work, that is, the meaning of *all* of the author's writings in their entirety. The work is precisely that which is wholly there, and the task of interpretation is to express *the* meaning which transpires in it. In this sense, interpretation works with the conviction that, as Heidegger has said, "every thinker thinks but a single thought." But any faithful interpretation is equally conscious of the fact that this central and in some way single thought is a historical thought, that is, that the work was done through gropings worked out in contingency. Interpretation is thus, as it were, a regressive reading: one attempts to show how the work arrived at its full meaning, for every path includes its twists and turnings.

This therefore is the method we propose to follow. We have absolutely no intention of projecting Merleau-Ponty's writings beyond themselves and of speculating on what the author might or should have said if he could have continued to follow and disentangle the thread of his thoughts, projecting more light on what he had written, which must, henceforth, carry for us and for always a certain aura of ambiguity. Our only aim is to disengage and lead to its full expression the deep meaning, the invisible life, the inner movement of the work itself, even though the work is an unfinished creation, recalling these words of Merleau-Ponty's about the dead whom we attempt to understand after their disappearance: "The only memory which respects them is the one which maintains the actual use they have made of themselves and of their world, the accent of their freedom in the incompleteness of their lives." (IPP, 65; *EP,* 105)

We thus turn to the use Merleau-Ponty made of his world and his life, a use which for us is his work; and we attempt to speak out the quasi-silent meaning which inhabits it by lending it the support of our voice. If we succeed in freeing and delivering up this meaning, this study will, it is true, be less a presentation or a commentary than an interpretive reappropriation. Let us then return with Merleau-Ponty to the things themselves and to our shadowy life, to that source beneath us full of inexhaustible riches, and let us attempt with him to wrest from it its secret. Let us follow his thought in its constant attempt to awaken a primordial, covered over, and forgotten logos and make the "voices of silence" speak.

## Chapter I

# The Phenomenal Field: Being in the World

Nihil est in intellectu
quod non prius fuerit
in sensu.

## I.  Discovery of Being in the World

WITH *The Structure of Behavior* Merleau-Ponty accosts the problems which will occupy him in the rest of his work. As well by its content as by its incompleteness in itself, this first book (finished, it appears, in 1938 but published only in 1942) constitutes an introduction to all his future work. The contrast between this youthful work and *Eye and Mind,* for instance, the last writing published in his lifetime, is striking. In the first work Merleau-Ponty speaks the language of psychologists and scientists; in the last work he has completely discovered his own tone of voice, one which is so foreign to scientists that it has made some people feel they are listening to a mystic of Nature. If, however, we wish to come to hear and understand this voice which speaks of the Flesh, of Nature, of the Earth, and of deep Being, we must listen to it attentively here at the moment when it begins to speak and discover itself. Merleau-Ponty's itinerary—that

1

path which leads to vertical Being—has its point of departure in *The Structure of Behavior* where the author opens up and traces in a first rough way the boundaries of the field of phenomenal Being. We shall first set forth briefly the various forms of behavior described by Merleau-Ponty in this work and then, before passing to the description itself of the phenomenal field constituted by the *Phenomenology of Perception,* we shall pause to take note of some of the guiding ideas which emerge from this reading.

## 1.   The Structures of Behavior

He who reads *The Structure of Behavior* after the *Phenomenology of Perception* (and this is the way most readers proceed) cannot but note the great difference in tone between the two works. Indeed, it is not only a few years which separate the two essays, but also and above all a difference in point of view. While in the *Phenomenology of Perception* Merleau-Ponty attempts to work out a phenomenology of *lived* experience, his aim in *The Structure of Behavior* is altogether different. The work begins with a critical study of experimental psychology, behaviorism, and Gestalt psychology, and then develops into a critical reflection on these sciences. Thus *The Structure of Behavior* does not, in the first instance, deal with natural and lived experience but rather with the interpretation or account of this experience by science. In a sense, this work is a confrontation between the data obtained by experimental psychology and the notion of "form" or "structure" that certain German psychologists had set out and popularized under the name of Gestalt.

It is, however, necessary to add that Merleau-Ponty is not content to remain at this level and accept without question the formulations and presuppositions of laboratory psychology, and that he does not attempt merely to formulate a critique of experimental psychology and behaviorism from the point of view of Gestalt psychology. For if it is true that he found his starting point in the research conducted by Gestalt psychologists, it is equally true that this school of psychology represents, along with the experimental psychology which it attacks, a level of discussion which, in his eyes, needs to be transcended. Gestalt psychology itself presupposes an implicit philosophy which is nowhere brought out and discussed: that of objective and causal realism.[1] In short, if Merleau-Ponty is interested in Gestalt psychology and speaks its language, it is not qua psychologist but rather qua philosopher. His aim is not to work out a psychology of Form but to do what the Gestaltists did not do: establish the groundwork for a *philosophy* of Form, of Structure.

However, his going beyond Gestalt psychology will take place on its own ground which is also that of all exact psychology—that of *behavior.* Taking therefore as his object the behavior—or, more exactly, the manifest activity—of physical and vital entities, he attempts, with the aid of the work of the psychologists of Form, to show first of all how the "reductionist" explanations of physics and psychophysiology do not stand up, and how behavior must be approached and analyzed from the point of view of Form or Gestalt. He applies the notion of Form to three orders of activity: the physical, the vital, and the human.

THE PHYSICAL ORDER

Referring to the body of knowledge obtained from analyses of the distribution of force in cases such as an electric current or a drop of oil suspended in water, Merleau-Ponty shows how, even in regard to the definition of physical systems, the activity in question can be explained only with the aid of the notion of Form. The reason for this is that the "physical experiment is never the revelation of an isolated causal series," which means that "the truth of physics is not found in the laws taken one by one, but in their combinations." (SB, 139; *SC,* 150) It is not possible to hold that a physical system, such as the distribution of forces in an electric current, is composed of a mosaic of physical activities, each of which obeys its own law. On the contrary, one cannot hope to explain a physical phenomenon and articulate its law if one does not look upon this phenomenon as part of an integrated whole apart from which it has no meaning and is not even conceivable. The law of falling bodies, for instance, presupposes a whole system of interrelated facts, and it has meaning only in regard to this dynamic and integrated, which is to say dialectical, structure: the law of falling bodies as we know it depends on the speed of the earth's rotation; were this to increase, the centrifugal force thereby generated could eventually equal and even surpass the force of gravity.

Physical laws, therefore, only have meaning in relation to certain global structures: "...the reference to a sensible or historical given is not a provisional imperfection; it is essential to physical knowledge." (SB, 145; *SC,* 157) A physical form must be defined as "an equilibrium obtained with respect to certain given external conditions". Or again: "The notion of form which was imposed upon us by the facts was defined like that of a physical system, that is, as an ensemble of forces in a state of equilibrium or of constant change such that no law is formulable for each part taken separately and such that each vector is determined in size and direction by all the others." (SB, 137; *SC*, 147–8) Thus what is essential to an understanding of a physical activity or essence is its form, the dialectic of laws in a given system, its structure.

To be sure, all of this had already been said by the Gestaltists. They themselves asserted that the nature which we have to deal with is neither a mere collection of independent, juxtaposed parts linked by simple causal action and determined by a number of laws, each of which would hold eternally, nor, again, a mixture wherein "everything would literally depend on everything else and in which no cleavage would be possible". (SB, 140; *SC*, 151) But even though Gestalt psychology, in discovering the notion of Form, freed itself from the atomistic explanations of traditional physics and the views of a naive materialism which takes nature to be "a multiplicity of events external to each other and bound together by relations of causality" (SB, 3; *SC*, 1), it nonetheless remained bound up with the implicit ontology of this science, one which is that of a naive *realism*. In fact, the Gestaltists did no more than substitute, in the place of a complex of independent, externally related causes and actions, the notion of an integrated whole wherein "causes" are now interdependent but where the motive force is nonetheless causality. In a word, they only touched up the notion of cause, and, for them, the form remains a real *thing* which acts by means of physical causality. Gestalt psychology remains a prisoner of an objectivistic and causal philosophy in that it holds that forms can be discovered *in* nature, taken by itself.

For Merleau-Ponty, however, this idea is no more acceptable than that of a causal positivism. He emphasizes that structure and law are "two dialectical moments and not two powers of being." And he adds, "Form is not an element of the world but a limit toward which physical *knowledge* tends and which it itself defines." (SB, 142; *SC*, 153; emphasis ours) The physical form is therefore not a fact of nature taken in itself but only insofar as it is discovered through consciousness. The form is thus not a *physical reality* but an *object of consciousness*: "a law is an instrument of knowledge and structure is an object of consciousness." (SB, 145; *SC*, 157)

When therefore, Merleau-Ponty asserts that the form is "the idea under which what happens in several places is brought together and resumed" (SB, 144; *SC*, 155-6), it could be wondered if he is not quite simply reverting to criticist and transcendental philosophy. We prefer to leave this question in suspense for the time being, keeping in mind nonetheless that the form or structure of which he speaks is, as he himself emphasizes, that of *perceived* objects.

THE VITAL ORDER

This order of behavior—and here the word has its full meaning and is no longer metaphorical—presents two sorts of forms for consideration: "syncretic" forms and "amovable" forms.[2] These two types of forms are qualitatively different, the distinction being that the first type designates structures which are for the most part submerged in the content itself of behavior, while the second type describes those which tend to impose their own demands on the elements of a situation. And this distinction corresponds roughly to two groups of animals: the invertebrates which act by what is generally called instinct, and the vertebrates where one begins to notice "intelligent" behavior. In the case of the ant, for instance, what one observes is a behavior which is imprisoned in its own conditions: "At this level behavior is tied either to certain abstract aspects of the situations or to certain complexes of very special stimuli. In any case, it is imprisoned in the framework of its natural conditions and treats unexpected situations only as allusions to the vital situations which are prescribed for it." (SB, 104; *SC*, 114) To give it its name, that behavior "which responds literally to a complex of stimuli rather than to certain essential traits of the situation" can be called "adherent." (SB, 105; *SC*, 115)

When one turns to more advanced organisms, one discovers "amovable" behavioral forms which are characterized by the fact that the behavior in question is meaningful. Here behavior is a response to "*signals* which are not determined by the instinctual equipment of the species". (SB, 105; *SC*, 115) On this level one observes structures which are relatively "independent of the materials in which they are realized." A chimpanzee, for instance, can adapt a bamboo stick with a small diameter to one with a larger diameter, and can use the instrument constructed in this way to reach a banana placed outside the bars of its cage which would otherwise remain unattainable. Here we are in the presence of a behavior which uses materials from its environment to intend a goal which is immediately present to the organism.

The animal does not merely respond to a given overall situation but "selects" itself certain givens in order to obtain others. The natural situation thereby receives a meaning by being integrated into the very structures of the animal's behavior.

Whether the equilibrium between the animal and its environment be obtained by means of instinct or by means of a kind of intelligence, what distinguishes it from the dynamic equilibrium between physical forces is that the structures of vital behavior are, in one way or another, meaningful: "The unity of physical systems is a *unity of correlation*, that of organisms is a *unity of meaning* [*signification*]." (SB, 155-6; *SC*, 168-9) Thus it must be said that animal behavior has a *meaning* (*sens*).

An organism's behavior cannot therefore be explained by physiological mechanisms which would be essentially autonomous and simply activated by isolated physical stimuli. On the contrary, in the case of the invertebrates it is a global structure of the organism, called instinct, which in a given situation adapts itself to a structural complex of stimuli. In the case of vertebrates, the organism does not merely react to a prescribed complex of stimuli but itself brings about the equilibrium with its environment by taking certain stimuli as signals so as to intend by means of them a goal which the organism sets itself. One is thus led to speak of *meaningful* behavior, since the behavior in question is not a chance result but seems to display a *meaning*. However, a criticist philosopher might answer that a meaning can exist only for an intelligence, and one which knows itself as such. There is therefore no meaning *in* organic life, but only for the *human* onlooker who describes this behavior. Indeed, these descriptions of vital behavior in terms of forms and structures give rise to a more radical question than those raised by the Gestaltists, and which, for its part, remains inescapable for whoever wants to formulate a philosophy of form: what is the justification for saying that a *structure* is *meaningful*? Or, more exactly: what is the relation between "structure" and "meaning"? These two terms, as Merleau-Ponty observes, cannot be mere synonyms. It should rather be said that behavior *is* a form or Gestalt or structure which *has* a certain meaning. We shall return to this question later; for the time being it is sufficient to note that this question is one raised by the very description of behavior, and we would like to point out that with this question one enters into the central problematic of *The Structure of Behavior*.

THE HUMAN ORDER

The difference between animal behavior and human behavior is that in the case of the animal signs are but "signals" and do not become "symbols." (SB, 120; *SC,* 130) A chimpanzee will use a stick which it has been given to seize a piece of food beyond its normal reach; it will not break off a branch of a nearby tree for the same purpose, even though the latter could serve equally well as an extension device. What the animal thus lacks is the capacity to orient itself by means of symbols—a capacity which consists in removing an object from its natural context, viewing it from different points of view, and, in short, treating it as a thing-in-itself open to a multiplicity of uses.

For man, on the contrary, a sign can cease to be a mere event in nature and become the proper object of a thematic activity. While animal behavior loses itself in the real transformations it effects, "for man the tree branch which has become a stick will remain precisely a tree-branch-which-has-become-a-stick, the same *thing* in two different functions and visible *for him* under a plurality of aspects. This power of choosing and varying points of view permits man to create instruments, not under the pressure of a *de facto* situation, but for a virtual use and especially in order to fabricate others." (SB, 175; *SC,* 190) Genuinely human consciousness is thus a symbolic consciousness; it has the ability to orient itself by the *possible,* the *virtual.* What indeed defines man is just this power he has of "going beyond created structures in order to create others." (SB, 175; *SC,* 189)

## 2.   The Essential Features of Structure

It seems to us that in *The Structure of Behavior* there are two dominant motifs which call out for our attention. We could designate these two themes, each of which has to do with spelling out the implications of form or structure, as (1) that of the *verticality* of behavioral structures, and (2) that of the relation between nature and idea, or, again, between structure and meaning. By becoming aware of these two themes at this moment in our study, we will be in a position to see how in Merleau-Ponty's later work they gradually take on ontological resonances and become the indispensable landmarks for revealing the "Being that we inhabit."

LINEAR CAUSALITY OR VERTICAL STRUCTURATION?

In order to make clear the *dialectical* and *vertical* nature of form or structure, we shall take as paradigmatic cases (1) the reflex and (2) the properly human behavior of man.

The Reflex.

When classical psychology—Pavlov, for example—attempted to explain nervous activity, it had recourse to the notion of reflex behavior. In its classical form this notion takes stimulation and reaction to be events in nature which have a purely extrinsic relation between them. A physical or chemical event serves only as the occasion for setting off an autonomous response in the organism which was simply waiting to occur in this mechanical fashion. This view of nervous activity "is but the application" of the traditional and materialist concept of *causality*.

The elements which explain reflex activity—the physical stimulus on the one hand, and the anatomical course on the other—constitute a *"linear* series of physical and physiological events." (SB, 9; *SC*, 7; italics ours) To a given stimulus there automatically corresponds a particular reflex response which is defined in advance. Thus the only relation between these two objective events is the *real* action of one *thing* on another. "The object of science is defined by the mutual exteriority of parts and processes." (SB, 9; *SC*, 8)

Actually, however, this way of understanding reflex activity reflects only an abstract and intellectualistic theory and does not describe what really happens in nature. Merleau-Ponty alludes to the work of German authors such as Weiszäcker and Goldstein in order to show that the reflex is not merely the result of independent, juxtaposed mechanisms and is not to be had by adding up elements, each of which would have its own reality. For the Gestaltists the reflex can be understood only by means of the notion of form.[3] A reflex occurs only in response to a stimulus which "is not a sum of partial stimuli...but rather a constellation, an order, a whole". (SB, 14; *SC*, 12) There are, therefore, no predetermined "reflex arcs." What exists is a reciprocal conditioning or constitution between stimulus and reaction where the reflex is a response to a global constellation of stimuli, but also where the stimuli form a whole only by being subjected to "the descriptive norms of the organism." (SB, 28; *SC*, 28) A "cause" is therefore a cause only in regard to an organism which "constitutes" it as such. Thus, in order to describe the relations between the organism and its environment, one is led to give up the notion of *linear causality* for that of *circular causality.* (SB, 15; *SC,* 13)

This needs to be made still more specific. By taking as his starting point the notion of the reflex in classical psychology Merleau-Ponty was able to show—by means of the work of certain physiologists and psychologists—the insufficiency of this notion. In fact, however, and even with the notion of form, the reflex cannot be understood if it is isolated from the total behavior of the organism. Gestalt psychology has indeed shown that the reflex is understandable only in relation to the whole of nervous activity and is but a dependent part of a more encompassing form than that of stimulus and reaction. So-called "pure" reflexes are the abstractions of an isolating intellectualistic analysis and are not to be found in nature. This is not to deny the existence of reflexes. On the contrary, reflexes exist, but their existence must be viewed in a way different from that characteristic of classical psychology. If this science was successful in isolating "pure" reflexes, this was only due to the artificial procedures of the laboratory. In the normal life of the organism there are not to be found, side by side, "reflex" activities and "instinctive" or "intellectual" activities. (SB, 43; *SC,* 44) What is to be found is rather an integrated nervous activity which is in harmony with the total situation in which the organism exists, and "reflexes" are themselves part of the global structure of the nervous system. In the real behavior of the organism, reflexes are an integral part of the higher nervous system. Thus the "effect of intervention of cerebral influences would be to reorganize behavior, to elevate it to a higher level of adaptation and life, and not merely to associate and disassociate pre-established devices." (SB, 21; *SC,* 19–20)

What Merleau-Ponty retains from this study of nervous activity and purely biological behavior is thus the realization that, even on this primitive level, life is defined by structurations which are *circular* and, precisely as such, *vertical.* Already in its beginnings life is oriented upwards; there already exists here a kind of movement of transcendence.

Higher-Level Behavior.

In his description of the human order, Merleau-Ponty had said that this order constitutes a new level of existence in relation to the physical and vital orders. It remains, though, to see how in regard to Freudianism—which Merleau-Ponty takes here as a special example of a causal and reductionist explanation of man's higher-level behavior—properly human behavior must be understood in a positive fashion and also how the notion of structuration which is involved here is further illuminated when Merleau-Ponty links it to the traditional problem of the relation between soul and body. The distinctive characteristic of human existence, the reference point of all existence, will become apparent in this way.

What Merleau-Ponty objects to in Freudianism at the time of *The Structure of Behavior* are not the facts discovered by Freud and which he referred to under the names of repression, complex, regression, transfer, sublimation, etc. These notions are, on the contrary, fully representative of certain phenomena of unbalanced behavior. Merleau-Ponty's criticism aims rather at the causal notions by means of which Freud interprets these phenomena. Instead of considering the complex, for instance, as a real force which "would subsist deep within us" (SB, 178; *SC,* 192) and would from time to time produce its effects in a semi-mechanical and "energetic action," Merleau-Ponty views it as a certain "weakening" (SB, 178; *SC,* 193) in the normal and real structuration of behavior. Thus, instead of considering normal behavior as an exception to pathological behavior—as being merely free from the influence of certain archaic psychological forces—it is, on the contrary, necessary to understand abnormal behavior in relation to so-called normal behavior, it being precisely a "weakening" or "breakdown" of normal behavior.

Normal behavior should thus be defined as a structuration which has succeeded in integrating the psychological order or the order of impulses into that of properly human intentions, into the "spiritual" life of man: "Normal structuration is one which reorganizes conduct in depth in such a way that infantile attitudes no longer have a place or meaning in the new attitude; it would result in perfectly integrated behavior, each moment of which would be internally linked with the whole." (SB, 177; *SC,* 192) It is not from out of the past that the experiences of an unhappy childhood deform behavior; there are no persistent *forces,* rather a lack of current structuration: the person has not succeeded in giving a meaning to these experiences and in integrating them so defined into his personal existence as an adult.[4] "Thus, the pretended unconsciousness of the complex," Merleau-Ponty writes, referring to Goldstein, "is reduced to the ambivalence of immediate consciousness."[5] (SB, 179; *SC,* 193) What therefore exist are not *energetic* forces but more or less *meaningful* structures.

This means that, to the degree that behavior is organized so that the structure or form constituted thereby confers on behavior an integrated meaning, it is normal and successful behavior; to the degree that this integration is lacking, it is abnormal, that is, "fragmentary," behavior. "What is required by the facts which Freud describes under the name of repression, complex, regression or resistance," Merleau-Ponty emphasizes, "is only the possibility of a fragmented life of consciousness which does not possess a unique significance at all times." (SB, 178; *SC,* 193) Just as Freud himself rejected the physiological explanation of dreams which, as he said, have their own meaning, so Merleau-Ponty likewise calls for an abandonment of the causal and "energetic" explanation of higher-level behavior and a recognition that at this level life is defined by structures[6] which it itself brings into existence, and that it possesses its own meaning and is not reducible to the play of lower-level structures. Thus, "Mental acts would have their own proper meaning and their own internal laws." (SB, 180; *SC,* 195)

From an abstract point of view one can, of course, discern three orders of behavior or life in man: the vital, the psychological, and the spiritual. However, precisely because normal existence is an integrated structure, one should not consider these three orders real and distinct levels. "The relation of each order to the higher order," Merleau-Ponty insists, "is that of the partial to the total." (SB, 180; *SC,* 195) The "total" character of behavior becomes even more apparent when one considers the developmental process that constitutes a person's history as a constant dialectic, wherein the past and the structures of a more simple and archaic life are taken up and transformed by the advent of more developed and complex structures. "The advent of higher orders, to the extent that it comes to be, eliminates the autonomy of the lower orders and gives a new signification to the steps which constitute them." (SB, 180; *SC,* 195)

*The relations between soul and body* must then be thought of as relations between two relative and varying terms in a single dialectic where the first term encompasses and surpasses the second, but where the second serves as a foundation and condition of possibility for the first. To the degree that the psychological order in man, his instinctual life, is integrated into a new and higher-level type of behavior and taken up in a properly human expression—such as loving a person for his own sake and not simply as an object of satisfaction—one can no longer speak of a psychological and bodily order as such in man.

Psychological and bodily life must thenceforth be conceived of as being part of a totality or higher-level structure which takes it up and re-expresses it in a symbolic intention, one which, in depriving it of its own autonomy, makes it vanish as such.[7] And thus, "It is not a question of two *de facto* orders external to each other, but of two types of relations, the second of which integrates the first." (SB, 180–1; *SC*, 195)

But if this prevents us from speaking of man's bodily life as if it were a distinct region of his being, the same holds for his "spiritual" life.[8] If, in the presence of the order of properly human intentions, the vital and psychological orders cease to exist as such and become the means for expressing a higher-level structuration, the opposition between body and soul must be conceived of as a "functional opposition" and not as a "substantial opposition." (SB, 181; *SC*, 196) In this case spirit is not a new kind of being but a new form of *unity*. Since, therefore, spirit is not a kind of substance or a being-in-itself, it would be better to speak, not of a spiritual order and a bodily order, but quite simply of a human order. In reformulating in this way the notions of soul and body, Merleau-Ponty abandons realism and succeeds in conceiving of what is human as a mode of behavior expressive of a certain Gestalt.

But if body and soul are not two substances or two orders of reality and must be "relativized," Merleau-Ponty in no way seeks to *reduce* one to the other. This refusal of a pure and simple *monism* is of the greatest importance, and we should be careful to take note of it. The integration of body and soul is in no way a *fusion*, and the bodily orders are not simply absorbed by the higher-level order. There are certainly not two substances in man, but nevertheless man is not a rigidly monolithic entity. There is indeed a "soul" and a "body," but the body is a *human* body only in being the very foundation of the soul, the visible expression of a "spiritual" life; and the soul is a soul only by means of the body which is like its very appearance. Between body and soul there is, as it were, a tensional polarity, and the total man is nothing other than this tension which is continually renewed. If therefore Merleau-Ponty categorically rejects all *dualism* in man, he still argues for a certain *duality* in his being. "There is always a duality," he says, "which reappears at one level or another." This is to say that "integration is never absolute and it always fails—at a higher level in the writer, at a lower level in the aphasic." (SB, 210; *SC*, 226)

Human existence is thus a structure. But this structure includes a duality; it is dialectical, and this means that it is composed of two terms which imply each other, which stand out against one another, and which exist only in this constant reference to one another. The structure in question is therefore *circular*. But we have not yet gotten to the bottom of the matter.

What appears to be the essence of Merleau-Ponty's thought and, as it were, its inner motivation, can be seen in the following passage where the author attempts to give a kind of ultimate definition to the body-soul duality: "there is the body as mass of chemical components in interaction, the body as dialectic of living being and its biological milieu, and the body as dialectic of social subject and his group; even all our habits are an impalpable body for the ego of each moment. Each of these degrees is soul with respect to the preceding one, body with respect to the following one. The body in general is an ensemble of paths already traced, of powers already constituted; the body is the acquired dialectical ground upon which a higher 'formation' is accomplished, and the soul is the meaning which is then established." (SB, 210; SC, 227)

It can therefore be seen that the dialectic which constitutes human behavior is a *dialectic of transcendence* and that the structure is a vertical circularity. Human existence thus bears witness to a power of transcendence (of *échappement*, as the *Phenomenology of Perception* will put it) embedded in it. While remaining faithful to its past, existence is something dynamic. Its nature, according to an expression of Hegel that Merleau-Ponty takes over himself, is to preserve while overcoming.

In short, therefore, this analysis of nervous activity and of higher-level behavior has served to bring out the circular characteristic of form or structure and, in addition, its aspect of verticality. As soon as one gets beyond the physical order one observes a vertical dialectic displaying itself, one wherein the terms merit being called moments; one has to deal with a kind of unfolding of a power of going beyond. On the one hand there are the foundations—in man his vital and psychological life—and on the other there is that towards which they surpass themselves—man's spiritual life. This "double relation" is a genuine dialectic of transcendence in the sense that the higher-level structuration surpasses the lower-level ones, but does so only being "founded" on them and by using them as means for passing beyond. Although they are not yet fully unraveled, Merleau-Ponty is already in possession of the guiding threads of his thought in *The Structure of Behavior;* the rest of his work will be a following up of these clues, a philosophical adventure which will finally direct him to their ultimate source, vertical Being, which will lead him to run up against the supremely unexplainable, the miracle of the "there is" [*il y a*]. Here it is enough to note that the circular, dialectical, and vertical characteristics of structure brought out by this work directly anticipate the analysis in the *Phenomenology of Perception,* where Merleau-Ponty will show that existence is defined by, and in fact is nothing other than, a dialogue with the world, intentionality, transcendence.

THE RELATIONS BETWEEN "STRUCTURE" AND "MEANING" AND THE PROBLEM OF PERCEPTUAL CONSCIOUSNESS

Already on two occasions we have touched upon the problem of the relation between structure or form and the meaning it manifests. Physical systems and organisms have been defined as "forms," that is, as meaningful structures. This came about in reaction to atomistic and materialistic thought which conceives of physical systems as simple collections of diverse forms, the totality of which could be explained by the mere addition of the activities of each element taken separately, and which likewise applies the same mechanistic explanation to the behavior of organisms which would be but corporeal aggregates *partes extra partes.* In point of fact, to say that an organism's behavior does not lend itself to a reductionist explanation, an explanation in terms of the mere interaction of its physical and chemical elements, but that it can be understood only in terms of the new structuration that it itself brings into existence amounts to saying that the form which comes about in this way is defined by the *meaning* it manifests. There are thus only two alternatives: the behavior in question can be understood by means of a "regressive analysis which goes back to its conditions" or, on the contrary, by means of a "prospective analysis which will look for the immanent signification" of life. (SB, 160; *SC,* 173) Gestalt theory has shown the insufficiency of the former explanation and has insisted on the irreducible and meaningful aspect of behavior.

But, as Merleau-Ponty remarks, Gestalt theory never pushed its investigations very far. When it was confronted with the apparent antinomy of materialism and spiritualism, it fell back into a materialism or an objectivism by maintaining the physical *reality* of form; for it, meaningful structures exist like things in a nature-in-itself. The psychology of form attempted to work out a philosophy of form without managing to do so; it was not successful in this endeavor because it had not freed itself "from the realistic postulates which are those of every psychology." (SB, 132; *SC,* 143) It was satisfied with pointing out the structural and meaningful character of behavior and did not raise any questions as to the *mode of existence* of form.

If, therefore, Merleau-Ponty devotes a great deal of time to presenting the work of the Gestaltists and to a discussion of their discovery—the notion of Form—it is not with the simple intention of popularizing this notion by showing that it alone is capable of expressing physical activity and vital and human behavior. In point of fact, while making detailed descriptions of the forms or structures of behavior, he has something "other in view." (SB, 127; *SC,* 138) This primary goal of his is, as he had said in the introduction to the book, "to understand the relations of consciousness and nature". (SB, 3; *SC,* 1) Or again, the relations of the objective and the subjective, the exterior and the interior. This question constitutes the central problem under discussion in this book.[9] Here the notion of Gestalt serves as a starting point and as an occasion for attacking this problematic which itself constitutes the aim of the work.[10]

When one sets about constructing a philosophy of form, all the difficulties one encounters derive indeed from the antinomy which inevitably seems to arise between nature and idea. It would indeed appear that form must be either a thing in nature or an idea of a constituting consciousness. Merleau-Ponty attempts to overcome this antinomy.

To this end he first of all shows that forms or meaningful structures cannot exist *in* nature. To say that behavior is a form is to say that it is not the juxtaposition of "exteriorly combined" terms, that it is meaningful, and that it is therefore not a thing, a material reality *partes extra partes.* Since, therefore, behavior does not exist like a thing, it must be "the *idea* under which what happens in several places is brought together and summed up." (SB, 144; *SC,* 155–6; emphasis ours) There is no other choice but to maintain that the law which expresses a certain physical or organic structuration is "an instrument of knowledge and [that] structure is an object of consciousness." (SB, 145; *SC,* 157) On the vital level the behavior-form manifests an irreducibly "ideal" nature. If vital acts have a meaning, it is because "they are not defined, even in science, as a sum of processes external to each other, but as the spatial and temporal unfolding of certain ideal unities." (SB, 159; SC, 172) The behavior of an animal cannot be explained by the mere addition of physical and chemical elements; this behavior has its own *meaning*. But this is certainly not to say that the animal is meaningful for itself and that it is the reflective consciousness of itself; "it is only to say that it is a whole which is meaningful for a consciousness which knows it, not a thing which rests in-itself." (SB, 159; SC, 172) Animal behavior has a meaning for the human onlooker who perceives it: "the object of biology cannot be thought of without the unities of signification which a consciousness finds and sees unfolding in it." (SB, 161; SC, 175)

We have seen that in order to construct a philosophy of form it is not enough to describe structures, but that one must analyze their mode of existence. And what a first movement of reflection shows is, as we have just seen, the essential "ideality" of form. The very description of form presupposes a consciousness which takes note of it. Influenced by Hegel, Merleau-Ponty says that what one designates by the name of life is already the consciousness of life. And he cites the following text of the German philosopher: "The mind of nature is a hidden mind. It is not produced in the form of mind itself; it is only mind for the mind which knows it: it is mind in itself, but not for itself." (SB, 161; SC, 175) This is an interesting text and a curious quotation since it seems to indicate that Merleau-Ponty has opted for transcendental and idealistic philosophy.

The "first conclusion" (SB, 206; SC, 222) to be drawn is thus in fact of a manifestly transcendental or criticist nature. The description of physical systems and vital forms is the description not of things which exist in themselves but of a nature which is *present to consciousness*. Structure is thus "the joining of an idea and an existence which are indiscernible". (SB, 206; SC, 223) By way of a first approximation, the Gestalt is to be understood in a "Hegelian sense": form is in a way a "concept before it has become the consciousness of itself." (SB, 210; SC, 227)

But just what exactly is a concept before it has become conscious of itself? It is the answer Merleau-Ponty gives to this question which prevents him from taking the "short cut" of critical philosophy. For a concept of this sort cannot be such as would be held in full lucidity by a consciousness in perfect possession of itself, one which could spread out the world in front of itself like a spectacle produced by itself where the world would be but "the ensemble of objective relations borne" (SB, 3; *SC*, 1) by this sovereign thought. A concept as murky as this can only belong to a consciousness which is equally ambiguous and opaque for itself. If therefore one maintains—and one is forced to do so—that form is not a thing but an object of perception, that it exists only in being perceived, and that it is what a consciousnesss discerns as soon as it looks about, one is forced to acknowledge that a concept such as this can nevertheless not belong to a constituting consciousness which is its own master, rather, such a concept belongs only to a consciousness which finds itself face to face with a world, one which looks about and which, at this stage, is nothing other than its look, one which lives outside of itself in the world. The key to the problem of meaningful forms is therefore to be sought in "perceptual consciousness," in "beginning consciousness": "Thus, it is perceptual consciousness which must be interrogated in order to find in it a definitive clarification." (SB, 210; *SC*, 227)

It is thus not on the level of the *Cogito* but beneath it in primary perception that is to be found the means of overcoming the antinomy of nature and idea, of objective and subjective. If one does not want simply to cover over this antinomy, it must be admitted that, on the one hand, when I begin to perceive I find myself confronted with a sensible ensemble which, for instance, has for me the meaning "triangle," and that it is on the sensible thing itself that this meaning stands out, that it is an "embodied" meaning. (SB, 211; *SC*, 228) But, on the other hand, I know—and critical philosophy will be quick to emphasize this—that the meaning I perceive does not exist *in* the thing like a natural property, spread out in space and time, but *for me*, the onlooker. If therefore one wants to understand this meaning as it shows itself, it must be taken in its nascent state: one must return to beginning perception as to a primordial experience and the place of the first upsurge of meaning (or "rationality") in the world. What is demanded is a kind of phenomenological reduction,[11] for what is in question is precisely the *phenomenon* of meaning, the advent of rationality.

It is thus consciousness which lives in the world which must be questioned, not consciousness which has arrived at the complete possession of itself (supposing that this consciousness exists or even could exist). The meaning of physical or vital forms is in the first instance something which is perceived and not an idea in the proper sense of the word. The antinomy of nature and idea or the problem of meaningful structures inevitably leads us to the problem of naive perception: "If one understands by perception the act which makes us know existences, all the problems which we have just touched on are reducible to the problem of perception." (SB, 224; *SC*, 240) It is the onlooker himself, an onlooker bound to the world by primary perception, who must be interrogated in order to understand the meaningful existence of forms. In this sense what remains is "to define transcendental philosophy anew" (SB, 224; *SC*, 241); what is important is to undertake a regressive or archeological inquiry which would reveal, not the "conditions of possibility" of perceptual meaning, but its real and fundamental structures. The very last lines of *The Structure of Behavior* sum up the final lesson of this work: "The natural 'thing,' the organism, the behavior of others and my own behavior exist only by their meaning; but this meaning which springs forth in them is not yet a Kantian object; the intentional life which constitutes them is not yet a representation; and the 'understanding' which gives access to them is not yet an intellection." (SB, 224; *SC*, 241)

This final lesson is not really an answer to the problem but only a crystallization of it. The *Structure of Behavior* comes to a close by confronting us with the real problem, that of the onlooker who participates in the scene he perceives. This first book does not solve anything, therefore. Quite to the contrary, it calls for the *Phenomenology of Perception* as for a natural continuation of the inquiry on another level, that of "natural and unsophisticated experience" (De Waelhens). In order to understand the existence of those structures which define physical and vital being, we are thus referred back to a study of perception and, even prior to this, to a study of the perceiving subject.

Who then is the perceiving subject? And what is the relation between him and what he perceives? In order that the scene appear meaningful to him, is it not necessary that he have, so to speak, a real interest in it, that he be himself an integral part of it? Is it not necessary that in the final analysis he be, as it were, the other side of Nature, its lining and something like a doubling-back of Nature on itself? Is it not necessary that he thus be something like Nature's own self-articulation? These questions refer us to the *Phenomenology*, but it may not yet be there that we will find the answers to them.

## II.  Exploration of Being in the World

THROUGH its criticism of the causalistic explanations of physiology and psychology, *The Structure of Behavior* has unearthed and
formulated the problem that will henceforth occupy a central place in
Merleau-Ponty's philosophy. As we have seen, this problem is that of
the existence of a meaningful, rational world; it is, in short, the problem of rationality. As it reveals itself in perception, the world is not
a chaos wherein everything acts indiscriminately on everything else,
but an ensemble of units which manifest a meaning. But this meaning
is not something real and does not belong to the world as a natural
property. The world is meaningful only for a *consciousness* which perceives it. However, since consciousness perceives a meaning which is
precisely the meaning of the world, the meaning in question is not an
idea, and perceptual consciousness is not constituting consciousness.
The problem is thus, first of all, to know what exactly a perceptual
consciousness is. Since the meaning of the world belongs inseparably
to the world and to consciousness, we must take up an examination of
the relations between object and subject, nature and consciousness.
*The Structure of Behavior* has outlined the field of investigation and
singled out the problem to be investigated. The *Phenomenology of
Perception* (1945) will undertake the exploration of this field of
perception and will be an "inventory of the perceived world." (PhP,
25; *PP,* 33)

In his long introduction to the *Phenomenology,* Merleau-Ponty
attacks the "classical prejudices" in regard to perception and calls for
a "return to the phenomena." Here he sums up and elaborates on his
criticism of the presuppositions of science and Gestalt psychology—
which is criticizable in what it does not say—and exposes at greater
length the weaknesses of transcendental or critical philosophy.

With its notion of "sensation" *empiricism* conceives of perception
as an event in nature. Perception for it is the action—physical or chemical, but always causal—of a thing on an organ, and sensation is the
mere registering of this action. For empiricism, everything takes place
in the objective world, and for this reason there is here no *subject* who
perceives.

In opposition to this complete objectivity, *intellectualism* posits
an absolute subjectivity. Intellectualist reflection recognizes that in
all sensation there is a kind of transcendental Ego which is the subject
of experience, and rejects the materialistic objectivism of empiricism

in favor of a pure interiority, a *Cogito* whose whole existence is to think.

Actually, however, intellectualism only constitutes an apparent antithesis to empiricism, for, even in opposing empiricism, it continues to share its fundamental prejudice. This is the prejudice of "a universe perfectly explicit in itself." (PhP, 41; *PP,* 51) For empiricism the subject is but an object in the objective world; for intellectualism the world is still an objective world only with this difference, that now it exists as such only for a consciousness which projects it before itself: "We started off from a world in itself which acted upon our eyes so as to cause us to see it, and we now have consciousness of or thought about the world, but the nature of this world remains unchanged: it is still defined by the absolute mutual exteriority of its parts, and is merely duplicated throughout its extent by a thought which sustains it." (PhP, 39; *PP,* 49)

In thus holding to a ready-made, objective world, empiricism and intellectualism both pass over the *phenomenon* of perception. Empiricism does so because it makes of the subject an object in the objective world where there is consequently *no one* who perceives. Intellectualism does so because it makes of perception an operation of thought, an act by which an absolute consciousness projects before itself "a universe perfectly explicit in itself." Empiricism thus renders perception impossible, while intellectualism makes it useless. In the empirical explanation of "sensation," perception does not yet exist—there is no Ego here who perceives—and in intellectualism, which rediscovers by means of a regressive analysis the "conditions of possibility" of the world in a consciousness which has already fully constituted it without knowing it, perception has already been supersceded.

But for Merleau-Ponty, before things can be the pure objects of which science speaks, they are dimensions of my existence in them and address me in a natural and immediately meaningful language. There is, he says, a "pre-objective realm that we have to explore in ourselves if we wish to understand sense experience." (PhP, 12; *PP,* 19) In lived experience there are not yet any pure objects, but there is already a subject who perceives. The error of intellectualism lies not in postulating the existence of this subject but in mistaking its nature. The subject who perceives and who is immediately in contact with a world of perceptual meanings is a *pre-subject,* a natural subject. It is a subject which only exists through what is worldly in it, its body.

There is thus a pre-subjective realm in ourselves to be explored if we wish to understand perception. We must recognize the existence of a body-subject: we must view the body as our living bond with the world and as the umbilical cord which attaches us to it. We must undertake the exploration of this phenomenal field where the world is not yet an objective world and the subject is not yet a reflective *Cogito,* but where the world and the subject reflect each other and, so to speak, flow into each other. In raising the questions, Who is it that perceives?, and, What is the perceived world?, Merleau-Ponty undertakes to revise the notions of *object* and *subject, nature* and *consciousness,* so as to view them as being as intimately related as a question and an answer and as two moments of a single circular system which is *being in the world:* "Let us then return to sensation and scrutinize it closely enough to learn from it the living relation of this perceiver to his body and to his world." (PhP, 208; *PP,* 241)

The *Phenomenology of Perception* has for its sole object what Merleau-Ponty calls "being in the world." In order to facilitate the analysis of the book, which embodies, according to the expression of De Waelhens, an "arduous and disconcerting" mode of thought, we will consider it from three points of view, those of *circularity, transcendence, rootedness.*

After this examination of the *Phenomenology,* we will be in possession of the main elements of Merleau-Ponty's ontology. This, however, does not mean that we will have encountered an ontology in the proper sense of the term, one which will be conscious of itself as ontology. It only means that with the *Phenomenology* Merleau-Ponty's eventual ontology has already taken its start, that the itinerary of this nascent ontology is already indicated, and that the resultant ontology will amount to a deeper analysis of the phenomena this book will have brought to light. It will then remain to be seen how the traits of existence set out here take on a definitively ontological dimension in Merleau-Ponty's subsequent works. It will remain to be seen how human existence finally shows itself to be a phenomenon of Being.[12]

## 1. Being in the World as Circularity

This first part of our analysis will be concerned above all with the first two parts of the *Phenomenology.* Merleau-Ponty there attempts to set out the constitutive relations which hold between (1) consciousness and the body, (2) the embodied subject (consciousness plus body) and the world, and (3) the self and other people. Each one of these dialectical relations constitutes a *system* in the proper sense of the word wherein the two terms are interdependent and mutually form a *circular structure*. Each system is taken up by the following one, thereby constituting a more encompassing system: so that all together these systems form, as it were, concentric circles and express a certain dimensionality of existence. I am a subject only by means of the many unbreakable bonds which tie my consciousness and my body together; I am an embodied subject only by being in a direct mutual relation with the world; and I am in the world only through my co-existence with others who, themselves, are also so many beings in the world. Inversely, the other exists for me only because I am directly linked to the world by a body which is inseparable from my existence.

THE LIVED BODY

The problem of meaning or rationality comes down to the problem of perception. In order to know what perception is and how it constitutes the bond between consciousness and nature, whence meanings arise, it is first of all necessary to know what the perceiving subject is. It is necessary to raise the question, Who is it that perceives? Both empiricism and intellectualism recognize that perception or sensation has to do in one way or another with the body. For empiricism sensation is the registering by a body-object of the causal action of objects on it. For intellectualism it is the recognition by an intellectual *Cogito* of what takes place in a body-mechanism with which it is confusedly associated. For the one, perception is thus the expression of a complete *passivity* and takes place in the world, while for the other it is essentially an *activity,* an intellectual operation which dominates the world. But these two conceptions have this in common, that they conceive the body itself as an object or an extended substance which is situated among other objects in an objective world.

But for Merleau-Ponty, my own body, before being an object that I can conceptualize or treat conceptually as a physiological thing, a mere material mass, is a dimension of my own existence. The body is in the first instance a *lived body.* If, as Merleau-Ponty demonstrates, the empirical and intellectualist conceptions do not succeed in accounting for perception, it is because they misunderstand the nature of the body and, for the sake of abstractions, lose sight of the body-subject.

Let us consider the example of the phenomenon of the phantom limb—the much discussed case where someone who has lost an arm or a leg still continues to "feel" it. How can this phenomenon be explained? Physiological and psychological explanations do not succeed in doing it justice, for they concern themselves with the body conceived of as an object independent of all personal history. In point of fact, the phenomenon can be understood only from the point of view of a subject for whom his body is not an object outside of his consciousness, but is rather his very way of being present in the world (of being conscious of the world). The subject who feels a phantom limb is not a consciousness which would in some mysterious way be merely attached to a body; it is rather a consciousness which is itself corporeal, that is, a subject which, in this case, is nothing other than its bodily presence in the world. Feeling an arm which one no longer has is a way of refusing a handicap, of continuing to live by means of a "bodily schema" which one had formerly learned through a real contact with the world. "To have a phantom arm is to remain open to all those actions of which the arm alone is capable; it is to keep the practical field that one had before being mutilated." (PhP. 81–2; *PP*, 97) The case of the phantom limb points to the existence of a subject intimately bound up with the world by a whole number of intentional threads which are nothing other than its body. The body is first of all a way of viewing the world; it is at one and the same time the way a subjective attitude both comes to know itself and express itself. The lived, phenomenal body must therefore not be thought of as an object in itself, but as the way a subject is *present* in the world and is aware of it. And correlatively, perceptual consciousness must not be understood as an absolute interiority, as the pure presence of the self to itself, but as a *bodily* presence in the world, a *bodily* awareness of the world. Here Merleau-Ponty is breaking with the Cartesian tradition and with, in fact, a conception present in all of modern philosophy that there are "two senses, and two only, of the word 'exist': one exists as a thing or else one exists as a consciousness." (PhP, 198; *PP*, 231) The perceiving subject is for him a worldly subject, and essentially so. The relation between the subject and his body is, so to speak, an inner relationship: at the level of perception the subject *is* his body. One could thus say, as does Marcel, that "I am my body," or, as Merleau-Ponty prefers, that "I have a body," that is, that *qua consciousness* I have a body. My body properly belongs to me. The body of which science and objectivistic philosophy speak is a secondary, thematized body, and that body does not *exist;* it is but a thought body.

The body considered merely physiologically is a body in itself; it is a body which belongs to no one. The lived body, the body which is for everyone his particular way of inhabiting the world, is, on the contrary, a strange *mixture of being-in-itself and being-for-itself.* This is what a consideration of the spatiality of the lived body serves to bring out. Indeed, to say that the body is the subject's very presence to the world, his way of inhabiting the world, amounts to saying that the body is not *in* space. To say that it is not a mere object is to say that it is not just an extended substance. Merleau-Ponty writes: "...far from my body's being for me no more than a fragment of space, there would be no space at all for me if I had no body." (PhP, 102; *PP,* 119) My body teaches me what space is, because it is itself the author of space. It is the body which makes it be that there is for me a far and a near, a low and a high. The world is spatial for me because I inhabit it by means of my body: "Consciousness," Merleau-Ponty says, "is being towards the thing through the intermediary of the body." (PhP, 138–9; *PP,* 161) Thus at the level of perception I am not a *Cogito* but a "knowing-body." "Consciousness is in the first place not a matter of 'I think that' but of 'I can'." (PhP, 137; *PP,* 160)

The phenomenal *body* thus escapes in a fashion from the realm of the in-itself and is already a kind of subject. It is, in fact, the true subject of perception. Perceptual *consciousness* is not yet a pure for-itself; it is a body-subject, a knowing-body. The experience that I have of my body thus teaches me a new mode of existence which properly belongs neither to the in-itself nor the for-itself. The lived body is not a "mechanism in itself," and perceptive consciousness is not a "being for itself." (PhP, 139; *PP,* 163) In short, this examination of the lived or phenomenal body allows Merleau-Ponty to overcome "the traditional subject-object dichotomy." (PP, 174; *PP,* 203) In summing up the first part of the *Phenomenology,* he is able to say, "The experience of our own body...reveals to us an ambiguous mode of existing." (PhP, 198; *PP,* 231) It is ambiguous because it calls into question the traditional distinctions of object and subject. "The body is thus not an object. For the same reason, my awareness of it is not a thought". I can only know the phenomenal body by living it, for, not being an object, an in itself, it is me myself; it is what I am, me inasmuch as I am conscious of the world. "I am my body...and cor-relatively my body is as it were a natural subject". (PhP, 198; *PP,* 231)

The lived body is that place where the in itself and the for itself mix and lead an ambiguous life. At the level of perception, conscious-ness and the body together constitute "the junction of the for itself and the in itself" (PhP, 373; *PP,* 427) and thereby form a *system* which is approachable from two sides. This system, which Merleau-Ponty calls being in the world, is thus one which could be termed *circular.* The knowing-body possesses the strange power of turning back on itself, that is, of re-flecting itself. There are times when the "body catches itself from the outside engaged in a cognitive process". (PhP, 93; *PP,* 109) I am in the process of touching an object with my right hand. Suddenly my two hands cross, and I touch my right hand with my left one. The hand which was "touching" becomes at that very second "touched"; it ceases for a moment to be a sensing "subject" and becomes a sensed "object." The body turns back on itself and takes itself for its own object. And thus it shows itself a being with two "sides"; at one moment it is a subject, existing for itself, at another an object, existing in itself. But in this situation the body is neither completely a subject nor completely an object; it manifests an ambig-uous union of the two; it is a reversible circularity.

It is in this way therefore that the phenomenal body "initiates 'a kind of reflection'." (PhP, 93; *PP,* 109) It is important to take note of this, for if the body were not a *power of natural reflection* it would never be a "power of natural expresssion," and language would never exist. This power that the lived body has of doubling back on itself is the source from which creative and symbolic expression will spring forth.

But we must also note the irreducible or dialectical aspect of the lived body's circularity. Even though the body can turn back on itself, take itself for its own proper object and in this way accomplish a kind of reflection, it never succeeds in *coinciding* with itself. This circularity never results in an *identity.* When for instance one's two hands touch each other, there is always one which acts as subject and another which exists as an object; a single hand is never subject and object at the same time. Even in perception the subject never succeeds in being qua "reflecting" what he is qua "reflected." All of this is a reaffirmation of what Merleau-Ponty had said in *The Structure of Behavior,* where, while maintaining the "relativity" of the two moments of body and soul, he had insisted on the impossibility of reducing one to the other. Being neither a simple object nor a pure spirit, the lived body is a dialectic of the in-itself and the for itself, and bodily existence is an ambiguous existence.

It is ambiguous; at the level of perception existence is not in-itself existence, as the being of things is, but it is still not a "personal" existence. The subject of perception is not the free subject, the master of itself which realizes itself to be a unique individual. It is not quite yet "the most irreplaceable of beings," according to the expression of André Gide. It is only an opening, a possibility for a meaningful life. It is a subject without personal identity which lives outside of itself and which loses track of itself in the perceived spectacle. As *The Visible and the Invisible* will say, the perceiving self is "the anonymous one buried in the world, and that has not yet traced its path." (VI, 201; *VI, 254*) In perception, existence is an unreasonable promiscuity with the world. My existence as perceiving consciousness is closely *tied up* with my existence as a body, and consciousness and body are but two sides or aspects of a certain presence to the world. In perception, subjectivity is but a "natural" subjectivity. Perceiving consciousness is that "I can" which is not yet an "I think that." In a word, the subject of perception is not that *I* which is familiar to me; it is only an anonymous "One." "Perception is always in the mode of the impersonal 'One'." (PhP, 240; *PP, 277*)

Such then is the perceiving subject. It is, so to speak, a subject without name, a "natural self." It is not a *Cogito;* it is a knowing-body. We will come back later to this prepersonal characteristic of our existence in order to see how, as a conscious and personal subject, I am supported by an entire prepersonal existence, an entire prehistory. Here we only wished to point out the circularity which Merleau-Ponty detected in the being of the perceiving subject—the indivisible but nonetheless dialectical joining of a consciousness and a body. The perceiving subject is the phenomenal body; perceptual consciousness is bodily consciousness. And thus our body "is a *natural self,* a current of given existence, with the result that we never know whether the forces which bear us on are its or ours". (PhP, 171; *PP, 199*)

THE PERCEIVED WORLD

As Merleau-Ponty points out, the new conception of the lived body as a circular system wherein "consciousness" and the "body" are but two aspects which are to a certain extent reversible requires a new conception of the *world* in relation to which the perceiving subject is but a global and massive presence. The new notion of perceiving subjectivity will result in fact in a new idea of the world and the perceived object; the theory of the lived body is implicitly a "theory of perception" and "the sensible world." (PhP, 206; *PP, 239*) This way of proceeding must be emphasized: what Merleau-Ponty will say about the world is for him already "implied in the rediscovery of the lived body [*le corps propre*]." (PhP, 199; *PP, 232*) The world of which he will speak will thus be a world which exists *for* the subject and which gets defined in relation to it.

Indeed, Merleau-Ponty cannot define the perceiving subject as a relation or presence to the world without the world itself being a relation to the subject. If the perception of the body is at the same time the perception of the world—as was seen in the case of the phantom limb—the perception of the world must be the other side of the perception of the body. It is thus within perception, *within the intentional relationship* of perceiving subject-perceived world, that Merleau-Ponty will define both the subject and the world. The experience of the body will be the reverse side of the perception of the world and vice versa. In a word, the lived body and the perceived world will be seen as *correlatives.* (PhP. 205; *PP, 237*) Merleau-Ponty reveals very clearly the essence of his thought in the very first lines of the second part of the *Phenomenology:* "The lived body [*le corps propre*] is in the world as the heart is in the organism: it keeps the visible spectacle constantly alive, it breathes life into it and sustains it inwardly, and with it forms a system." (PhP, 203; *PP, 235*)

The relation of the perceived world and the lived body is thus an *internal* relation, such that the world and the body together constitute a *system.* Let us see in somewhat more detail what all of this means by taking as an example the perception of the "qualities" of things.

In regard to the perceiving subject, that is, embodied consciousness, the qualities of things are not objective facts existing outside of perception and merely observed by the subject. Colors, for instance, get defined and distinguished from each other because they are so many different meanings lived by the body. Red is that aspect of a thing which "repels" us; it "dives into the eye." Green, on the contrary, is "restful." One could in this way spell out an ontology of colors and other sensory qualities, such as Sartre does in *Being and Nothingness* where he sketches an "existential psychoanalysis" of qualities and things. But beyond the various descriptions that one could and that Merleau-Ponty does provide here, it is important to recognize that qualities can appear as concrete propositions made to my being only because I *co-exist* with things. Inspired perhaps by Claudel's famous definition of *connaissance* (knowledge) as *co-naissance* (co-birth) Merleau-Ponty writes, "The subject of sensation is neither a thinker who takes note of a quality, nor an inert setting which is affected or changed by it, it is a power which is born into, and simultaneously with [*qui co-nait*] , a certain existential environment, or is synchronized with it." (PhP, 211; *PP,* 245)

Sensation is described by Merleau-Ponty as a "communion" (PhP, 212; *PP,* 246) between body and thing, as their "natural transaction" (PhP, 226; *PP,* 262), their "co-existence" (PhP, 213; *PP,* 247). It is a matter neither of the physical impression of the thing on the body nor of the thematic consciousness of the thing which would constitute it in such and such a way. It is quite simply a question of a bodily cohabitation with things, of a "life in common," by which things receive a meaning which is the meaning of my life in them.

Sensation thus expressses a *circularity* between the lived body and the perceived world. The "gaze pairs off [*s'accouple avec*] with color" as does "my hand with hardness and softness," and in "this exchange" (PhP, 214; *PP,* 248) the thing and the body correlatively come to be as sensed object and sensing subject. The subject "plunges" into the thing and the thing "thinks itself" in him. (PhP, 214; *PP,* 248) Their relation is entirely internal. The perceiving subject is in the midst of things; it is the thing "itself as it is drawn together and unified, and as it begins to exist for itself" (PhP, 214; *PP,* 248); it is the "contextuality of all objects [*la texture commune de tous les objets*] " (*PP,* 272) without itself being a thing and also without being a "nothingness" or a "hole in being." The lived body is rather a "hollow" or a "fold" (PhP, 215; *PP,* 249) in the world, the place where there occurs a "dialogue" between consciousness and thing, subject and object.

*Space* furnishes us with another example of the circular system that is constituted by the lived body and the perceived world together. In the second chapter of the second part of the *Phenomenology,* Merleau-Ponty attempts to show how "objective" space, "objective" movement, etc., are in reality *founded on our being in the world* and are "encompassed [*enveloppés*] in the hold that our body takes upon the world". (PhP, 275; *PP,* 318) In the "in-itself" world there would be no here or there, no high or low. Everything would be at an equal distance from everything else; nothing would stand out from anything else, and there would be no movement since there would be no place— a "here" and a "there"—to change. If in the last analysis such a world is unthinkable, it is so for a good reason: the world that we know is something altogether different. The world we rediscover through reflection is a world we have always inhabited through our bodies: and the body is that "I can" which gives structure to the world by dividing it up and making things stand out from each other because of its presence at a certain "here." The "here" is nothing other than the body's presence in the world, and it is thus inseparable from this presence. As Bergson and Sartre have emphasized, each in his own way and in the context of his philosophy, perception is not a "function of knowledge" but the sketch of what I can do; it expresses a possible action. The perceived world is structured according to the hold that the body has or can have on it. The spatiality of the perceived world is thus a *reply* to the body's dimensions and its possibilities for action. From this point of view the lived body is not *in* space as things are; it is the point or rather the hollow from which space radiates and around which things arrange themselves in order. "What counts for the orientation of the spectacle is not my body as it in fact is, as a thing in object space, but as a system of possible actions, a virtual body with its phenomenal 'place' defined by its task and situation." (PhP, 249–50; *PP,* 289) This means that the body "inhabits the spectacle" and that space comes from "a certain *hold* of my body on the world." Thus, "everything throws us back onto the organic relations between subject and space, to that hold of the subject on the world which is the origin of space." (PhP, 251; *PP,* 291)

Magnitude, height, depth, and all other variations of the perceived world's spatiality are in the last analysis "existential dimensions." (PhP, 267; *PP,* 309) "Things co-exist in space because they are *present* to the same perceiving subject" (PhP, 275; *PP,* 318), because things and subject co-exist through the body. The body and the world form as it were a *circuit* and co-exist *internally,* and it is because of this that there can be something like space: "we have been led to bring out, as the condition of spatiality, the establishment of the subject in a setting, and finally his inherence in a world." (PhP, 280; *PP,* 325)[13]

Let us see what in this context the perceived thing and the perceiving subject must be. If a "compact" (*PP,* 359) exists between them, and if the lived body forms together with the perceived world a *sys-*

*tem* or *circular structure,* then the two terms of this dialectical system imply each other and are *correlative,* that is, neither has existence and meaning without the other. To the unity or the dialectical synthesis of the body considered as a system in its own right would *correspond* the thing as an integral unity of all of its properties. "The sensory 'properties' of a thing together constitute one and the same thing, just as my gaze, my touch and all my other senses are together the powers of one and the same body integrated into one and the same action." (PhP, 317–8; *PP,* 367) For me the thing is a kind of individual which manifests a certain mode of existence or, to use a technical term of Merleau-Ponty's, a certain *style,* just as I am myself a certain way of treating the world. In Husserlian language, one could thus characterize the relation between the lived body and the perceived thing as an *intentional* relation, where the "knowing-body" represents the side of the "noesis" and the perceived thing the side of the "noema." Unlike Husserl, however, for whom the intentional relation is *irreal* or *ideal,* Merleau-Ponty holds that it is not a question here of a relationship having to do with *knowledge* but a lived relationship, a "real implication" (PhP, 350; *PP,* 402) where the two terms mutually come to be what they *are.* The perceived thing is thus the "absolute fullness which my undivided existence *projects* before itself." (PhP, 319; *PP,* 368; emphasis ours) In short the perceived world is a *projection* of the perceiving subject and is *relative* and *correlative* to him.

What makes up the unity of the thing is thus not an "unknown X," a certain interior "substance" hidden behind and upholding the thing's "properties" or "accidents," but rather a certain "symbolism which links each sensible quality to the rest." (PhP, 319; *PP,* 368) But it should be noted that this symbolism in the thing which makes it a thing, that is, an individual with a definite physiognomy, is at the same time a symbolism *of*—and not simply "for"—my body and my entire existence. Things are for us *signs* which teach us what we are, precisely because it is we who make them be what they are.

The perceived thing is thus the "correlative of my body and, in more general terms, of my existence." (PhP, 320; *PP,* 369) Body and world are strictly inseparable; a thing can never exist "in itself because its articulations are those of our very existence". (PhP, 320; *PP,* 370) The body is the medium of things, and its presence to the world *makes it be* that *there are* "things": "The relations between things or aspects of things having always our body as their vehicle, the whole of nature

is the setting of our own life, or our interlocutor in a sort of dialogue."
(PhP, 320; *PP,* 369–70)

In this way a *first layer of expressivity* becomes apparent. The
corporeal subject and the perceived world lead one another to expression; through their mutual reference they come to know and *articulate*
themselves.

Just as the lived body is a circular system wherein the body as
consciousness and the body as object form the two moments, so also
the lived body and the perceived world form between them a true system, one which includes the system of the lived body. We live with
things and are tied to the world, which is, as it were, "our homeland,"
the ground towards which, as corporeal existences, we are "magneti-
cally attracted." (PhP, 322; *PP,* 372) Does this mean that basically we
*coincide* with things and with the being of the world, and, inversely,
that *the world is reducible to nothing more than an existential project?*
It would seem that although Merleau-Ponty's thought has a tendency
to go in this direction and to "relativize" the being of the subject and
that of the world by defining these two terms as correlatives of each
other, there is also in his work a wish to safeguard the fullness of the
world's being.

It is indeed unthinkable, as Merleau-Ponty remarks, to conceive
of a thing which would exist completely in itself, apart from all relation to a consciousness. But as he also observes, the thing nonetheless
*appears* to us as if it were a thing in itself; it is opaque and indifferent
to our hold on it, an "insurpassable plenitude." We encounter the
thing as that which withdraws from our complete possession, as that
which draws along with it an entire elusive world. Were we to formulate this experience of the thing, it would be necessary to say that
paradoxically it is an *in itself for us.* The experienced thing is "something transcendent standing in the wake of subjectivity." (PhP, 325;
*PP,* 376)

Thus, just as the bodily subject is never, as consciousness, what
it is as object and never coincides with itself, so also the circularity
and reciprocal implication between the perceiving subject and the perceived thing never result in an identity; between the two there is always
a certain *duality.* "To 'live' a thing is not to coincide with it, nor
fully to embrace it in thought." (PhP, 325; *PP,* 376) The thing is lived
by us, but it "is nevertheless transcendent in relation to our life".
(PhP, 326; *PP,* 377) It always escapes from us in the final analysis,

and it thus brings us face to face with "a background of nature which is alien to us" (*un fond de nature inhumaine*) (PhP, 324; *PP,* 374) from which it emerges and into which it retreats. As an overflowing fullness the thing reveals to us the existence of a depth of being which transcends us.

What is this "background of nature which is alien to us," this "inhuman nature"? What finally does Merleau-Ponty understand by "world"? And what is the relation between "world" and "being"? The problem encountered here is analogous to that raised by a reading of *Sein und Zeit:* it is the problem of the relations between the world and being. In the *Phenomenology,* just as in Heidegger's work, these two terms tend to get confused and, moreover, to be defined solely in relation to the notion of being-in-the-world. Merleau-Ponty's analysis of the thing and the natural world raises and leaves in suspense a question which is in fact the "*bête noire*" of phenomenolgy. It is the question of the ontological status of the world, of the being of the world. Phenomenology (in the case of Heidegger as well as in that of Merleau-Ponty) seeks to overcome the idealism-realism antinomy. Husserl in fact already believed that he had dealt with the question of the world's being by placing the "in-itself" world between parentheses. In the framework of Husserl's notion of intentionality, being is being-for-a-subject.[14] Like Heidegger, Merleau-Ponty reacted against Husserl's idealism and his notion of a transcendental Ego as the constituting source of everything which appears to consciousness. But he had not for all that—at the time of the *Phenomenology*—called into question the notion of intentionality itself. He wanted in fact to hold on to this Husserlian notion while rejecting its idealist implications. This may have been an impossible project; it is in any event the source of all the ambiguity in Merleau-Ponty's work.

Thus the world is no longer the correlative of a transcendental consciousness; it is instead the opposite pole of our preconscious bodily existence. For intellectual consciousness the world is a kind of absolute which this consciousness has absolutely not constructed or constituted. But this world is not for all that the objective, in-itself, "real" world of realism, because it remains entirely *relative* to the existential projects of the *bodily* subject. Thus Merleau-Ponty says (taking his inspiration from Heidegger), "The world is inseparable from the subject, but from a subject which is nothing but a project of the world, and the subject is inseparable from the world, but from a world which it projects itself. The subject is being-in-the-world and the world remains 'subjective' since its texture and articulations are delineated by the subject's movement of transcendence." (PhP, 430; *PP*, 491-2) When Merleau-Ponty says that the world is the "open and indefinite unity in which I have my place" (PhP, 304; *PP*, 351), that it is "the primordial unity of all our experiences standing on the horizon of our life and the one goal of all our projects" (PhP, 430; *PP*, 492), the "familiar setting of our life," he seems to want to define the world exclusively in terms of its *relation to the subject.* In his attempt to overcome objectivistic and realistic thought for which the world that we know is only the "subjective" appearance and a weak image of the world in itself, independent of us, Merleau-Ponty indeed tends to idealize or subjectivize the world, that is, to define it solely in relation to (bodily) subjectivity. He says in fact that the "thing and the world exist only in so far as they are experienced by me or by subjects like me, since they are both the concatenation of our perspectives," adding however that the thing and the world transcend our perspectives since their concatenation is temporal (PhP, 333; *PP*, 384-5)—all of which, in fact, does not attenuate in the least the ontological dependence of the world in relation to the subject since, as he says elsewhere, subjectivity is itself temporality. He thus grounds the transcendence of the world on subjectivity itself, which amounts to removing from the world any real transcendence. In this sense the world is a sort of Kantian idea, only transposed into the preconscious, existential order. This is what he calls the *phenomenological, perceived* or *natural* (since it corresponds to our natural, that is, bodily, existence) world. This world is the "correlative" (*corrélatif*) (*PP*, 381) of our undivided existence, a sort of ultimate horizon of our perspectives, the correlative of a "bodily teleology." (PhP, 322; *PP*, 373) It is what our incarnate existence projects before itself. The phenomenological world, Merleau-Ponty says, is "inseparable from subjectivity and intersubjectivity." (PhP, XX; *PP*, XV) Merleau-Ponty postulates the "radical subjectivity of all our experience" (SNS, 93; *SNS*, 163) and maintains that the only mode of being of which one can speak is "being-for-me." (SNS, 93; *SNS*, 164) Thus with him the world is still defined in the light of Husserlian intentionality; that is, it is what exists *for* a subject, this subject being, however, not Husserl's transcendental Ego but the lived body. Husserl's thematic intentionality and constitution become with Merleau-Ponty operant, bodily intentionality and constitution. But, underneath these new forms, the notions remain basically the same.

Merleau-Ponty believed that in phenomenology and its notion of intentionality he had found the means of overcoming objectivistic thought, whether it be realistic or idealistic. In conformity with the program announced at the beginning of *The Structure of Behavior,* he wants to understand the true relations between consciousness and nature. He thereby discovers that the world of our experiences, the perceived or phenomenal world—the only world of which we in fact have any experience and of which we can therefore speak—is a world which cannot be in itself, indifferent to our relation to it, since its dimensions and structures exist only as the correlatives of the lived body. The objective, in-itself world is only a conceptual world; the world with which we have our dealings is a world of which it would be meaningless to say that it could be absolutely transcendent to us since it is only in *our experience* that the world appears to us as it is. In opposition to naive realism and its conceiving of consciousness as a "representation" or "reproduction" or even "reflection," Merleau-Ponty refuses to admit that the world of our experience could be a lesser world, a weak image of a world fully determined in itself. He thus ties together or dialecticizes the objective and the subjective: there is no subject which is not a project of the world, a being in the world; and there is no world which is not "existential," the correlative to our existence. Together the world and the subject form a system and are relative to one another. If the world appears in such and such a way, it is because it is itself the correlative and the response to our existence and is structured (constituted) by the lived body. On the other hand, Merleau-Ponty believes that he is avoiding idealism, and Husserlian idealism in particular, by maintaining nonetheless that if by definition the world is what corresponds to our existence, this existence is not for all that conscious and autonomous existence. It is true that it is by means of the subject that the world is a "world," but this subject is not constituting consciousness; it is the preconscious and involuntary existence which is our body itself. It is not ourselves as personal subjects who constitute the world; and, in this sense, the *perceived* world is a *natural,* ante-predicative world that we do not constitute but take up.

There is therefore an ambiguity in Merleau-Ponty's analysis stemming from the presence of two points of view between which he oscillates almost imperceptibly. He indeed conceives of subjectivity in two different ways. Normally, when in describing or analyzing an experience Merleau-Ponty says "us," he is speaking of us as personal subjects, and conceives of subjectivity here in the more or less usual sense of the term, even if in the last analysis this subjectivity is that of the thinking, philosophizing subject, that of the intellectual and reflective *Cogito.* But for him subjectivity is also the lived body, a subjectivity beneath our personal and conscious existence, an anonymous and "natural" subjectivity. Thus when he says that "we" do not constitute the world, that does not mean for all that that the world retains its full autonomy, for the "us" here is the us in the first sense of the term. And although Merleau-Ponty does not usually say so, what he means by such an affirmation is that it is not we, as thinking subjects, who constitute the world, but it it we, as impersonal, bodily subjects, who do so. In this second sense subjectivity is radically redefined, no longer coinciding in any way with the usual sense of the term; and it is according to this meaning that one is obliged to say that Merleau-Ponty "subjectivizes" the world. It is thus necessary always to keep in view the multi-dimensionality of the argument of the *Phenomenology* under pain of misconstruing its import.

But even if the world in *the proper sense of the term* is that which has existence only in relation to our bodily existence, the question still remains: Is the world therefore nothing more than that? Where does the phenomenal world itself come from? To say that the world exists only for the (bodily) subject and that the subject exists only for the world seems to be a conception which in the last analysis does not account for the ontological status—the being—of either the world or the subject. In fact, Merleau-Ponty lets it be understood that the phenomenological world emerges from a sort of *pre-world* existing prior to the dialectical-intentional structure bodily subject–perceived world. It would seem to be our bodily presence in the midst of this pre-world which calls into being space, movement, time, things, and finally the world itself in the proper sense of the term as the contextuality of all things, the horizon of all horizons. It is necessary to admit however that Merleau-Ponty's thought is very fuzzy here, and that it is impossible to arrive at a precise idea of what this pre-world, prior to the intentional relation subject-world, might be, and if, in the last analysis, it is *really* a pre-world. Merleau-Ponty seems to be alluding to it when he speaks of the nondifferenciation of being-in-itself in which the subject exists as a "crack," opening up horizons and perspectives and constituting the world properly so called. He seems also to be aiming at a sort of pre-world when he speaks of a "a ground of inhuman nature," of the "density of being," (PhP, 196; *PP,* 229) of the "plenitude of being," or, quite simply, of "natural being" (PhP, 197; *PP,* 229). When he says that the world is the "inexhaustible reservoir from which things are drawn" (PhP, 344; *PP,* 396), it is difficult to see how this world could be the phenomenological world, the only world which according to him pre-exists, which is prior to our conscious and reflective existence. Logically speaking, it would seem that the world can have here three meanings: as the construction of objectivistic thought (the thought world, the objective world), as the correlative to our incarnate life (the perceived, natural world), or as a depth of being prior to subjectivity in whatever way one chooses to conceive of it (the inhuman world?). The entire difficulty for us is to know when and if Merleau-Ponty is speaking of the world in this last sense.

Thus in regard to the question of the being of the world, Merleau-Ponty's thought remains very ambiguous. It is as if there existed in the heart of his phenomenology a conflict of badly resolved philosophical positions.[15] The question which the *Phenomenology* raises, but which it does not succeed in elucidating, is the age-old question of the relations between being and appearing, being and phenomenon, a question as old as philosophy itself. In regard to this fundamental question about the ontological status of the world, Merleau-Ponty's thought is thus rather obscure. As he has said, his is a philosophy of ambiguity, only, it would seem, in the bad sense of the term. For the reader who would like to get to the bottom of this question that phenomenology has for so long left unanswered—the question of the meaning of the being of the world—Merleau-Ponty's attempt to formulate a philosophy which would be capable of overcoming the antinomies of idealism and realism leaves in the end much to be desired. Truth to tell, in the *Phenomenology* Merleau-Ponty is not overly concerned with this problem and, it would seem, is not even fully aware of it. Here he is interested almost exclusively in the *subject* of perception, and it will be necessary to await his other writings in order to see his interest turn towards the other term of the perceptual and intentional relation and towards the relation as such. We will then see him in the process of attempting to formulate a philosophy which can definitively overcome (while realizing it) phenomenology and the Husserlian notion of intentionality. We will then see his ontology take shape.

OTHER PEOPLE

If the *Phenomenology,* as some people have remarked, does not give to the intersubjective dimension of existence the consideration it merits, it has, notwithstanding, clearly formulated the problem that goes along with any analysis of the perception of other people from within a phenomenological point of view.

What is this problem? In its most impartial formulation it is the question: How is the other person *present* to me? We say that this is the most impartial formulation for, in fact, the question which is most often asked is altogether different: How can I *know* that other people exist? For a philosophy of consciousness the existence of other people constitutes a very real and serious problem. If subjectivity is in the first instance defined as being essentially an interiority, as the immediate and direct presence of the self to itself, as, in short, reflective *Cogito,* I could never have but the immediate experience of a single ego, my own. In this context the concept of an alter ego seems to become a contradiction, for if I constitute the world and all that I perceive, it would be necessary that this other that I perceive be constituted by me, but in this case he would not be a true alter ego, an ego like my-self; he would be what I constitute and would thus not be himself a constituting ego. From the point of view of subjectivity conceived of as constituting consciousness, there are but two possibilities: either I constitute the other, in which case he is not himself a constituting ego and is thus not a true ego, or he is a constituting consciousness and I myself am neither a constituting consciousness nor an ego.

Although Merleau-Ponty does not mention Husserl when using this argument, it is not difficult to recognize that this criticism is in fact directed against him. And, indeed, a few years later in one of his courses at the Sorbonne, Merleau-Ponty explicitly criticizes Husserl's position. As it is presented in the Fifth Cartesian Meditation, Husserl's thought takes as its point of departure consciousness which coincides with itself, constituting consciousness, the transcendental Ego. Husserl attempts to show "how I can constitute in myself another Ego or, more radically, how I can constitute in my monad another monad, and can experience what is constituted in me as nevertheless other than me." (par. 55) Husserl tries to avoid the contradiction which such an idea seems to include by making a distinction between perception and what he calls "apperception." I do not perceive the other as I perceive things in the world; his body does not exist for me as a simple physical reality. Behind the body that I perceive I divine the presence of another psychical life, or, rather, I do perceive this life, but in a mediate fashion— I "apperceive" it. Husserl is proposing a notion which in fact resembles a sort of reasoning by analogy (cf., e.g., par. 54 of the *Cartesian Meditations*). But if such a notion suffices to conceive of the other as another "psychical life," it does not suffice to posit the other as an alter ego, that is, as another transcendental Ego, another constituting consciousness. The idea of "apperception" or "appresentation" tends to make the solution too easy, and Husserl himself did not fail to recognize its insufficiency. In the last analysis he always comes back to the requirement which he formulates in the following way: "The only conceivable manner in which others can have for me the sense and status of existent others, thus and so determined, consists in their being constituted *in me* as others." (par. 56) And this means, "The question after all concerns, not other men, but the manner in which the Ego (as the transcendental onlooker experiences him transcendentally) constitutes within himself the distinction between Ego and Other Ego." (par. 44) In the Fifth Meditation Husserl constantly reaffirms the prejudice which serves as his point of departure: "the Cartesian conception of the *Cogito*" (CAL, 43; *BP*, 239), the notion of a transcendental Ego which *constitutes within himself* and by himself the other as other. For Merleau-Ponty there is throughout the Fifth Meditation an internal vice which Husserl does not manage to overcome. Like Descartes, "Husserl also refuses to *overcome* the constitutive contradiction in the perception of the other," and "on the brink of an intersubjective conception Husserl maintains in the last analysis an integral transcendental subjectivity." (CAL, 45; *BP*, 240)

What we see here—there can be no question about it—is a whole way of doing philosophy which is being called into question. What Merleau-Ponty takes exception to in Husserl is in the last analysis the notion of an *intuitive* or eidetic philosophy. It is the prejudice of the *Cogito,* the notion of an "apodictic ego" which would be in an immediate and fully clear possession of itself, a transcendental onlooker for whom its own body, things, and the other's body would be but objects spread out before its consciousness. It is therefore, at an ontological level, the notion that "There are two modes of being, and two only: being in itself, which is that of objects arrayed in space, and being for itself, which is that of consciousness." (PhP, 349; *PP,* 401–2)

Now, for Merleau-Ponty the rediscovery of the lived body enables us to overcome the alternative of the in itself and the for itself and to give an account of the genuine presence of the other, a presence that every idealistic philosophy recognizes or presupposes, even if it does not succeed in justifying it in its theory. Merleau-Ponty believes that he has discovered in the experience of the lived body "a third genus of being" (PhP, 350; *PP,* 402), that is, a mode of being which is neither that of being in itself nor that of being for itself but, as it were, the dialectical synthesis of the two. As perceptual consciousness I am not a pure subject, I am not a consciousness *of* my body; I *am* this massive and opaque body which *knows itself.* For Merleau-Ponty the solution to the "problem" of other people is to be found in the revelation of this mode of being which undercuts the antinomy of the in itself and the for itself: "If I experience this inhering of my consciousness in its body and its world, the perception of other people and the plurality of consciousnesses no longer present any difficulty." (PhP, 351; *PP,* 403) Indeed, if my body is not an object for me, the body of the other is not one either. In this case my body opens me onto the other who is himself an open, bodily existence. If I am not a pure interiority,[16] but rather a being which lives outside of itself (which transcends itself), the other, who is like me, exists in the same way, and it is that which allows for our encountering each other.

The secret of the presence of the other resides therefore in the perception that I have of my own body.[17] There is a prefiguration—to be understood in an ontological and not a temporal sense—of the perception of the other in the natural reflection of the body on itself wherein, when one's two hands touch each other, the subject is for himself an *other.* The experience of the other "presupposes that already my view of myself is half-way to having the quality of a possible 'other'". (PhP, 448; *PP,* 511) It is the lived body as a circular structure which, by accomplishing the synthesis of the in itself and the for itself, makes it be that my field of bodily experience intertwines with that of the other. There is no "reasoning by analogy" in the perception of the other, because this perception here involves not two *Cogitos* which infer each other's existence, but two knowing-bodies which "couple up" (*s'accouplent*) and which know each other "diametrically." Just as my body knows itself by "a sort of reflection," so also my body and the body of the other reflect each other and instigate between themselves a "reflection": "...when my gaze meets another gaze, I re-enact the alien existence in a sort of reflection." (PhP, 352; PP, 404) As Merleau-Ponty will say in the Preface to Signs, here there is but one life, two gazes which reflect each other and which coexist "one in the other." (S, 24)

Thus between one's own lived body and the body of the other there is a circularity such that these two bodies together form a *single system,* just as, between consciousness and the body and between the lived body and the perceived world, there are internal relations which make it be that all these elements are moments of a single circular structure: "Between my consciousness and my body as I experience it, between this phenomenal body of mine and that of the other as I see it from the outside, there exists an internal relation which causes the other to appear as the completion of the system." (PhP, 352; PP, 405) For me as a bodily existence the existence of the other does not constitute a problem because as being in the world I am immediately present to the other who is himself being in the world. *The relation with the other is thus mediated by the world;* I and the other are "brought together in the one single world in which we all participate as anonymous subjects of perception." (PhP, 353; PP, 406) Inasmuch as the system myself–the other is the system myself–the world–the other it is to be understood as the system which encompasses the two systems we have already analyzed (me–my body, the lived body–the perceived world) and as the ultimate and most complete dimension of being in the world.

Underlining the complementarity of the lived body and that of the other and the fact that these two bodies together form one single circular structure, Merleau-Ponty says, "as the parts of my body together comprise a system, so my body and the body of the other are one whole, two sides of one and the same phenomenon, and the anonymous existence of which my body is the ever-renewed trace henceforth inhabits both bodies simultaneously." (PhP, 354; PP, 406) At the basis of my being I come across myself not as the personal owner of my life but as the trace of a life current which has no proper name and in which both I and the other participate. The passage that we have just quoted directly anticipates that strange passage in Signs: "We must conceive—certainly not of a soul of the world or the group or the couple, of which we would be but the instruments—but of a primordial *One (On)*... which is experienced anew in each of our perceptions." (S, 175; *S,* 221) If one wished to project these short and obscure allusions onto an ontological plane, one would have to say that in the depths of his being the subject is but a relation and a participation, that the self and the other are relational and that they exist only on the ground of a more vast generality, that they both spring from a single source and are animated by a single life.

We are not going to follow up these remarks, for they would lead us directly into the ontological field and beyond the *Phenomenology.* In order to see Merleau-Ponty pursue and elucidate what is here but a vague allusion, we will have to await his last writings. Besides, we are faced with a more immediate question. For if indeed subjectivity is conceived of as being primordially an *anonymous* intersubjectivity, this would seem to deny precisely that which must be clarified, namely, the community of *subjectivities.* If at the level of bodily existence the subject is inextricably mixed with a life which is not properly its own but rather the life of a "one," a life of generality and anonymity where there are not yet any *I*'s, there is, to be sure, a kind of communion or exchange; but this can cannot properly be said to be an "intersubjectivity" for the simple reason that here there are not two subjectivities properly speaking, two subjects each of which has its own, first person existence. At first glance it would seem therefore that if the philosophy of the *Cogito* does not succeed in accounting for intersubjective life, Merleau-Ponty's phenomenology fares no better. In the former instance the subject is closed in on himself, thereby ruling out any knowledge which is not a constitution; in the latter instance the very notion of subjectivity seems to be denied and, consequently, any possibility of a genuine intersubjectivity. This is the objection that Merleau-Ponty raises after having described the myself–the other relation as an integral system of two "natural" or bodily subjectivities: "if the perceiving *I* is genuinely an *I,* it cannot perceive a different one; if the perceiving subject is anonymous, the other which it perceives is equally so." (PhP, 356; *PP,* 408)

But, as we have seen, this is exactly the case: the perceiving subject is an anonymous existence. It would thus seem to follow as a consequence that the communion of "subjects" at the perceptive level can only be a "mute," anonymous communication. At the level of perception there can only be a natural subjectivity and an anonymous intersubjectivity. Everything we have seen about Merleau-Ponty's phenomenology forces us to this conclusion. We must nevertheless not discontinue our analysis at this point, for the whole meaning of Merleau-Ponty's philosophy is summed up in his attempt to overcome the alternative of a purely transcendental subjectivity and a subjectivity which would be no more than a dispersion and a loss of itself.

The course entitled "Consciousness and the Acquisition of Language" from which we have already quoted throws a helpful light on this situation. If Merleau-Ponty is unequivocally opposed to Husserl's position in the *Cartesian Meditations,* he does not for all that accept Scheler's conclusions. While Husserl takes the Cartsian *Cogito* as his point of departure, Scheler—Merleau-Ponty tells us—places himself in a directly opposite position by starting out from the "total *undifferentiation* between the self and the other." (CAL, 45; *BP,* 240) Merleau-Ponty sees in these two antithetical positions difficulties from which neither of the two philosophers managed to escape: "For Husserl the problem is to go from consciousness of self to that of others. In Scheler's view, it is a question of understanding how the consciousness of self and of others can arise out of a background of primitive indistinctness."

In the analysis of the perception of the other there are two theses to be reconciled: the certain and immediate consciousness of self and the certain and immediate consciousness of the other. This phenomenon cannot be accounted for by suppressing one or the other of these two requirements. In the last analysis Merleau-Ponty sees in Scheler's position a forgetfulness of what is individual and irreducible in the *I* as well as in the other. He asks, "Does he not bring the consciousness of self and of the other down to the level of a neutral psychism which is neither one nor the other?" And he draws the conclusion: "Scheler's conception skirts a kind of panpsychism, at the heart of which there is no individuation of consciousnesses." (Cal, 48; *BP,* 241) Thus even though Merleau-Ponty wants at all cost to avoid the Cartesian notion of the *Cogito*, in no way does he wish to deny the ipseity of the subject.

Indeed, by analyzing the phenomenon of the perception of the other and by attempting to reconcile the two requirements it seems to put to reflection—the presence of the other, the presence of the self to itself—Merleau-Ponty is finally led to attempt a renewal of the notion of subjectivity itself. The question is finally that of knowing how I, as *Cogito,* as reflecting subject, can be open to that which is not me and experience it as other. It would seem that the paradox can be overcome if the lesson of the analysis of the perception of the other is drawn: I am, qua *Cogito,* given to myself. "The central phenomenon, at the root of both my subjectivity and my transcendence towards others, consists in my being given to myself. *I am given,* that is, I find myself already situated and involved in a physical and social world—*I am given to myself,* which means that this situation is never hidden from me, it is never round about me as an alien necessity, and I am never in effect enclosed in it like an object in a box." (PhP, 360; *PP,* 413)

We said that *at the level of perception* the subject is inextricably mixed with the other and that there is here only a natural subjectivity, an impersonal and anonymous life "in the third person." Viewed from the point we have now reached, however, this is obviously an abstraction. For as a matter of fact what exists is not first of all a "One" and then afterwards an *I*; the case is rather that it is an *I* which discovers the One as a dimension of its *own* being. Rather than say that what exists is a natural subjectivity and that this subjectivity is impersonal and anonymous, it would be better to say that nature penetrates to the very heart of the personal, thinking subject and that the latter encounters *in himself* an anonymous element, a certain abyss into which his being escapes (or rather, perhaps, an abyss out of which his being arises). For it must not be forgotten that the discovery of the One was *already an act of reflection,* that is, the act of a conscious and reflecting subject. Unlike Husserl and Scheler, one must hold together the two ends of the analysis—reflection and anonymity—and see *in reflection itself* their reconciliation. He who speaks and writes and asks himself how the other is present to him is a subject reflecting on an experience—that of the presence of the other—which he first of all lived naively and unquestioningly; he thus discovers within himself a depth of lived and unreflected experience which he carries in the heart of his personal being. Reflection discovers itself as reflection on an unreflected out of which it emerges and which continues to envelop it like a persistant haze. An analysis of the perception of the other thus inevitably leads to a reflection on reflection, and what is in question is the very nature of reflection and the *Cogito,* of subjectivity. From this point of view, "What is given and initially true is a reflection open to the unreflected, the reflective assumption of the unreflected— and similarly there is given the tension of my experience towards another whose existence on the horizon of my life is beyond doubt, even when my knowledge of him is imperfect." (PhP, 359; *PP*, 413) And in order to emphasize that these two problems are basically one and the same and that in the last analysis it is reflection (subjectivity) itself which is in question, Merleau-Ponty adds, "There is more than a vague analogy between the two problems, for in both cases it is a matter of finding out how to steal a march on myself and experience the unreflected as such." (PhP, 359–60; *PP*, 413)

Certain commentators have directed their criticism onto this central project, characterizing the notion of a reflection on the "unreflected as such" as paradoxical. We shall return to this question in a future chapter; for the time being it is enough to note that the analysis of the perception of the other essentially leads in the end towards a new way of conceiving of *subjectivity*, of the *Cogito*. The phenomenological reduction, such as practiced by Merleau-Ponty, leads us to the reflecting subject, but unlike the Husserlian epoch it brings us face to face, not with a subject which is the constituting source of all that is, but with a subject which discovers itself to be *derived*. Thus, "Transcendental subjectivity is a revealed subjectivity, revealed to itself and to others, and is for that reason an intersubjectivity." (PhP, 361; *PP*, 415)

Transcendental (reflective) subjectivity is thus a *founded* subjectivity. The impersonal life of the One, one's life as intermixed with that of others, is not an "object," a region of being, but is rather a "permanent field" or a "dimension" (PhP, 362; *PP*, 415) of personal existence, of the *Cogito*. The "problem of other people" comes down in the final analysis to the problem of the transcendence and rootedness of the personal subject; and the question is to know *"how the presence to myself (Urpräsenz) which defines me and conditions every alien presence is at the same time de-presentation (entgegenwärtigung) and throws me outside myself."* (PhP, 363; *PP*, 417) We must therefore see how the subject is at one and the same time *"naturans* and *naturatus"* (PhP, 365; *PP*, 419), how he is a transcendence but is such only on the ground of what is "natural" in him.

It is clear that Merleau-Ponty wants to conceive of subjectivity as a dialogue and interchange with the world and with the other and that he wants to do so by conceiving of the *presence* of the self to itself, which is the very definition of subjectivity and which makes of it something "undeniable", as precisely a derived presence (subjectivity as given to itself), and that he wants to reconcile the notions of anonymity and personality. It is not certain however that in the *Phenomenology* he succeeds in this attempt.

## 2. Being in the World as Transcendence

At the beginning of our analysis of the *Phenomenology* we pointed out that this work displays three major themes: circularity, transcendence, and rootedness. As we turn now to the theme of transcendence we must be aware that we have already touched on what is essential to the question in our analysis of being in the world as circularity. To say that the lived body constitutes along with the perceived world a rigorous system and that it cannot be conceived of outside of this intrinsic relation is to say that it *transcends itself* and that this fact of transcendence is its *very definition.* We need, though, to better clarify what we have seen only in a vague way.

The notion of transcendence lends itself, indeed, to two possible interpretations. One could understand it in a "Hegelian" sense, that is, as a vertical overcoming wherein existence would transcend itself towards a greater perfection and a greater degree of being; or again one could rule out any notion of this sort by allowing a solely horizontal transcendence, that is, a transcendence which would include only the intentional relations between man and the world. The latter conception is proposed to us by Sartre's philosophy, which, in presenting itself as an explicitly atheistic humanism, refuses to recognize a vertical transcendence in the case of man, the possibility whereby man could, in good faith, commit himself to a movement of being which surpasses him. With Merleau-Ponty, on the contrary, we encounter a thought which, basing itself on a concrete analysis of the human phenomenon, attempts to unify the two notions of vertical and horizontal transcendence according to the requirements that the phenomenon itself seems to call for when one attempts to think it. That for Merleau-Ponty there is a horizontal transcendence between the body and the world is something we have already clearly seen. But what must finally be seen is that this constitutive intentionality between the body and the world only exists because bodily existence embodies a movement of vertical transcendence in relation to the world and natural being.

Between the perceived world and the lived body there exist intentional relations such that the two together form a single system, a circular structure. As perceptual consciousness I am but a project of the world, and the perceived world is constituted as the correlative to this project. The world is here "inseparable from our views of the world." and, correlatively, subjectivity is to be understood as "inherence in the world." (PhP, 405; *PP*, 464) Between the two there is an internal relation: "The world is wholly inside and I am wholly outside myself." (PhP, 407; *PP*, 467) The subject is essentially an "ex-stasis"; there is "a relationship of active transcendence between the subject and the world." (PhP, 430; *PP*, 491) Existence is thus to be understood as *ex-sistence*. With Merleau-Ponty the word "existence" takes on a very special meaning, because, for him, to say that man exists is to say that he ex-sists—that he transcends himself towards that which is not him and that this act of transcendence constitutes and defines him, is his very essence.

Thus the primordial fact that the *Phenomenology* takes note of is that of the *presence* of the subject to the world (and, at the same time, to others). What Merleau-Ponty's phenomenology has uncovered has not been a new kind of transcendental Ego, an acosmic subject which would find within itself the justification and reason for everything it perceives; it has been a subject which is but a presence to the world—the *Phenomenology* has conceived of existence as being in the world.

The fact which serves as a basis for all others is thus that of the *presence* of the bodily subject to the perceived world. It is this contingent fact without apparent reason that thus reveals itself to reflection as the source of all "explanations," the origin of all *rationality*. The "only pre-existent Logos is the world itself," Merleau-Ponty writes (PhP, XX; *PP*, XV), understanding by world here the "phenomenological" world, that is, the presence of the subject to the world, being in the world. The presence of these beginnings, this primordial opening, this *Offenheit*, is for him the foundation and the ground of all rationality. What we have seen in connection with circularity enables us to understand what he means. The "relation of active transcendence" which is the circularity between the subject and the world is what makes it be that for us there is a *meaningful* world, that there is *meaning*. The meaning of the world is the meaning of man's existence in the world: those "natural" meanings that we call colors are, for instance, expressions of the different ways in which the subject inhabits the world; they are expressions of his presence to the world. We have thus seen that our cohabitation with the world is a relation of *expressivity* (the manifestation, therefore, of a "logos") where, in intermingling in "a sort of dialogue," the body and the world *articulate* themselves, *express* and *define* themselves. If, as basically every great philosophy does, one looks for the origin of rationality or meaning, one must in this perspective look for it there where as a nascent logos or meaning it reveals itself for the first time: in the transcendence that bodily existence manifests.

But if, through the fact of its explosive presence to the world, the lived body causes to spring up in the featureless world of the in-itself those concrete meanings that things and the "qualities" of things are (which, as meanings, are the diverse expressions of this presence itself), it does so only because it is not a mere part of the world and is not itself a thing. The lived body transcends itself towards the world because it transcends itself as a worldly thing. The intentionality between the bodily subject and the perceived world (this horizontal transcendence) is thus but the expression of a transcendence that the lived body realizes in regard to itself. This is why the body is the world but is so only as a "hollow" or a "fold." The lived body is that in-itself which exists for-itself; it is a consciousness of the world, a natural subject. As we have seen, what is unique about the body is that it can reflect on itself; to express the matter in another way, it transcends itself as a mere physical object.

*The Structure of Behavior* had already tried to point out the essential difference between the human and the animal bodies. The human body is either more or less but is never the same thing as an animal body, because it is the bearer of a power of signification; as a human body it is "a power of natural expression." (PhP, 181; *PP,* 211) Bodily existence is "always a prey to an active nothingness." (PhP, 165; *PP,* 193) As an incarnate existence, "I never become quite a thing in the world; the density of existence as a thing always evades me, my own substance slips away from me internally, and some intention is always foreshadowed." (PhP, 165; *PP,* 192–3) The lived body reveals a power of "escape" or transcendence (*échappement*) (*PP,* 199) by which that which is natural in it is taken as a means for achieving and expressing a "figured," human meaning.

This is what an examination of human sexuality reveals. In the chapter "The Body in Its Sexual Being," Merleau-Ponty attempts to show that bodily existence is transcendent in regard to itself as mere biological existence. In the case of the normal individual, sexuality never functions as an autonomous physiological mechanism. It is already penetrated and transformed through and through by personal attitudes, and, conversely, personal existence always has a sexual meaning or coloring. This means that sexuality in the case of man—that aspect of his being which is most obviously corporeal—is not a chance thing but a meaningful expression of his being, of his humanity.

In fact, there is nothing purely "natural" in man. Or, rather, in him everything is natural and everything is "invented." "It is impossible to superimpose on man a lower layer of behavior which one chooses to call 'natural', followed by a invented cultural or spiritual world. Everything is both invented and natural in man". (PhP, 189; *PP*, 220-1)

There exist meanings which are engendered by bodily behavior and from which they are inseparable but which at the same time transcend it. Sexual love which expresses more than mere desire, which literally incarnates love and brings it into being, is an example. It is one of the more striking examples, but in fact all bodily gestures are uses of the body which possess meanings, ones which are inseparable from the very movement of the body expressing them, but which are nonetheless transcendent to the body as a mere anatomical apparatus. A gesture as "natural" as the kiss, for instance, is in reality a cultural and invented usage of the body.[18]

For Merleau-Ponty all of this shows that the "use a man is to make of his body is transcendent in relation to that body as a mere biological entity." (PhP, 189; *PP,* 220) This leads him to say that "Man is a historical idea and not a natural species" (PhP, 170; *PP,* 199)— by which he means that "there is in human existence no unconditioned possession, and yet no fortuitous attribute."[19] In man everything is natural and everything is invented, and this is true because "there is in human existence a principle of indeterminacy". (PhP, 169; *PP,* 197) The "equivocal" is constitutive of human existence which is always more than it is. Existence is thus not a factual state of affairs, and man is not a "substance," a sort of super-thing, an animal endowed with a "soul." Existence is an *act;* it is "the very process whereby the hitherto meaningless takes on meaning, whereby what had merely a sexual significance assumes a more general one, chance is transformed into reason." And this "act in which existence takes up, for its own purposes, and transforms such a situation" is, as we know, what Merleau-Ponty calls transcendence. In the final analysis therefore, what is "natural" in man is his transcendence of the natural: "the human body is defined in terms of its property of appropriating, in an indefinite series of discontinuous acts, significant cores which transcend and transfigure its natural powers." (PhP, 193; *PP,* 226)

Even *speech,* which is often treated as being essentially an operation of thought and spirit, must be viewed in the context of the power
the lived body has of reflecting on and expressing itself (that is, of
turning back on itself, doubling up, and taking itself for an object).
For Merleau-Ponty it is but "one particular case" (PhP, 189; *PP,* 221)
of this "primordial process of signification" (PhP, 166; *PP,* 193).
In the chapter entitled "The Body as Expression, And Speech," he
attempts to expose the link between these two functions—natural
expression and speech—and to show how speech is founded on the
expressive function of the body and how it extends it.

Directing his criticism to intellectualistic and empiricist explanations, he maintains that speech is neither the mere translation of an
already fully selfconscious thought nor a mere physiological operation
where the "meaning" of words would be but the existence of paths
traced out in the nervous system. In both of these conceptions the
meaning expressed by a word is conceived of as being essentially exterior to the word itself. But for Merleau-Ponty the word's meaning
is inseparable from it[20] —which is what he means when he says that
*"the word has a meaning."* (PhP, 177; *PP,* 206) Speech possesses its
meaning exactly "like" the gesture does, which means that speech is
essentially a use that body makes of itself: the word is "one of the
modulations, one of the possible uses of my body." (PhP, 180; *PP,*
210) "The spoken word is a genuine gesture, and it contains its meaning in the same way as the gesture contains its." (PhP, 183; *PP,* 214)
Speech is therefore to be understood, not as an "operation of knowledge," but as an existential function of the body wherein it takes
itself for an object in order to project itself outside, in order to signify.
Like the gesture, speech is born of a "natural" use of the body and is
inseparable from it; although, not being the foreseeable result of the
anatomical structure of the body, it is, like the kiss, transcendent to
the body taken as a mere biological entity. It thus demonstrates that
bodily existence is already more than natural and biological existence,
that it is already a "natural" movement of transcendence.

It is however necessary to add—and Merleau-Ponty does not
hesitate to do so—that if speech is but "one particular case" of the
body's expressive function, it is nonetheless a *very* special case. For
of all the expressive operations of the body speech is unique in that it
contains a *claim on the absolute.* While the meaning of a gesture is
strictly inseparable from the gesture itself and can only be repeated
by a repetition of the gesture, the meaning of a sentence, once expressed,

seems to us to be like an acquisition which does not need to be said to be thought. It seems able to settle itself in eternity and detach itself from its bodily origin. Speech introduces us to the notion of truth as infinite *telos*: "speech implants the idea of truth in us as the presumptive limit of its effort. It loses sight of itself as a contingent fact, and takes to resting upon itself; this is, as we have seen, what provides us with the ideal of thought without word". (PhP, 190; *PP*, 221) Precisely because speech, of all the expressive operations of the body, seems to be the only one capable of transcending itself as a bodily expression and of effectuating a double reflection (a reflection on itself precisely as a natural reflection of the body on itself), we reserve for later (Chapter III) a detailed analysis both of speech and its creative use by the writer and the thinker. What should be noted now is that speech, like every transcendent use of the body, bears witness to a "natural" power of transcendence the lived body brings about in relation to natural being. Corporeal existence is already a crack in the "plenitude of being" (PhP, 196; *PP*, 229); and speech does no more than take up and extend "that productivity which is man's deepest essence," that "surplus of our existence over natural being." (PhP, 197; *PP*, 229)

We see therefore that for Merleau-Ponty bodily existence is already a movement of transcendence, that transcendence is the very definition of man as an incarnate being and is thus not a secondary element which would only make its appearance at the level of spirit and explicitly symbolic expression. The lived body is itself an instigator of meaning, a transforming opening in the undifferentiation of natural being.

In unveiling the expressive operation of the lived body and in showing that it is itself a power of expression, Merleau-Ponty feels that he has discovered an "enigmatic nature" (PhP, 197; *PP*, 230) in it. The whole enigma seems to come from the fact that, while being a visible part of the world, the lived body is not for all that a thing like the other visible parts of the world and other biological bodies, but is, in its very corporeity, more than it is—it is that "opening" in the world whence an invisible world, a world of meaning, emerges in the midst of *visibilia*. The "ambiguity of the body" stems from the fact that it is more than a mere physical and natural reality, that it is endowed with a "metaphysical structure." (PhP, 167; *PP*, 195) "Metaphysics—the coming to light of something beyond nature—is not localized at the level of knowledge: it begins with the opening out upon 'another', and is to be found everywhere, and already, in the specific development of sexuality" (PhP, 168; *PP*, 195)—as well as in the gesture and in speech.

Having recognized the existence of "an immanent or incipient significance in the living body" (PhP, 197; *PP*, 230) and having consequently discovered in it an "enigmatic nature," Merleau-Ponty is led to characterize bodily existence as a "miracle." (PhP, 194; *PP*, 226) Indeed, if "that incarnate meaning" which constitutes the central phenomenon of bodily existence is born from an immanent use of the body itself and is thus not to be explained as a derivative product of spirit or reason, if it is not a free and conscious production, there can be no explanations for it. Existence appears to be nothing other than "the perpetual taking up of fact and hazard by a reason nonexistent before and without those circumstances." (PhP, 127; *PP*, 148) In this case it is necessary to recognize that this act of transcendence is "like an ultimate fact" (PhP, 194; *PP*, 266) and must be made the definition of man. This is obviously a definition which resolves nothing, which only brings out more clearly the enigmatic, mysterious nature of man. At the bottom of his being, in the deepest parts of that involuntary and preconscious region, he is a transforming and creative existence. There can be no other definition of this foundation of personal and spiritual life than that one which refuses all "explanation," which recognizes that bodily existence is more than it is, that it cannot be explained, and that it is the expression of a drive of transcendence which arises through it, for which it lacks the "secret," and which it only embodies. There is a "drama" which transpires in the body of which we are not the authors.

The ultimate definition of man is thus that he is a "movement of transcendence." Here in the *Phenomenology* Merleau-Ponty's last word will be to call this power of transcendence—this "mystery of reason"—a "miracle" or a "mystery" without explanation; and we will have to wait until his last writings to see him return to this notion of a "drama" which transpires in the body and of which the body is the expression in an attempt to elucidate it better and to ask what in the final analysis all of this *means*.

## 3.  Being in the World as Rootedness

The argument of *The Structure of Behavior* was directed primarily against empiricism. In the *Phenomenology* the principal adversary is always intellectualist philosophy. Whether the question concerns perception, sexuality, or speech, the constant goal of Merleau-Ponty is to show that so-called bodily operations are precisely that—they secrete and contain in themselves the meanings they manifest and, as expressive functions, are not be be understood as mere reflections of an operation of a sovereign spirit or a pure intelligence. In fact, in the third part of the *Phenomenology* which bears the title "Being-for-Itself and Being-in-the-World," he attempts to show how the conscious and free subject who unfolds intellectual or spiritual powers is rather to be understood as a derived subject in regard to the bodily subject; if, at the level of personal existence in the proper sense of the term, the subject is capable of original operations, this is so only because he rests on a layer of existence which is already meaningful and from which he draws his strength. In writing his chapter on "the Cogito," he could well have used this sentence from Saint-Exupéry: "It is thought that man can advance straight ahead. What is not seen is the cord which attaches him to the well-spring, which, like an umbilical cord, attaches him to the stomach of the earth."[21]

All bodily or perceptual experience, then, does not depend on an intellectual function which would structure it in accordance with certain norms or criteria possessed by virtue of its own nature; on the contrary, it is intelligence or reason which is supported by perceptual life. Already on page 31 (*PP*, 40) of the *Phenomenology*, Merleau-Ponty had revealed the central aim of his efforts: "Consciousness must be faced with its own unreflected life in things and awakened to its own history which it was forgetting: such is the true part that philosophical reflection has to play".

This is not to say that Merleau-Ponty wants to *reduce* consciousness to perception. The path of empiricism has been left behind, even if with intellectualism it remains always a temptation which reflection must at all cost resist. The existence of a reflective consciousness, the existence, in short, of the *Cogito,* is on the contrary an indubitable fact, and there is no question with Merleau-Ponty of denying its originality and transcendence in regard to bodily existence. However, this *Cogito*—which everyone can ascertain as soon as he reflects on the fact that all knowledge is at once reflective knowledge, that is, that to know is to know that one knows and that in the last analysis there would be no knowledge if knowledge were not a presence to and possession of oneself—this *Cogito* is not to be conceived of as *causa sui,* as being its own origin, but as hailing from an obscure region which is none other than the prepersonal and anonymous life of the subject. It is thus a matter of revealing, at the heart of the thinking subject, obscure zones and a certain "unreason;" but it is not in any way a matter of making reason into a mere transposition or derivation of perceptual or bodily functions, in short, of *explaining* consciousness in terms of the body. Merleau-Ponty's fundamental problematic is to *"understand how subjectivity can be both dependent and undeniable [indéclinable]."* (PhP, 400; *PP,* 459; emphasis ours) For as the self's possession of and presence to itself, as an original and irreducible realm, consciousness is indeed undeniable. But, on the other hand, if consciousness possesses itself and is to a certain degree transparent to itself, for Merleau-Ponty this is due precisely to the fact that it has originally been *given to itself,* and thus at the basis of its activity there exists an insurpassable passivity which is thereby nothing other than the mark of its *birth.* For him it is therefore a question of undertaking an "archeology" or a "genealogy" of the thinking subject in order to unearth the sedimented layers of prepersonal existence which support and foreshadow this subject.

This is why we have chosen the term "rootedness" ("*enracinement*")[22] to refer to this theme of the *Phenomenology* which in so many ways constitutes its central project. One does not explain the flowers and fruits of a tree by its roots, but on the other hand, through its roots the tree takes the nourishment that it afterwards transforms into fruit, and through its roots, in the last analysis, it exists. In the *Phenomenology* one can find a great number of expressions referring to the inherence of the *Cogito* in the body and the world—among which the term, borrowed from Husserl, of *Fundierung,* which plays the role of a technical term—but we prefer to sum them all up with this other word, "rootedness," which seems to us to depict best the essentially *organic* links which exist between the thinking subject and his body and between him and the world.

As we know, the decisive discovery of the *Phenomenology* has been that of the lived body, the realization that the body is like a *natural subject.* In opposition to empiricism, Merleau-Ponty had indicated in *The Structure of Behavior* that if nature shows itself to be meaningful, the meaning which it thus manifests does not exist *in* nature considered as an object in itself but is rather a *perceptual* meaning; that is, it does not exist apart from the onlooker who perceives it. But in opposition to intellectualism, he has shown in the *Phenomenology* that the onlooker for whom the world is meaningful is not yet thematic consciousness and that the meaning of the world is not constructed or constituted by "an act of significance or *Sinn-gebung.*" (PhP, 428; *PP,* 490) The various Gestalt forms or meaningful structures are rather to be understood as the expressions of a corporeal dialogue between the body and the world, and the perceiving subject as a subject which forms a "circuit" with the world. The meaning of the world stems from "our collusion with" it (PhP, 429; *PP,* 491), from our bodily cohabitation with it.

If therefore the world has an immediate meaning for me, this is not an intellectual meaning but the very familiarity of my body with it. The lived body is itself an instigator of meaning: "the gaze is that perceptual genius underlying the thinking subject which can give to things the precise reply that they are awaiting in order to exist before us." (PhP, 264; *PP,* 305) Thus if I, as *Cogito,* reflective subject, ascertain the existence of a meaningful world, this *is not* because "my actual contact with the thing awakens within me a primordial knowledge of all things and because my finite and determinate perceptions are the partial manifestations of a power of knowing which is co-extensive with the world and unfolds it in its full extent and depth." (PhP, 370; *PP,* 424)

It is thus necessary to recognize, beneath all active or thematic intentionality, an "operative intentionality already at work before any positing or any judgment, a 'Logos of the aesthetic world'" which is the very "condition of possibility" (PhP, 429; *PP,* 490) of all constitutive operations on the part of the thinking subject. Before any intellectual operation of signification, existence is already fully significant; and thus, if the *Cogito* or reflective consciousness is undeniably a fact, it is in a way a secondary fact, that is, a *founded* fact: "the 'mental' or cultural life borrows its structures from natural life and...the thinking subject must have its basis in the subject incarnate." (PhP, 193; *PP,* 225)

Having thus discovered a power of signification in the lived body at work before all intellectual operations, Merleau-Ponty's effort in writing the chapter on "The Cogito" will essentially be limited to showing how intellectual life rests on a life which precedes it and how, as he says, "All knowledge takes its place within the horizons opened up by perception." (PhP, 207; *PP,* 240) Although if, Merleau-Ponty will say, the subject qua *Cogito* thinks itself original in that its business is with truth, it only takes up and transforms here what it had initially learnt in the unreflected life of perception, it is "the perception of the world…which ever serves as the basis for our idea of truth." (PhP, XVI; *PP,* XI)

Merleau-Ponty sets about substantiating this thesis by showing how the act of perceiving cannot be reduced, as Cartesian analysis would like, to the *thought of perceiving.* To be sure, as Cartesianism rightly insists, there would be no perception if the act of perceiving were not indissociably the *certainty* of perceiving. This is to say there would be no perception if the perceiving subject were not aware of himself and did not possess himself precisely as a consciousness of perceiving; the doctrine of the *Cogito* claims to be but the statement of the fact that to be conscious is at the same time to be conscious of being conscious. But what for Merleau-Ponty is to be noted is that the certainty which the subject has of seeing (the presence of the self to itself) comes, not from a prior coincidence of his consciousness with itself, but occurs in the very *act* of perception; that is, the subject discovers and possesses himself only on the basis of his actual contact with things and the world.

Consciousness possesses itself only by belonging to the world, and the certainty of seeing is but the certainty of being present to the world, of transcending oneself to what is not oneself. The subject does not step out from his being in order to discover things; rather he returns to himself and becomes conscious of his being by associating with them; one is certain of seeing only when one is certain of seeing something. It is therefore essential to perception to be related to what is not it, and the certainty that it necessarily includes is one with its transcendence; it is but the result and the expression of it. Hence, Merleau-Ponty concludes, "The acts of the *I* are of such a nature that they outstrip themselves leaving no interiority of consciousness. Consciousness is transcendence through and through". (PhP, 376; *PP,* 431)

But if this conclusion seems to be imposed on us by an analysis of perception, is the situation not otherwise when it is a question of "pure" thought and of intellectual operations in the full sense of the word, where, it would seem, the *Cogito* finds within itself its own *cogitata*? Consider for instance the science of geometry. The idea of the triangle would seem to be, purely and simply, an eternal idea which reason discovers within itself and by its own resources: by triangle I, as thinking subject, mean a figure formed with three straight lines, the sum of whose angles is equal to two right angles and whose area is equal to the half product of its base by its altitude. The figure which I define in this way does not exist, has never existed, and will never exist at any time anywhere in nature; it is a product of the understanding understanding itself. "The knowledge of the circle cannot be drawn from the vicissitudes that a circle in iron or wood suffers in nature.... There is no truth but what relates to essences and essences must be looked for in eternal and immutable things such as the sphere and the circle." [23] The triangles, circles, spheres, and all the other geometrical forms that I can perceive with the senses are never real triangles or circles or spheres; they are but the always more or less imperfect approximations to the *idea* of triangle, circle, or sphere which I discover in myself and which is precisely that by means of which I can recognize a "triangle" and any other geometrical form in nature. The metal or concrete triangles which border our highways are so many material and disparate things which merely resemble one another; whereas the idea "triangle" is identically one and the same for me who thinks it at the present moment in Paris and for someone who at the same time thinks it in Tokyo, the same as was thought over two millenia ago by Euclid and the same as was rediscovered and thought in solitude and isolation by the young Pascal. Geometrical ideas, like all other acts of "pure thought," lead an immaterial and eternal life; material things are but the occasions for recalling them to me, and when I contemplate them I rejoin a thought which exists "outside of time."

What must be remembered, however, is that the triangle is in fact nothing if it is not a certain modulation or structuration of *space.* Now space is not a Cartesian idea engendered by mere reflection but, as we have seen, is rather the expression of the hold the subject has on the world by means of his body. If the words "high" and "low," "right" and "left," etc., have a meaning for us, it is because we are present in the world through our bodies; and it is this which calls forth from the nondifferentiation of the in itself "directions" and "meanings" (*sens*). If we therefore have recourse to these expressions to describe our idea of the triangle, it is because the geometrical idea is not self-dependent but borrows its structures from perceptual and bodily life. If space is one of the expressions of our being in the world, the idea "triangle," which is but one of the possible structurations of space, must be considered to be *founded* on bodily existence and to be, as it were, a certain conceptual formulation of perceptual life. The "essence" of the triangle or circle which Spinoza talks about does not therefore belong to a transcendent region of being but is a variable of the phenomenal world.

Merleau-Ponty thus concludes that the "subject of geometry is a motor subject." (PhP, 387; *PP,* 443) And lastly he observes that the body would not be able to fill this role of an instigator of meaning if, before all "intellectual" operations, it were not an indigenous faculty of signification, "an original intentionality" (PhP, 387; *PP,* 444), in relation to which scientific knowledge is always "an abstract and derivative sign-language, as is geography in relation to the country-side in which we have learnt beforehand what a forest, a prairie or a river is." (PhP, IX; *PP,* III)

After having analyzed in his chapter on "The Cogito" the "thought of thinking," "psychic states,"[24] and the "pure ideas" proposed by geometry, and having shown that in all these areas intelligence or thought is not first of all an absolute coincidence with itself but is essentially a transcendence of itself founded on a perceptual or bodily life from which it emerges and which it always presupposes, Merleau-Ponty is able to draw the following conclusion: "Our body,...to the extent that it is inseparable from a view of the world and is that view itself brought into existence, is the condition of possibility, not only of the geometrical synthesis, but of all expressive operations and all acquired views which constitute the cultural world." (PhP, 388; *PP,* 445) This is a decisive conclusion which reveals the central aim of his "archeological" phenomenology and which rests precisely on the fact that any idea, however clear and distinct it be in itself, derives from the fundamentally obscure operation of *speech,* which, as we know, is bound up with a power of expression of the lived body.

For Merleau-Ponty the idea is to speech what the soul is to the body;[25] that is to say, it is its very meaning, its "other side". Thought is not self-sufficient but finds and possesses itself by means of words. To be sure, we possess ideas for which no externalization in words is necessary every time we wish to evoke or recall their meaning. But these are "already acquired" thoughts, and we possess them only because one day we discovered or learned them, either by *reading* or *listening* to them or by working them out for ourselves by means of certain *words.* It is indeed necessary to distinguish between two kinds of speech. There is a "secondary speech," and thought can indeed dispense with this since it only translates already acquired thoughts or already expressed feelings. But beneath constituted speech, which only functions as the vehicle for already discovered thoughts, there is an "operative" or "originating" speech which is precisely the coming to light of thoughts in search of themselves. New ideas are born and become fully conscious of themselves only by "speaking themselves out"; before being expressed they are only vague feelings of dubious value. It can thus be said that "all words which have become mere signs for a univocal thought have been able to do so only because they have first of all functioned as originating words, and we can still remember with what richness they appeared to be endowed, and how they were like a landscape new to us, while we were engaged in 'acquiring' them". (PhP, 389; *PP*, 446) As Scheler remarks, "An emotion, for example, which everyone can now perceive in himself, must once have been wrested by some 'poet' from the fearful inarticulacy of our inner life for this clear perception of it to be possible."[26] Even that height of clarity and rational self-evidence which is the *cogito ergo sum* is a thought which, in fact, is "humming with words." (PhP, 400; *PP*, 459) The *Cogito* is a cultural work and acquisition which we possess as an intimate thought of our own only because at one time in the past it was found and expressed in words; and this is the way we too have learnt it. What is peculiar about language is that once we have discovered a worthwhile thought through it, the words which served to reveal the thought are forgotten in the clarity of the idea: "Expression fades out before what is expressed, and this is why its mediating role may pass unnoticed, and why Descartes nowhere mentions it. Descartes, and *a fortiori* his reader, begin their meditation in what is already a universe of discourse." (PhP, 401; *PP*, 459)

But is not, at least, the idea of triangle of a different sort? For if all the books of geometry were to disappear from the face of the earth and if not a single man were to remain to remember its definition, it would still remain true that the triangle "itself" has a sum of angles equal to two right angles. For Merleau-Ponty this kind of objection stems from "objective" thought which claims to express ideas in themselves and to be the translation of a world in itself indifferent to any presence or absence of man. But the idea of triangle which Euclidian geometry proposes to us is not an impartial translation of an "in-itself" space if it is true that one can quite legitimately construct non-Euclidian geometries. Our awareness of nature is always a certain way of structuring it, and we cannot divorce the truth of the world from the truth-of-the-world-for-us.[27]

In short, every idea is a cultural object and rests on a spoken or written tradition. This observation enables us to understand the claim that the true idea makes to *eternity* and to put it in its proper perspective. Merleau-Ponty's thought on this subject is completely summed up in these words: "The non-temporal is the acquired." (PhP, 392; *PP*, 450) The eternal is not the opposite of the temporal; it is precisely that which persists throughout and by means of time; it is that which *endures.* So far is it from being the case that thought transcends time that we have but a slippery hold on time and never succeed in immobilizing or dominating it. Euclidian geometry, just like the Ninth Symphony, was born at a certain moment and, having called out to other minds and having been taken up by them, has entered into the history of the human race to become a cultural acquisition; its fate henceforth coincides with that of the culture of which it is one of the expressions and determinants. Taking up an idea which he had perhaps first of all come across in Proust[28] and to which he will often return, Merleau-Ponty understands the eternity of the true idea or work of the mind to be that persistent power it has of *teaching itself.* It is eternal in the sense that as a worthwhile creation of the human mind it calls out to all possible men and all possible times. And it becomes "eternal" from that moment when it is taken up by other men and enters in this way into the history of culture. To eternalize an idea "is to insure, by the use of words already used, that the new intention carries on the heritage of the past, it is at a stroke to incorporate the past into the present, and weld that present to a future, to open a whole temporal cycle in which the 'acquired' thought will remain present as a dimension, without our needing henceforth to summon it up or reproduce it. What is known as the non-temporal in thought is what, having thus taken up the past and committed the future, is presumptively of all time and is therefore anything but transcendent in relation to time." (PhP, 392; *PP*, 450)

And, likewise, when I discover in myself an "eternally worthwhile" thought, this is not done by leaping outside of time and making contact with some intelligible heaven or some world of Ideas. It is only that I take up and transform ideas which already figure in some way or other in the horizon of my history and the history of humanity. It is known for instance that the first clear and distinct ideas that Descartes thought he had drawn out of nothingness in the solitude of his mind, such as the idea of God as *ens realissimum,* unlimited perfection, supreme goodness, infinite being, etc., were in fact inheritances from medieval philosophy—ideas that the young Descartes had encountered at the Jesuit college at La Flèche—which he takes up and subjects to a new use. To be sure, Descartes' transformation of these ideas was revolutionary, but it was still not any the less grounded and, perhaps, even anticipated. One can never predict creations of the mind which represent precisely a novel use of a culture and, sometimes, the calling into question of this culture, but one can always find in them motivations and already existing elements. This is true because we carry within us "historical sedimentations"[29] on which our thought secretly nourishes itself and which constitute for it the horizons between which it moves.

Thus the true and eternal idea rests on originating speech which takes place in time, and everything that is most original and universally valid in us is carried along by a stream of generality and brute being which is nothing other than anonymous, bodily existence: "every act of reflection, every voluntary taking up of a position is based on the ground and the proposition of a life of pre-personal consciousness." (PhP, 208; *PP,* 241) The *Cogito* is the awareness of a flow of life which bears no proper name and which loses sight of itself in anonymity. It is as though there were in me another subject which I hardly know, one which leads an ambiguous and obscure life of which I am only partially conscious. In every act of my conscious and free being I dimly experience obscure motivations that I have never taken the time to bring to light and analyze; they stem from what inevitably escapes any serious attempt to get hold of and thus testify to a pre-personal and pre-conscious life. I am indeed conscious of my existence for otherwise I would never be able to say "I think," but this thought of existing never succeeds in summing up my actual existence nor in exposing its inner mechanisms; rather than explain it, it presupposes it. Thus it is that "my life slips away from me on all sides and is circumscribed by impersonal zones." (PhP, 331; *PP,* 382)

It is in this sense that the subject carries within himself a "prehistory." Before I began to reflect and found within myself the irrefutable truth, "I think, I exist," I in fact existed; I led a perceptual and meaningful life. When I gain hold of myself I discover myself as "already there." I become aware that I presuppose many things. And even this perceptual life clouds over for me to the degree that I plunge into it and attempt to get into contact with its origins; the first memory I have presents itself as the sequel of an unknown history which preceded it; it finds me already "in a situation": "the earliest years of my life are lost in the general existence of my body". (PhP, 331; *PP,* 381) Thus the *Cogito* that I am exists between horizons which it has not itself instituted and which are my birth and my death. These are insurmountable obstacles for any absolute knowledge and total grasping of me by myself. "I can, then, apprehend myself only as 'already born' and 'still alive'." (PhP, 216; *PP,* 249) Truthfully, my birth and death are "prepersonal horizons: I know that people are born and die, but I cannot know my own birth and death." Thus that which prevents the reflecting subject from coinciding with himself and from becoming a *Cogito* through and through is precisely this movement and this loss of my being which is *time.* It is not I who make my heart beat; I did not choose to be born, and I will not be able to do anything when my death steals upon me: "I am borne in my personal existence by a time which I do not constitute". (PhP, 347; *PP,* 399) This "natural time" is something I do not constitute because *it is my being* itself as a being in the world. Reflection encounters time by discovering before itself the life of a natural subjectivity which for it is "already there." To say therefore that reflective consciousness is upheld by an entire perceptual life which precedes it and which is already meaningful is at the same time to give it a temporal thickness and to make of subjectivity "the upsurge of time." (PhP, 428; *PP,* 489) The conclusion is thus inescapable: "reflection does not itself grasp its full significance unless it refers to the unreflected fund of experience which it presupposes, upon which it draws, and which constitutes for it a kind of original past, a past which has never been a present." (PhP, 242; *PP,* 280)[30]

Consciousness is present to itself only through the density of lived experience (the density of time), and thus the presence of the self to itself which serves to define the *Cogito* is a mediated, derived presence. Consciousness rests on an "unreflected fund" which can indiscriminately be called bodily existence or temporality.

But in denying to reason any priority in regard to meaning, in giving subjectivity an impenetrable thickness, and in according to consciousness only an imperfect possession of itself, is not Merleau-Ponty destroying all possibility of *certainty*? If the subject cannot bring to the complete light of day the motivations and intimations which operate beneath all voluntary initiatives and all intellectual thematizations, is he not in the last analysis condemned to total uncertainty, and in this case is not truth made impossible in principle? We will close our discussion of the rootedness of the subject by thus analyzing what, for Merleau-Ponty constitutes *the basis of certainty and evidence.*

The subject is not first of all a total possession of itself, an immediate presence to itself, and the "true *Cogito* is not the intimate communing of thought with the thought of that thought." (PhP, 297–8; *PP,* 344) Consciousness is not a consciousness of itself except by being a consciousness of something other than itself, and the first truth for me is not "I think that I think," but rather "something appears to me," "there is something." Obviously I can always cast doubt upon the phenomenon which appears to me, declare it illusory, but this can only be done by appealing to other perceptions and by awaiting from them either a rectification or a confirmation of my present perception. This is to say that there is no apodictic evidence and that consciousness is always to a certain degree ambiguous to itself. There is however, on the other hand, no question for Merleau-Ponty of a skepticism which calls into doubt the existence of everything; and if everything is not absolutely certain, it is not because everything is absurd. To say "I know nothing" is to affirm at least one certainty—that of knowing nothing. Basically, Merleau-Ponty says, both rationalism and skepticism are self-contradictory. If the philosophy of the absurd, in declaring that truth is but an illusion, affirms by that very fact a truth, rationalism is a scandal and an absurdity in that "it has to be formulated as a thesis." (PhP, 295; *PP,* 341) For Merleau-Ponty rationalism and skepticism draw upon a life of consciousness which they presuppose and wherein "it is impossible to say that *everything has a meaning* or that *everything is nonsense,* but only that *there is meaning.*" (PhP, 296; *PP,* 342) I can only call into doubt the perception of something in particular by affirming that there is "something in general" (PhP, 360; *PP,* 414) to see; and if "Each thing can, after the event, appear uncertain,...it is at least certain for us that there are things, that is to say, a world." (PhP, 344; *PP,* 396) For the subject there is a naive and always presupposed certainty which is that of its undivided and unarticulated existence before a world in general. It is in this sense that Merleau-Ponty can say that "There is an absolute certainty of the world in general, but not of any one thing in particular." (PhP, 297; *PP*, 344)

Thus it is that all explicit certainty is supported by a *primordial belief in the world*, an *Urdoxa*, a primitive assurance that there is something *to be known*. The thematized *Cogito* is nothing other than this "originating opinion" which has been made explicit. All rationality for me comes from the *fact* that with my first perception the world is "there." All certainty is the translation of an "all-embracing adherence to the world" (PhP, 241; *PP*, 279) and stems from my actual presence to the world. The world is for me indubitably real,[31] and reflective consciousness exists only as the unfolding of this fundamental "faith" in the world.

In insisting on the necessity of a return to perceptual life so as to take hold of that actual existence which we are, Merleau-Ponty's works thus aim at accomplishing what Paul Ricoeur has referred to as the "letting-go" of the *Cogito*. What is involved is an effort to dig beneath the *Cogito* with the goal of uncovering the foundations on which it rests (archeology of the subject); but—we have already said this but it bears repeating—in no way does this involve an attempt to *deny* the "truth" of the *Cogito*. For a philosophy such as Merleau-Ponty's which calls itself "reflective"—but in no way introspective—there can be no question of rejecting the *Cogito;* on the contrary, what is important is to *understand* it. It could in fact be said that the *Cogito* is the first of all truths, but it is so not in the way conceived of by idealist philosophy, namely as a constituting source; it is first not as a fact but as a "value-fact." (PhP, 398; *PP*, 456) It is by means of the *Cogito,* by means of reason, that prepersonal existence receives its full meaning and is understood: the *Cogito* is the "recuperation" of the latter. The *Cogito* is thus not first chronologically but teleologically, that is to say, as being the ultimate *telos* of philosophical reflection. Since reflection presupposes an unreflected, it must, in order to grasp itself precisely as a reflection on the unreflected, pass by way of an arduous road which is the rediscovery and exploration of the unreflected; and the *Cogito* is first by being at once the instigator and the goal of all this archeological work.

This is to say, therefore, that it is necessary not to abandon but to *revise* the notion of the *Cogito*. As Merleau-Ponty will say in the preface to *Sense and Non-Sense,* "we must form a new idea of reason." (SNS, 3; *SNS*, 8) For him the true *Cogito* must be established by means of the "reconquest" or the "recuperation" of perceptual, unreflected consciousness. In a word, it must be the "coming to awareness" (by reason or reflection) of this beginning consciousness, this encompassing atmosphere of its own operations. It is thus in the last analysis a question of an "attempt to explore the irrational and integrate it into an expanded reason". (SNS, 63; *SNS,* 109)

What, then, is the unreflected life on which consciousness is based? We have already observed that is an "opinion," a "faith," a "belief" in the existence of the world. At this stage existence is only a project of the world; it is precisely ex-sistence, ec-stasis. However—Merleau-Ponty insists on this point and it is important to note it—life at this level is already a form of *consciousness,* for, were it not, there could—so Merleau-Ponty believes—never be any consciousness. How indeed could a *thing* ever begin to think? (cf. PhP, 404; *PP,* 463) It is indeed necessary that perceptual life not be completely hidden from itself, that it already be a possession of itself, a consciousness of itself, in short, a *Cogito.* Merleau-Ponty does not deny this "requirement" and in fact he reiterates it. Only for him perceptual existence is a consciousness of itself only by being a consciousness of the world. These two consciousnesses are rigorously reciprocal and simultaneous: "There is a world for me because I am not unaware of myself; and I am not concealed from myself because I have a world." (PhP, 298; *PP,* 344) However, since the fundamental faith in the world only constitutes a "global and inarticulate grasp upon the world" (PhP, 404; *PP,* 463), the hold on the self which corresponds to it is equally slippery and vague. The unreflected consciousness or operative intentionality which supports the reflective consciousness or thematized intentionality is what Merleau-Ponty calls "silent consciousness" (PhP, 404; *PP,* 463), or again, "pre-reflective" (PhP, 298; *PP,* 344), "tacit *Cogito*" (PhP, 403; *PP,* 462). The tacit *Cogito* is indeed "an experience of myself by myself," but it is essential for it to be so only in a kind of quasi silence and in ambivalence. It is therefore what could be called the unconscious, if—like Merleau-Ponty at the time of the *Phenomenology*—one understands by this term, not a non-knowing, but a state of consciousness where the subject is not unaware of his existence, but where on the other hand, he does not have of himself an explicit consciousness. All of this could be summed up by saying that the tacit *Cogito* is a self-revelation, a self-premonition. At the same time that something appears to me, I exist for myself as the consciousness of what

I perceive, and thus I experience my existence as a dialogue with the world; that is to say, I manage to secure only an indirect hold on myself, on the margins of my life.

In a word, therefore, the tacit *Cogito,* the basis of all evidence and certainty, is *being in the world* itself. It is the movement of active transcendence that we are in our bodily existence, the presence of us to ourselves through our presence to the world and our body. It is quite simply an "opening upon a world" (PhP, 297; *PP,* 344), an original opening where, for the first time, *the world becomes a world and the subject a subject.* It is thus the initial upsurge of meaning, the basis of all possible truth, all rationality.

We must not however bring our analysis to a halt here for, as Merleau-Ponty says, "The essential point is clearly to grasp the project of the world that we are." (PhP, 405; *PP,* 463) The question is thus to know what exactly this "tacit *Cogito*" or this "operative intentionality" is and just how it is the basis of all certainty and rationality. Merleau-Ponty's belief that the *Cogito* or reflective consciousness and all intellectual life are based on our perceptual participation in the world calls for a clarification of what for him is *the true relation between the subject and the world.*

The first thing to be noted is that the presence of the world to the subject is not the result of a constituting activity on the part of the subject. Rather is it the case that the world appears *in perception* as that which consciousness "has not given itself"; rather than something constituted by consciousness, the world is that which consciousness vaguely apprehends as surrounding itself. This is not, however, to say that the world is fully what it is before the apparition of consciousness and that consciousness is but the reflection of this in-itself reality. It must on the contrary be said that the world has meaning only in relation to the subject and that it is impossible to conceive of a world which would not be a world for a consciousness. This is why Merleau-Ponty says that nothing can make us understand what would be a nebula seen by no one. Laplace's nebula, supposed to have existed at the beginning of the universe, is not, he says, "behind us, at our remote beginnings, but in front of us in the cultural world." (PhP, 432; *PP,* 494) This is not to say that the world is only what we constitute; it only means that the world of which science speaks is not fully in-itself, indifferent to all relation to subjectivity. There is not, so to speak, any in itself which would be absolutely in itself. The formulas of science are not the translations of the world as it would be apart from all relation to man or as it would have been before him. The theories of science are so many constructions, so many ways of structuring or constituting *the world to which we are present in perception*. Thus the world that science makes for itself is a *derived* world; it is a certain formulation of the *lived, perceived* world. The explanations of science presuppose our actual experience of the world and cannot put themselves before it.

When therefore Merleau-Ponty says that "there is no world without an Existence that sustains its structure" or that "there is no world without a being in the world", he does not mean "that the world is constituted by consciousness, but on the contrary that consciousness always finds itself already at work in the world." (PhP, 432; *PP*, 494) When one returns to perception one finds, not a non-temporal and worldless *Ego,* but a subject which possesses itself only in the world; and, correlatively, one discovers a world which is "already there," a world which exists only by being present to consciousness. The *primordial fact* is thus this *simultaneity* of the perceiving subject and the perceived world. If, therefore, the world gets defined only in terms of this "project" which subjectivity itself is, and if it is but the correlate of a "logic of the world" at the heart of the subject (PhP, 405; *PP,* 463), it is just as true that the subject himself is completely polarized towards the world and exists only in relation to it. In this sense the world is "the native abode of all rationality," "the cradle of significations, the meaning of all meaning, and ground of all thinking." (PhP, 430; *PP*, 492) The *to be* of the world is to be a correlate of the subject, and the *to be* of the subject is to be a project of the world. "We do not say that the *notion* of the world is inseparable from that of the subject, or that the subject *thinks himself* inseparable from the idea of his body and the idea of the world; for, if it were a matter of no more than a conceived relationship, it would *ipso facto* leave the absolute independence of the subject as thinker intact, and the subject would not be in a situation." (PhP, 408; *PP,* 467) The relation between the subject and the world is, in short, not a *conceived* relationship but an *ontological* one; it is not a *"relationship of knowing"* but a *"relationship of being."* (SNS, 72; *SNS,* 125)

If therefore Merleau-Ponty *relativizes* the subject and the world, and if he says that the world *exists* only for the subject, this is not for all that a pure and simple *subjectivization* of the world. The world exists and has meaning only in relation to the subject, but it is not the subject who constitutes the world's presence. This is why Merleau-Ponty says that we are *in* the truth. (PhP, XVI; *PP*, XI) When we reflect on our unreflected life we find ourselves to be, as it were, "thrown" into the world; we find the world as that which is "already there." The first *truth* or evidence for us is this unmotivated presence of the world; this is therefore a truth which is for us a brute fact, a truth which is "already there" and which we do not constitute but take up. It can be said either that the meaning and existence of the world are its meaning and existence for us, or, equally as well, that the existence of the subject is to be a project of the world and that whatever truth he can have comes from his participation in the world; these two statements come down to the same. As Merleau-Ponty says, "It is before our undivided existence that the world is true or exists; ...which is to say...that we have in [the world] the experience of a truth which shows through and envelops rather than being held and circumscribed by our mind." (PriP, 6; *Inédit*, 404–5)

It is thus that Merleau-Ponty believes he has solved the "problem of rationality" (PhP, 408; *PP,* 467) which is for him the most fundamental of problems. For him, in fact, the "chief gain from phenomenology is no doubt to have united extreme subjectivism and extreme objectivism in its notion of the world or of rationality." (PhP, XIX; *PP,* XV) The ground of all possible truth is the "phenomenological world" (PhP, XX; *PP,* XV), the *presence* of the world, being in the world. This is for him "the only Logos which pre-exists." (PhP, XX; *PP,* XV) The ultimate truth for the subject and one which is the basis of all other truths, the primordial evidence, is the world itself as the "open and indefinite unity in which I have my place." (PhP, 304; *PP,* 351) The first of all evidences is: "There is meaning, something and not nothing, there is an indefinite train of concordant experiences". (PhP, 397; *PP,* 454) All our knowledge, everything that is true for us, is based "on our communication with the world as primary embodiment of rationality." (PhP, XXI; *PP,* XVI)

Now, as we have just seen, the presence of the world, the subject-world structure, being in the world, is a brute fact, a real and irreducible a priori as regards reason, for it stems neither from the world nor from the subject. It is only within the subject-world relation that the world is a "world" and that the subject knows himself and knows evidences; and thus this presence, this foundation of all rationality, is itself without a foundation, without justification or reason. Beneath perceptual rationality, beneath the brute presence of the world, there exists no transcendent reason, and thus this presence appears to be a totally gratuitous and contingent fact having no possible justification. There is truth for me because the world is "there" and because I possess myself as a consciousness of the world; it is this primordial fact which is the ultimate foundation of all evidence and truth, and thus there is no reason which could justify it in return. Rationality thus rests on an insurpassable contingency: "Ontological contingency, the contingency of the world itself, being radical, is...what forms the basis once and for all of our ideas of truth." (PhP, 398; *PP*, 456) The subject and the world are "two abstract 'moments' of a unique structure which is *presence*" (PhP, 430; *PP*, 492), and since presence is time itself, it must be said that truth or rationality is but "the accident [*hasard*] of time" (PhP, 396; *PP*, 452), that everything comes down to the "fundamental accident which made us appear and will make us disappear." (S, 202; *S*, 255)

But even if this way of conceiving of things actually does reveal the factual foundation of *rationality* (of meaning), it can still be wondered if it also takes account of (the ideality of) *reason*. For indeed, as Merleau-Ponty himself recognizes, to speak of reason is in the last analysis to speak of a "presumption of reason," an "invocation of truth," a truth which is presumably for all possible times and men. Taking up an expression of Husserl, he speaks of a "teleology of consciousness" (PhP, 396, 398; *PP*, 453, 456); but can one really justify such a "teleology" if one merely links up with pure contingency and considers it to be an "accident"? The two notion of teleology and accident would seem rather to be mutually exclusive if one situates them at *the same level*. In fact, in order to justify this *teleology* of consciousness—which is most assuredly a fact of consciousness—would one not need a more radical *archelogy* than is to be found in the *Phenomenology*? In the following chapters we will indeed see how Merleau-Ponty radicalizes his search for the "originating," and how this search leads him to descend into the "basement" of phenomenology,[32] underneath phenomenal being in the world, in such a way as to discover there the truly fundamental *archē*—Being.

## Conclusion

THE *Phenomenology of Perception* is essentially a work of "archeological" research. Its principal discovery is that of the lived body—of corporeity as a natural subjectivity, a spontaneous power of meaning and expression. In the light of this discovery Merleau-Ponty sets about showing how what is "natural" and indigenous in the subject is at the root of all thematic reflection and all conscious and free action. The powers of expression and meaning which the personal subject displays draw all their impetus from a "movement of transcendence" at work below this subject, a movement which in a sense he possesses but which he does not in any way initiate. With a certain affinity to the work of Marx and Freud, the *Phenomenology* attempts to accomplish a "letting-go" of the thinking subject and show him to be a dependent subject—dependent in regard to a life or current of existence which properly possesses a meaning on its own. The personal subject merely continues on in a tradition which he did not initiate but received as an inheritance.

While maintaining the truth of the *Cogito* and the reality of freedom, Merleau-Ponty attempts to show how all thinking and all voluntary decisions are never without support in pre-reflective life. It is in this sense that he was able to say of the *Phenomenology* that "I have tried, first of all, to re-establish the roots [*l'enracinement*] of the mind in its body and in its world". (PriP, 3; *Inédit*, 402)

But if the *Cogito* and freedom are not called into question as to their reality, it is because, unlike Marx and Freud, Merleau-Ponty never ceases to reject vigorously all attempts to *explain* existence in terms of its infrastructures. If man does not walk on his head, it is also true that he does not think with his feet. The subject is rooted in his body and finally in the world which is quite literally his homeland, the ground of his existence. The subject irrupts in the midst of the world and never ceases to be situated in it. He is through and through and for always *of* the world. Under pain of falling back like Freud or Marx into rationalism, one cannot, however, make the Unconscious or Nature into *explanatory* concepts of man and his mental and spiritual life. Strictly speaking, nature, for instance, explains absolutely nothing, for whatever meaning it has comes precisely from man's emergence in it, from that irreducible subject who will transcend it and lead it to expression. In this way the birth of an infant in the world is not a mere event *in* the world, rather an "advent or again [a] transcendental event." (PhP, 407; *PP*, 466) From this opening which springs up like a miracle in the plenitude and nondifferentiation of natural being, the world receives "a new layer of meaning." With the advent of man the world becomes an invitation to the unforeseeable and is *pledged to reason.*

Through its descriptions of being in the world the *Phenomenology* thus raises problems of a properly *metaphysical* sort. It raises questions about man and about the world and about the relation of man to the world, about rationality and about reason. But while joining up in this way with the classic problems of metaphysics it insists on breaking with rationalism, that is to say, with all attempts to explain these phenomena once and for all by subsuming them under a ready-made category such as Nature or Reason. (cf. PriP, 10; *Inédit*, 408) It says that the subject inheres in the world but also that at the same time he is transcendent to the world. And it presents this movement of transcendence, which is incarnate existence, as a brute, ambiguous, mysterious fact—as a *miracle* without any possible explanation. As a power of natural expression, the subject can be explained neither in terms of the world nor in terms of a transcendent Reason. The subject is in the world precisely as a transcendental event. The difficulty comes therefore when one attempts to *think* of existence as a transcendental incarnation; and, by insisting above all on the rootedness of the subject, the *Phenomenology* teaches an ambiguity which in the last analysis, as Merleau-Ponty himself admitted, is a "bad ambiguity." (PriP, 11; *Inédit*, 409) One cannot understand that *lumen naturale* which is man as long as one does not make it the explicit theme of one's inquiry. What is important is to see more clearly how *man is in the world as the very transcendence of the world.*

This is to say that we must turn back to consider an already noted but still insufficiently clarified fact: that human existence expresses an absolutely irreducible dialectic. Man is rooted and transcendent *at one and the same time.* We have seen that bodily existence is already transcendent to merely biological and natural existence, that transcendence is the very definition of incarnate existence (and that for this very reason there can be no definition of man) and is thus not a secondary trait of man, proper only to the "second level" of mind or spirit. Being in the world is indivisibly a limitation and an overcoming of this limitation. Indeed, the incarnation of man must be considered to be the other side of his transcendence. Man is capable of bestial acts only because he is inevitably more than a beast. Anonymity and impersonality haunt his being only because he is a personal and conscious being. There is an unreflected for us only because we reflect, which is to say only because always and from the very first we transcend our factual condition.[33] Man is "condemned" to meaning as he is to being free. Decidedly, there is a "privilege of reason" which all naturalism ignores, but also which all spiritualism renders incomprehensible.

In 1945 Merleau-Ponty wrote, "My involvement in nature and history is at one and the same time a limitation of my view on the world and the only way for me to approach the world, know it, and do something in it." (SNS, 72; *SNS,* 125) But in accordance with the internal requirements of his thought itself, it would be necesary to say more than this. It would be necessary to say that my incarnation is experienced by me as a limitation of my possibilities only because I encounter it as such, which is to say that the experience of a limitation is already in some way an overcoming of it. As Hegel says, consciousness is "immediately the act of overcoming the limit."[34] If the involvement of the subject in his body and in the world is fundamentally ambiguous, it is "because it both affirms and restricts a freedom." (SNS, 72; *SNS,* 125) Limits exist only for an intention which aims beyond them. Like the feeble reed that Pascal speaks of, the greatness of man is visible in his very wretchedness.

This movement of active transcendence is precisely what is eminently attested to by the *phenomenon of expression.* In order to understand the dialectical relation between man and the world (how man is in the world as the transcendence of the world), it is now necessary to consider in more detail this pivotal phenomenon wherein man shows himself to be at once *naturata* and *naturans,* inheritor and creator, rooted and transcendent.

There is, Merleau-Ponty says, a "teleology of consciousness," a wave of transcendence which rises up through man, an opening of man towards the virtual, a "Logos which assigns to us the task of bringing to speech a hitherto mute world." (PriP, 10; *Inédit,* 408) And it is this which we must understand—how in the radical and forever inexpungible contingency of his own existence and that of the world man is open to truth and to universality. It is now the "origin of truth" with which we must concern ourselves. The "fundamental philosophic problem," Merleau-Ponty writes in the *Phenomenology,* is "this *presumption* on reason's part." (PhP, 63; *PP,* 76) What must be elucidated is thus this "mystery of reason" (PhP, XXI; *PP,* XVI) which the *Phenomenology* has indeed revealed but which it has at the same time neglected by considering it a philosophically incomprehensible fact. It will be by means of a meditation on symbolic expression (the teleology of consciousness) in painting, language, and philosophy itself that Merleau-Ponty will come to substitute a "good ambiguity" for the "bad ambiguity" of the *Phenomenology*; for if the entire work of the artist is, as we shall see in the following chapter, polarized towards an "infinite Logos" (SNS, 19; *SNS,* 33), this can only be because the ground of reason and of its infinite *logos* or *telos* is not the mere *finitude* of phenomenal being in the world but is itself an *infinite* ground or *archē*.

## Chapter II

# Painting

*In whatever civilization it is born,
from whatever beliefs, motives, or thoughts,
no matter what ceremonies surround it—and
even when it appears devoted to something
else—from Lascaux to our time, pure or im-
pure, figurative or not, painting celebrates
no other enigma but that of visibility.*

"Eye and Mind" (PriP, 165–6; *OE*, 26)

THAT the philosopher who formulated his initial theses on the basis of a confrontation with the sciences and, in particular, with Gestalt psychology, should afterwards interest himself in the art of the painter has, basically, nothing surprising about it. For here it is still the same theme that he is pursuing—perception. And, indeed, where could perception manifest itself with more magnificence, more expressivity and evidence than in that privileged operation which is the inspired vision of the painter? "Painting," Merleau-Ponty writes, "awakens and carries to its highest pitch a delirium which is vision itself". (PriP, 166; *OE*, 26)

What therefore a reflection on painting can teach us is the very relation which we entertain with the world; for, by bringing to expression the phenomenon of visibility, painting illustrates nothing other than our bodily insertion in being. Painting thus has a "metaphysical significance" (PriP, 178; *OE*, 61); it is "a central operation which con-

73

tributes to the definition of our access to being." (PriP, 171; *OE*, 42) What is proper to painting is that it renders visible, in a work accessible to everyone, the world which we inhabit. Its theme is that great spectacle which is being, and, like the metaphysician, the painter "lives in fascination." (PriP, 167; *OE*, 31) As the expression of a passion for the colors and forms of life, painting is a celebration of our participation in the world. By this fact it constitutes a concrete meditation on our relation to being—that relation which is visibility—and for him who makes it the theme of a philosophical interrogation it has many things to say. In Africa, in Europe, man, awakened to the fact of his existence, had painted, had traced designs on the walls of his cave, before he began to reflect in language; and, finding itself face to face with this primordial operation of signification, philosophy should have for its task to speak the meaning which, in painting itself, is still only a mute meaning.

In this chapter we shall consider successively the three writings of Merleau-Ponty which are expressly devoted to painting: "Cézanne's Doubt," "Indirect Language and the Voices of Silence," and "Eye and Mind." This way of proceeding will give rise to a certain amount of repetition, but it is perhaps preferable to an attempt aiming at imposing on what Merleau-Ponty has said about painting a systematization which is not to be found in his work itself. Rather than a linear progression, Merleau-Ponty's reflection on painting represents a vertical, on-the-spot fathoming of the matter. In these three essays which extend over the philosophical life of Merleau-Ponty, we will indeed be able to see his phenomenology transform itself little by little into an ontology. In "Cézanne's Doubt" (1945) the author's attention is fixed essentially on the attempt of the *painter* to express being, to capture it alive on his canvas. "Indirect Language and the Voices of Silence" (1952) appears as a transition between this phenomenological approach and a more intensive interrogation; it sets out in fact the first elements of an *ontology* of painting. Finally, in "Eye and Mind" (1960) a sort of "reversal" becomes manifest in that now painting is envisaged rather as an ontological function, as a demand, it would seem, that Being places on man. The painter's operation is here viewed as an operation of Being, as the primordial and privileged instance where Being *manifests and sees itself.*

Thus in these three writings we assist at the slow maturation of the philosopher's thought. In the first Merleau-Ponty finds in *percep-*

*tion,* such as it was understood in the *Phenomenology,* the basis of the act of painting. It is the original perceptual relation of man to the world that Cézanne attempted to unveil and expose on his canvases. In the second essay, written seven years later, Merleau-Ponty enlarges the horizon of his investigations and, on the basis of his notion of perception as the foundation of the act of painting, attempts to understand in its light the meaning of cultural *history*—how there can be a single history (a cultural Logos) which unites all the painters of all times. But this meditation on history and on a historical truth which transcends painters taken individually results in notions which, in the last analysis, conform rather poorly to his theory of perception. It is thus that, eight years afterwards in his last publication, Merleau-Ponty returns to *perception* in order to analyze it anew and in a much more radical way than he had up to that point. It is here that we see his "new ontology" take shape.

## I.  Cézanne

ALL the greatness, as all the misery, difficulty, and anguish, of Cézanne's work comes from the fact that he wanted—over and beyond a naive realism which takes nature to be the scientific constructions we make of it and an Impressionism which paints only *our* impressions of nature—to return to nature itself and paint it as it manifests itself to us in our primitive experience of perceiving subjects. The nature which Cézanne wanted to paint is the nature which is the ground of our life, "this primordial world" in which "we are anchored" (SNS, 13; *SNS,* 23);[1] in a word, he wanted to get hold of "nature in its origin." It is this project of Cézanne's such as Merleau-Ponty understands it which interests us here, for one cannot fail to notice the resemblances it bears to Merleau-Ponty's own desire to return to and express the "originating"—our primitive experience of the world; it is the entire problem of recuperating the meaning of the world as we live it, and it is known that Merleau-Ponty found in Cézanne a kind of prefiguration of his own efforts.

## 1.  Art and Nature

Just as Merleau-Ponty only came to formulate his own thought in a dialectical confrontation with empiricism and intellectualism, so also

Cézanne's work came to be only through a struggle with two antagonistic conceptions of painting: naturalism or realism, and Impressionism.

The decisive encounter in Cézanne's career would seem to have been the one he made around 1870 with the Impressionists and, in particular, with Pissarro. It is here that he learned that painting can be something other than the mere expression of the subjective fantasies of the painter and acquired a knowledge of painting conceived of as "the exact study of appearances, less a work of the studio than a working from nature." (SNS, 11; *SNS*, 19) The actual confrontation of the Impressionist painter with the landscape, the exact study of appearances, and, in short, the idea of painting "from nature" excited him. Concerning nature he said that "the artist must conform to this perfect work of art. Everything comes to us from nature; we exist through it; nothing else is worth remembering." (SNS, 12; *SNS*, 21) But it must be added that even if Cézanne found in Impressionism a fruitful source of inspiration, he soon detached himself from it.

He did so because basically the Impressionist aesthetic seemed to him to be too timorous and to have failed to achieve a genuine painting "from nature." The goal of Impressionism was to depict "the very way in which objects strike our eyes and attack our senses." (SNS, 11; *SNS*, 19) In order to express this luminosity of things it limited itself to the seven colors of the prism, eliminating the earth colors, ochres, and black. The result of this was that objects seem to be, as it were, dissolved in the air, fuzzy, ephemeral, and lost behind the reflections which they project into the atmosphere and which are the only things that an Impressionist painter seeks to express on his canvas. What is lacking to things here is thus the weight, the solidity, the fullness of *real* objects. And it was precisely this density of things, their massive *presence*, that Cézanne wanted to seize and render visible. He wanted to paint not "sense data" but the object itself in all its reality and all its presence; he wanted to "represent the object, to find it again behind the atmosphere." (SNS, 12; *SNS*, 20) Thus Cézanne's palette included rich and substantial colors, earth colors and black; it included a great variety of colors not to be found on the Impressionists' palettes. And Cézanne's technique was different too. With him the "object is no longer covered by reflections and lost in its relationships to the atmosphere and to other objects: it seems subtly illuminated from within, light emanates from it, and the result is an impression of solidity and material substance." (SNS, 12; *SNS,* 21) It is the entire substantiality and reality of the object that Cézanne found again in his painting.

But even if Cézanne effectively went beyond Impressionism, he did not want in any way to abandon it. "One must therefore say that Cézanne wished to return to the object without abandoning the Impressionist aesthetic which takes nature as its model." What he wanted, as he himself said, was to make of Impressionism "something solid, like the art in the museums." He wanted to rediscover and paint the object itself *in its appearances.* This is the "paradox" of his painting: "he was pursuing reality without giving up the sensuous surface, with no other guide than the immediate impression of nature." An impossible project, as Emile Bernard said: Cézanne aims at "reality while denying himself the means to attain it." It is in this paradox—expressing nature itself without any abandonment of "sensation"—that Merleau-Ponty locates the supreme significance of Cézanne's work. The "meaning of his painting" is summed up for him in Cézanne's attempt to escape from this apparent antinomy: either nature as it is "in itself" or our "subjective" impression of nature, an antinomy which, on the philosophical level, is that of realism and idealism.

If therefore Cézanne wanted to "conform himself" to nature and to paint it in all its nascent state, to make it be seen as the first man on earth could have seen it, it was not because he wanted to *identify* painting with nature. It was rather a question of rediscovering nature using all the resources of *art.* Concerning nature and art Cézanne said, "I want to unite them." His painting is thus not a naturalism or a primitivism, and the painter of reality is not, as Bernard said, a mimicking ape. "Cézanne," Merleau-Ponty writes, never wished to "paint like a savage." (SNS, 14; *SNS,* 23) Let us therefore be careful. It is not a question of *reproducing* reality but of *expressing* it, which is an altogether different matter. Just as "speech does not *resemble* what it designates, painting is not a *trompe-l'oeil.*" (SNS, 17; *SNS,* 30) Those who have visited Cézanne's studio in Aix or who have seen elsewhere photographs made of the very spots the artist painted cannot fail to be struck by the poverty of these images compared to the living canvases of the painter. What photography lacks is the entire movement, the entire life of reality which only art, *by means of its free inventions,* can express. There can be no question of copying or imitating nature;

it must be re-presented, made to live again in painting. Since it is a *creative* endeavor, it is essential to art that it follow its own exigencies, and thus it can rediscover and preserve nature only by transcending it.

It is in this context that one must look for the full meaning of those famous "deformations" which Cézanne introduces into his pictures. To cite only one example, in the portrait of Mme. Cézanne the freize of the tapestry in the background passes behind the subject but does not form a straight line from one side of the body to the other, as it "should." It is known what meaning Merleau-Ponty discovered in these perspectival deformations. On a practical level, he said, Cézanne was implementing a knowledge that Gestalt psychology was later to formulate in theses. Here what is "arbitrary" is called into the service of what is real, and it is by means of the artist's *constructions* that *nature* becomes present in its own reality: "it is Cézanne's genius that when the over-all composition of the picture is seen globally, perspectival distortions are no longer visible in their own right but rather contribute, as they do in natural vision, to the impression of an emerging order, of an object in the act of appearing, organizing itself before our eyes." (SNS, 14; *SNS,* 25) And thus he concludes, "Nothing could be less arbitrary than these famous distortions." (SNS, 15; *SNS,* 25) It was by following up the exigencies of his *art* that Cézanne was able to make the full meaning of *nature* itself appear on his canvas.

Cézanne could thus say of the portrayal of a face, "I realize that the painter interprets it. The painter is not an imbecile." (SNS, 15; *SNS,* 27) The task of saying what is is a difficult undertaking which can have a successful outcome only if the artist brings to it all the resources of his intelligence. This is why Cézanne was of the opinion that he could not succeed in his attempt to paint "from nature" by ignoring the history of painting and the knowledge of techniques—tradition and science. When in Paris, he visited the Louvre every day. Likewise, before painting a landscape he informed himself about its geological structure, and before starting to paint he meditated, "germinated." All of this abstract knowledge had to be present and reunited in the spontaneous act of painting, so that it became the most faithful means of saying what nature itself was. "Nothing could be farther from naturalism than this intuitive science," Merleau-Ponty writes. "Art is not imitation, nor is it something manufactured according to the wishes of instinct or good taste. It is an expressive operation." (SNS, 17; *SNS,* 30) And this is the reason why "Cézanne was able to revive the classical definition of art: man added to nature." (SNS, 16; *SNS*, 28)

As Cézanne's work attests, art thus has a bipolar nature. This is to say that it cannot be understood unless one takes account of the fact that it is, at one and the same time, a representation of nature and a human creation, that it is, precisely, man added to nature. Cézanne's painting has no other vocation than that of expressing nature, of grasping hold of it and making it live in a picture. Thus the "meaning Cézanne gave to objects and faces in his paintings presented itself to him in the world itself as it appeared to him. Cézanne simply released this meaning: it was the objects and the faces themselves as he saw them which demanded to be painted in this way, and Cézanne simply expressed what they *wanted* to say." (SNS, 21; *SNS*, 35) As Cézanne said, what he wanted was to "conform himself" to Nature. But if Cézanne wanted to say no more than what the things themselves wanted to say and to deliver up the meaning of nature itself, he was nonetheless able to achieve his goal only by means of his art, which is to say—and Cézanne himself says it—by an *effort of interpretation.* His art is thus at one and the same time a *recuperation* of nature and a *creative* endeavor. To say what the things themselves want to say is the work of man.

We are now in a position to understand the goal of Cézanne's efforts. It was, in the first instance, reality itself. But since art is not an imitation of nature and is not to be confused with it, it can express it only by making it live again. Cézanne's pictures do not make us think of nature, they present it to us.[2] And if they can do this, it is because the nature which appears in them is that of our initial perceptions. This nature is that of the "immediate impression" (SNS, 12; *SNS*, 21); it is the "primordial world" (SNS, 13; *SNS*, 23) in which "we are anchored," not that of civilized man who has surrounded himself with cultural worlds which hide from him the natural world, but that which the first man on earth could have seen; it is "nature at its origin." (*SNS*, 23) When we contemplate Cézanne's pictures we get the impression of being present at a primordial spectacle, at the first appearance of the world; they convey to us the impression of "an emerging order, of an object in the act of appearing, organizing itself before our eyes." (SNS, 14; *SNS*, 25) This happens because nature here is that which *corresponds* to and is a *correlate* of naked vision, that "vision which penetrates right to the root of things beneath the imposed order of humanity." (SNS, 16; *SNS,* 28) Cézanne thus shows himself to be faithful to his desire of uniting nature and vision, of "searching for reality without abandoning sensation," for his painting leads us back to the instant when the world and perception are *born together and mutually define themselves.* He was looking for primordial perception, and he "arrests the spectacle in which men take part without really seeing it and makes it visible to the most 'human' among them." (SNS, 18; *SNS,* 31) We could thus ascribe to Cézanne, such as Merleau-Ponty presents him, Merleau-Ponty's own program: "We must discover the origin of the object at the very center of our experience; we must describe the emergence of being and we must understand how, paradoxically, there is *for us* an *in-itself.*" (PhP, 71; *PP,* 86)

This is to say therefore that what Cézanne wanted was to "make *visible* how the world *touches* us." (SNS, 19; *SNS,* 33) He wanted to convert into a visible spectacle our perceptual *relation* to the world, the original perceptual contact between man and the world, the instant when the *non-human* world appears *for* man. He wanted to express on his canvas that *circularity* between man and the world which is *perception.* What is expressed in his work is neither mere "sensations" nor an "in-itself" reality but the primordial encounter of man and the world, the moment when they *mutually come into being,* one as perceiving, the other as perceived.

We can understand from this how it can be said that the work of art does not exist *in* the world, why it is that "the picture as a work of art is not in the space which it inhabits as a physical thing and as a colored canvas." (PhP, 287; *PP,* 333) It is because "aesthetic perception in its turn opens up a new spatiality," and for this reason: as a creative attempt to express our perceptual relation with the world, painting is a *reflection on* being in the world. Since it is the very expression of the phenomenological world, painting is necessarily in some sense transcendent to it; it is an interpretation, a becoming aware of it. As Hyppolyte says in regard to Hegel: "The self-consciousness of life becomes other than life by manifesting its truth, by making itself able to be its truth."[3] The work of art exists as a symbol or a sign: it translates and expresses existence (being in the world), and it is by its means that man comes to an awareness, comes for the first time to the full awareness of his own existence, grasps reflectively what he *is.* The work of art is a recuperation of our being in the world, of the phenomenological world, of that original Logos of which the *Phenomenology* speaks (cf. PhP, XX; *PP,* XV) and which is our very being in the world. Like all creative expressions, painting is thus a manifestation of that effort which man, as a movement of transcendence, expends to consummate "in a precise language the confused discourse of the world." (SNS, 187; *SNS,* 331)

By being the very inauguration of a transcendent (because reflective) meaning, painting rules out all attempts to "explain" it. One cannot link it up with a principle exterior to it, to the perceived world for example; for painting is not an imitation or a "representation" of the world, but the *coming to awareness* by man of his own existence in the world. The meaning that painting offers us does not exist before it, for this meaning is the very *recuperation* of our actual existence. "The meaning of what the artist is going to say *does not exist* anywhere— not in things, which as yet have no meaning, nor in the artist himself, in his unformulated life." (SNS, 19; *SNS,* 32) Cézanne's difficulties, Merleau-Ponty remarks, are precisely those of "the first word."[4] His mission is to deliver up a meaning which, however, does not yet exist as a meaning. Hence the doubt, the anguish, the uncertainty; "only the work itself, completed and understood, is proof that there was *something* rather than *nothing* to be said." The work of expression addresses an appeal to our actual existence whose meaning it wants to grasp, but this immediate meaning of our being in the world manifests itself as a meaning only by and in the act of expression. We become conscious of our existence only by expressing it; before expression the meaning of existence is confused and is concealed in the many everyday experiences which have not yet been thematized. This concealment of the meaning of being in the world is essentially the same phenomenon that Heidegger refers to under the term *Alltäglichkeit.* Or again, in a Hegelian language, one could say that being in the world, bodily, perceptual existence, is meaningful *in* itself but not, properly speaking, *for* itself; it is fully meaningful only *for us* who reflect on it and deliver up its meaning.

This is, at a higher level, the same relation as that, alluded to in the preceding chapter, between structure and meaning. Just as the perceived world contains structures which are meaningful only *for the consciousness* which detects them, so also being in the world is fully structured, but this structuration is not properly speaking a meaning except for the reflective or thematic consciousness which doubles back on existence in order to become conscious of it. One can thus say that the work of art invokes a primordial, covered over logos—this primitive logos being the configuration or structuration of our actual existence—which outstrips itself since it awaits from the work itself its own manifestation or actualization as meaning. The artist, Merleau-Ponty says, calls out "towards a reason which would be able to encompass its own origins." (SNS, 19; *SNS,* 32) This is to say that by means of reflection and expression he attempts to take hold of the unreflected (perceptual life) on which reflection (painting, in this case) rests and to which it refers back. With a heightened consciousness of the difficulties of this sort of endeavor, Cézanne said that he turned "towards the intelligence of the *Pater Omnipotens.*" "He turned himself, in any case," Merleau-Ponty comments, "towards the idea or the project of an infinite Logos." (SNS, 19; *SNS,* 33) In other words, if the painter's work is motivated by his way of living and seeing, it nonetheless has meaning as a *work* or act of expression only because it is not the mere reflection of this primitive logos but is, rather, the attempt to deliver up the primitive logos and understand it. The work has meaning only because it is turned towards a logos which is not beneath but beyond itself, an "infinite Logos," only because the work is animated by the idea or the project of a total manifestation or *justification* of its own grounding. It is polarized towards the idea of an infinite telos, a *reason* which would be able to assure itself of "its own origins." If therefore the act of expression is the attempt to turn back upon and un-cover and express its own grounding or its *archeology,* this is so because in the last analysis it itself is part of a *teleology* of consciousness or reason which makes it be that consciousness wants to justify itself by seizing hold of its own grounding.

## 2.  Nature and the Universal

Born in this way of an individual life and resting on a covered over logos, the work of art is turned towards an "infinite Logos"; it attempts to actualize a *universal* meaning. The work of art is a sign, as we have said, a sign which translates or expresses the phenomenological world, our being in the world. More than this must, however, be said, for by expressing the phenomenological world, this original logos, the work brings to it a meaning which is no longer individual and diffused but universal. "It is thanks to symbols," M. Eliade writes, "that man emerges from his individual situation and 'opens' himself to the general and the universal."[5] Onto the individuality of an existence which has not yet become conscious of itself and its universal significance, the "artist's creations...impose...a figurative sense which did not pre-exist them." (SNS, 20; *SNS,* 34) The artist raises the nature which everyone lives through in his amorphous spiritual solitude and in the flow of individual life to the level of the universal, and transforms it into a general signification which is accessible to everyone and for always: he "recaptures and converts into visible objects what would, without him, remain walled up in the separate life of each consciousness: the vibration of appearances which is the cradle of things." (SNS, 17-8; *SNS,* 30) It is by means of the work alone that the world receives its own meaning and that man becomes conscious of himself; the artist "is he who arrests and renders accessible" (*SNS,* 31) to men the meaning of their own life in the world. At the same time therefore that the work renders unto the world its meaning, it reunites those beings capable of appreciating it and establishes a universal community. The meaning of being in the world is thereby saved, singularity and dispersion are transcended, and a history is founded.[6] "Then the work of art will have united these separate lives; it will no longer exist in only one of them like a stubborn dream or a persistent delirium, nor will it exist only in space as a colored piece of canvas. It will dwell undivided in several minds, with a claim on every possible mind like a perennial acquisition." (SNS, 20; *SNS,* 34) As the deciphering and recuperation of an original, primordial logos, the work of art is the establishment of a history and a universal logos.[7]

Thus with the example of Cézanne, Merleau-Ponty seems to want to say that the meaning of the world is not the meaning of the world "in itself," that it is inseparable from our existence in it, and that it becomes and is fully meaningful only through the creative work of man. By bringing the world to expression, by transforming it into signs, man also confers a meaning on his own life, for to define being is at the same time and necessarily to define our relation to being; it is to contribute to the establishment of a universal logos which, in the last analysis, justifies us and renders our own life meaningful. Cézanne said that the landscape thought itself in him and that he was its consciousness. (SNS, 17; *SNS,* 30) It is in man that the transmutation of a concealed logos into a revealed, professed logos is brought about, and thus it is that at certain moments man finds himself surrounded by a "glow from out of nowhere." (SNS, 25; *SNS,* 43) "Here," Merleau-Ponty says, "a light bursts forth." And thus it is that we have to do with "a being the whole essence of which, like that of light, is to *make visible.*" (PhP, 426; *PP*, 487) It seems then that in the final analysis man should be understood as *lumen naturale,* as the illumination of Being itself.


## II.   The Voices of Silence

BY its date of composition, "Indirect Language and the Voices of Silence"[8] occupies a position midway between "Cézanne's Doubt" and "Eye and Mind." It is also a significant step in the author's thought and enables us to witness a decisive moment in the evolution of this thought. Here Merleau-Ponty goes more deeply into certain elements of the act of painting which his essay on Cézanne had already set out, and he introduces new distinctions which will inevitably lead him to make the transition from phenomenology to ontology.

The occasion for this essay or, if one prefers, its point of departure, was provided by a certain number of studies which André Malraux had devoted to painting. In *Le Musée imaginaire* the latter had made a rather clear-cut distinction between classical painting and the abstract or "absolute" painting of today, seeing in the former an essentially "objective" character, a faithfulness to reality, and in the latter a return to the "subjective" where the painter is above all—and excessively—preoccupied, not with "representing," but quite simply with "expressing himself." It is this hiatus which Malraux introduces into the history of painting that Merleau-Ponty cannot accept. And so he proposes to "re-examine [Malraux'] analysis" (S, 47; *S,* 59), to "put Malraux' analyses in their proper perspective" (S, 75; *S,* 94), and to do so by treating the entire enterprise of painting as a continuous effort to speak the same "language," by showing "that there is a tacit language and that painting speaks in its own way." (S, 47; *S,* 59) In order to make evident this silent discourse which is uninterruptedly pursued throughout the entire history of painting, Merleau-Ponty's analysis will consist in bringing together these three problems: *perception, history, expression.*[9]


### 1.   The Unity of Painting

As a matter of fact, one cannot draw an essential distinction between classical and modern painting except by treating the history of painting as a balance sheet wherein would be progressively registered the invention and perfection of techniques or procedures whose purpose would be to *reproduce* with the greatest precision possible nature as it is "in itself." Let us call history conceived in this way *empirical* or *linear.* For this kind of thinking the only thing to be considered is "a general technique of *representation* which, at the limit, should reach the thing itself". (S, 47; *S,* 60) It is clear that this conception of painting leads one to posit, and even requires, a rupture between traditional painting and modern painting which has explicitly renounced any attempt to imitate things.

Now, we should remember that a painter can apply a technique or invent one only if he is *already a painter;* it is not techniques which make the painter; it is the painter who makes use of and invents them. Malraux himself admits that the conception of painting as creative expression is not exclusively characteristic of modern painting but that it applies to all painting. Merleau-Ponty, however, does not hesitate for a moment; for him "no valuable painting has ever consisted in simply representing." (S, 48; *S,* 60) Indeed, because the great painters of the past did not *paint* in accordance with the objectivistic theories they held about painting, because, in the very act of painting, they operated below the level of their theories, they still speak to us today and have not simply "fallen out of style." There is another meaning to their art than that of representation, a meaning other than the one they for the most part thought they were investing in it; and it is this subterranean element which turns their works into *classics*, which confers on them the power of touching us even today.

Merleau-Ponty thus concludes that "classical painting cannot be defined by its representation of nature...modern painting by its reference to the subjective." (S, 48; *S,* 60) The unity of painting does not come about in a time composed of sporadic events, in the accumulation of techniques aimed at capturing an in-itself nature, but in that unique vocation of painting which is to effectuate a *metamorphosis,* to *transmute* the perceived world into a professed symbol.

The language of painting—a language spoken by all painting which is genuinely art, that is, creative expression—is therefore not "prose," the exact reproduction of a world already sufficient unto itself, but *poetry,* the evocation and taking up of a world in the process of being born. Painting "must be poetry; that is, it must completely awaken and recall our sheer power of expressing beyond things already said or seen." (S, 52; *S,* 65) As Paul Klee said, the artist sees the creative side of the world. "*Natura naturans* is of more importance to him than *natura naturata.*" He assigns himself, "instead of a finite image of nature, that—the only one which counts—of creation as genesis". And thus, as Klee goes on to say, "art does not reproduce the visible; it makes visible."[10]

To sum up, therefore, Merleau-Ponty is attempting to bring into relief the unity of painting, and he is doing so by showing precisely that there is *another dimension* to painting: not that of reproduction or resemblance to "a pre-established Nature" (S, 52; S, 65), but that of creation, metamorphosis, pure expression. Thus the problem raised by modern painting, he observes, is "a problem completely different from that of the return to the individual"; it is that of knowing how, without making ourselves conform to a nature which is fully actualized and rests in itself, to an "objective" world, we nonetheless succeed in joining up with a universal meaning whereby we enter in communication with others—"how we are grafted to the universal by that which is most our own." (S, 52; S, 65) It is precisely this problem which we have to explore. We must know what the "silent world" of the painter, that generality at the bottom of his individuality which furnishes him with the means of joining up with the universal, consists in. What is the origin of his "poetry"? What is the *spontaneous source* of painting?

## 2.  Silence and Expression

What the painter puts into his picture is thus not a thing, a world which is already self-sufficient; and the success of the picture cannot be measured by its degree of resemblance to the object painted. What the painter puts into it is not, however, a private vision of the world which he enjoys in the solitude of his mind; it is not merely his own subjectivity, his "immediate self." To maintain that the painter expresses only himself would be to fall back into the subject-object antinomy which Merleau-Ponty is seeking to overcome by asserting the unity of the history of painting. We must pass beyond this dichotomy to another dimension.

Let us then say that what the painter puts into his picture is his *style.* But let us be careful. The painter's style must not be thought to be the outwardly visible expression, for others, of a system of equivalences for which he himself would hold the key. The painter does not freely dispose of his own style; he is never himself fully conscious of it. Thus for the painter himself his style is not what it is for others: a certain visible aspect of his work, an "object of predilection." (S, 53; *S*, 66) The artist's style exists for him in the same way his body does; it is not an instrument, a mere vehicle, but his very way of inhabiting and taking up the world, his way of presenting himself to others, and, in short, his existence; like the body, it is as imperceptible to him as it is manifest to others.

We can thus see that for the artist his style is not an *end* in itself. It is not what he seeks to express but is rather the operative, latent, silent meaning which animates him; this meaning is present in everything he sees or, rather, is his very way of seeing, of responding to the visibility of his world. We must therefore, Merleau-Ponty says, conceive of his style as, in the first instance, a *demand* placed on the painter. This is to say that as the diffuse meaning which is present in everything he *sees* and which impels him to paint, the painter's style is *a demand on him issuing from perception:* "We must see it appear in the context of the painter's perception as a painter; style is a demand that has issued from that perception." (S, 54; *S*, 67) We need not comment on this observation here, having already encountered the idea in the *Phenomenology* in the context of the psychology of form. What is peculiar to the painter is that he transforms the natural stylization of indigenous perception into a professed, figurative, created symbol and makes of the object he perceives and paints a precise "emblem of a way of inhabiting the world, of handling it…—in short, the emblem of a certain relationship to being." (S, 54; *S*, 68) The painter makes his already stylizing perception submit to a "coherent deformation"; he makes it undergo a metamorphosis and change into a pictorial meaning.

But if what is peculiar to the painter as such is that he reorganizes his natural perception, interprets it, and draws from it figures which he himself brings into being, what is essential for us to see here is that this creative interpretation is "already sketched out in the painter's perception," that it "begins as soon as he perceives." (S, 54; *S*, 68) The painter's style is thus the concentrating of a "still scattered meaning of his perception" which he "makes exist expressly." (S, 55; *S*, 68) The painter expresses nothing other than "his communication with the world." (S, 54; *S*, 67) We must not look for the secret of the painter's style in his arbitrary and merely conscious deliberations; it is his operative perception itself which proposes it to him. If the painter is to find his style, it is thus necessary for him to deliver himself over to his spontaneous perception, to that delirium which is vision (as "Eye and Mind" will put it). It is necessary for him to listen to the "voices of silence" which speak in him, for it is from them that issue forth initiatives which—worked over and expressed—could prove worthwhile. "What one too deliberately seeks, he does not find; and he who on the contrary has in his meditative life known how to tap its spontaneous source never lacks for ideas and values." (S, 83; S, 104)

If therefore the painter's style springs from the encounter of his "gaze with the things which solicit it," it must be in his perception itself, in this "spontaneous source," that he discovers the means of joining up with a universal meaning through which he succeeds in communicating with others. The perceived world is full of initiatives which it makes to the gaze—it is, as the *Phenomenology* said, like an interlocutor in a dialogue—and this gaze, which "throws out of focus and regroups" (S, 56; S, 71) the spectacle, draws from it a meaning which it itself seems to propose. The painter's work is the response he makes to the "call" of things, to the "questioning" of the world. (S, 58; S, 73) It is the "question spread out through the world's spectacle" which he believes he is merely making explicit. Rejoining the lesson of his essay on Cézanne, Merleau-Ponty asks, "How would the painter or poet express anything other than his encounter with the world?" (S, 56; S, 70) In *Le Temps retrouvé* Proust had already written, "Style, for the writer just as much as for the artist, is a matter not of technique but of vision." And as Proust also said, "everything priceless is in the gaze of the painter."[11]

Thus the painter always speaks a language which he has learned through his contact with the world. Even abstract art speaks of nothing else, even if what it has to say is a "negation or refusal of the world." (S, 56; S, 70) It is from the world's spectacle in which he himself is involved as the partner in a majestic discourse that the painter receives his "vocation" to paint. If therefore today's "absolute" painting refuses simply to reproduce the world, it is not because it rejects the world in favor of an isolated subject; it is actually because it is searching for a new idea of what the meaning, the truth, of painting is. The moderns' refusal of tradition stems from the fact that they "want nothing to do with a truth defined as the resemblance of painting and the world." (S, 57; *S,* 71) Whether they recognize it or not, they are still looking for the truth, only another kind of truth, a truth which would not be that of resemblance: "Modern painting, like modern thought generally, obliges us to admit a truth which does not resemble things, which is without any external model and without any predestined instruments of expression, and which is nevertheless truth." (S, 57; *S,* 72)

Merleau-Ponty is here touching on a central idea in his analysis, that of *truth.* Let us see how this notion of a truth which stems from spontaneous perception[12] is the same for all of the history of painting, and how, in the last analysis, it obliges us to revise our idea of what history itself is.

3. History and Truth

The important thing is to understand that pictorial expression, that metamorphosis which the painter effects, is an operation which comes to pass "through him." (S, 57; *S,* 72) Since it is not an act on the part of a pure "subjectivity," since the meaning of painting has its ground in the spontaneity and generality of bodily existence, in the perceptual contact of the painter with his world, it must be admitted that the painter is caught up in a movement, in a desire to paint, which does not originate in his will or intelligence; he is possessed by his art, and consequently all painters of all times have experienced the same problem, the same visual relation with the world, and are thus united in the same enterprise. "The unity of painting...exists in that single task which all painters are confronted with". (S, 60; *S,* 75) This is to say that the painter is he who has been pushed by his sensitivity towards the marvels of vision to want to bear witness to it and to make works of his vision and of the visibility of the world; and that it is thus this "vocation" to paint which makes it be that all painters are united together in the same enterprise.

The first effort made by man to respond freely to the visibility of his world—and even before that, the first perception of the seeing man who drew out *figures* from the nondifferenciation of natural being—already announced modern painting, for it opened up a field and established a tradition, just as the birth to the world of a new individual is an event which announces and calls for a follow-up, a history, and is, as the *Phenomenology* said, an advent or a transcendental event.

"The first sketches on the walls of caves set forth the world as 'to be painted' or 'to be sketched' and called for an indefinite future of painting, so that they speak to us and we answer them by metamorphoses in which they collaborate with us." (S, 60; *S,* 75) The first attempt to express the world goes completely beyond itself and founds a community which ignores temporal and spatial distances: *expression is by its nature transcendental or teleological.*[13]

At this point in his analysis Merleau-Ponty makes a distinction whose importance must be emphasized. Indeed, we are assisting here at a turning in his philosophy where his phenomenology becomes radically deeper and begins to change into an ontology. Having characterized the beginnings of painting as a direct prefiguration of our own present wherein they continue to live, Merleau-Ponty writes, "There are thus *two historicities."* (S, 60; *S,* 75; emphasis ours)

The first historicity, the most evident and usually the only one to be recognized, is what Merleau-Ponty at different times calls "empirical history" (S, 62; *S,* 77), "historicity of death" (S, 63; *S,* 79), "the order of events" (S, 64; *S,* 80), "the empirical order of events" (S, 68; *S,* 85). This is *visible* or phenomenal history, what we have already called linear history. Here one unites the moments in the history of painting as so many events which are *external* to each other. Here painting makes its way across time in an evolution which is sometimes hesitant, sometimes hasty, accumulating procedures and techniques which each generation augments in its turn. Here there is but *succession* and *replacement.* This history "is forgetfulness rather than memory; it is dismemberment, ignorance, externality." (S, 60; *S,* 75)

There is, however, another historicity. This one is not made up of successive events which have only empirical relations among them; it is not visible, it does not go from a beginning towards an end. Merleau-Ponty calls this history "cumulative history" (S, 60; *S,* 75), "true history" (S, 61; *S,* 77), history of "advents" (S, 62; *S,* 77), "secret, modest, non-deliberated, involuntary, and, in short, living historicity" (S, 62; *S,* 78), "historicity of life" (S, 63; *S,* 79), "the order of expression" (S, 64; *S,* 80), and "the order of culture or meaning" (S, 68; *S,* 85). Here one does not have to do with a mere succession of events but with the continuous life, the integral and cumulative becoming of painting as a modality of human expression, which, like an uninterrupted discourse, continues throughout time, underneath time, and in which each painter "revives, recaptures, and renews the entire undertaking of painting in each new work." (S, 60; *S,* 75)

And it is this secret, silent, invisible history which makes empirical, phenomenal history possible. It is because all painters live the same problem that one can compare two pictures from different eras and say how they resemble each other and how they differ. Painters can be arranged in an empirical history, and relations can be traced between works as events—this constituting a "historicity of death"—only because there is another historicity, that of life, which makes it be that each painter is "a certain speech in the discourse of painting which awakens echoes from the past and future....he is linked to all other attempts to the exact degree that he busies himself resolutely with his world." (S, 62; S, 77)

Merleau-Ponty thus states: "We propose...to consider the order of culture or meaning an original order of *advent,* which should not be derived from that of mere events, if they exist, or treated as simply the effect of extraordinary conjunctions."[14] (S, 68; S, 85) It is important that we grasp this point.

Let us begin by ruling out the idealist interpretation of this true historicity which Merleau-Ponty believes he has uncovered. In "positing a field distinct from the empirical order of events," he insists that he is not positing "a Spirit of Painting which is already in possession of itself on the other side of the world that it is gradually manifested in." (S, 68; S, 85) He refuses to have recourse to this kind of "Hegelian monster." Thus we must not conceive of cultural or true history as taking place in a "supra-sensible world": it does not constitute "a second causality" over and above empirical history. It must rather be looked for underneath events, in the *generality* of bodily existence. It could thus be said that the efforts of different painters converge "by the sole fact that they are efforts to express." (S, 69; S, 86)[15] The unity of painting is of the same sort as that of the style of an individual; in both instances we have to do with a kind of "envelopment": the beginnings of painting continue on indefinitely in the rest of its history, just as the birth of an individual is never an event which is purely and simply past but rather constitutes an expressive opening which announces a series of reappropriations and which will cease to express itself and signify only when it will have ceased to exist. All efforts of expression are accomplished beyond or through distances in space and time, for they are all reappropriations of the natural expressivity of the lived body, that anonymous and general opening perpetually recreated in the nondifferentiation of natural being. Just "as the hold our body has upon every possible object founds one single space," so also "the continued attempt at expression founds one single history". (S, 70; *S*, 87) Thus this unity of painting which is like a "provisional eternity," this true history, stems from the fact that painting has its source in the *generality* of bodily existence and is the taking up or reappropriation of our power of natural expression. "The quasi-eternity of art is of a piece with the quasi-eternity of incarnate existence." And thus Merleau-Ponty is able to conclude, "it is the expressive operation of the body, begun by the smallest perception, which is amplified into painting and art. The field of pictorial meaning has been open ever since one man appeared in the world."[16]

With the appearance of man, the world is, so to speak, committed to truth; a teleology of consciousness is established (the "task" of becoming conscious), and the ground of this teleology, this rationality, is bodily existence, that is, the *contingent* appearance of man. Here, as in the *Phenomenology,* Merleau-Ponty's last word is that of the contingency of rationality. In the last analysis, therefore, bodily existence, in this essay as in his major thesis, is conceived to be the ultimate foundation beyond which there is nothing to be understood.

We can see that what occupies the center of Merleau-Ponty's preoccupations is the notion of *history* as a milieu engendered by expression: how the power of expression which springs up in man, and which is like a *miracle* in that it has no explanation but is rather precisely that which makes possible all man's explanations and marvels, establishes by virtue of its generality a recuperative or cumulative history, wherein all men of all time and all efforts of expression are *reunited* in a single movement, a single explosion of meaning.

If, however, there is something that this essay passes over in silence and does not seek to clarify, it is precisely this "miracle" which is human existence. Merleau-Ponty says in effect that this is a ground which is itself irrational, devoid of reason. However, can one, legitimately and without contradiction, conceive of the history of culture and expression as a single project, as the manifestation of a teleology of expression, if one only assigns to it as a ground and condition of possibility irrationality and contingency? How can Merleau-Ponty say that cultural history belongs to the order of *advents* and neither stems from "pure events" nor results merely from "exceptional encounters" if he does no more than link it up with bodily existence, which is itself, in the last analysis conceived of as an incomprehensible, mysterious, and reasonless fact, as, in a way, merely a happy *accident*?

In any event, to tie up the notion of history with that of expression and, more basically still, with that of perception, which is to say, with bodily existence, is at the same time to conceive anew the idea of *progress*. It is indeed essential to history that it happen, that it have movement, for without this history obviously would not exist. Nonetheless, the kind of progress appropriate to the history of meaning cannot be the same kind which characterizes the history of empirical events. We have seen that for Merleau-Ponty true history does not proceed from a beginning towards an end; there can be no question here of a "finality" of history. This is not to say, however, that there is no development here, for if the order of meaning "does not follow each zigzag of empirical history, it sketches out, it calls for, a series of successive steps." (S, 69; S, 86) Precisely because the unity of painting is not a supra-sensible metaphysical entity which governs events, the true history of painting is not an eternity wherein nothing moves. It is neither more nor less eternal than incarnate existence, which means that it is like a "provisional eternity," an "eternity which has always to be reconstituted." Or again, that the history of painting is "in principle a meaning in genesis." (S, 69; S, 87). There is progress in culture, for each painter takes up and starts anew the entire enterprise of painting. There is, however, no progress if this life of painting is conceived of as an *evolution* whose course is broken up into stages which replace former ones.[17] The history of meaning is a history without a beginning and without a foreseeable end, and, consequently, it is without any hierarchical ordering; it is nothing other than the *universal* community of men within the phenomenon of expression: "It is the perceptual conversation carried on between all spoken words and all valid actions, each in turn contesting and confirming the other, and each recreating all the others." (S, 74; S, 92)

Thus conceived, true history is not a Power outside of man. It lives only in the efforts made by men to express themselves: "True history gets its life entirely from us." (S, 75; S, 93) If the efforts of all painters come together in that they are all efforts of expression, there is, nonetheless, *a* universe of painting only because *certain* men chose to devote their life to painting. History must not be conceived of as a principle outside of us, and we no more than the *occasion* for its self-expression. It would be more true to say that we are ourselves History transcending itself, making itself, that we are ourselves its will: "Transcendence no longer hangs over man: he becomes, strangely, its privileged bearer." (S, 71; S, 88)[18]

Even if history conceived of in this way does not affect any of man's privileges or diminish his value, it nonetheless ends up by conferring another dimensionality on his actions and by situating them in another field. When, concerned with the "validity" of his work, a painter appeals to "the judgment of history," he is invoking, no doubt unknowingly for the most part, a reason which can justify him; his appeal to posterity is not an appeal to the "complacency of the public... It is inseparable from the inner certainty of having said what waited to be said in the particular situation and what consequently could not fail to be understood by X." (S, 74; S, 93-4) The artist's work situates him in the *field of truth*. Man is animated by the "desire for a total manifestation" which will justify his efforts and his existence: "Except perhaps in the case of some wretched men who think only of winning or of being right, all action and all love are haunted by the expectation of an account which will transform them into their truth. In short, they are haunted by the expectation of the moment at which it will finally be known just what they were all about." (S, 74; S, 93)[19] It is in expression, in the creative taking up of the native significance of his existence, that man brings about the "junction of the individual and the universal" (S, 73; S, 91), joins up with "a second-order value" (S, 78; S, 97), and at once places himself in the field of History and what, later on, Merleau-Ponty will call the field of Being.

In "Indirect Language and the Voices of Silence" Merleau-Ponty has succeeded in envisaging the painter's style as the advent or coming to light of a power of expression which emerges from incarnate existence. If the painter brings to the total enterprise of painting his own initiative and makes his perception undergo a "coherent deformation," the fact remains that he is haunted by a desire to paint, a demand for manifestation of truth, which impels him to express himself. The true history of painting is thus, not a mere succession of events in time which follow upon and replace one another, but a series of events which mutually confirm themselves; efforts at expression do not die like empirical facts, nor do they become simply past and done with; they continue to live in a universe of truth. True history is a "cumulative" history; it is the historicity not of death but of life. The unity of painting stems from this simple fact that all painters do no more than take up and re-express their bodily insertion into the world; they simply give universal symbols to the signifying existence of the perceiving body.

What, however, in the last analysis is perception or bodily exist-ence if it is capable of instituting a history and a universe of truth? In this essay, Merleau-Ponty has discovered the field of history, but he has said nothing about its basis, perception, which he had not already said in the *Phenomenology*. When he will write "Eye and Mind" eight years hence, he will reconsider perception itself. In this last of his pub-lications, Merleau-Ponty will think of perception itself as a demand arising from Being. Thus painting, the advent of perception, will be thought of in the final analysis as an advent of Being, as Being mani-festing and expressing itself. Here it will be less a question of the vision of the painter or the visibility of the world, than of a Being which views itself through the creative vision of the painter and the visible spectacle of the world.

Thus the desire to paint, to celebrate the mystery of visibility, will in the last analysis be Being which desires itself, which desires to get hold of itself, to re-flect itself—to see itself. And man, to the de-gree that he responds to this demand with a creativity and a meta-morphosis which are peculiar to him, will be the com-prehension of Being—Being getting hold of and realizing itself; man will be the place where Being transforms itself into logos. In "Eye and Mind" the *voca-tion* to paint, the *teleology* of consciousness, will be understood as expressive of a movement of transcendence which is nothing other than Being itself.

## III.   Eye and Mind

THE small essay "Eye and Mind"[20] is the last writing of Merleau-Ponty published in his lifetime, and, as Sartre remarked, it "says every-thing provided one knows how to decipher it."[21] Indeed, although one reads it with a great deal of pleasure, "Eye and Mind" is basically a difficult work wherein the reader discovers "beneath its manifest content the surplus and thickness of meaning" (PriP, 179; *OE*, 63), of which he often feels he is getting only a glimpse. To borrow an ex-pression from Heidegger, this essay is easy to read but difficult to think. It seems that here Merleau-Ponty has pushed to the limit the possibilities of the philosophical discourse and of that way of reflect-ing and writing which is altogether his own. As if to attest to his con-viction that all modes of expression are rigorously bound up together, his thought here, like the painting on which it reflects, is less prose than poetry, less a designation than an evocation. The quotation from Cézanne which prefaces the work is thus the articulation of Merleau-Ponty's own goal: "What I am trying to translate to you is more mysterious; it is entwined in the very roots of being, in the impalpable source of sensations." Since the truth he is trying to discern is hidden in "the impalpable source of sensations," since it is a question of bringing to the pure expression of its own meaning that mute experience which is the act of painting, "Eye and Mind" cannot be but allusive. For us it remains, as Sartre says, a work which must be deciphered.[22]

The act of painting, like the language of the writer and the thought of the philosopher, is an act of expression; it does not coincide with life but is rather the attempt to "speak" it, to deliver up its meaning. Painting is a reflection on being in the world. It thus contains an implicit philosophy of being, and one could say with Klee that the painter is "a philosopher unbeknownst to himself."[23] Since, however, the painter's reflection is precisely an operative, spontaneous, non-thematized reflection, painting does not result in ideas, concepts, or propositions. It takes place in that original and silent milieu which is perception, and it is, in this sense, closer to the spontaneous meaning of being in the world than are literature and philosophy. It would thus be in the interest of a philosophy which assigns to itself the task of undertaking "the prospection of the actual world" (PriP, 177, OE, 58) to interrogate painting, for it is precisely this philosophy "which animates the painter—not when he expresses his opinions about the world but in that instant when his vision becomes gesture, when, in Cézanne's words, he 'thinks in painting'." (PriP, 178; OE, 60) By means of painting there appears "a Logos of lines, of lighting, of colors, or reliefs, of masses," and in this way painting constitutes "a conceptless presentation of universal Being." (PriP, 182; OE, 71) It is thus important for reflection to know what "this secret science" is which is present in the work of the painter, this "fundamental of painting, and perhaps of all culture." (PriP, 161; OE, 15)

We should add one last word: the uncertainty one feels in reading this essay stems not only from the fact that the style of the work is allusive and its meaning fugitive, but also from the fact that almost all elements of the analysis and all phenomena described seem to be the same as those we have already encountered, and that yet, nevertheless, everything here seems to be *turned upside down*. The phenomena are indeed the same, but underneath them a disconcerting depth appears into which Merleau-Ponty has not up to now reached with so much insistence and assurance. And it is this unshakable conviction which he seems to manifest of having finally put his finger here on the heart of the phenomenon which is surprising. He speaks here of "vision" rather than of "perception," of "carnal" (*charnelle*) existence rather than "corporeal" existence, and the word "being" now begins with a capital letter. These are so many lexical changes pointing to a certain shift in his way of viewing things. It is indeed in this essay that Merleau-Ponty is going to get to the bottom of the problem raised by "Indirect Language and the Voices of Silence." This problem is perception itself. Perception may indeed be the basis of the act of painting and of a universal history of meaning, but is this the last word that can be said? Must one not rather ask what indeed perception itself is? It is in "Eye and Mind" that Merleau-Ponty is going to revise his ideas concerning the primacy of perception and, consequently, concerning the contingency of existence and the gratuitousness of the teleology of consciousness.

## 1. The Flesh of the Sensible

The operant meaning of painting, its implicit philosophy, the "secret science" which animates the painter's efforts without his knowing it, must be looked for, Merleau-Ponty says, in the painter's own body. By means of his body and, more precisely, by means of that primordial modality of bodily existence which is vision, the painter is a painter. "It is by lending his body to the world that the painter changes the world into paintings." (PriP, 162; *OE*, 16) In order to understand the expressive operation of the painter it is thus necessary to see how it comes to him or is proposed to him by his body. It is necessary to raise the questions which were not raised by "Indirect Language and the Voices of Silence": What does it mean, in the last analysis, to have a body, to be open to the world by perception? What is perception?

The first fact discovered by this analysis—and which is no less surprising for being first—is that the active body which I am, this seeing body, is also and at the same time *visible;* it is numbered among the things it sees. We must take careful note of this "first paradox" which will not fail to call forth others. For it prevents us from conceiving of vision as an operation of thought, as an inspection or over-flight of the world. Vision is not, as Descartes would have us believe, a view *on* the world; it takes place *in* the world; it springs forth at that moment when a visible thing which we call the body turns back on itself and begins to see. Since then the body which sees is also visible and is a part of the world it sees, we must not conceive of the world of which the body is a part as "in itself or matter." As soon as one takes notice of the existence of this "extraordinary overlapping" between vision and the visible in the body itself, one must say that it recognizes in what it sees the "other side" of its visionary powers. Precisely because the body which sees is itself a thing, a visible, be-cause it is "a thing among things" (PriP, 163; *OE,* 19), it must be said that *in the body it is the visible which sees itself* and that the body and the world are thus "made of the same stuff." (PriP, 164; *OE,* 21) In our analysis of the *Phenomenology* we have already seen that the body and the world reflect one another, mutually articulate one another. But here Merleau-Ponty is involved in making his thought more explicit and says without equivocation what in the *Phenomenology* was said only obscurely if indeed it was said at all. He now insists on the fact that the world and the body come from the *same stuff.* The world is not merely the correlate of the body; the reversibility which exists between them makes it be that they are together a *single* reality, a single being, a single Whole: the world is a part—and here appears what is perhaps *the* key term of the later Merleau-Ponty—of the *flesh* of the body.

It will be worth our while to assimilate this idea properly, for it is without a doubt the cornerstone, the key concept of Merleau-Ponty's ontology. In his essay "The Philosopher and His Shadow," which appeared in 1959 a few months before "Eye and Mind," and in which he speaks of the later Husserl and also—if not above all—of himself, Merleau-Ponty returns to that phenomenon which had never ceased to intrigue him: the fact that the body announces in itself a kind of "natural reflection." In the moment when the body touches itself touching or sees itself seeing, it manifests itself as a "sensing thing," as a "subject-object." (S, 166; *S,* 210) What is important here, Merleau-Ponty insists, is to recognize that such a phenomenon "also overturns our idea of the thing and the world, and that it results in an ontological rehabilitation of the sensible." For, precisely, if "the distinction between subject and object is blurred in my body..., it is also blurred in the thing". (S, 167; *S,* 211) Since the thing and the world "reflect my own incarnation and are its counterpart," it must be said that there literally exists a *flesh* of the sensible. The body and the thing are included in the same stuff; they have the same flesh. When therefore that visible which is the body sees itself, it is the visible world which is seeing itself. "Here we have," Merleau-Ponty observes, "a type of being, a universe with its unparalleled 'subject' and 'object'." The sensible is no longer merely things; it is also the subject which sees them. Vision takes place among things, and here there is a single flesh which, paradoxically, is subject *and* object.

In the *Phenomenology* Merleau-Ponty had said that if I comprehend the world it is because it comprehends me. In "Eye and Mind" this affirmation receives its justification. If I see, it is because I am in this way a part of the world. If I can explore the visible with my eyes, it is because I am situated in it, because *I am of it (j'en suis),* because, as a seeing body, I am included among visible things and inhabit along with them a single universe. Thus "vision happens among, or is caught in, things—in that place where something visible undertakes to see, becomes visible for itself". (PriP, 163; *OE,* 19) It can be said without distinction that vision takes place in the visible or that the visible doubles itself with a vision.

And it thus can be understood how Cézanne could say that "nature is on the inside" (PriP, 164; *OE,* 22), that the landscape thought itself in him and that he was its consciousness. For the painter it is indeed not a question of a vision which he commands—the painter's gaze is not the inspection of an in-itself world—but rather of a Vision which occurs in him. "The world no longer stands before him through representation," Merleau-Ponty writes, "rather, it is the painter to whom the things of the world give birth by a sort of concentration or coming-to-itself of the visible." (PriP, 181; *OE,* 69) And thus Merleau-Ponty agrees with Max Ernst when the latter says: "Just as the role of the poet since [Rimbaud's] famous *Lettre du voyant* consists in writing under the dictation of what thinks itself, of what articulates itself in him, the role of the painter is to grasp and project what sees itself in him." (PriP, 167; *OE,* 30)[24] Painting expresses nothing other than these "inversions" *(renversements)* (PriP, 163; *OE,* 19) between vision and the visible. It does nothing other than awaken and carry "to its highest pitch a delirium which is vision itself". (PriP, 166; *OE,* 26) In their work painters thus attest to "the metamorphosis of seeing

and seen which defines both our flesh and the painter's vocation."
(PriP, 169; *OE*, 34)[25] To speak of definition is to speak of *logos;* this
primitive *articulation* of the body in terms of the world and the world
in terms of the body, this "chiasm," this phenomenon which Merleau-
Ponty calls the flesh, this he also calls a wild or brute logos. Let us
now see how this fleshly logos is precisely the logos of the act of
painting.

## 2.  The Seeing Vision

Since the seeing body is also a visible thing, it carries within itself the "carnal formula" (PriP, 164; *OE*, 22) of things. Why, in giving
himself over to that delirium which is vision, should the painter therefore not discover the secret of the *presence* of things, of *visibility?*
The "interrogation of painting in any case," Merleau-Ponty says,
"looks toward this secret and feverish genesis of things in our body."
(PriP, 167; *OE*, 30) The work which the painter accomplishes by letting his vision reconstitute itself, this "second-order visible," is not "a
faded copy, a *trompe-l'oeil,* or another *thing.*" (PriP, 164; *OE*, 22) It
is not the image of an image[26] but is the visible itself which is seeing
itself in the vision of the painter and, afterwards, in that of the spectator. It could thus be said that the picture is the visible thing seeing
itself anew or, rather, for the first time, or else that it is vision making
itself visible, that it is the "inside of the outside and the outside of
the inside." (PriP, 146; *OE*, 23) As a work of the imagination, a picture is not a real thing, nor is it immediate, straightforward vision. It
is the "diagram of the thing's life in my body," "its pulp and carnal
obverse exposed to view for the first time, " (PriP, 164–5; *OE*, 24)
just as it is the outward presentation of "the inward traces of vision."
The picture reinstates in the visible "the ciphers of the visible" (PriP,
166; *OE*, 28) which are engraved in vision. It gets us under the skin of
things in order to show us how "things make themselves into things
and the world into a world."[27] And it shows us how we see things
by reintroducing our vision into the visible. The painter brings to expression and installs in the realm of the available the internal relation
with things that for the most part we merely live. As a recuperative
work, painting renders visible the phenomenon of visibility.[28]

A picture is thus a second-order visible only by being a transcendental visible. It is transcendental or reflective, for it reveals, enables

us to see, the means by which things make themselves be seen by us. What a painting takes as its theme and recreates are the relations existing between "light, illumination, shadows, reflections, colors," all those exchanges and performances which we do not normally see because we are too taken up by the thing which they present to us. For this reason, it can be said that painting is "a central operation contributing to the definition of our access to Being." (PriP, 171; *OE*, 42) Is it therefore so surprising or so hackneyed when, in order to describe the beauty of a landscape, one has recourse to the worn-out expression of saying that it is "as beautiful as a picture"—since painting is nothing else than the *coming to awareness* of that marvel which is visibility? Who could better express the miracle of this "there is" *(il y a)* than the painter who "lives in fascination" (PriP, 167; *OE*, 31) and experiences more than anyone else the delirium of vision?

However, if we can say that painting pertains to a transcendental order, we know that this expression cannot have for Merleau-Ponty the same meaning it would have in the context of a critical or idealist philosophy. The meaning engendered by the act of painting does not belong to a sovereign Spirit which claims to govern the world and bestow its meaning upon it. It is the meaning of being in the world, of carnal existence itself, with the only difference that it is now delivered up. Thus it cannot be said that the painter institutes the transcendence which painting realizes; it must rather be said that he incarnates it and is, as it were, its bearer. Here again the painter's words have something to teach us: "The work is in the first instance a genesis, and its history can be briefly represented as a mysterious spark which bursts out from one knows not where, which inflames the spirit, activates the hand, and, transmitting itself as a movement to matter, becomes a work."[29] The painter himself cannot say whence stem the resources of his art. What he is going to say on canvas does not pre-exist in his mind but comes to be only on the canvas. Similarly, "Art is not construction, artifice, meticulous relationship to a space and a world existing outside. It is truly the 'inarticulate cry', as Hermes Trismegistus said, 'which seemed to be the voice of the light'." (PriP, 167; *OE*, 70) The artist feels himself to be "penetrated by the universe" (PriP, 167; *OE*, 31); he is, quite literally, inspired: "There really is inspiration and expiration of Being, a respiration in Being, action and passion so slightly discernible that it becomes impossible to distinguish between what sees and what is seen, what paints and what is painted." In his work the painter sets off again the "genesis of the visible," as Klee says; he exalts the coming-to-itself of the visible, and thus it is that his vision is like "a continued birth." (PriP, 168; *OE,* 32)[30]

In the picture it is thus nature which is born anew, which undergoes a metamorphosis and makes itself into something which sees. What is speaking here are the "voices of silence" of which Merleau-Ponty has spoken; it is that silent logos of the world which is the "spark between sensing and the sensible." (PriP, 163; *OE,* 21) What comes to light is "that fire" which burns in the sensible, that *illumination of the flesh (éclair de la chair)* which elsewhere Merleau-Ponty calls *lumen naturale.* The painter seeks to express this "internal animation, this radiation of the visible." (PriP, 182; *OE,* 71) The painter attempts to transpose this light which bursts forth in his flesh, which is also the flesh of the visible, into his picture. "We ourselves," Klee says, "are charged with this force down to the very marrow of our bones. We cannot say what it is, but we can draw nearer to its source to some degree or other. We must in any event reveal this force; we must show it in its functions just as it shows itself in us."[31] Since, as Merleau-Ponty says, it is "impossible to say that nature ends here and that man or expression starts here," it must be said that "It is, therefore, mute Being which itself comes to show forth its own meaning." (PriP, 188; *OE,* 87)

## 3.   The Deflagration of Being

Visibility, we have seen, is possible only if the visible doubles itself with a vision. Vision is that hollow, that absence (vision is an absence since it is not, as such, visible), that invisible doubling of the visible which makes it visible and which thus figures in its definition: "the proper essence of the visible is to have a lining *(doublure)* of invisibility in the strict sense, which it makes present as a certain absence." (PriP, 187; *OE,* 85) Here is announced the title of Merleau-Ponty's last manuscript, *The Visible and the Invisible.* We can thus expect from it clarifications of what must necessarily remain obscure in our reading of this essay. However, before we undertake this analysis, let us attempt to take note of the references in this writing to a Being which reveals itself as a visible-invisible, which comes to manifest its own meaning in the metamorphosis of seeing and the visible, a metamorphosis which serves to define the vocation of the painter and which assigns to him his task.

When the painter unveils the phenomenon of visibility, when he elevates it to expression, it is "mute Being which itself comes to show forth its own meaning." (PriP, 188; *OE,* 87) This meaning is "a Logos of lines, of lighting, of colors, of reliefs, of masses—a conceptless presentation of universal Being." (PriP, 182; *OE,* 71) Let us attempt to sum this up by saying that the logos of which Merleau-Ponty speaks is the original presentation of Being, that it is Being presenting itself, articulating itself, phenomenalizing itself. Now the Logos of the visible is also—we have only to recall this—the Logos of vision; or, rather, it is the reversibility between seeing and the visible, their common flesh. This is to say that the Logos is a natural light, that "spark between sensing and the sensible": a Logos—light, illumination, "intelligibility," rationality—exists when the visible doubles itself with an invisible, when for the first time the "chiasm" visible-invisible appears. We must thus say that that the upsurge of the articulation, the chiasm sensing-sensible, the appearance, the advent of this Logos is the presentation, the *Erscheinung,* of Being,[32] that it is Being *radiating.*

It will be noted that what we have just said is not, as such, said in "Eye and Mind," but we would like to think that it is no less faithful to the text for not being said by it, that it is no less its "unthought thought." Merleau-Ponty writes, "Vision is not a certain mode of thought or presence to self; it is the means given me for being absent from myself, for *being present at the fission of Being from the inside.*" (PriP, 186; *OE,* 81; emphasis ours) The upsurge of the articulation, the configuration sensing-sensible, is the coming to articulation of Being itself; it is Being *articulating itself, transforming itself into logos.* "Every visual something...gives itself as the result of a *dehisence* of Being" (PriP, 187; *OE,* 85), of a "*deflagration* of Being" (PriP, 180; *OE,* 65). Being explodes and makes its advent as Logos, articulation, configuration, meaning, when, in the midst of the visible or the sensible, vision or sensation springs forth—or, rather, this springing forth, this dehiscence of the sensible, is *the very definition of Being.* It is necessary that the encounter of the visible and the seeing occur on a certain "ground," in a certain "location"—it is indeed necessary that these two "relatives" stem from a certain "irrelative"—in "a unique Space which separates and reunites, which sustains every cohesion".

(PriP, 187; *OE,* 84) This "unique Space" which is *the ground of all presence* (being in the world) is Being as dehiscence or *opening.* The ultimate ground, the "irrelative," is Being as radiance, explosion, transcendence, opening.

Thus in his work the painter—like the poet and the thinker—consolidates and advances a wild logos which is a primordial articulation or dehiscence—an *"aus-eindersetzung"* or *polemos,* as Heidegger would say. In this originating opening all of man's efforts at expression inscribe themselves. As a lens collects the sun's rays, reorganizes them, and concentrates them on a precise point, so also the painter concentrates on a canvas the light which is dispersed throughout the sensible; he recuperates, confirms, and exalts the radiance of Being.

Since man lives in a Logos which is neither himself nor the in-itself world—nor, above all, an in-itself Principle—but rather the reversibility between the two which makes it be that the world is a world and man is man; and since the Logos which he expresses is precisely the fact that he is there and that the world is there, that they exist face to face, inseparable, complementary, and reversible, and that they see each other; then it can be understood that the idea of a progress which would culminate in the perfect possession of this Logos is an impossibility, is nonsense. The history of painting does not make its way towards a perfect painting; and, in this sense, because there is no hierarchy among the different modes and periods of painting, there is no progress in paintng: "The idea of a universal painting, of a totalization of painting, of a fully and definitively achieved painting is an idea bereft of sense." (PriP, 189; *OE,* 90) In painting it is always the same adventure which is relived, as "Indirect Language and the Voices of Silence" said, and painting never expresses anything other than the miracle of bodily existence—the miracle of visibility. Painting is not a succession of events in time but a series of advents—of Being. Painting does not copy anything whatsoever which exists before it; it expresses only visibility, that opening in Being; and an opening is nothing at all, merely the fact that something begins to appear. "Painting celebrates no other enigma but that of visibility" (PriP, 166; *OE,* 26), and the drawings at Lascaux do so as well as the pictures of Picasso. The idea of an "intellectual adequation" (PriP, 189; *OE,* 91) is what always confuses one's analysis, that is, the idea that somewhere an in itself exists to which one can attain and that because of this one can trace a progress, "draw up an objective balance sheet."[33] There is, however, no objective in itself, for the ultimate foundation, Being, is *nothing;* it is nothing but explosion, radiance, and opening, and thus, as Merleau-Ponty says, "never fully *is.*" (PriP, 190; *OE,* 92)

But even if there is no "in-itself progress" it still must not be said that everything is immobile, that the history of painting and of every creative endeavor goes nowhere, that it turns in circles and is vanity and failure, that we are condemned to remaining always entangled in our origins. For here the Origin, the ἀρχή, the dehiscence of Being, is not to be understood as an *event,* as a temporal *beginning,* as a mere starting point which exists only to be left behind; it is not something which occured *in illo tempore.* It is, rather—as the first Greek thinkers said and in so doing demonstrated just how much they had left mythical thought behind—the ground or always present principle of all events, their spontaneous and constant source; it is precisely the always renewed fact that *there is (il y a)* something. Since, therefore, the Origin is the world's own internal possibility, a world whose essence is to be in development, it is also a not yet realized τέλος; it is an origin which exists as having yet to exist; it gives to reflection its alpha and omega; it is itself the *teleology* of consciousness. It is a truly insurpassable fact when man sees the world and sees himself in it—for, as the actualization of a movement of transcendence, this is a fact which surpasses all others. A world wherein consciousness, even a single conscious being, exists transcends by this very fact and by an infinite distance a world which is plunged into the night of the unconscious; and thus this essential, qualitative difference is itself insurpassable. Consciousness or subjectivity, Merleau-Ponty would say with Husserl, is the miracle of miracles. The first attempt to express this miracle is insurpassable, for it too surpasses everything: "if we cannot establish a hierarchy of civilizations or speak of progress—neither in painting nor in anything else that matters—it is not because some fate holds us back; it is, rather, because the very first painting in some sense went to the farthest reach of the future." (PriP, 190; *OE,* 92) The original Opening is not a former moment in the life of the world which is now past; it is the continual advent of Being, of a Being which is pure radiance, transcendence, *there is.* Thus all efforts at expression are contemporaneous and live together in an infinite future; they all aim at an infinite Logos, for they all belong and attest to "one sole explosion of Being which is forever." (VI, 265; *VI,* 318) It is precisely this eternal explosion of Being which grounds for us the possibility of the idea or project of an "infinite Logos," which grounds rationality itself.


## Conclusion

BUT even if painting speaks to us of our insertion in the world, of the appearance of being for us, it still remains that it conveys to us only "mute meanings." (PriP, 169; *OE,* 35) The language of painting is a language which says without saying. If it is a "central operation contributing to the definition of our access to being," it is so because it teaches us a great many things when we reflect *on* it. In itself, it is much less definition than evocation; it constitutes an access to the universal, but a *conceptless* access. Painting reveals and expresses our relationship to the world, to the visible, that primordial and original relationship which occurs in vision; but at the same time that it reveals it it dissimulates it in another visible which is the picture. As a sign or symbol the picture hides as much as it reveals. The meaning it expresses is an ungraspable meaning which withdraws from us at the very moment we think we have grasped it in all its evidence. When we look at a picture we never receive more than fleeting illuminations. "Thus painting as a whole presents itself as an abortive effort to say something which remains always to be said." (S, 79; *S,* 99)

"Speech, on the contrary, tries to gain possession of itself." (S, 80; *S,* 100) Painting is a reflection on the world, transcendence; but language goes "much farther toward true creation" (S, 79; *S,* 99), for it seems to be able to reflect on itself, to be able to catch up and grasp its own meaning—it seems able not only to transcend lived experience but, even more, to *transcend itself.* "It is possible to speak about speech whereas it is impossible to paint about painting" (PhP, 190; *PP,* 222); for this reason the painter turns to language when he wants not only to live but to understand, to grasp the meaning of his acts (Klee's *Théorie de l'art moderne* is a good example of this). With language there thus appears a new idea of truth—truth as absolute gathering together, absolute recuperation: "Speech, not content to push beyond the past, claims to recapitulate, retrieve, and contain it in substance." (S, 80; *S,* 99) And at the limit "there is a critical, philosophic, universal use of language which claims to retrieve things as they are—whereas painting transforms them into painting—to re-trieve everything," including language itself. (S, 80; *S*, 100)

Language thus includes in its essence the ideal of a total mani-festation, of "thought without words" (PhP, 190; *PP*, 221)[34] whereas the idea of a painting without forms is an idea devoid of meaning. Unlike what happens in painting, in speech one has the feeling of "going beyond signs toward their meaning." (S, 81; *S*, 101) Signs here carve out for us an access to truth, "such a complete access that we seem to have no further need of them to refer to it." Between the "oneiric universe of carnal essences, of effective likenesses, of mute meanings" (PriP, 169; *OE*, 35) of painting and the spoken, professed, fully available universe of speech there would seem to be a radical difference.[35] "In short, language speaks, and the voices of painting are the voices of silence." (S, 81; *S*, 101)

It still remains to examine language's claim to the absolute. In order to understand the ideal of a thought without words which speech itself gives rise to in us, we must begin by putting language back among expressive phenomena in order to see *how it expresses.* We must take a closer look at the relation between meaning and expression, between the visibility of the sign and the invisibility of meaning. It may be that, like painting, language too expresses tacitly that, beneath what appears to be evident, transparent, *selbstverständlich* in language, there exists "an operant or speaking language whose words live a little-known life and unite and separate from one another as their lateral or indirect signification demands, even though these relations seem *evident* to us once the expression is accomplished." (S, 75; *S*, 94)

# L

*Chapter III*

> *Perhaps all men, as well as the man of letters,
> can only be present to the world and others
> through language; and perhaps in everyone
> language is the basic function which con-
> structs a life as it constructs a work and
> which transforms even the problems of our
> existence into life's motives.*
>
> TFL, 18; *RC*, 30

IN one sense, language is everything or it is nothing. So much so that
man himself is inconceivable without the communication with others
and the powers of speech that this communication presupposes. "We
are involved in the world and with others," Merleau-Ponty writes, "in
an inextricable tangle." (PhP, 454; *PP*, 518) Everything which we have
been able to realize which is most properly our own and of the greatest
worth we have done on the absolutely fundamental basis of our encounters with others. Man is indeed for man a mirror, and this reflection, this mutual back and forth takes place above all in speech. Man
tends towards communication as towards his own being; he is desire,
the desire of another human consciousness, as Hegel said. He is the existent which speaks; and thus, as other beings live in a natural world,
man is born and lives in a Logos, a cultural world. Language, Merleau-
Ponty emphasizes, is "our element as water is the element of fishes."
(S, 17; *S*, 25)

Thus the question as to what language is is an inescapable question for all reflection, for every philosophy which wants to grasp and understand our actual existence. The problem of language is an absolutely central one, for in it one comes across all the others: "more clearly than any other it takes the form of both a special problem and a problem which contains all the others, including the problem of philosophy." (S, 93; S, 116) Philosophy itself is perhaps nothing other than the attempt to turn language back on itself, the last effort of man to be as consciousness what he is as existence. The narrow gate leading to truth is the linguistic reflection of language. That Logos which is language is light for those who speak and listen, and this light, as St. John said, is the life of men. Everything that one says will thus remain superficial so long as one does not manage to understand how, by the grace of what power, in function of what gift, one says it. What is language?

## I.  The Phenomenology of Speech

### 1.  Speech

Even though there is convergence and confrontation between the linguistics of Ferdinand de Saussure and the phenomenology of Merleau-Ponty, and even though one comes across a great many references to Saussure in writings by the French philosopher, one would no doubt be pursuing the wrong path by wanting to see in the *Phenomenology of Perception* merely a revival of certain Saussurian themes. Let us therefore proceed directly to the view of speech that Merleau-Ponty proposes in his first great book.[1]

The argument in the *Phenomenology* is essentially summed up, as we saw in Chapter I, in the thesis that "the word has a meaning." With this watchword Merleau-Ponty launches his attack against the empiricist and intellectualist accounts of language, both of which try to discover *causes* susceptible of explaining the relation—a completely external one—between thought and speech. In language as in the perceived world, causal thought discerns only a *partes extra partes* whole: on the one side are words which are so many particular entities, and on the other is the meaning they express. But between these two elements there is no common measure, and whether it be thought of as the path traced in the nervous system which is associated with a certain movement of the articulatory organs or as something first held by a sovereign intelligence which freely chooses the sensory vehicles for projecting it outside into the intersubjective world, meaning remains external to the word. It is above all, however, the intellectualist explanation which is singled out in the *Phenomenology*. Against intellectualism and all objectivist thought, a *phenomenology* of language will adopt the opposing point of view of the *speaking subject:* "The phenomenologist tries to recover an awareness of what a speaking subject really is." (PriP, 80; *SHP*, 41) Now, for the speaking subject an objective history of language does not exist; he encounters his language only in that *act* which is *speech*.

The expressive operation by which a meaning emerges for the first time is what Merleau-Ponty calls "speaking speech" or "originating speech," or again "transcendental" or "authentic speech" (in opposition to "spoken speech" or "secondary speech" which is but the repetition of already expressed ideas). Before the act of expression, thought, as Saussure said, is but a "floating realm": "'Pure' thought is reducible to a certain emptiness in consciousness, to an instantaneous desire." (PhP, 183; *PP*, 213) Speaking speech is the bringing into being of this mute "desire"; it is the appropriation or accomplishment of thought for itself, and thus speaking speech and thinking thought are two terms designating a single phenomenon. I cannot say that I have found my thought so long as I have not found the formulas which make it concrete. Speech is not the "sign" of thought as smoke is of fire, but its very presence "in the phenomenal world, and, moreover, not its clothing but its token or its body." (PhP, 182; *PP*, 212) Speech is the bringing to light of thoughts themselves: "I say that I *know an idea* when there is set up in me a power of organizing around it words which make a coherent meaning."

Like the painter, therefore, he who speaks or writes brings into being first of all a certain *style*. And here it is a matter not of a mere analogy but of a true solidarity between these modes of expression. No one would think of saying that the meaning of a picture, its special impression, results from the mere addition of the colors which compose it, or that its meaning can exist independent of the picture. The picture is precisely a composition wherein a given color has meaning only in relation to the *whole* of the picture. Here the meaning of the work is not in each color taken separately but somewhere between them, in their mutual references to each other, in their "harmony." Language, too, is just as "structural" as painting or music. Here also we have to do with an initial clarity which dissolves as soon as we attempt to reduce it to its constitutive elements. In a direct line with what Saussure said, Merleau-Ponty writes, "the clearness of language stands out from an obscure background, and if we carry our research far enough we shall eventually find that language is equally uncommunicative of anything other than itself, that its meaning is inseparable from it." (PhP, 188; *PP*, 219)

This dialectic or mutual dependence between meaning and expression, thought and speech, is no doubt most apparent in poetry. A poem cannot be summed up; it does not exist apart from the play of words which constitute it, and, when one translates a poem into another language, one does not seek to reproduce its words or ideas but to recreate the same system of correspondences. The case is not otherwise with prose, even the most philosophical and, in appearance, most transparent prose. It is always the case in language that "meaning is not so much designated by it as it is implied by the word structure." (S, 83; *S*, 103) In its conformity to linguistic discoveries, Merleau-Ponty's thought differs radically on this point from Sartre's. For the latter, indeed, the function of prose is wholly other than that of poetry, which, he does admit, speaks tacitly like painting, expresses *itself* like music, and carries its meaning with it. While Sartre allows that poetic language has itself for its object and expresses itself, he holds that the language of prose is but "a certain kind of instrument,"[2] a kind of tool. The prose word is for Sartre a "sign," that is, something which does not have its own being and merely serves to represent an object which exists independent of it. The sign immediately transcends itself towards its meaning and is but a way of arriving at it. "Prose," Sartre writes, is utilitarian by nature." Ordinary (nonpoetic) language does no more than refer to a world of ideas which has its own reality and resides elsewhere.[3]

Criticizing this "Cartesian" conception of language, Merleau-Ponty remarks, "In this perspective, language belongs to the order of things and not the order of the subject....one ends us with a devalorization of language, one considers it only as the clothing of a consciousness, a facing on thought. Even for an author like Sartre, who however is not oblivious to the problem of other people, it is impossible that language should contribute something to thought: The word has no 'power'; it universalizes and summarizes what already exists. Here, thought owes nothing to the word." (CAL, 4; *BP*, 226) Indeed, for Merleau-Ponty there is only a difference of degree and not of nature between prose and poetry and, therefore, between language in general and painting and music.

Let us return to the comparison of language to painting. It may indeed be that in the last analysis language has a decisive privilege over painting, but, as Merleau-Ponty observes, if we wish to appreciate this difference for what is is, we must first begin by seeing how these two forms of expression resemble each another. Thus, like the meaning of a picture, the meaning of language "is inseparable from it." In order to understand this statement which, at first glance, might appear to be rather surprising, we must reinsert it into the linguistic perspective which justifies it. The expressive value of language, Merleau-Ponty says, recalling Saussure, does not result from the partial values of the words which make it up; on the contrary, words themselves have value only through the total system which is language itself. (S, 88; S, 110) A word has meaning only in opposition to all other words.[4] A given meaning is but a certain value having to do with its use; it does not exist in or alongside the word but *between* that word and all others.[5] Meaning comes down to the *divergence* (*écart*) between words. In a crucial passage Merleau-Ponty writes, "What we have learned from Saussure is that, taken singly, signs do not signify anything, and that each one of them does not so much express a meaning as mark a divergence of meaning between itself and other signs." (S, 39; S, 49)

If this is the way things stand and if language is quite literally a system, a structure wherein sound and sense, thought and speech, are two sides of a single phenomenon, and if the meaning of a word exists somewhere between this word and all others and is the divergence which sets them apart; then it becomes possible to understand the nature of the creative act, that for instance of the writer whose creative act calls forth a new meaning in the cultural world. There can be no question of his merely translating already worked-out thoughts into a given vocabulary. The voices of language are the voices of silence, and the writer does not work with thoughts existing in themselves but with words or, more exactly, with the "threads of silence" (S, 46; S, 58) with which speech is mixed together and which make of speech a signifying structure. The writer has to do only with "the visible and the invisible" (S, 76; S, 95) of an architectonics of signs. If he wishes to express a new meaning, he must erect a new construction of signs;

he must bend "the resources of constituted language to some fresh usage." (PhP, 389; *PP*, 445) If this expressive operation succeeds, the word arrangement will provide for his reader as well as for himself the meaning which they could possess in no other way. Animated by a meaning-intention, he will act in a way such that the "available meanings suddenly link up in accordance with an unknown law" (PhP, 183; *PP*, 213); he decentralizes, breaks up, and reorganizes (PhP, 194; *PP*, 226) the given system of correspondences in a language. The truth and meaning one searches for can be found only in and by words, by working with them, by linking them up together: "Like the weaver, the writer works on the wrong side of his material. He has to do only with language, and it is thus that he suddenly finds himself surrounded by meaning." (S, 45; S, 56)

The important thing to understand is that one can bring an idea into being only by reorganizing the relations between words themselves, since the meaning of language is nothing other than the silence which surrounds words, their other, "invisible" side. In the expressive operation it is a question of "shaking the linguistic or narrative apparatus in order to tear a new sound from it." (S, 46; S, 58) Like the painter, therefore, the writer brings about a "coherent deformation"; he decentralizes and rearranges words, makes them enter into a new style: "For that speechless want, the significative intention, it is a matter of realizing a certain arrangement of already signifying instruments or already speaking significations (morphological, syntactical, and lexical instruments, literary *genres*, types of narrative, modes of presenting events, etc.) which arouses in the hearer the presentiment of a new and different signification, and which inversely (in the speaker or the writer) manages to anchor this original signification in the already available ones." (S, 90; S, 113)[6]

For Merleau-Ponty the authentic expressive operation is violent, spontaneous, nonnecessitated—but it is always *motivated*. In expression thought does not precede speech; it results from it at that moment when language realizes what it *meant to say*—the *meaning-intention* which impels the writer to express himself. This means that, even though speech is not directed from the outside, it becomes *meaningful* because it is animated by an operative *intention*. When the writer breaks up and reorganizes the structure of language, he is guided by a certain "unknown law." This "unknown law" or "intention to signify," which precedes and serves to motivate speech, we would now like to attempt to clarify by raising the question, What is it which precedes speech?[7]

There is no "inner man," Merleau-Ponty said in responding to Husserl (PhP, XI; PP, V): "internal experience...is meaningless." (PhP, 276; PP, 319) And again, "Thought is no 'internal' thing, and does not exist independently of the world and of words." (PhP, 183; PP, 213) And finally, the inner life is an "illusion." In reading texts like these, however, we must always remember that the argument in the *Phenomenology* is always directed principally against the excesses of intellectualism.[8] Thus, if Merleau-Ponty insists that thought does not exist outside of speech, he does so not to simply deny its existence but in order to consider it anew, as Saussure would say. And indeed, he says of thought, "It does indeed move forward instantaneously and, as it were, in flashes, but we are then left to appropriate it for ourselves, and it is through expression that we make it our own." (PhP, 177; PP, 207)

We can thus see quite clearly that for Merleau-Ponty speech does not receive its meaning from nowhere; it is always motivated, and this motivation, this thought which precedes speech, is what could be called "momentary desire" (PhP, 183; PP, 213), a "new signifying intention," a "thought which is struggling to establish itself" (PhP, 389; PP, 446). This "yet unspoken meaning" (S, 88; S, 111) is not something we can make use of; it is but a "vague fever" (SNS, 19; SNS, 32), an initial orientation, a "certain void of consciousness" (PhP, 183; PP, 213)—a "determinate" void, however (S, 89; S, 112)—which "seeks to fill itself." The filling of this void, the coming-to-itself of thought, is the act of expression, speaking speech or authentic language.

We thus arrive at this definition which sums everything up: "Speech is, therefore, that paradoxical operation through which, by using words of a given sense, and already available meanings, we try to join up with an intention which necessarily outstrips, modifies, and itself, in the last analysis, determines the meanings of the words which translate it." (PhP, 389; PP, 445)

Still, it must be noted that in the *Phenomenology* Merleau-Ponty ends up by calling this "speaking silence," this meaning-intention, a "tacit *cogito*" and that he morevoer identifies this silent *Cogito* with being in the world itself, with our bodily existence. This is to say that he attempts to ground the signifying function of language in our *perceptual* contact with the world.

He writes, "Thus language presupposes nothing less than a consciousness of language, a silence of consciousness embracing the world of speech in which words first receive a form and meaning." And, "Behind the spoken *cogito*...there indeed lies a tacit *cogito,* an experience of myself by myself." (PhP, 403; *PP,* 462) But this "undeniable subjectivity" is not, he insists, a reflective *Cogito,* a transcendental Ego; it is nothing other than "existence itself," that is, the lived body's project of the world, *bodily* existence. This conclusion is understandable and points in the right direction if one's aim is to expose the insufficiencies and presuppositions of intellectualist analysis, which locates the condition of possibility of language and of truth in a transcendental Ego possessing itself beyond the world and bodily existence. But at the same time this conclusion appears highly insufficient in that it seems unable to account for what is unique about language in relation to the other functions of the lived body. It is hard to see in the conclusion a true foundation, a true *Urgrund.* It does not seem able to clarify the "meaning-intention" and the "teleology of consciousness" which Merleau-Ponty speaks of, or again "that Logos which gives us the task of bringing to speech a hitherto mute world." (PriP, 10; *Inédit,* 408)

It is indeed in the context of these remarks and, notably, of what we have just said about the meaning-*intention* that it would perhaps be best to discuss the thesis of the *Phenomenology* which postulates that language has its basis in "a *motor power* given to me along with the first experience I have of my body and its perceptual and practical fields." (PhP, 403; *PP,* 462; emphasis ours) It is in the light of what Merleau-Ponty says about the "thought which is struggling to establish itself" and about the "desire" which seeks to realize itself in speech that one can perhaps best appreciate both the meaning of his thesis as to the bodily and perceptual basis of language and also its radical insufficiency. For as a matter of fact it seems that this thesis raises more problems than it resolves. As Merleau-Ponty himself noted a few years later, the "archeological" investigations of the *Phenomenology* teach us a "bad ambiguity." (PriP, 11; *Inédit,* 409) Conceived of as perception or "motor power" the tacit *Cogito* is not sufficient to solve the problems of language and, notably, the "problem of the passage from the perceptual meaning to the language meaning, from behavior to thematization." (VI, 176; *VI*, 229) The perspective of the lived body alone can no more account for the miracle accomplished by language—the "excess of the signified over the signifying"—than it can justify us in speaking of a "task" which imposes itself on the painter.

Thus, even though Merleau-Ponty always insisted that the symbolic function can be understood only in the context of an archeological investigation, he does not, in the *Phenomenology,* seem to be certain as to what exactly is implied by this regressive analysis. Does such an analysis aim at identifying the symbolic expressivity of language with the natural expressivity of the lived body? It does not seem so, even so far as the *Phenomenology* is concerned; for what he insists on above all is that the speaking subject is *rooted* in the perceptual subject—which does not necessarily mean that the speaking subject does not have his own dimensionality, even if he does not exist independent of perceptual life. In the phenomenology, the author is above all preoccupied with refuting the illusion of a "transcendent thought" (PhP, 392; *PP,* 449) of which language would be but a feeble image. He thus does not deny that by means of language the subject *transcends himself* towards a meaning or truth which is not reducible to the perceived world; and, as a matter of fact, he seems to aim precisely at this notion, though he insists that the transcendence of speech, this teleology of consciousness, is realized only in the perceived world, that the natural expressivity of the lived body is the womb or the soil wherein this transcendence is engendered.[9] It would then be necessary to say that language does not coincide with existence and also that it is not something purely and simply transcendent, but that it is the very act of transcendence.

Thus thought does not direct speech from the outside; the latter is rather the act by which the "teleology of consciousness" discovers the symbols which incarnate it and, to a certain degree, make it transparent for itself: "language transcends itself in speech". (PhP, 392; *PP,* 449) The relation between language and perceptual life cannot be a one-way relation, and language cannot be simply derived from the motor power of the body but must also be the mark of the speaking subject's transcendence over the motor subject. This properly dialectical relation between speech and motricity would be "that two-way relationship that phenomenology has called *Fundierung:* the founding term...is primary in the sense that the founded presents itself as a determinate or explicit form of the founding, which prevents the latter from ever reabsorbing the former, and yet the founding is not primary in the empiricist sense and the founded is not simply derived, since it is through the founded that the founding is made manifest." (PhP, 394; *PP,* 451) We should say that the speaking subject is founded on the motor subject, but that the latter is not the cause of the former; by transcending the motor subject the speaking subject is precisely that which reveals its meaning. Language is not a matter of a pure *I know,* but neither is it—or so it would seem—identical with a mere *I can.* Or rather, the *I can* which the speaking subject is does not coincide with the *I can* which the motor subject is. The natural expressivity of the lived body would be a kind of "first language" (PriP, 7; *Inédit,* 406) and a kind of partial figure or announcement of language in the proper sense of the term, which, itself, would be the reappropriation or "sublimation" of the first order of expressivity, founded on it but also, to a certain degree, transcendent in regard to it.

The archeology of the *Phenomenology* would thereby be a way of arriving at a new kind of teleology, which, however, it does not explicitly take into consideration. In this work Merleau-Ponty writes, "Silent consciousness grasps itself only as a generalized 'I think' in face of a confused world 'to be thought'." (PhP, 404; *PP,* 463) But what makes it be that the perceived world is in the last analysis *to-be-thought*? How can bodily being in the world impose the task of "becoming conscious"? How can it contain the demand for a *teleology* of consciousness? "Any particular seizure, even the recovery of this generalized project [being in the world] by philosophy, demands that the subject bring into action powers which are a closed book to him and, in particular, that he should become a speaking subject." (PhP, 404; *PP,* 463) The phenomenological and perceived world calls for its own overcoming by the speaking subject, who thereby incarnates a movement of transcendence and "brings into action powers which are a closed book to him". Is Merleau-Ponty going in the direction of a phenomenology of mind in the Hegelian sense? The *Phenomenology* does not permit us to say so, for, as to the nature of these "powers" and this teleology, it remains, in the final analysis, silent.

In any event, the return to the lived body effected by the *Phenomenology* seems to express less an intention of reducing thought to speech and speech to perception than a desire to show how bodily existence contains in itself the seeds of an active transcendence which makes its first appearance in it, but which, afterwards, grows and transcends itself into other forms.

The bodily subject is thus not in the world like a thing but as the active transcendence of the world. Its appearance in the thickness of being introduces a "principle of indeterminacy" (PhP, 169; *PP,* 197) into the world; it is itself an "ever-recreated opening in the plenitude of being." (PhP, 197; *PP,* 229) In this way, therefore, the fact that man speaks and thereby has access to truth "is neither more nor less miraculous than the emergence of love from desire, or that of gesture from the unco-ordinated movements of infancy." (PhP, 194; *PP,* 226) Speech is "merely one particular case" of "this irrational power" (PhP, 189; *PP,* 221) that human existence has of introducing a world of meanings into the natural world. Thus Merleau-Ponty aims above all at showing how bodily existence is not mere biological existence, how it is "a power of natural expression" (PhP, 181; *PP,* 211), and how, in this way, there exists in man "a sort of *escaping* [*échappement*]" which can serve to define him. (*PP,* 221) And Merleau-Ponty sees a whole itinerary to "this act of transcendence": one encounters it first in the motor subject who can move about in the perceived world, then in the "silent communication of the gesture"; and then in language and the system of thoughts to which it affords access. In short, a kind of itinerary of spirit or mind...

If such is the argument of the *Phenomenology,* the speaking subject (and thus the thinking subject) is not reduced to the motor subject, for the lived body is not itself an explanatory factor; it merely incarnates the "mystery" or the "miracle" of an expressive power which is defined by its transcendence over natural being—which, therefore, has no definition. By fathoming language and unveiling its roots in the lived body one does not succeed in explaining it; one does not make it more clear than bodily existence, which itself, by its power of natural expression, only underlines all the more emphatically the "mystery of reason." (PhP, XXI; *PP,* XVI) The *Phenomenology* does no more than recognize "as an ultimate fact this open and indefinite power of giving significance...by which man transcends himself towards a new form of behavior, or towards other people, or towards his own thought, through his body and his speech." (PhP, 194; *PP,* 226) Speech thus shows itself as the "surplus of our existence over natural being" (PhP, 197; *PP,* 229), and it bears witness to a wave of transcendence which bodily existence but incarnates: "Such is the function which we intuit through language, which reiterates itself, which is its own foundation, or which, like a wave, gathers and poises itself to hurtle beyond its own limits." (PhP, 197; *PP*, 229–30) This mounting wave, this "drama" which transpires in the lived body and embodies itself in a series of forms and which remains as the great "unthought thought" of the *Phenomenology*—we will see in the rest of this study how Merleau-Ponty finally comes to give it the name "Being."

## 2.   Language

Rather than reduce the symbolic and expressive function of language to the motricity of the lived body, it would no doubt be more correct to uphold the originality of the "linguistic and cultural world" (PhP, 197; *PP*, 229) in relation to the perceived world; and Merleau-Ponty's work seems, in the final analysis, to have this intention.[10] If, however, Merleau-Ponty was not able to do this very well in the *Phenomenology*, it was perhaps because the dominant perspective of this work remained that of the *subject*—the subject of perception, of language (the speaking subject), etc. As we have already observed, Merleau-Ponty is above all interested in the side of the subject in the subject–world relation, and much less in the other side or in the relation as such. Thus, as concerns language, Merleau-Ponty concentrates primarily on speech, as the individual act of expression, rather than on language itself, as the signifying intersubjective system inside of which speech occurs. This is a very significant fact. For even if language (or *"la langue,"* in Saussure's terminology) is manifest only in the speech act (in the wide sense of this term) and is understandable only in relation to the speaking subject, it still has its own proper autonomy. I, as speaking subject, do not constitute language; on the contrary, I am a speaking subject only because I have been able to grasp its possibilities. Language's paradox is that it exists only through speaking subjects and yet, when one considers it at any given moment, is not something produced by them. What is the nature of this transcendence which is peculiar to language? It is of the same sort as that characteristic of history, which lives only by men but also transcends them all and is the milieu which forms them and in which they live. Man is not mere being in the world; unlike all other existents, he is separated from the perceived world by that other world which is culture, "that interworld which we call history, symbolism, truth-to-be-made." (AD, 100; *AD*, 269)

Indeed, the important thing is to take account of the far reaching changes that language produces in the perceived world. To be initiated into the symbolizing function by mastering language is not only to continue but to be capable of reorganizing perceptual experience at a higher level. As is shown by the case of Schneider, to which Merleau-Ponty alludes frequently in the *Phenomenology,* the act of speaking is, not the immediate presence of the subject to things, but a new way of making them present while keeping them at a distance. To give a name to something, a color for instance—something which Schneider was incapable of doing—is to draw that thing out from the mere here and now of immediate consciousness and make it participate in a life which is not only its own or that of the perceived world but that of a world more enduring and at the same time more difficult to grasp (since it is only by means of symbols that one has access to it), a life belonging to what could be called the cultural world or the universe of truth. Language is the transcendence of merely lived experience, for it is the way the subject mediates that experience. As Humboldt observed, language is "a veritable world that the mind is obliged to place between it and its objects."[11]

We must therefore recognize that there exists a *linguistic field* as there does a perceptual one, and that the former is in fact the truth of the latter (for the word is the truth of the thing). But we must not permit ourselves to take the path of criticism by subsuming the symbolic function of language under an operation of *Sinngebung* or meaning-giving on the part of a freely constituting consciousness. For, as we shall see, it so happens that in the end language is not something which is made by anyone, and this is precisely the problem it poses: language is the subject's transcending of the perceived world, but its mediating function was never instituted by the subject. Every subject is born into language and inherits its symbolic power without ever having constituted it. Language precedes all speaking subjects, and, since it is inseparable from acts of expression which have occurred in the past, it is a wholly historical phenomenon.

Language is thus not a natural but a cultural phenomenon—it is "transnatural." (CAL, 84; *BP*, 253) However, as a cultural phenomenon it is not the *product* of the speaking subject. First of all, viewed transversely, that is, synchronically, language appears as an *intersubjective* rather than a subjective phenomenon. The language one speaks is also that of all the other members of the linguistic community to which one belongs. This amounts to saying that it belongs to everyone and to *no one*. This characteristic of language is quite evident, yet it merits being considered more closely. For, if the language I speak is not primarily or essentially a "subjective" phenomenon, to the degree that I lead an intellectual life, which, as we have seen, depends upon the use of language, I live outside myself in a symbolic world which I have never constituted and in which I *participate* with others. In this sense, the speaking subject is for himself an "other." (S, 97; *S*, 121) Nothing is more intimate to me and more my own than language which is thoroughly intermixed with my personal life, and even with my dreams; and yet there is nothing which better reveals my dependence on other people and how my life is immersed in a universal life. To the degree therefore that my life appears to me to be absolutely individual, it is also absolutely universal.

If, therefore, we are obliged to admit that, taken at a given moment, a language is not something produced by speaking subjects, we must say that in some way it has its proper existence or being, that it is "in the air *between* the speaking subjects but never fully realized in any of them." (PriP, 81; *SHP*, 41) "Language must *surround* each speaking subject, like an instrument with its own inertia, its own demands, constraints, and internal logic." (SNS, 87; *SNS*, 153) This is the conclusion arrived at by modern linguistics. Language exists like a "collective spirit"; it has an incarnate logic. Indeed, language is a signifying system; and, since when considered transversely it appears as something "already there," something the members of a linguistic community have inherited and not constituted, it is impossible to reduce the inner logic of language to a constitutive operation on the part of these subjects. There can be no question, as there was for Husserl in his *Logical Investigations,* "of making us leap beyond language into a universe of thought in which it would be included as a particular sector." (PriP, 82; *SHP*, 42) On the contrary, to reflect on language is to rediscover "a reason already incorporated in these means of expression." (PriP, 82; *SHP*, 42) It is to recognize that there is a kind of "objective spirit" present in language. "It is the collective spirit living in language," von Wartburg writes, "which, every time a new human life is created, little by little transforms and shapes the

individual."[12] And Merleau-Ponty writes, summing up linguistic investigations which point in the same direction, "At the heart of every
language one should find laws of equilibrium, maybe even a theme,
a fundamental project, or, as G. Guillaume says, a 'sublinguistic
schema'". One must recognize the existence of a "general spirit
which we all constitute by living our life in common, that intention
already deposited in the given system of the language, preconscious
because the speaking subject espouses it before he becomes aware of
it and elevates it to the level of knowledge, and yet which only sub-
sists on the condition of being taken up or assumed by speaking subjects and lives on their desire for communication". (SNS, 88; *SNS*,
154)

Language is thus a cultural acquisition; and although it owes
its existence to speaking subjects alone, it precedes them all, such
that each and every subject becomes a speaking and thinking subject,
not by constituting language, but by taking it up. To speak is thus to
live in a reason or a logos which exists, not as a thing or an idea, but
as the permanent and sedimented trace of subjectivities. Thus in the
first instance language transcends me because it belongs to others
just as much—or just as little—as it belongs to me. But language's
transcendence is also vertical: it transcends the members of a linguistic
community taken all together; it is a phenomenon which has its own
history. Present-day French, which everyone is obliged to take up, is
to a large extent the outcome of what happened to it in the past.
Thus the signifying system of language is a *historical* system; and it
should be possible to overcome the dichotomy which Saussure saw
between synchronic linguistics and diachronic linguistics—between
the descriptive study of language conceived of as a Gestalt or structure
wherein the meaning of words results from the oppositions between
them and is a matter of use value, and the historical study of language
where one attempts to account for its present state by comparing it
to what it was in the past. This reconciliation of viewpoints cannot,
however, take place as long as one persists in thinking of language as
a nomenclature, that is, as a collection of word-things. Indeed, one
does not clarify the development of a language by linking up a present
word in French, for instance, with a Latin word which preceded it.
This is to do no more than point out a succession of facts without
understanding the dynamism of language, that which causes it always
to orient itself towards new forms which, for the speaking subjects,
will be more expressive.

The past as such cannot explain the present state of language, and it is above all here that Saussure was right. One must, on the contrary, start from the present and from the structural concept of language to understand diachrony, for, as Merleau-Ponty observes, the "past of language began by being present." (S, 86; *S,* 108) If, at any given moment, language is a system, it must have been such in its development too. Thus, in order to think the development of language, it is necessary to apply the notion of structure to history and conceive of the development of language as that of an equilibrium or a Gestalt in movement. In this way the history of language would not be a series of causes and effects but "the history of successive synchronies." (S, 87; *S,* 109)

Language would be a structure, a Logos or incarnate logic which moves always towards more expressivity or meaning. Indeed, in language conceived of as a diacritical structure, there are cracks, gaps, or weak zones which prevent it from being perfectly clear for the speaking subjects and which make for difficulties in communication. In order to fill these gaps in the means of expression language would reorganize itself, would seek a new equilibrium through the introduction of new expressions or the modification of the relations already existing between words.[13]

When we start from synchrony, we can succeed in conceiving diachrony anew; we can in fact succeed in reconciling or dialecticizing synchrony and diachrony, for now development shows itself part of the very being of language: "we must understand that since synchrony is only a cross-section of diachrony, the system realized in it never exists wholly in act but always involves latent or incubating changes." (S, 87; *S,* 109) In short, the phenomenology of language teaches us "a new conception of the being of language, which is now logic in contingency—an oriented system which nevertheless always elaborates random factors, taking what was fortuitous up again into a meaningful whole—incarnate logic." (S, 88; *S,* 110)

The phenomenology of language thus has an "ontological bearing." (S, 86; *S,* 108) It shows us that language belongs neither to a constituting consciousness nor to a natural world, nor even to a merely perceptual consciousness, but to a third kind of being, that of a generalized spirit, a cultural logos, or an incarnate logic. And it enables us to view the development of language as that of a "theme" or a "fundamental project"; a language always extends itself towards greater meaningfulness, up to the point sometimes of becoming another language, just as Latin became French in the case of certain subjects. In its development, language operates, as it were, a natural selection by assimilating certain chance events, by eliminating others, and in this development it is always animated and directed by a certain general spirit or a certain logos. "In language everything happens as though the mind's play were that of a constant reappropriating of chance events. What is in question is thus a kind of blind spirit." (CAL, 90; BP, 255) When an individual radically assumes his language, expresses himself creatively, and makes it say what it had never before said, he is always guided by the general spirit of his language, its incarnate logic, which permits and even solicits certain innovations and excludes others. The writer espouses and is guided by the "instructive spontaneity" of his language.

These remarks make even more pressing the question as to the mode of being of this Logos or this general spirit.[14] Shall we say that it is an in-itself Spirit which seeks to know itself, to become for itself what it is in itself, and which uses men to this end? This Hegelian notion does not suffice, or, rather, it is superfluous; for if language transcends men taken individually, it lives only in and by them. In the last analysis, it is only men who speak: "Everywhere there are meanings, dimensions, and forms in excess of what each 'consciousness' could have produced; and yet it is men who speak and think and see." (S, 20; S, 28) Language and, in general, the symbolic function were never invented by man, but we have no justification for saying that it is only a ruse of Reason with itself. Modern linguistics admits the existence of a collective spirit in language which orients its users, but it also recognizes that this reason invested in the linguistic system is, as Merleau-Ponty says, a blind spirit. The dynamic force in language— the factor which insures its existence and development—is not an in-itself Spirit or Reason but *men* and, more specifically, their *need* to express themselves and communicate. It is the use individuals make of language which makes it live, while at the same time the use changes the language little by little. Language is an inheritance which subjects are obliged to assume, a logic or a logos which imposes itself on them, but which lives only by them and is finally modified and transformed by them. Wartburg has summed up in an admirable way this relation between individual creativity and the general spirit in a passage which Merleau-Ponty must have read: "Individuals are the living but also changing carriers of the collective spirit; it is their creative action which moves it and advances it, even though the movement itself, as a uniform continuity, belongs only to the spirit and not to its carriers. And, inversely, the collective spirit is what supports spontaneity and the individual creative force."[15] A reflection on language reveals to us the existence of a *reason,* a *logos,* or a *light* transpiring in men and constituting a history, which in the end is the history of men and of their expressive efforts.

We thus arrive at the conception of a cycle or a circuit of reason. As an intersubjective milieu, the possession of everyone and no one, an incarnate logic, language in the first instance imposes itself on the individual and shapes him in its image.

But language is not only transmitted by means of speech from one generation to another, for, once assimilated, it is destined to undergo transformations in certain individuals. Impelled by what linguistics has called the expressive need or instinct, the individual puts forth creative powers, takes up his language, and makes it say what it had never said before. "Speech, as distinguished from language," Merleau-Ponty writes, "is that moment when the significative intention (still silent and wholly in act) proves itself capable of incorporating itself into my culture and that of others—of shaping me and others by transforming the meaning of cultural instruments." (S, 92; *S,* 115) If these transformations brought about by the individual find an echo in other speaking subjects and are taken up by them, they become in their turn cultural acquisitions, available meanings, and language is enriched. The contribution of the individual then gets *sedimented* in language and becomes a new starting point for other expressive acts. It can thus be said that *"languages* or constituted systems of vocabulary and syntax, empirically existing 'means of expression', are both the repository and sedimentation of acts of *speech,* in which unformulated meaning not only finds the means of being conveyed outwardly, but moreover acquires existence for itself, and is genuinely created as meaning." (PhP, 196; *PP,* 229)

This dialectic of speech and language, individuality and universality, existence and truth, man and Logos, is what could be called *history.*[16] Since the Logos of the cultural world is another name for sedimentation, it must be recognized that this is a Logos which is always undergoing transformation, becoming enriched, and, as it passes from one attempt at expression to another, developing. Basing itself on a world of meanings in order to extend it even further, the symbolic function insures the development of this world; and, since what has been creatively expressed gets sedimented in the cultural world and is preserved there as an acquisition, the Logos of the cultural world is the recuperation (gathering together = logos) of all the acts of expression—this Logos is their history, their Memory. Thus, to reflect on culture, on that inter-world which occurs by means of symbols (and of which language is only one particular, even if privileged, instance) is to reflect on history, on a Logos which develops and makes its advent in the simultaneous and successive community of subjectivities.

We thus find ourselves in possession of the elements of an *ontology of expression* which is beginning to make its appearance. There is, on the one hand, language or a Logos of the cultural world which is neither a natural process nor an idea, but a symbolic milieu among men, the locus of truth, and, in a word, history. This Logos transcends men, but it is not for all that something transcendent, for it is by men that it is brought into being and carried along.

There is, on the other hand, speech or, more generally, the act of expression itself. This is the motive force of history and insures the development of culture. In this sense, the act of expression is the ground of the Logos, for it is in it that there springs up the creative force, the expressive instinct, which realizes or crystallizes itself in language. As far as "this productivity which is man's deepest essence" (PhP, 196; PP, 229) is concerned, we have seen how Merleau-Ponty refuses to "explain" it by subsuming it under some prior principle, such as Nature or Reason. Man's expressivity is a "miracle" precisely because it does not merely reflect already existing meanings, but is the place where that which did not have a meaning until then receives one. The "miracle of expression" can be reduced neither to the objective world nor to the personal subject; the subject unfolds powers which are a closed book to him. Existence is transcendence, the advent or institution of a Logos; and thus, as elements of an ontology, we have, besides the Logos, man's active transcendence which is transformed into a cultural acquisition, into Logos. We shall thus have to elucidate better this second element, this transcendence which is not created by man but rather sublimated by him. "The problem is to grasp *what,* across the successive and simultaneous community of speaking subjects, *wishes, speaks,* and finally *thinks.*" (VI, 176; *VI,* 230) This "what" which the *Phenomenology* refers to as a "movement of transcendence" is what *The Visible and Invisible* will take to be Being itself.

We are thus, as of now, in possession of the elements of Merleau-Ponty's ontology. But just exactly *how many* do we have? There is the instituted Logos and there is man's active transcendence. What, however, is the relation between the individual and "his" creativity, that wave of transcendence which rises in him and which he does not himself create but assumes or incarnates? Should we take man to be a mere modality of Being in itself which seeks to gain possession of itself as a for itself, as Logos or Truth? Or should we, on the contrary, take subjectivity to be an absolutely central, irreducible, and unsurpassable fact, characterize Merleau-Ponty's ontology as an integral and resolute humanism, and thereby assert the existence of an unbridgeable gap between his ontology and, for instance, Heidegger's, which, in seeking to overcome all humanism, could alone be a truly fundamental ontology?

## II.    The Phenomenon of Expression

SINCE man, or to be more exact, the act of authentic expression shows itself to be a central phenomenon, as the place where Being (which for the time being we can take to be the force or creative transcendence in man) becomes Logos, the place where a spontaneous desire, a "teleology" of consciousness, is transformed into symbols and truth, it is incumbent upon us to examine more closely this moment "without equal" when man begins to speak and to deliver up what in him wanted to express itself, to "endow with a name what has never been named." (S, 233; *S,* 296) The phenomenon of expression is the joint or *articulus* between existence and truth, Being and Logos. In this section we will attempt to describe this active relation between the silent intention in man and its transformation into professed symbols and available truth. We shall then in the third section of this chapter inquire into the "philosophical foundations" (PriP, 7; *Inédit,* 405) of the creative act of expression and into the dual movement—archeology-teleology—it requires of philosophical reflection.

If, like Merleau-Ponty, one is interested in the question of the "origin of truth," the example of literary language would seem to be particularly suitable for revealing "above the perceived world, the field of knowledge properly so called—i.e., the field in which the mind seeks to possess the truth". (PriP, 6; *Inédit*, 405) Like painting, literature is the revelation of a transcendental field of experience; it does not *coincide* with lived existence, but is rather a *reflection* on our usual commerce with the world and with others, a revealing of a logos of the sensible world. To speak as the writer speaks is not only to continue the miracle of expression which is already manifest in bodily existence—in perception as in sexuality—not only to inherit and to blindly use the expressive power of language; on the contrary, the writer is he who, in the context of the creativity which is sedimented and incarnated in already existing language, personally assumes this language and takes it up for himself. "To become a writer is to learn a personal language; it is to create one's own language and public; it is thus to rebegin at a higher lever the creation of language." (CAL, 10; *BP*, 228) As the painter is he who not only sees but who transforms his vision into something visible and thereby brings about a transmutation of visibility, so the writer is he who not only lives as other men do but who again thematizes this life in order to *express* it, to reflect it in a work and thereby transform it into its truth. And just as Merleau-Ponty saw in Cézanne a striking example of the painter's activity, so also the work of Proust seems to us to constitute a privileged example of literary expression considered as a manifestation of reflective and transcendental experience. Thus by referring to the work of Proust we shall now attempt to bring out what for Merleau-Ponty is the essence of the expressive act, the significance of this higher and transcendental layer of human existence.[17]

## 1.   The Expressibility of Life

The feeling which dominates Proust's work is the feeling for the expressibility (*dicibilité*) of life. In his infancy Proust often had the impression that things held in themselves an insurpassable wealth, an inexhaustible beauty, and that they called out to him to enter into them and to deliver up the secrets they contained. In *A la recherche du temps perdu* he describes many experiences of this sort, such as the one occasioned by the church towers of Martinville which he glimpsed in the course of an automobile ride: "At a turning in the road I suddenly experienced a special pleasure resembling no other in noticing the two steeples of Martinville, illuminated by the setting sun, and which the movement of our car and the twists in the road seemed to make change place.... In witnessing, in noticing the form of their spires, the movement of their lines, the illumination of their surface, I felt that I was not getting to the bottom of my impression, that there was something behind this clarity, something that they seemed to contain and to conceal at the same time." (I, 180)[18] Three trees near Balbec inspired a similar experience: "I looked at the three trees, I saw them clearly, yet my mind felt that they were covering something which it could not get hold of.... Again I felt that there was behind them the same known but vague object, which I could not draw forth.... In their naive and passionate gesticulation, I recognized the impotent regret of a being which has lost the use of speech, feels that it is not able to say what it wants, and which we are not able to guess at. Shortly, at a crossing in the road, the car left them behind. It drew me far from what alone I believed to be true, from what would have made me truly happy; it resembled my life." (I, 717-9)

It was from moments such as these that Proust received, as he says, his vocation to be a writer by feeling himself called upon to re-discover in himself the secret which things seemed to be suggesting to him. What destines a man to be a writer, Merleau-Ponty would say, is the conviction that "the sensible is, like life, a treasury ever full of things to say" (VI, 252; *VI*, 305); it is the feeling that the world and experience contain in themselves a "scattered," "buried" (S, 55; *S*, 68), "captive," or "hidden" (VI, 36; *VI*, 58) meaning, a meaning which is *to-be-said*. The writer is precisely he who attempts to bring to light "those notions 'without equivalent,' as Proust calls them, that lead their shadowy life in the night of the mind only because they have been divined at the junctures of the visible world." (VI, 152; *VI*, 200) The work of Proust thus appears as an archetype of literary experience; for, more clearly than in the case of many other writers, the work presents itself here as the realization of the conviction that lived ex-perience is eminently expressible, that life is full of things to be said, and that the task of the writer is to exploit this bed of lived and al-most forgotten experiences by extracting from it what wanted to be said and by transforming it into an enduring work, into its truth.

The crucial moment in Proust's life, as he himself relates it in *Le Temps retrouvé*, was the instant when it dawned on him that, in order to realize the work which ever since his youth he felt himself called to write, he had only to turn back on his own past life, that his life was carrying within itself a work which had only to be released: "And I understood that all the materials for a literary work were in my past life." Indeed, the entire structure of what was to be *A la recherche du temps perdu* revealed itself to Proust in 1909 when his mind was triggered by the discovery of the involuntary memory, when he realized that the subject of his work could be nothing other than Time. Past times, lived experiences, are never, for him who still lives, totally past; everything one believes to be past is but a forgotten part of one-self, for time *is* the self: "I experienced a feeling of fatigue and dismay in realizing that all this time which had been so long had not only, without an interruption, been lived, thought, secreted by me, that it was me, but again that I had at every moment to keep it attached to me, that it supported me, me, perched at its dizzying peak, that I could not move without moving it." (III, 1047)[19] To write the *Recherche,* to recount his past life, would be thereby to seize hold again of "all this unfolded past which I did not know that I carried"; it would be to recuperate oneself in a work which makes present everything which has been and which saves from non-being everything which is no longer. Proust's case perfectly illustrates what Merleau-Ponty takes to be the "human moment *par excellence*"—the moment "in which a life woven out of chance events turns back upon, regrasps, and expresses itself." (S, 240; *S,* 305)

What is above all remarkable in the case of Proust is the intensity of the need he felt to write his work once he had understood its theme. "Instead of working," he said, "I had lived in laziness, in the dissipation of pleasures, in sickness, treatments, follies, and I under-took my work on the eve of dying, knowing nothing of my craft." (III, 1041) However, with the realization that with the passage of time the self disappears little by little and tends toward non-being, Proust could no longer put off the elaboration of his work. He now felt him-self to be relentlessly pursued and menaced by this flight of time which, perhaps, was going to conquer him before he could triumph over it by tearing from it its meaning and by placing it "in greater security in a book." (III, 1037) "Yes, in regard to this work, this idea of Time that I had just formed said that it was time to set myself to it. It was indeed time; but, and this justified the anxiety which had grabbed hold of me..., was there still time and was I even still in form?... I had lived like a painter ascending a path overlooking a lake which a wall of rocks and trees hides from his view. Through an opening he glimpses it, he has it wholly before him, he takes up his brushes. But already the night arrives in which one can no longer paint, and on which the sun does not rise." (III, 1035)

As Sartre says in regard to Merleau-Ponty, Proust too had "a painful and full feeling for fleeting time." The work he projected was immense, and he was not sure that he had either the force or the time to realize it. Whence a terrible anxiety. He compared himself to Scheherazade in *The Thousand and One Nights* over whom was suspended the imminence of death: "I lived in anxiety at not knowing if the Master of my destiny, less indulgent than the sultan Sheriar, would be willing, when morning interrupted my tale, to postpone my death sentence and allow me to continue on the following evening." (III, 1043)

As a matter of fact, this anxiety in the face of time manifests a dual consciousness. In the first instance it presupposes the conviction that life is full of things to say, that it is, as Proust says, "worthy of being lived," above all "now that it seemed to me capable of being illuminated—that life which one lives in darkness—brought back to the truth of what it was—that life which one is constantly falsifying— finally realized in a book." (III, 1032) The demand that one feels to sum up the past in a work is in fact, Merleau-Ponty would say, an "invocation of truth"; it stems from "that desire for a total manifestation... which makes man sometimes become a writer, and which in any case makes man speak and everyone want to account for himself in the eyes of X". Except in some rare cases, he insists, "all action and all love are haunted by the expectation of an account which will transform them into their truth; in short they are haunted by the expectation of the moment at which it will finally be known just what it was all about." (S, 74; S, 93) The project of his great work seemed to Proust to be the only means of "attaining what I had at times felt in the course of my life, in brief intimations when I was in the vicinity of the Guermantes, in my automobile excursions with Mme. de Villeparisis, and which had made me feel that life was worth living." (III, 1032)

But if this anxiety in the face of time presupposes and immediately stems from the "desire for a total manifestation," it is crystallized and a man actually becomes a writer only when, instead of merely living in time, only feeling that life is worth the trouble of being lived, he turns back and reflects on time and on life in order to seize hold of them and express them. Even if the greater part of mankind experiences the premonition that life is, as Proust says, "the bearer of a work"—contains in itself a surplus of meaning—they do not, however, become writers or artists except by crossing the threshold of transcendental experience, by passing from lived experience to reflected experience. Indeed, even if life hides a truth within itself, it is not and does not become true, in the proper sense of the term, unless man knows how to extract this truth, save it from its dissimulation in daily experience, and make it exist in an explicit manner. Life's truth is thus already there, but as that which is not yet there; it is there precisely as a truth to be made: "Search? not only: create. [The mind] has in front of it something which is not yet and which only it can bring into being, and then give to it its light." (I, 45) It is necessary not only to live but to pass from life to a reflection on life. Now, to take life as a theme is, for the writer, to gather it together and transform it into a work. The passage from the man to the writer, from natural experience to transcendental experience, is effected by the *work of reflection.* "At this moment," Merleau-Ponty writes, "something has been founded in signification; an experience has been transformed into its meaning, has become truth." (S, 96; *S,* 120) The phenomenon of expression is a key phenomenon, for it affords access to a Logos which is the recapitulation and transmutation of life and phenomenal being.

Proust experienced with a growing intensity this necessity of transforming life into a work in order to save it. He was constantly afraid that an accident would happen which would put an end to his life before he was able to finish his work: "I felt myself augmented with this work that I bore within me (like some precious and fragile thing which had been entrusted to me and which I desired to render intact into the hands for which it was destined and which were not mine). Now, to feel myself the bearer of a work, made an accident wherein I would have died more fearful for me, even (to the degree that this work seemed to me necessary and enduring) absurd, in contradiction with my desire, with the drive of my thought". (III, 1036)

## 2.  Time Reflected, Recaptured

The meaning of a life is indeed something fragile, as Proust observes, and is without guarantee, is in fact transitory and destined to dissipate like so much smoke, so long as it is not placed "in greater security in a book." Whence the curious paradox of Proust who, though animated by a desire for life, withdraws from daily life and, totally devoting himself to his work to the great detriment of his physical well-being, leads the life of a recluse until death comes to find him. Here transcendental experience appears as the negation of life as lived experience; but this negation of life is in fact its realization, its metamorphosis into a work and into truth. Giving himself over to death, Proust overcomes his fate—Time—transforms it into a reason for living and thereby attests to the fact that man, according to Hyppolite's commentary on Hegel, is "essentially that being who can transgress the limit by appropriating it to himself and confer throughout all his history a spiritual significance on death, convert the negative into being."[20] A life makes a theme of itself and transforms itself into a work; and this work, surviving the empirical life of the man, continues to exist as the guarantee of the truth of his life or, as Proust said in regard to the works of Bergotte, as the "symbol of his resurrection."

This difference between life and reflection on life or between the empirical and the transcendental that we see in an operative, phenomenal state in Proust reminds us of the distinction Merleau-Ponty drew, in regard to painting, between two kinds of historicities—between empirical historicity and true historicity, that of events and that of culture. The example of Proust or any creative man indeed reveals to us the existence of *two kinds of temporality.* In "this world where everything gets used up, where everything perishes" (III, 695), creative expression succeeds in opening up a new dimension; it introduces us into "a more occult time than natural time." (PhP, 390; *PP,* 447) Instead of simply carrying on with the past, he who expresses himself creatively draws together his past, reshapes it, generalizes it, and draws from it universal meanings which have the power of being indefinitely of value. And he thereby contributes to the institution of a Culture or a History of meaning which transpires otherwise than phenomenal time, the time of empirical events, of merely lived existence.[21] "The novelty of the arts of expression is that they make tacit culture come out of its mortal circle." (S, 79; *S,* 99) In empirical historicity, there is, Merleau-Ponty said, but succession and replacement; one event merely succeeds another by pushing it back into the obscurity of the past. This is the "historicity of death." (S, 63; *S,* 79) Here there is no truth, for what is or could become true in a life is forgotten and disappears. Here there are but experiences external to one another; there is but dispersion and dissimulation. Now, it is essential for truth to be, to gather itself together and grasp itself as true. "Cultural" history is, consequently and by definition, the recuperation of men's expressive acts; it is the gathering together and conservation—the Logos—of what was most worthwhile in what they saw and did; it is the domain *par excellence* of Being. "Cumulative" history, Merleau-Ponty says, is the "history of life". And, at the limit, this Life or this Logos engendered by expressive efforts is the life or the meaning of no one in particular but, in a way, of everyone. There is, Merleau-Ponty says, but a single culture which from work to work always sets off again and which advances like the waves of a mounting tide. This continuous and cumulative advent is that of an infinite Logos—of Being.

Thus the example of Proust enables us to grasp concretely the *two dimensions* which Merleau-Ponty pointed to in his reflections on painting—those of the empirical and the transcendental. The example of Proust illustrates in a perfectly exemplary way the passage from the ontical to the ontological; but, as a matter of fact, the situation is no different when a man, without much literary pretension, merely sums up his life in a book, when he relates the story of his travels, his impressions, his loves, his hopes, and his deceptions, when he attempts to extract the essence of his life. At these times something has always taken place; a life has been transformed into its truth. Just as the studio of Elstir, the painter, seemed to Proust to be "the laboratory for a kind of new creation of the world" (I, 834), so also the operation of reflective or creative expression realizes a new field of existence; it throws our phenomenal and passing life over onto the side of an infinite Logos. As Hyppolite says, "The self-consciousness of life becomes other than life by manifesting its truth, by making itself capable of being its truth."[22] The work of reflection thus reveals a new dimension of existence which we could call transcendental or ontological. In a crucial passage Merleau-Ponty writes, "The operation of expression, when it is successful, does not merely leave for the reader and the writer himself a kind of reminder, it brings the meaning into existence as a thing at the very heart of the text, it brings it to life in an organism of words, establishing it in the writer or the reader as a new sense organ, opening a new field or a new dimension to our experience." (PhP, 182; *PP*, 212) The point of transition between the phenomenal and the transcendental is always and solely that "fundamentally obscure operation which has enabled us to eternalize within ourselves a moment of fleeting life." (PhP, 389; *PP,* 446)

It must however be added that the ontological is not something other than the phenomenal; it is not a supra-sensible world; it is only the truth and the gathering together—the Logos—of the phenomenal world and life, its other, "invisible," side. *A la recherche du temps perdu* does not afford access to Eternity; it is not time overcome but time *recaptured (retrouvé).* One ends up by saying what is and what has been, and it is that which counts, which saves, which makes all the difference.

The purpose of this eidetic consideration of Proust's work was to obliquely suggest some of the guiding themes of Merleau-Ponty's thought. What stands out the most are the dialectical relation between life and the reflective consciousness of life, or between the phenomenal and the transcendental, and the privileged place occupied by reflection as the mediation between the two dimensions, as the institution of the second. But Proust's work illustrates not only the content of Merleau-Ponty's philosophy, its themes, but also its own form or "methodology." Just as Merleau-Ponty saw in Cézanne's attempt to escape from the naturalism-impressionism dilemma a kind of prefiguration of his own attempt to overcome the antinomies of empirical and intellectualist thought, so also it is clear that the structure of the *Recherche* very much resembles Merleau-Ponty's "radical reflection." The result is that one could say that Proust accomplishes in the realm of literature what Merleau-Ponty attempts to do in philosophy.

Proust's work is unique because it is not only the account of a life but, again, the *account of this account.* Indeed, in addition to being the search for a covered over, hidden logos, Proust's work is itself the *reflective consciousness* of this search. Its theme is not only life but its author's reflection on life. The *Recherche* relates its *own* genesis in the author's mind, its slow preparation, and ends at the very moment when the narrator sets about writing. The book is thus the book of a book; it does nothing other than relate itself; it turns back on itself and takes itself for an object. Proust's work is in this way a work not only of reflection but of transcendental reflection, for its theme is precisely the author's reflection on his life, a reflection which is the work itself.

Thus it resembles Merleau-Ponty's thought, which seeks to be not only a reflective thought but, as he says in *The Visible and the Invisible,* "a sort of *hyper-reflection* [*sur-réflexion*] that would also

take itself and the changes it introduces into the spectacle into account."
(VI, 38; *VI, 61*) We will have the occasion in the following chapter to
examine Merleau-Ponty's philosophy as a philosophy and to see how,
from its very beginnings, it aimed at being a "truly transcendental"
philosophy, a "reflection on reflection," or a "radical reflection."
Throughout his philosophical career Merleau-Ponty never ceased to
question himself as to the meaning of his philosophical effort, and, in
a working note of February 1959 where he seeks to define his philosophy, he writes, explicitly invoking the example of Proust, "The end
of a philosophy is the account of its beginning." (VI, 177; *VI, 231*)

In the preface to the *Recherche* which he composed for the
Pléiade edition of the work, André Maurois says that throughout his
life Proust was pursuing an *absolute* and that he finally discovered it
in his work, "in art, such that the novel merges with the life of the
novelist and the book ends at the moment when the narrator, having
recaptured [*retrouvé*] time, can begin *his* book, the long serpent
thus turning back on itself and looping itself in a giant loop." (I, XV)
A life applies itself to itself and seizes hold of itself through the mediation of a work which, issuing from a life and turning back on it, takes
it up and transmutes it into a kind of absolute. We find once again
here, in literature, the same phenomenon already encountered in the
context of painting, where painting seems to realize a kind of absolute
when painters paint themselves in the act of painting, "adding,"
Merleau-Ponty said, "to what *they* saw then, what *things* saw of
them, as if they were claiming that there is a total or absolute vision,
outside of which there is nothing and which closes itself over them."
(PriP, 169; *OE, 34*)

Absolute truth would be the total grasp of the self by the self, the
perfect recuperation of life by reflection. Can, however, reflection ever
realize this complete doubling-back? "Reflection cannot be thoroughgoing, or bring a complete elucidation of its object, if it does not arrive at awareness of itself as well as of its results," Merleau-Ponty
writes in the *Phenomenology*, adding however that, if this condition
is actually realized, "philosophical knowledge can become absolute
knowledge, and cease to be a speciality or a technique." (PhP, 62;
*PP, 75*) It remains for us to see if this condition can be and ever was
realized by Merleau-Ponty. *It remains for us to see what actually is
the fate of this "desire for a total manifestition" or this teleology of*
consciousness which Merleau-Ponty sees at work in all expressive

forms and existing in an explicit and manifest state in philosophy. However the matter might stand—and we shall return to it in the following chapter—it is clear that the "fundamental philosophical problem" in Merleau-Ponty is, as he himself observed in the *Phenomenology*, "this *presumption* on reason's part." (PhP, 63; *PP,* 76)

## III.   The Ontological Foundations of Expression

THE main object of phenomenology as a reflective philosophy is rationality itself. Finding himself confronted with a world which includes autochthonous meanings, the phenomenologist attempts to describe them, to draw up an "inventory" of them; but in doing so he realizes that the meaning of the world is not a meaning existing *in* the world but that of a world which *appears to*— This calls for a philosophy which, as *The Structure of Behavior* expressed it, will be not only a description but a reflection on this description. How does it come about that the world is meaningful? What is basically in question is thus the meaning of meaning. If the world's truth is not a "natural property" of an in-itself world but what a *consciousness* discovers in contact with it, it is because truth is not itself an in itself which can be unveiled but somehow the result of an operation on the part of consciousness. Truth is inseparable from the expressive operation which says it.

Truth thus has a bipolar nature: it is at one and the same time the truth of what is revealed and something which is realized by saying itself. Truth thus does not precede reflection; it is a result of it. But, *once it has appeared,* it presents itself as that which preceded and motivated reflection. The problem thus lies entirely in the "retrospective reality" (VI, 252; *VI,* 306), this "retrograde movement" of the truth. "What we call expression is only another formula for the phenomenon...of the retroactive effect of the true. The experience of the true cannot keep from projecting itself back into the time which preceded it. ...To think, or, in other words, to think an idea as true, implies that we arrogate to ourselves the right of recovering the past, either to treat it as an anticipation of the present, or at least to place the past and the present in the same world. What I say of the sensible world is not in the sensible world, and yet it has no other meaning than to say what the sensible world means. The expression antedates itself and postulates that being comes towards it." (IPP, 29; *EP,* 49) Truth is a *creation* but a creation which presents itself as an *adequation.* How can this apparent antinomy be resolved?

Merleau-Ponty's *ontology,* his philosophy of Being, takes shape in the effort he makes to clarify this problematic of expression and truth.

## 1.  Archeology

If what I say has a meaning, it is because it finds a confirmation in the unspoken experience which I am attempting to formulate. Truth is not a free invention but the deliverance of what "wanted to be said." Truth is thus always motivated and solicited and speech *(le dire)* is a success or a failure depending on whether or not it is faithful to prelinguistic experience. In this sense, truth as the work of expression has an "archeological" nature;[23] it is the manifest existence of a meaning which is already at work in the perceived world or in lived existence before all expression: "to understand is to translate into available significations a meaning first held captive in the thing and in the world itself." (VI, 36; *VI,* 58) In order to know what the truth is, we thus have to return to the *archē* on which it rests and to which it refers.

In lived and not yet expressed experience there is thus a raw *(brut)* meaning, a *wild logos,* which, so to speak, *calls out* to thematic expression and serves as a motive for reflection. There is, Merleau-Ponty writes, "that which...summons all things from the depths of language beforehand as nameable. There is that which is to be said, and which is as yet no more than a precise uneasiness in the world of things-said." (S, 19; *S,* 27) Expression must be viewed as a *response* to a solicitation coming to it from below. The world contains in itself a surplus of meaning; it demands that we speak and deliver up this meaning which is "operant and latent" (S, 53; *S.* 66) in it. It can thus be said that "True speech...speech which signifies...frees the meaning captive in the thing." (S, 44; *S,* 56)

If, however, to speak is not to speak in a void, if true speech is motivated by prior experience and is not a work of pure fantasy, we must, nonetheless, recognize what is *ruled out* by this notion of the expressibility of the lived world. There can indeed be no question of a truth which would already exist ready-made and to which reflection would have only to conform itself. Whether that truth would belong to an intelligible heaven, a world of ideas, or whether it would be that of a world perfectly intelligible in itself (like the world of scientism which is supposed to contain in itself "laws" which the physicist merely "discovers"), it is always the kind of truth posited by objectivistic thought. Now, Merleau-Ponty never ceases to call this form of thought into question under its dual, empiricist-intellectualist aspect. Thus if Merleau-Ponty recognizes the existence of an inspiration prior to expression, he nevertheless does not allow that it can direct expression from outside or from above. "We would be wrong," he says in speaking of Bergson's notion of inspiration, "in believing, though Bergson said so, that the philosopher speaks all his life *for want of* being able to say this 'infinitely simple thing' forever concentrated 'in a single point' of himself. He also speaks *to say it,* because it demands to be said, because it does not fully exist before it has been said." (IPP, 18; *EP,* 32) We must resolutely reject all *causal* notions and, as a consequence, the notion of objective truth.

The problem, therefore, is that of working out a philosophy of expression and of truth (of rationality) which can account for the at once recuperative (archeological) and creative (teleological) nature of expression. To express the matter another way, the difficulty is that of resolving the "enigma of a becoming-conscious which is an authentic creation," as Hyppolite says.[24] We would not look for anything at all if in some way we did not know what we were looking for, but we would also not look for anything if we had already found what we were looking for. The situation is thus as follows (according, again, to the formulation Hyppolite gives to Hegel's problematic): "Everything happens as if there existed an immediate lived experience which it is a question of expressing, this expression being at once a discovery, in the etymological sense of the term, and an invention, since its expression has not yet been formulated."[25] This is an excellent way of formulating Merleau-Ponty's own problem.

## 2. Teleology

In a working note of June 1959 where he invokes the name of Proust, Merleau-Ponty says that what is needed is a theory of the lived world, of the *Lebenswelt,* as that which in one sense contains in advance everything that we will say about it and which yet leaves us free to create it. The problem is that it is only by means of philosophy, a cultural *construction*, that we rediscover and become conscious of the lived world, the world of silence. Thus, in what sense do we *rediscover* this antepredicative, prelinguistic world? Certainly not in the sense that what philosophy *says* existed before it and as such in the lived world. As a matter of fact, Merleau-Ponty concludes that there is no dilemma here between expression and silence and that the expressibility of the phenomenal world does not prevent philosophy "from having value, from being something else than and more than the simple partial product of the *Lebenswelt*," because, as he says, "it is philosophy that discloses it." (VI, 170; *VI*, 224) The "archeological" investigations of reflection—the rediscovery of lived existence and of its expressibility—is thus in reality a promotion of existence to its meaning; and, far from pointing to a subordination of reflection to the unreflected, as if the former were but a feeble image of the latter, it bears witness to the privileged and transcendent state of reflection. The "world of silence, the perceived world," includes "nonlanguage significations, but they are not for all that *positive.*" (VI, 171; *VI*, 225) Truth appears as truth only by means of the mediation of reflective expession which, in transcending, in doubling back on existence, renders itself capable of being its truth. Existence is not true in itself, for its truth is precisely reflection.

Thus, to discover the foundation of language, the "ground" of truth, in bodily existence and in its expressibility—as Merleau-Ponty did in the *Phenomenology*— does not in any way resolve the problem. This he himself clearly and unambiguously admitted several years later: "The tacit Cogito does not, of course, solve these problems. In disclosing it as I did in *PhP*, I did not arrive at a solution (my chapter on the Cogito is not connected with the chapter on speech): on the contrary I posed a problem. The tacit Cogito should make understood how language is not impossible, *but cannot make understood how it is possible*——There remains the problem of the passage from the perceptual meaning to the language meaning, from behavior to thematization. Moreover the thematization itself must be understood as a behavior of a higher degree—the relation between the thematization and the behavior is a dialectical relation: *language realizes, by breaking the silence, what the silence wished and did not obtain.*" (VI, 175-6; *VI*, 229-30; emphasis ours)

As we can therefore see in this note of February 1959 where Merleau-Ponty himself criticizes the *Phenomenology,* truth is not only an archeological affair but also a *teleological* one. One discovers the meaning of lived experience only by transcending it through reflection, through language: the "very description of silence rests entirely on the virtues of language. The taking possession of the world of silence, such as the description of the human body effects it, is no longer this world of silence, it is the world articulated, elevated to the *Wesen,* spoken." (VI, 179; *VI,* 233) Thus reflection is not a *coincidence* with a meaning or a brute logos; it is its *realization,* the promotion of a wild logos to a spoken Logos, to truth. It is not the perceived world, unreflected life as the ground or de facto foundation of rationality, which accounts for language or reason; they do not tell us how it is *possible;* on the contrary, the notion of a return to and a rediscovery of a de facto foundation of reason is meaningless if there is not a teleology of consciousness or reason.

With Merleau-Ponty therefore, as with Hegel, "becoming-conscious entails a real development."[26] The silent logos which is to be recovered cannot be grasped in its silence; to be recuperated, it must be *transformed* into a spoken Logos. It is through the mediating work of reflection that existence receives it meaning, that its truth appears. This is why expression is a *task.* The meaning of the world and of our existence is not given in advance; it is a conquest on the part of reflection.[27] The perceived world imposes a task, a vocation, on the painter, for the painter can grasp the visibility of the world in its meaning (this meaning being that of his presence to the perceived world) only by reflecting it in a picture which expresses it. Existence is that which demands transcendence, reflection, of us in order to be understood. And thus, "what there is is a creation that is called forth and engendered by the *Lebenswelt* as operative, latent historicity, that prolongs it and bears witness to it." (VI, 174; *VI,* 228)

## 3. Vertical Being

If this is the way things stand, the phenomenon of expression necessarily teaches us something about the very structure of Being. For if the being of man and of things is such that it receives its meaning only through the mediation of reflection, is genuinely grasped only through transcendence and the self's doubling back on itself, the theory of expression contains an entire theory of Being. Since reflection appears as the coming to light of a phenomenal or wild logos and as its own proper manifestation, but since too this revelation is a creation, reflection seizes hold of itself as an essential moment of phenomenal being which is seeking to know itself, as a figure of being in search of itself. Reflection—seizing hold of itself precisely as a reflection on the unreflected—thereby knows itself as comprised within being, as being's grasp of itself by itself.

Let us turn back to what we have just said in order to consider it more carefully and with textual support. In one of his most important working notes Merleau-Ponty writes, "Philosophy, precisely as 'Being speaking within us,' expression of the mute experience by itself, is creation. A creation that is at the same time a reintegration of Being: for it is not a creation in the sense of one of the commonplace *Gebilde* that history fabricates: it knows itself to be a *Gebilde* and wishes to surpass itself as *pure Gebilde,* to find again its origin. It is hence a creation in a radical sense: a creation that is at the same time an adequation, the only way to obtain an adequation." Philosophy makes contact with phenomenal Being precisely as a *creation,* which makes it such that "Being is *what requires creation of us* for us to experience it." (VI, 197; *VI, 250–1*)

One will note the presence here of several "Heideggerian" themes. In the text just quoted, man appears as an *opening* in Being through which Being becomes *present* to itself; he is the place where an *advent* of Being occurs. And, as transcendental, creative experience, man is an essential moment in the advent of Being. If one can grasp Being only by way of creation, it is because the Being which is in question is a Being which is realized (made real) only in and through reflection, and reflection must thus be conceived of as a moment or a figure of Being. Expresssion has a teleological nature because it stems from a movement of transcendence which is Being itself.

But an important ambiguity remains in all this. What indeed is the relation between Being and the *Lebenswelt?* This is, in part, a question of terminology: if one can call the world "being," what then is "Being"? Is there even a difference between these two terms? We shall return to this question in our last chapter in order to treat it in more depth; here we only want to raise the question. In any event, it is already apparent that in Merleau-Ponty's late philosophy "being" does not have only one meaning; indeed, for him as for Aristotle, being is said in many ways: τὸ ὂν λέγεται πολλαχῶς. Being is first of all phenomenal being, that is, the structure lived body–perceived world, and as such it is the de facto foundation of rationality. But if this being "calls for" and "demands" expressive efforts and presents itself to the teleology of consciousness as a "task" to be accomplished, it is because it is not itself, qua *fact,* the ultimate source of reason or what grounds the *possibility* of the teleology of expression. Rather, it is itself derived in regard to a Being which, as "Eye and Mind" says, "never fully *is,*" a Being which is *nothing* in itself but which is rather the active transcendence of *everything,* which first expresses itself and makes its advent in the perceived world and then, better still, in reflection which expresses and testifies to it best precisely because reflection is a transcendence which knows itself as such. Language, Merleau-Ponty writes, "continues an effort of articulation which is the Being of every being" (VI, 127; *VI,* 168), and it thus expresses "an ontogenesis of which it is a part." (VI, 102; *VI,* 139) In the final analysis Being would be the very genesis and advent of the world and of reason, and it would thus not be a fact, a foundation, a ground, but an abyss, a spontaneous, eternal, and inexhaustible source of transcendence.

## Conclusion

IN the "movement of transcendence" that human existence is, transcendental, authentic expression occupies an altogether special and irreducible position. But in regard to transcendental experience, reflection properly so-called—philosophy—appears as a privileged modality. Whereas "other forms of symbolism exercise only in a limited way" the expressive power which first makes its appearance in bodily existence, philosophy "recovers this meaning, and also pushes beyond all limits the becoming of truth". (IPP, 58; *EP,* 92)[28] Philosophy is not only the unveiling of a logos; it also knows itself as such and thus attempts to seize hold of this relation between it and brute or wild being, a relation which in the last analysis is Being itself. Like literature, philosophy is language; but it is a language which takes itself for its theme—it is speech concerned with speaking speech—and which attempts to express the relation itself which exists between language and prelanguage so as to understand thereby how it is itself possible. Thus, if creative language is the advent or articulation of Being, if it stems from "an effort of articulation which is the Being of every being" and thus "expresses, at least laterally, an ontogenesis of which it is a part," philosophy must in addition be the consciousness of language as an articulation of Being and must thus be the reflective self-consciousness of Being itself. It would seem that the "fundamental thought" (VI, 183; *VI,* 237) that Merleau-Ponty proposes in one of his working notes is related to Heidegger's *wesentliche Denken,* or again to Hegel's phenomenology. If, however, this is the case, how can Merleau-Ponty avoid a *Logik* or a *Seinsdenken* which makes of reflection a mere event of Being or a ruse of Reason?[29] Can philosophy forget itself as philosophy—as the thought of man—so as to become the thought that Being has of itself? Can reflection ever be complete? This is what we now have to examine.

# Chapter IV

# Philosophy

*Far from thinking that philosophy is a
useless repetition of life I think, on the
contrary, that without reflection life would
probably dissipate itself in ignorance of
itself or in chaos.*

"The Primacy of Perception" (PriP, 19)

THE central theme of Merleau-Ponty's philosophy, from *The Structure
of Behavior* to his last manuscript, *The Visible and the Invisible,* is
philosophy itself. Even if Merleau-Ponty was always certain of the goal
to be pursued—understanding the world as we live it—the philosophy
which would afford access to it did not for all that cease to be problematic, such that in *The Visible and the Invisible* we see him in the
process of beginning everything again, as if his other writings, and the
*Phenomenology of Perception* in particular, had missed their target.
This is to say that the subject of his reflection was always not only
the *Lebenswelt,* the lived world, but also, if not above all, this very
reflection on our unreflected life. It is often not noticed that the
*Phenomenology* is in fact not a dogmatic work, a collection of theses
and propositions—about the lived body, the perceived world, the
*Cogito,* etc.—but the proposition, analysis, and explication of a way
of thought, that underneath the presentation and analysis of various
phenomena another discussion is pursued, one which turns back on

145

phenomenology itself, on its nature and its ability to return to and express our unreflected life, on the very relation between philosophy and non-philosophy. Merleau-Ponty's work occupies in this way a place in the tradition of transcendental and reflexive philosophy, even though it seeks to overcome its weaknesses and its "subjectivism." A transcendental philosophy which does not want to be a philosophy of mere consciousness—such was in fact Merleau-Ponty's philosophy. And it is this double polarity in his thought which makes it a philosophy of ambiguity, an "arduous and disconcerting" thought (De Waelhens).

## I.   Towards a Phenomenology of Phenomenology

### 1.   The Point of View of the Spectator

The first of Merleau-Ponty's two doctoral theses, *The Structure of Behavior,* is, as we have seen, devoted to a discussion of and an application to various orders of existence of the notion of Form or Gestalt. But even while describing existence—physical, vital, and human—in terms of structure, Merleau-Ponty attempts to show here that this notion of Form, however essential it might be, is not enough by itself. This notion, such as it was worked out by Gestalt psychology, represents a decisive advance over the causal and atomistic explanations of classical psychology and behaviorism, and it is indeed necessary to understand nature; but it itself overflows the confines of descriptive psychology and raises a problem of a properly philosophical sort— that of the relation between *consciousness* and *nature.*

Gestalt psychology, for Merleau-Ponty, is implicitly linked to a *realist* philosophy. It contents itself with substituting structural descriptions for mechanical explanations of nature considered as a *partes extra partes* ensemble; and, although it proposes a new way of conceiving of natural processes, it does not for all that escape from objectivistic thought, for it holds that Forms exist *in* an objective, in-itself nature. This is to say that it does not push its inquiry in the Form's mode of existence very far; it remains a *descriptive* science and holds itself to the point of view of the "outside spectator" (SB, 162, 184; *SC,* 175, 199)

Now, as Merleau-Ponty says, critical or transcendental philosophy teaches us, and rightly so, that merely descriptive thought is a thought which is still naive. He who describes the spectacle and who believes himself to be forming a fully objective and impartial representation of it—from where does he speak? Is his presence to the world unrelated to the fact that the world *appears* this way rather than that way? In reality, the spectator is himself a part of the spectacle, for nature is a spectacle only inasmuch as it exists as an object for a *consciousness,* only inasmuch as it is *for* consciousness. There is in the final analysis no "outside spectator," because the human spectator is himself that which makes it be that there is a spectacle; it is he who is the producer of all spectacles, and it is for him that nature is a Gestalt. The observation of natural Forms thus does not have an essentially passive nature; it is not the mere reception by a perceiving subject of something which exists fully defined in itself. Consciousness of nature is, on the contrary, an *activity* which constitutes nature in what it is. Thus, having applied the descriptive method and having seen that it refers us back to that consciousness which was always actively present to the spectacle, Merleau-Ponty can conclude, "what we call nature is already consciousness of nature, what we call life is already consciousness of life and what we call mental is still an object vis-à-vis consciousness." (SB, 184; *SC,* 199)

Transcendental philosophy—by showing us that wherever nature is there also is consciousness and that consciousness is thus, far from being a mere part of the world, the very milieu of the universe which supports it from below; and by inviting us, consequently, to analyze not nature but the very relation between consciousness and nature—represents for Merleau-Ponty "a definitive acquisition as the first phase of reflection." (SB, 215; *SC,* 232) This is the "first conclusion" he is able to draw when towards the end of *The Structure of Behavior* he begins to sum up its implications. His analyses lead him in short to the *transcendental attitude.* (SB, 201; *SC,* 217) At the end of the work and after presenting the notion of Form from the point of view of the outside spectator, Merleau-Ponty thus joins up with the first requirement of Husserlian phenomenology by asserting the need for a "phenomenological reduction." (SB, 220 n; *SC,* 236) It is necessary to step out of immediate or natural experience, suspend the attitude of the outside spectator, and turn natural experience into the very object of reflection precisely in order to become conscious of it. Perceptual consciousness, our experience of nature, is indeed a consciousness which knows itself only by perceiving things; in other words, it is unaware of itself  as an active consciousness, as that without which there would be nothing perceptual at all, and takes itself to be a mere impartial witness of what exists objectively.

Forms are not *real* properties of things but their way of presenting themselves to a perceptual consciousness; they are therefore not real but perceived things. It is thus necessary to cease living in things, taking them unquestioningly as existing outside of perception the way we know them only by perception, and return to perceptual conscious-ness itself so as to see in it the essential condition of Forms, the essen-tial condition of the very objectivity of experience.

Up to this point Merleau-Ponty's analysis is inspired by critical philosophy; it leads us back underneath the world to the conscious-ness of the world and discovers that it is absurd to speak of the world as though it existed completely in itself, indifferent to every relation to consciousness, and to conceive of perception as a mere passivity and as a natural event. But criticism does not stop there: not only does it trace the world which is supposed to contain consciousness back to the perceived world and discover that consciousness is coextensive with the world, but again it reduces perceptual consciousness to intel-lectual consciousness. And at this point Merleau-Ponty feels obliged to abandon the criticist route. For criticism perception is itself but a con-fused thought: it is transcendental, constituting consciousness itself, but is unaware of itself as such; and because of this unawareness of itself it can initially think that it takes place in the world and is merely a registering of the spectacle of nature. The realist thesis according to which perception takes place in the objective world and is a function of the biological body reveals itself, in the light of reflection, as an error and an illusion; for, not being a thing or a part of the world but the very condition of its appearance as world, consciousness cannot be determined by the world; it can be determined only by meanings, and it is precisely it itself which confers on the world its meaning or Form.

Merleau-Ponty asks, however, Whence arises this notion of passivi-ty given to us by perception if it has no basis at all in our actual exper-ience and does not express a real fact about the life of consciousness? Is it really possible that a consciousness which would be all act could, even at the beginning of its reflection, be so seriously mistaken as to its true nature by believing itself to be, not the absolute and transcen-dental source of the world, but, as it were, its at once active and passive partner? Realism, which makes of perception a mere effect of the world and an event inside of it, a function of the objective body, is an error, but it is nevertheless a motivated error: "it rests on an authentic phenomenon which philosophy has the function of making explicit." (SB, 216; *SC*, 233) The experience of passivity is an essential element in perceptual consciousness, and we cannot begin to understand it if we say that it is a mere illusion. In order to understand our actual experience of the world, we must not begin by looking for its conditions of possibility in constituting consciousness; we must return to perception itself, to this "beginning consciousness" which criticism is too quick in assimilating to reflective self-consciousness, and we must attempt to understand it as such, just as it presents itself, as an experience of passivity.

Transcendental consciousness, the full consciousness of the self by itself, the notion which criticism ends up with and afterwards attempts to posit, not as the end result of its reflections, but as the eternal a priori from which it proceeds, is not in fact, Merleau-Ponty emphasizes, a de jure possession of consciousness. What is first of all given is not an active thematizing but a reflection which is open to an unreflected experience which it seeks to take up; it is the *active* experience of *passivity*. If transcendental consciousness is at all possible, it can be had only through a clarification of the concrete and actual being of consciousness, of unreflected and perceptual life; it does not lie ready-made elsewhere in some intelligible heaven but is to-be-made. The task Merleau-Ponty sets himself here is thus a radicalization of criticism's task, for he wants to *think* perception, understand it, without however destroying its specificity by making of it a confused thought, a "variation of intellection"; he wants to think it precisely as an original and irreducible mode of our experience. Just as Hegel wanted to give a foundation to Kant's transcendental attitude, so also Merleau-Ponty seeks to realize the ambition of Hegel's phenomenology: the reflective recuperation of what we effectively are. "We want," he says, "to make consciousness equal with the whole of experience, to gather into consciousness for-itself all the life of consciousness in-itself." (SB, 223; *SC*, 240)

Thus, to the degree that criticism makes of the Form a pure idea, it is to be rejected; for if the Form exists only through its meaning, this perceived meaning is not for all that "a Kantian object," a construction of pure intellect. What is indeed unique in the notion of Form, as it emerges from the analyses of *The Structure of Behavior*, is that it unites the two notions of *structure* and *meaning*. (SB, 223; *SC,* 240) Form belongs *at one and the same time* to the world (it is a structure) and to consciousness (it is a meaning); and thus its proper locus is neither in-itself nature nor pure internal self-consciousness, but rather perception which is the life of a subject engaged outside of himself in the world and who is at once active and passive. The Gestalt is precisely "the joining of an idea and an existence which are indiscernible, the contingent arrangement by which materials begin to have meaning in our presence, intelligibility in the nascent state." (SB, 206; *SC,* 223) It is thus necessary to return to perception, to this beginning consciousness, and to attempt to discover exactly how matters stand with it in order to find out what is in fact the true relation between the subject and the world. Having thus defined at the end of *The Structure of Behavior* the task lying before him, Merleau-Ponty pauses however to ask if such a project is fully realizable and if it is, strictly speaking, *reasonable.* "Can one conceptualize perceptual consciousness without eliminating it as an original mode; can one maintain its specificity without rendering inconceivable its relation to intellectual consciousness?" (SB, 224; *SC,* 241) What is certain is that if criticism can treat of perception only as a confused thought and as a first rough sketch of intellection, destined to be replaced by it, it is to be rejected, and what remains is thus "to define transcendental philosophy anew in such a way as to integrate with it the very phenomenon of the real." This redefinition of transcendental philosophy, whose goal is to seize hold of the immediate meaning of perceptual life and to think it as such, will be the *Phenomenology of Perception.*

## 2.   The Transcendental Point of View

Thus, Merleau-Ponty seeks to "make reflection equal the unreflected life of consciousness." (PhP, XVI; *PP,* XI) In the very first lines of *The Structure of Behavior* he had written, "our goal is to understand the relations of consciousness and nature." This is the program which the *Phenomenology of Perception* attempts to carry through and which, moreover, constitutes the constant theme of all his work. We will indeed see in the seond part of this chapter how *The Visible and the Invisible* appears as a renewal and a radicalization of this problem which transposes it from the phenomenological field to the ontological field.

For the time being, however, it is important to follow Merleau-Ponty's first attempt to clarify this problem of the relations of subject and world, such as it is worked out in the *Phenomenology*.

*The Structure of Behavior* has thus outlined the dimensions of the problem. To understand the relations between consciousness and nature it is necessary to return to perception, that realm of our experience where the problem first arises. But how can one and how must one conceive of perception?

In the eyes of Merleau-Ponty, as he expresses himself in the *Phenomenology*, the descriptive, precritical method practiced by psychology is valid in itself as an inventory of the perceived world. Its insufficiency as a method stems, therefore, not from what it has to say about the structure of the world we perceive, but from what it does not say—that the world thus described is not a world external to consciousness, an in-itself, objective world, but a world which exists only as the correlate of consciousness. The error of the psychologist or the empiricist philosopher, who thinks that perception is a natural event like others, is that of not "being aware that he himself perceives, that he is himself a perceiving subject". (PhP, 206; *PP,* 240) Empiricism gives itself a world of ready-made relations and does not see that in regard to this world perceptual consciousness is a constituting factor. The empirical world is an objective, already constituted world; it is not the phenomenal world, the world which takes shape before us, which expresses itself in our experience. Thus, since it fails to take account of consciousness and has in fact lost sight of it as the place where the world appears, empiricism is "like a kind of mental blindness." (PhP, 25; *PP,* 33) It calls in this way for a more radical kind of reflection which will account for the essential condition of all objectivity, the *presence* of the subject. "The descriptive method," Merleau-Ponty emphasizes, "can acquire its proper status only from the transcendental point of view." (PhP, 7; *PP,* 13)

This is the point of view achieved by criticist or transcendental philosophy in the classical sense of the term. It leads us back beneath the objective world to the phenomenal world, the world which is appearance (and not being in itself, noumenon); and its great discovery is subjectivity itself, which is not an element of the world but its indispensable correlate. Intellectualism thereby represents indeed a progress in the process of becoming-conscious. But even if reflective (transcendental, criticist) philosophy represents a progress in the process of becoming-conscious, it is a becoming-conscious which is still incomplete.

Indeed, reflective analysis attempts, in regard to the phenomenal world which it has just exposed, to discover immediately its *conditions of possibility*. It claims to follow in an inverse direction a path of a prior constitution and thereby return to certain a priori structures, behind experience, which make it *possible*. It thus wants to ground what is on what must be, and claims to discover a transcendental Ego behind experience which has already constituted it without being aware of having done so. As a matter of fact, this kind of reflection only dissimulates the phenomenal world by at once transforming it into a transcendental world. It is thereby oblivious to the *appearance* of being to us for having linked it up to conditions of possibility given in advance. For this reason it cannot claim to be a description and clarification of our actual experience, because in this experience what is given is not a transcendental Ego which emerges from its inner being to search for things, but an incarnate subject who attempts to understand himself and get hold of himself on the basis of his association with things; what is given is a reflection which is open to the unreflected and which is inseparable from it.

This is to say, in the last analysis, that here reflection loses sight of itself as an *event*. By claiming to be merely making explicit a work of consititution which has already been accomplished "somewhere or other," by claiming to follow up in an inverse direction a path of constitution already traversed without the subject's knowing it, it is in bad faith. Reflective analysis wants to place itself behind its own beginning in experience and ground its facticity on its ideality, its reality on its possibility. It thinks that its possibility is given in advance and loses sight of its real origin. Like empiricism, it too is thus a kind of mental blindness; it thinks through everything except itself as thought. Whence does the criticist philosopher speak? This question which is ignored by a classical type of reflection is the one a "truly reflective" philosophy would have to answer. What is called for, Merleau-Ponty says, is "a more radical self-discovery. Reflection cannot be thoroughgoing, or bring a complete elucidation of its object, if it does not arrive at awareness of itself as well as of its results. We must," he says, "not only adopt a reflective attitude..., but furthermore reflect on this reflection, understand the natural situation which it is conscious of succeeding and which is therefore part of its definition." (PhP, 62; *PP*, 75)

This is a very important text, for it reveals the requirement Merleau-Ponty's philosophy sets itself and its program. Philosophy is the recuperation and interpretation of our actual experience, and it is necessary for it not only to effect this interpretation but again to grasp the relation between it and experience, a relation which makes it be that it is itself possible. It is only on this condition—on the condition that philosophy establish its own ground or possibility—that philosophy can cease to be a technique and become an "absolute knowledge". (PhP, 62; *PP*, 75) This reference by Merleau-Ponty to "absolute knowledge" may surprise us, but it is indeed a kind of absolute which his phenomenology aims at. It is this which we must seek to understand.

Merleau-Ponty's argument in the *Phenomenology of Perception* is not, however, easy to follow. The question as to the method and the nature of a truly reflective philosophy comes up very often, but the author never succeeds in treating it in a systematic way. More often than not he only makes passing allusions to this matter and unsettles the reader with innumerable repetitions. And yet it can be seen that this is for him a question of the greatest importance, that what he is trying to do here is to realize "a new type of reflection." (PhP 241; *PP,* 278) However, unlike an author who merely exposits an already formulated thought, in the *Phenomenology* Merleau-Ponty seems embarked upon a search to discover and master his own thought.

It would appear, however, that Merleau-Ponty is above all preoccupied with the question of what is ordinarily called the radical starting point. Merleau-Ponty's position could perhaps be clarified by viewing it in the context of the definition of philosophy as a search for what is first. According to Aristotle's expression, philosophy is ἐπιστήμη τῶν πρώτων αρχῶν χαὶ αιτίων θεωρητιχή, (*Metaphysics*, 982 b 9) Philosophy is a search for what is first and grounds everything else, the πρώτων or the ἀρχή. The ἀρχή. however, can be conceived of in two ways: as something real or as something ideal, that is, as a *beginning* or a *principle.* In transcendental philosophy of the traditional sort, the ἀρχή is discovered in the form of a principle or an a priori. For a radical reflection such as Merleau-Ponty advocates, however, the task is not only that of discovering the first principle of reality but also reflection's own principle. Reflection's radical question is the question of its own reality and its own possibility; it is the question of its grounding. This is to say that a philosophy which looks for its own ἀρχή is looking for the radical starting point; it is seeking to discover the principle which grounds it and guarantees its own beginning; it is, as Husserl said, *Wissenschaft des Anfangs*, a science of the beginning.

Reflective analysis does indeed discover principles which account for our experience of the world, but these are only logical principles which do not take account of the real and ontological beginning of reflection itself. Criticist philosophy explains everything except itself; it discovers principles which clarify everything except its own beginning *as* reflection. For this reason, Merleau-Ponty says, it is "naive, or at least it is an incomplete form of reflection which loses sight of its own beginning. When I begin to reflect my reflection bears upon an unreflected experience; it cannot be unaware of itself as an event". (PhP, X; *PP*, IV) The "new conception of reflection" which Merleau-Ponty is attempting to spell out "amounts in other words to giving a new definition of the a priori." (PhP, 220; *PP*, 255) Kant's fault, as Merleau-Ponty sees it, lay not in having attempted to unearth the a priori of experience, but in having done so, so to speak, behind the back of experience. Kant did not follow "out his programme, which was to define our cognitive powers in terms of our factual condition, and which would have compelled him to set every conceivable being against the background of this world." With its discovery of the logical a priori of experience, transcendental philosophy did indeed eliminate the notion of objective causes, but it failed to grasp its own ontological a priori. Merleau-Ponty is thus obliged to rediscover a principle of *reason* which will at the same time be a *factual* beginning.

If Merleau-Ponty never ceases to be interested in Descartes despite all the profound differences between his thought and Cartesian philosophy, it is because for him Descartes was one of those great thinkers who cannot be merely overcome and refuted, and who can be fought only by means of a creative reappropriation and a faithful correction of what they thought.[1] In modern philosophy it is indeed Descartes who was the first to recognize the absolute necessity for a radical starting point. His *cogito sum* is at one and the same time the principle which guarantees the rationality of experience and the foundation, the starting point, the beginning, of reflection. Reflection finds in it an archē, an a priori which is logical and ontological, rational and real. Descartes' own fault, for Merleau-Ponty, was to have reversed the relation between the *cogito* and the *sum*. For him it is not the "I think" which grounds the "I am"; it is rather the I think which is reintegrated into the movement of transcendence of the I am and con-

sciousness into existence. (PhP, 382; *PP,* 439) The certainty of thinking stems from its actual existence.[2] Thus the reduction set into play
by Merleau-Ponty leads us back to reflection itself; but this "second-
order reflection" (PhP, 63; *PP,* 77) discovers, not an impeachable
*Cogito,* "a source of intrinsic truth, but a subject destined to be in
the world." (PhP, XI; *PP,* V) The reflecting subject discovers that he
is present to himself only by being present to the world, that he is
reflective only insofar as this reflection is a reflection on a prereflective
experience. In Merleau-Ponty's phenomenology, consciousness, while
it is always at the center of his analyses, does not therefore possess an
ontological and logical priority, for it grasps itself as the consciousness
of a preconscious and prereflective life which is its absolute beginning.
And thus with him the phenomenological reduction ceases to be "a
procedure of idealistic philosophy" and becomes "that of an existential philosophy." (PhP, XIV; *PP,* IX)

If, therefore, "reflection consists in seeking the originating
[*l'originaire*], that by which everything else can be and can be thought",
(PhP, 289; *PP,* 334) this "originating" is the *fact* that as an event reflection is "reflection-on-an-unreflected-experience." (PhP, 62; *PP,* 76)
The originating is the fact that the subject is given to himself in his
reflection as something to be reflected. Reflection finds its beginning
in the fact that it is a reflection on the unreflected, and it is this
situation which it must think. Philosophy comes back to its center
when it returns to this "perpetual beginning of reflection, at the point
where an individual life begins to reflect on itself." The radical starting
point is attained when reflection recognizes that it is "an ever-renewed
experience of its own beginning, that it consists wholly in the description of this beginning, and finally, that radical reflection amounts to a
consciousness of its own dependence on an unreflected life which is its
initial situation, unchanging, given once and for all." (PhP, XIV; *PP,*
IX) From that point on there can be no question of the reflecting
subject's becoming wholly consciousness and reabsorbing his facticity
in his ideality of principle.[3] He is obliged, rather, to locate the origin of
rationality and the foundation of the "presumption on reason's part"
which animates him in the fact that he is given to himself as something
to be thought, and thus to recognize that reflection as reflection-on-
the-unreflected is itself a "gift of nature."

This amounts to saying, therefore, that if the subject wants to
radically think himself, if he wants, by means of reflection, to recuper-

ate himself, he must think himself in his beginning, as initially given to himself as something to be thought, as, therefore, the "upsurge of time." The ἀρχή φιλοσοφίας (Plato, *Theaetetus*, 155 d), philosophy's radical starting point in Merleau-Ponty, is the renewed consciousness of the perpetual beginning of reflection; it is the reflective consciousness of *time*. For, as he says, "if we rediscover time beneath the subject, and if we relate to the paradox of time those of the body, the world, the thing, and other people, we shall understand that beyond these there is nothing to understand." (PhP, 365; *PP,* 419) In leading us back by means of the reduction to a subject destined to be in the world, Merleau-Ponty's phenomenology reveals in all its depth "the mystery of the world and of reason" (PhP, XXI; *PP,* XVI), and it traces this mystery back to that of our temporality.

## 3.   The Radical Point of View

Thus, by means of the reduction, reflection finally discovers that which it must think: reflection itself in the way it is given to itself as a reflection-on-an-unreflected. Henceforth the task incumbent on reflective philosophy takes on a wholly new meaning. Everything changes indeed when philosophy no longer has to discover the "conditions of possibility" of experience but rather its own genesis in experience, and when it must rediscover in experience the origin and ground of the "presumption on reason's part" by which it is inspired. Since reflection brings to light, not a transcendental Ego which would be the constituting source of "everything that can be and can be thought," but a subject which is initially a perceptual relation to the world and a bodily dialogue with it, the task of a radical reflection is to formulate "an experience of the world, a contact with the world which precedes all thought *about* the world." (SNS, 28; *SNS,* 113) The task of reflection is to recover or recuperate the meaning of our actual life so as to discover in our bodily commerce with the world the ground and the guarantee of rationality. Phenomenology becomes in this way "a phenomenology of origins [*de la genése*] " (PhP, XVIII; *PP,* XIII) and, "through a process similar to that of an archaeologist" (PriP, 5; *Inédit,* 403), it retraces the "genealogy" of the conscious and reflective subject. Reflection sets out to recover our unreflected life and our bodily experience of the world and is "the act whereby we take up this unfinished world in an effort to totalize and to think it." (PhP XX; *PP,* XV)

The transcendental or reflective operation is, as we have seen in the two preceding chapters, animated by the "desire for a total manifestation." It claims to be able to transform the silent meaning of our perceptual and bodily life into a manifest and available meaning and, in so doing, to justify itself. However, as we have seen, pictorial and literary expression do not manage to arrive at a total manifestation and a perfect reappropriation of our facticity, at a reappropriation which would make it fully intelligible. The painter brings to light our original relation to the world, but, by making pictures, he at the same time dissimulates it by reintroducing it into the realm of things which are merely perceived and lived, the realm of facticity. In this regard literary language represents a progress, for the relation between language and what it signifies and reveals seems to be much more transparent; linguistic signs seem to immediately transcend themselves towards their meaning and to eclipse themselves before it, leaving us face to face with a pure intelligibility. This is not at all the case, however: language is only an invocation. The meaning of literary expression is never pure, because here language does not succeed in unveiling the relation which binds it to what is prior to language in such a way as to realize its own possibility. Like the painter, the writer is limited to exercising a power whose source he has not understood. Radical philosophy, finally, would like to return to its source, seize hold of the relation between language and what precedes it, transform into a fully available truth the hidden meaning of our bodily being in the world, realizing thereby its own possiblity. Being in this way the recuperation of a spirit lost in the world and in our prereflective experience, philosophy would be the Spirit which has become transparent to itself and which knows itself as the Spirit of the World; and the phenomenology of experience would become a Logic of experience; a truth of fact would transform itself into a truth of reason, facticity into necessity. However, for Merleau-Ponty this attempt at a total recuperation is in the last analysis doomed to fail, for, in becoming a radical reflection, what at the end of its efforts phenomenology discovers is *time*. Let us see what this means.

In rediscovering its own history reflection thus discovers itself as a reflection-on-an-unreflected; it grasps itself as being founded on the impersonal and as-yet-unreflected life of perception or corporeity. What it must therefore think is not only this prepersonal life but also its own relationship to it, how precisely it is reflection only insofar as

it is a reflection on the unreflected. Reflection discovers that what forever grounds its idea (one could even say, its ideal) of truth is the *fact*
that by means of perception the subject enjoys a primordial contact
with the world; all intellectual certainty is merely the translation of
this *Urdoxa,* this primitive project or belief in the world. Perceptual,
prereflective life is an "operative intentionality," and the world is
the correlate of the lived body's existential projects. The origin of
rationality lies in the fact that by means of perception the world appears for the first time like this rather than like that; that is, it manifests a certain *meaning* which is perfectly proportioned to the dimensions of our bodily existence. Now, the perceiving subject is a *temporal*
subject. This is not simply to say that the bodily subject exists in time;
he is rather time itself. "We are not saying that time is *for* someone....
We are saying that time *is* someone....We must understand time as
the subject and the subject as time." (PhP, 422; *PP,* 482) It is precisely the ex-static presence of the subject to the world which makes it
be that there is time, that is, a past, a present, and a future, just as it
is by means of the subject that there is space, a "here" and an "over
there," a "high" and a "low." The incarnate subject lives between the
two horizons of his birth and his death, and thus the meaning of his
existence—according to Heidegger's expression which Merleau-Ponty
takes over—is temporality. He is himself nothing other than a process
of temporalization, "one single temporality which is engaged, from
birth, in making itself progressively explicit, and in confirming that
cohesion in each successive present." (PhP, 407; *PP,* 466) Existing
always between a past and a future, in a present which is the retention
of the former and the protention of the latter, the subject of perception is "like a continued birth." (PriP, 6; *Inédit,* 404)

Thus when the subject returns to himself and attempts to get
hold of himself, he discovers a "prehistory" at the heart of his personal
and reflective existence. In his reflection the subject finds himself as
being "already there"; he realizes that in his personal existence he is
borne along by a time which he does not constitute, since this time is
his very being as a being in the world. The subject of reflection does
not coincide with his own origin, but rather presupposes a prepersonal
and prereflective life on the basis of which he possesses himself as something to be reflected. The subject who calls himself *Cogito,* who is a
reflective self-consciousness, can know himself only as "already born"
or "still living"; he finds himself as having been "thrown" into exis-

tence, given to himself, and can grab hold of his arché and his telos, his birth and his death, only as "prepersonal horizons." (PhP, 216; *PP*, 250) Thus a radical reflection discovers that what grounds forever its activity and what makes for its own possibility is its constitutional passivity, the fact that as an incarnate subject he possesses himself only because one day he was *born.* It is thus the subject's *birth,* this initial and insurpassable passivity, which is forever the ground of his activity. In thinking his own birth, the fact that he has been *given to himself* as something to understand, the reflecting subject thus discovers in himself a kind of "inner weakness" (PhP, 428; *PP*, 489) which forever prevents him from coinciding with himself and from being in the mode of knowledge or activity what he was in the mode of event or passivity. Thus the subject's birth is not for himself a mere event in time, a merely past event. The necessity of the *Cogito* is always derivative in regard to that contingent fact which is the subject's birth. As "a thinking subject, I still am that first perception, the continuation of that same life inaugurated by it." (PhP, 407; *PP*, 466)

By maintaining that what the *Cogito* rediscovers is its own birth and in thus conferring upon the *Cogito* "a temporal thickness" (PhP, 398; *PP*, 456), Merleau-Ponty is introducing into the very heart of the thinking subject a "prehistory," an "unreflected fund," an "original past, a past which has never been a present." (PhP, 242; *PP*, 280) And thus for him the reflecting subject can never coincide with his own beginning and cannot ground his de facto reality on a de jure necessity. For Merleau-Ponty reflective consciousness is, as Hegel said, a consciousness "split within itself."[4] In discovering his own archeology, the thinking subject discovers his radical and insurpassable *contingency* and realizes that he consequently cannot be the equal in knowledge to what he was as an event. It is only ambivalently and ambiguously that the subject can seize hold of himself; all absolute certainty and evidence are thereby automatically and definitively ruled out.

There can be no "total manifestation," for there is no Reason which is transcendent to our de facto condition and which grounds its reality on a de jure necessity to which reflection could return. The reflecting subject cannot reduce his being to his knowing, for in discovering his own arché he finds the contingent and gratuitous event of his birth. In thinking himself as given to himself as something to be thought, the subject is forced to recognize that what gives him to himself is not a Reason hidden in the world but the non-necessitated fact of his own unmotivated appearance in the midst of a world which, as reason, he has neither created nor constructed, but which for him has been "always-already-there." In the last resort reflection cannot become rational explanation; it can do no more than take note of the indissoluble "mystery" of rationality. In recognizing that it is "through temporality that there can be, without contradiction, ipseity, significance and reason" (PhP, 426; *PP,* 487), reflection thereby automatically forbids itself access to a "metaphysical entity," transcendent to time, which would be able to explain our temporality; and it considers irresolute any reflection which, like Descartes', can accept the fundamental irrationality of our condition only by grounding it on that "transcendent guarantee" which is "God as the rational author of our *de facto* situation." (PhP, 199; *PP,* 232) For Merleau-Ponty any recourse to any such notion of eternity is "hypocritical" since "eternity feeds on time." (PhP, 423; *PP,* 484) It is only on the basis of our de facto condition that we have an idea of the true; and since this is the way things stand there can be in return no absolute truth which would be able to ground and serve as a guarantee for our de facto situation.[5]

Insofar as it implies and constitutes a metaphysics, phenomenology is thus "the opposite of system" (SNS, 94; *SNS,* 166), because for it to explain the contingency of our condition is inevitably to destroy it as contingency, just as it is to render human freedom incomprehensible by subordinating it to divine predestination. Merleau-Ponty's "radical reflection" is through and through an existential philosophy, if one understands by this a philosophy which wants to hold itself rigorously to what is given in our experience and to explicate it faithfully, refusing thereby any notion which is not grounded in and justified by this experience as it is given, and refusing everything which is not immanent in it. Consequently only one attitude is possible for this philosophy: "the feeling of strangeness" (SNS, 18; *SNS,* 30), a perpetual astonishment in face of the "unmotivated upsurge of the world" (PhP, XIV; *PP,* VIII) and the upsurge of reason in the midst of contingency. Merleau-Ponty's philosophy is a refusal of the absolute, for it discovers at the end of its reflection that the *principle* of rationality is nothing other than its gratuitous *beginning.*

Thus for Merleau-Ponty philosophy cannot become an absolute knowledge in the Hegelian sense; that is, it cannot, according to Hegel's expression, "set aside its name *love of wisdom* so as to be an *actively real* knowledge."[6] Reflection cannot claim to discover a transcendental grounding of our actual experience; the only Logos which preexists, Merelau-Ponty insists, is the world itself (PhP, XX; *PP,* XV), that is, our contingent presence to the world and to ourselves. Reflection moreover cannot complete itself, for it is upheld and borne along by that time which it seeks to capture; it is "like a passenger at the rear of a train who sees only the places he has left behind."[7] For this reason philosophy is alway a perpetual beginning. (cf. PhP, XIV; *PP,* IX) If however reflection can arrive at at radical awareness of contingency and seize hold of its own relation to a prereflective life which is its constant and ultimate source, and if it makes of that time which prevents it from being complete the very object of its reflection, it can indeed become a kind of absolute knowledge; for then it ceases to be a mere technique in the service of a transcendent Truth and becomes a knowledge of its own limits, so as to understand that beyond time "there is nothing to understand." (PhP, 365; *PP,* 419) This "beyond these there is nothing to understand" is indeed the password of a philosophical discipline which seeks to be ultimate knowledge. Here philosophy is "the movement which leads back without ceasing from knowledge to ignorance, from ignorance to knowledge, and a kind of rest in this movement." (IPP, 5; *EP,* 12)

Contrary therefore to what at first might be thought and to what some critics have said, Merleau-Ponty's project of reflecting on the unreflected as such does not at all constitute a contradiction in terms. It would be a contradiction and an impossible project only for a rationalist philosophy which claims to reduce our being to our knowing, and which therefore seeks to reflect on our unreflected life only so as to transform it into life which is reflected and understood, *presupposing* thereby that there exists an eternal norm which can render all facticity intelligible. For Merleau-Ponty, however, to think perception does not mean to discover in perception a logical and a priori principle which renders it intelligible. To think perception as the unreflected life of consciousness means to recognize that perception is an absolutely fundamental knowledge for which there is no explanation and no justification, other than its own de facto existence. In the last resort, to reflect on the unreflected as such is the program of a philosophy which wants to understand, not what the unreflected or perception is in itself, but rather what exactly reflection itself is, inasmuch as it is reflection only on the basis of a situation which rules

out any intelligible grounding.[8] It is the program not of a phenomenology of the Hegelian sort, which attempts to transform the prereflective life of the mind into an intelligible meaning, but of a philosophy
for which the last word is not the basic intelligibility but the unsurpassable contingency of everything. If, then, the ground of reflection,
as it itself discovers it, is our bodily being in the world which appears
to reflection as a contingent and unmotivated fact, reflection is forced
to recognize that it itself exists and that consequently truth exists
only on the basis of a radical contingency, that the absolute is unthinkable, and that all meaning maintains itself on a ground of non-
meaning.

## 4.  Critical Considerations

The *Phenomenology of Perception* takes up a radical position. It
reminds us that we have access to no truth which does not find its
beginning in our de facto condition, in our own experience, in our
total and blind adhesion to the world; and precisely thereby it upholds
the contingency of all rationality. If, for instance, phenomenology rejects the idea of eternal truths, it is because we have no experience of
them. Thus the primary exigency of Merleau-Ponty's philosophy, at
the time of the *Phenomenology,* is that of the immanence of everything which can be and can be thought to our own experience. In regard to the notion of eternity, for instance, he says, "If we are in fact
destined to make contact with a sort of eternity, it will be at the core
of our experience of time, and not in some non-temporal subject
whose function it is to conceive and posit it." (PhP, 415; *PP*, 475) But
as to the possibility that at the core of our experience of time we might
perhaps make contact with a kind of eternity, that is (for this is what
is in question here), as to the possibility that our experience might
open on to what transcends it and which is absolutely not reducible
to it, Merleau-Ponty has nothing else to say; and this hypothesis is not
followed up in this book, for here all the author's efforts are directed
towards the second expressed alternative, whose impossibility he above
all wants to demonstrate. And Merleau-Ponty does not seem to be
well disposed even in regard to the first alternative—that a transcendence might reveal itself in the immanence of experience—for one
year after the *Phenomenology* in an essay on "The Metaphysical in
Man" he wrote, "I cannot introduce a 'transcendence in immanence'
behind me as Husserl did (as a hypothesis moreover), for I am not

God, and I cannot verify the co-existence of these two attributes in any indubitable experience." (SNS, 96; *SNS,* 169) Merleau-Ponty's refusal in this period to give consideration to the notion of a "transcendence in immanence" is perhaps but the consequence of the fight he feels himself obliged to wage against the excesses of objectivistic and intellectualistic thought, which transforms transcendence into something transcendent to and independent of phenomenal experience. If this is indeed the case, Merleau-Ponty's thought would at this point be negatively conditioned by the intellectualism he is fighting, just as at its origin psychoanalysis, in the formulation of its intuitions, was contaminated by the materialism it sought to overcome. In the *Phenomenology of Perception* one meets at the very heart of the analyses certain questions, which nonetheless remain dormant in this book and which Merleau-Ponty will be forced to take into consideration later on.

It is in fact interesting to note that in 1946, on the occasion of a meeting of the Société française de philosophie where Merleau-Ponty presented and defended the main theses of the *Phenomenology* ("The Primacy of Perception and Its Philosophical Consequences"), he had to defend himself against the accusation leveled by many discussants that by rooting the *Cogito* in perception he had thereby made rationality and all intellectual certainty impossible; and he had to show that even if there is no absolute, truth is still possible. Only one questioner, Jean Beaufret, saw things in a totally different light. The latter stated that in his opinion nothing was less pernicious than the *Phenomenology,* and that the only reproach he could make to the author was not that he had gone "too far" but rather that he had not been radical *enough;* for the really important question, as he said, is to know if a fully realized phenomenology does not call for an abandonment of the vocabulary of subjective idealism which is still present in the *Phenomenology.* It would appear that Beaufret meant that phenomenology must break out of the framework of a philosophy of consciousness, something, precisely, which Merleau-Ponty had not yet succeeded in doing. If this represents his meaning accurately, his remarks are extremely striking in retrospect, for it was precisely this criticism which Merleau-Ponty directed to himself in a working note concerning the *Phenomenology of Perception.* (VI, 200; *VI,* 253)

In this context, as concerns the limitations of the *Phenomenology of Perception* as an instance of a philosophy of consciousness, we should also note that the immanentist demand of Merleau-Ponty's

phenomenology—the refusal to recognize a "transcendence in immanence," the thesis which postulates that everything which can be and
can be thought must have its intelligible ground in our actual experience—goes hand in hand with the author's inability at this time to
see any real meaning in the notion of the *unconscious.* For the psychoanalyst the unconscious is that which could never, under any circumstances, be present to our consciousness as such and which is
immanent to conscious experience only by remaining irremediably
transcendent to it. For Merleau-Ponty in the *Phenomenology,* however,
the unconscious is not this wholly unfathomable realm of our being
but is in the last analysis reducible to the perceptual and prereflective life itself. Finally, the unconscious is the tacit *Cogito,* bodily
being in the world; it is thus not something beneath experience but
is this experience itself inasmuch as it is an indirect, ambivalent, and
ambiguous self-consciousness.[9] Although Merleau-Ponty's thought in
this regard is much more nuanced than Sartre's, for which the notion
of the unconscious is quite simply philosophical non-sense, it nonetheless betrays a philosophical motivation which is more or less similar
to Sartre's and which has to do with the demands of a philosophy of
consciousness. In his attempt to "form a new idea of reason" by taking account of the "experience of unreason" (SNS, 3; *SNS,* 8), Merleau-
Ponty goes much farther in the *Phenomenology of Perception* than
Sartre; but this attempt is not without its limits, and for it the notion
of the unconscious as such, as a kind of transcendence in immanence,
remains inconceivable. For phenomenology in general, which began
as a philosophy of consciousness, the notion of the unconscious is
indeed a veritable stumbling block. Merleau-Ponty's phenomenology
will be unable to conceive of the unconscious precisely as an *unconsciousness* until it radically deepens itself in such a way as to descend
into its own "basement."

The philosophical consciousness to which the *Phenomenology
of Perception* gives expression is in the last resort a kind of unhappy
consciousness. Radical reflection is the becoming-aware of the unreflected and unreflectable ground of reflection. Through reflection the
subject comes to a knowledge of self; the subject of life seizes hold
of himself as temporality, for life is time, and the consciousness of
self is the consciousness of time. Consciousness rediscovers itself as
given to itself; it becomes conscious of the fact that its origin is not
within itself and of how its own being escapes from it. The reflective

consciousness of life is thus the consciousness of a failure to hold onto life, for time never possesses itself but always flees from itself between two imperceptible horizons. The reflective consciousness of life is thus the consciousness of a failure on the part of the consciousness of life; it is, as Hegel said, the consciousness of the unhappiness of life; it is an unhappy consciousness. The desire for a total manifestation is destined to failure, for there exists no truth or intelligibility-in-itself to be revealed; there is only an opaque and contingent fact—the unmotivated presence of the subject to the world, the irrational source of all rationality—to be noted. Thus the consciousness which discovers at work within it a "presumption on reason's part" is, according to Hegel's expression, "the consciousness of its own contradiction."[10] "Today a humanism," Merleau-Ponty writes, "...begins by becoming aware of contingency. It is the continued confirmation of an astonishing junction between fact and meaning...It is the methodical refusal of explanations, because they destroy the mixture we are made of and make us incomprehensible to ourselves." (S, 241; *S,* 315)

Merleau-Ponty is perhaps right in wanting to oppose all systematic and objectivist metaphysics which attempt to *explain* the situation man finds himself in by linking it up with certain eternal a priori. The origin of rationality, that is, the ground of the possibility of perceptual and intellectual meaning, is to be found in the primitive fact, itself without grounding, that man is "thrown" into the world and that the world appears to him as though by miracle; the only reason for there being meaning is that man exists in point of fact, and thus there can be no explanation for this fact since it is presupposed by all explanations. Rationalist explanations thus amount to no more than a "retrospective illusion." Objectivistic metaphysics would like to transform the *mystery* of our existence into a *problem,* that is, a difficulty "which could be solved cheaply through the use of a few metaphysical entities constructed for this purpose." (PriP, 10; *Inédit,* 108)[11]

For Merleau-Ponty, on the contrary, philosophy can only be a perpetual astonishment; it is the awareness of the fundamentally and insurpassably mysterious character of existence. However, to refuse to problematize the mystery is not for all that to make it more understandable as a mystery. Merleau-Ponty's analysis in the *Phenomenology* bypasses, in fact, the issue; it teaches a "bad ambiguity." It has succeeded in bringing out the "mysterious" and "miraculous" character of our existence (qua signifying existence), and it has detected at the heart of our experience a "presumption on reason's part," a "teleology of consciousness," or, to put it another way, the desire for a total manifestation; but it has failed to clarify what that signifies. Can it be a merely contingent fact without positive meaning that we are, in spite of everything, animated by the desire to "render visible" (as Klee says); does that not mean more than what the *Phenomenology* allows for? If we experience the desire, the need, as the linguists say, to speak, to make manifest, to reveal and to be revealed to ourselves, must that not be because we have in some way or other already comprehended and are already com-prehended (included) in that which is to be revealed? If what we desire is a manifestation, must that not be because there is something in us which wants to manifest itself? If such were the case, it would be necessary to grasp that which in us "wishes, speaks, and finally thinks." (VI, 176; *VI*, 230) Truth to tell, the notion of the radical and unsurpassable contingency of everything is a rather unsatisfying response, above all on the part of a philosophy which seeks to be a form of ultimate knowledge or interrogation. The great discoveries of the *Phenomenology of Perception* are basically of a very indeterminate and imprecise sort, and the definitive meaning of this work remains in suspense.

It is thus time to see how *The Visible and the Invisible* "takes up again, deepens, and rectifies" (VI, 168; *VI*, 222) the *Phenomenology*.


## II.   From Phenomenology to Ontology

THIS attempt to take up again, deepen, and rectify his phenomenology is what Merleau-Ponty calls *ontology*. We know of it only through *The Visible and the Invisible* and a few other writings, notably "Eye and Mind" and the preface to *Signs*, all of which were written in the last years of the philosopher's life. This is to say, therefore, that we have a rather poor knowledge of it. The preface to *Signs* is an announcement and an indication of it rather than an exposition of it. "Eye and Mind," the last writing published in the author's lifetime, is the first work which presents the new orientation in depth, but it is also an extremely dense and enigmatic work whose meaning we can grasp only through an effort of interpretation and decipherment. It is *The Visible and the Invisible* which furnishes us with the necessary guides for this decipherment, but the meaning of this latter work is itself profoundly indeterminate. Indeed, although *The Visible and the Invisible* was intended to be the realization and systematic presentation of Merleau-Ponty's new orientation and would no doubt have been a work of sizable proportions, it is itself, because of the author's untimely death, an unfinished manuscript. Of what the work was supposed to be there are only four chapters, which in all likelihood were meant as a kind of introduction, and a certain number of working notes, which are for the most part very obscure and difficult to understand. Apparently, therefore, in its unfinished state *The Visible and the Invisible* is but the introduction to a thought which does not exist. But things are not quite that simple, or that unfortunate. Everything said in the hundred and fifty pages or so of the manuscript and in the working notes accompanying it is not only an *introduction* to Merleau-Ponty's last thought. Rather, these pages represent Merleau-Ponty's thought itself as it is beginning to make itself explicit, such that the whole thought is germinally present in the manuscript. If therefore we can interpret and unfold its latent meaning, it can tell us everything.

What makes for the "newness" of *The Visible and the Invisible* is that it reveals the conviction Merleau-Ponty had arrived at of the "necessity of a return to ontology." (VI, 165; *VI, 219*)[12] It is fully apparent that here Merleau-Ponty wants to "recommence everything" (VI, 130; *VI, 173*), that he wants to return to the notions of subject and object, intersubjectivity, and Nature (VI, 165; *VI, 219*) and treat them in a much more radical way than did the *Phenomenology of Perception.* We must thus not allow ourselves to be mistaken. *The Visible and the Invisible* is not merely a continuation of the *Phenomenology* and the author's other writings, but is rather a radical *calling into question* of them. Since absolutely everything has changed in this last work, under no circumstances could one simply juxtapose *The Visible and the Invisible* and the *Phenomenology* and interpret the one in terms of the other. It must on the contrary be recognized that *The Visible and the Invisible* takes up a position on a much *deeper level* than the *Phenomenology* and constitutes a wholly new starting point. But precisely because *The Visible and the Invisible* and the *Phenomenology* cannot be placed side by side and be compared, so to speak, in a linear fashion, it must also be recognized that *The Visible and the Invisible* appears as a *total taking up again* of the

*Phenomenology,* transposing it in its entirety into a wholly other field where alone the theses of this first important book receive their true and ultimate significance. This is why, on a first reading of *The Visible and the Invisible,* one might think that nothing in this philosophy has changed; it is precisely because it has "shifted" in its entirety that one does not notice the shifting which has in fact occurred. As Sartre observes, "in one sense nothing has changed in the ideas he defended in his thesis; in another sense everything is unrecognizable; he has plunged into the night of non-knowledge in search for what he now calls the 'fundamental.'"[13]

In the two preceding chapters we assisted at the working out of Merleau-Ponty's thought so as to see how, in regard to painting and language and starting from a phenomenology of the act of self-expression, it finally ends up in an ontology of expression. It only remains now to make this ontology itself the theme of our inquiry so as to see how and in what regard it is a "fundamental thought." (VI, 183; *VI,* 237) Thus in the following section we shall analyze the discovery—that of the *flesh*—which furnishes Merleau-Ponty's phenomenology with the means of becoming an ontology; and in the second section we shall inquire into the very structure, or, if one prefers, the method, of this ontology, this philosophy of the flesh. Along the way it will become evident that "flesh" is nothing other than Being, and the philosophy of the flesh, a thought about Being. We shall however put off to the following and final chapter a detailed discussion of the notion of Being in Merleau-Ponty; there, on the basis of all the available texts, we shall attempt to form an idea of the guiding themes of his nascent ontology.

## 1.  The Flesh

The notion of the flesh is the key notion in Merleau-Ponty's ontology, without which this ontology would not even be. His ontology is, as he says, a philosophy of "brute being," and brute being is the flesh. With his discovery of the flesh Merleau-Ponty gives a decisive significance to the problem of the relations between the subjective and the objective which is, as we have noted, the problem which is central to all his work. Let us therefore briefly recall the development of this problem.

In *The Structure of Behavior,* which set itself the goal of clarifying the relations between consciousness and nature, Merleau-Ponty arrived at the conclusion that a meaningful nature exists only for a perceiving subject, a subject which actively participates in the spectacle it perceives. At the end of our reading of this first book and in anticipation of the reading to follow we asked the following questions: In order for the spectacle to appear meaningful to the perceiving subject is it not necessary for the subject to be an integral part of the spectacle? Is it not necessary that in the last resort he should be something like the "other side" of Nature, its lining, and, as it were, a fold in Nature itself?

The *Phenomenology of Perception* did not go so far as to say that. But with his notion of being in the world, conceived of as *circularity,* Merleau-Ponty did, in that book, radically dialecticize the notions of subject and object. The subject and the world, he said, have no existence in themselves, independent of one another, but rather constitute one single *system* and are *correlates* of each other. The world is the field of existence, and existence is being in the world, a project of the world. "The world is inseparable from the subject," he wrote, "but from a subject which is nothing but a project of the world, and the subject is inseparable from the world, but from a world which it projects itself. The subject is a being-in-the-world and the world remains 'subjective' since its texture and articulation are traced out by the subject's movement of transcendence." (PhP, 430; *PP,* 491)

Although in his analyses Merleau-Ponty was led to touch on the question of the *natural world* or *natural being,* which he recognized as a kind of underside of the phenomenological world, as a kind of pre-world on which rests the perceived world qua correlate of existence, he did not pursue this question and did not attempt to unravel its implications, but returned rather to phenomenology's basic requirement, the notion of *intentionality,* by maintaining that the only world which pre-exists is the phenomenological world, being in the world, the intentional relation perceiving subject–perceived world.[14] He thus posited our bodily communication as a brute fact without any intelligible foundation. All that reflection can do, he insisted, is note the contingency of this fact and recognize in it "the primary embodiment of rationality" without looking any farther, because, as he said, beyond this fact there is nothing to understand. Phenomenology has no other mission than "to reveal the mystery of the world and of reason" (PhP, XXI; *PP,* XVI) and the mystery of their original presence: it is the courageous and constant acknowledgment of the radical and unsurpassable contingency of existence and of truth. It is precisely in this way, however, that phenomenology, believing itself capable of resting on itself or providing its own foundation (PhP, XX; *PP*, XVI), does not live up to its own mission, which is to be "a phenomenology of origins." (PhP, XVIII; *PP*, XIII) For the attempt to make of the subject a relation to the world and of the world a relation to the subject runs the risk of ending up in a confused philosophical relativism which can account neither for the origin nor the being of this dialectical relation itself. In the last analysis, the theory of intentionality illuminates everything except the very being of the intentional relation. The world exists for the subject and the subject exists for the world, but why do they exist for each other? After or at the limit of an intentional analysis there remains one last question, but one which is inescapable for any philosophy which wants to be a radical philosophy. It is a metaphysical question; it is the question which asks why the world is "there" for the subject; it is the question as to the *possibility* of intentionality, of *presence*, of self-evidence, of rationality.

It is in his essay "The Philosopher and His Shadow," which appeared in 1959, that Merleau-Ponty gives us a glimpse for the first time of the unsettling development which had occurred in his thought after the *Phenomenology of Perception.* In this essay he attempts to bring to light the implications of Husserl's late thought and to think his "unthought thought" [*impensé*], but the essay is no doubt more interesting for what it tells us about Merleau-Ponty's own late thought. For here, indeed, he recognizes the need to ground phenomenological relativism. "Does the descent into the realm of our 'archeology',"
he asks, "leave our analytical tools intact? Does it make no changes at all in our conception of noesis, noema, and intentionality—in our ontology? After we have made this descent, are we still entitled to seek in an analytics of acts [i.e., in an intentional analysis] *what in the last resort upholds our own and the world's life?*" (S, 165; *S,* 208; emphasis ours) Merleau-Ponty thus recognizes that the subject-world relation is a derived relation, that the subject's *being* in the world and the world's *existence* for the subject are upheld by something which encompasses them. Between the subject and the world is *that which* makes their relation, their complementarity and their opposition, possible and which thus cannot be reduced to this de facto relation. "It is," he says, "into this in-between [*entre-deux*] that we must try to advance." (S, 166; *S,* 209)[15]

The phenomenon to which this renewed investigation addresses itself is the natural reflexivity of the lived body, which already occupied the author's attention in the *Phenomenology*. When one hand touches the other which is itself in the process of touching an object, the body effects a reflection on itself and reveals itself to be a two-sided being; it is at once both subject and object, it is a "sensing thing." But whereas in the *Phenomenology* the analysis of the natural reflexivity of the body served only to demonstrate the circularity which exists in the body itself and the fact that the body and the world exist in a dialectical relationship, here Merleau-Ponty goes much further with his analysis and says that it requires us to consider anew the thing and the world and "that it results in an ontological rehabilitation of the sensible." (S, 166–7; *S*, 210) For if the distinction between subject and object is blurred in the body, which is a sensible, it is also blurred throughout all of the sensible, such that the sensible is no longer only things but also the subject which perceives them. Things, he says, "reflect my own incarnation and are its counterpart." (S, 167; *S*, 211) The subject and things are articulations of a single and common—and here Merleau-Ponty introduces the guiding notion of his late thought—*flesh*. "Here we have," he insists, "a type of being, a universe with its unparalleled 'subject' and 'object'". Indeed, these two "relativities," the subject and the object, are what they are only in regard to an "irrelative." (S, 167; *S*, 211) They are both included in one and the same "universe" and are the articulation and definition of an "inexhaustible richness" (S, 167; *S*, 212); both stem from a "brute being" (S, 172; *S*, 217) which inwardly upholds them and renders them *present* to each other. Thus, he says, if we want to understand the intentional relation and see it in its true light, we have no other option but "to interrogate this layer of the sensible or to become accustomed to its enigmas." (S, 168; *S*, 212)

In this essay, which is surprising by reason of its own inexhaustible richness, Merleau-Ponty touches on another notion which plays a prime role in his last thought and which must be linked up with the notion of the flesh—the notion of the *Earth*. The Earth—he spells it with a capital—is the "soil" or "stem" of our thought and our life; it is our "homeland" (*patrie*), the "matrix" of time and space. (S, 180; *S*, 227) Although Merleau-Ponty says no more, he lets us understand that the Earth is the original milieu in which man lives and in which he encounters things. The Earth, it seems, is that pre-world on which is based the phenomenological world, the object of our existential projects; that is, it is the invisible soil or ground which upholds the subject-world relation and which makes it possible. Since in Merleau-Ponty the notion of the Earth is intimately linked up with those of the flesh and of Nature, which are the focal points of his ontology, we shall return to this subject in the following chapter.

In "Eye and Mind," written the following year in 1960, Merleau-Ponty returns to this notion of the flesh and discovers in it the means of resolving the question as to the source or foundation of painting which he had already attempted to clarify, as we have seen, in "Indirect Language and the Voices of Silence." There is, however, between these two essays—separated by eight years of reflection and meditation—an enormous difference. In the former Merleau-Ponty made perception, bodily existence, the foundation of the act of painting, the source of the pictorial universal. All painters of all times, he said, are devoted to the same task, because their art stems from nothing other than perceptual life itself. Thus in this essay, as in the *Phenomenology,* Merleau-Ponty took perception (bodily being in the world) to be a brute and absolutely fundamental fact.[16] In "Eye and Mind," on the contrary, he succeeds in raising the question he had formerly left in suspense: What is perception itself? Or again: How is vision possible? The question which he treats here is basically, Why therefore is there visibility, how is it possible?

If there is vision and the visible—if there is visibility—it is, Merleau-Ponty says, because the seeing subject and the seen thing are "total parts of the same Being." (PriP, 162; *OE,* 17) There is vision when a certain visible thing called the body turns back on itself and becomes visible for itself. Precisely because the seeing body "is a thing among things, is one of them,...is caught in the fabric of the world" (PriP, 163; *OE,* 19), it must be said that in the body it is the visible itself which begins to see. Thus the seeing body and the seen thing are not only complementary to each other but are partners which, being "made of the same stuff" (PriP, 164; *OE,* 21), share the same *flesh.* Basically they are but differentiations of the same fabric, the same primordial Being.

If, however, "Eye and Mind" remains enigmatic and allusive and its meaning difficult to capture, *The Visible and the Invisible* provides us with the indispensable clarifications. This book would indeed have been, like the *Phenomenology of Perception,* a work of a systematic sort wherein the author would have worked out and presented the guiding ideas of his new ontology. Owing however to its incompletion, the manuscript contains only one chapter, "The Intertwining—The Chiasm," which sets out his thought in a positive way. Let us therefore attempt to disengage the fundamental intuition which takes shape here.

Merleau-Ponty begins his analysis with a massive rejection of the entire "bric-à-brac" (VI, 235, 253, 270; *VI,* 289, 307, 324) of objectivistic thought. Notions such as "acts of consciousness," "states of consciousness," "matter," "form," and "image" are all to be abandoned. *Even* the notion of "perception" is to be excluded, he says, to the degree that it presupposes an opposition and a separation between him who perceives and that which is perceived (VI, 158; *VI,* 209) and thus prejudges an experience which must be interrogated anew without philosophical preconceptions. Merleau-Ponty thus wants to "take up everything again" and forge new notions in contact with an experience which has not yet been "worked on." For him it is the experience which is still silent which must be brought to the pure expression of its own meaning.

Why, he asks at the start of his analysis, does the visible, that thing I see, seem to rest *in itself* at the same time that it appears *for me?* Why, being wholly present to me, does it appear dense and deep and more than the mere superficial correlate of my gaze? And how does my gaze know how to do just what it has to for the thing to reveal itself to it such as it is in itself? What is "this inspired exegesis"? (VI, 133; *VI,* 175) We might be able to discover the answer, he says, if we consider the case where the interrogator and the interrogated are closer to each other—touching. In order for my hand to tell me something about the texture of the thing, there must exist between the two "some relationship by principle, some kinship." (VI, 133; *VI,* 176) Indeed my hand could never sense anything were it not itself a sensible, so as to be able to be impressed by things. Thus if my hand is able to touch, it is because it is itself tangible at the same time that it is sensed from the inside, because it is a thing among things, because it "opens finally upon a tangible being of which it is also a part." (VI, 133; *VI,* 176) It cannot be otherwise with vision. If I can see it is because I have a body, that is, because I exist in the world among things, because I am precisely a certain carnal *here* around which things arrange themselves in depth. The seeing subject cannot be foreign to what he sees. I would never be able to see, indeed, were I not myself *visible*, were I not visible "from without, such as another would see me, installed in the midst of the visible, occupied in considering it from a certain spot." (VI, 134; *VI,* 177) Hence there is a certain "identity of the seer and the visible," and it must be noted "that he who sees cannot possess the visible unless he is possessed by it, unless he *is of it.*" (VI, 134–5; *VI,* 177) This "is of it" is one of the later Merleau-Ponty's favorite expressions, because it expresses not only a correspondence between the subject and the object but also their essential belonging to one another—the fact that the subject who sees things is himself included among them and is one of them, the fact that the seeing body and visible things are of the same *flesh.* It is precisely this "thickness of flesh" (VI, 135; *VI,* 178) between them which makes it be that he who sees things is alongside them and yet does not merge with them and does not exhaust them. The proximity and the distance between the seer and the seen stems from the fact— Merleau-Ponty is now able to answer the question he had raised at the beginning of his analysis—that they are differentiations of a single fabric, such that while not at all coinciding they are still included in the same generality, the same phenomenon of visibility. This flesh which is common to them is what constitutes the visibility of the thing as well as the corporeality of the seeing subject.

Thus that body by which I am in the world is itself a part of the world, a bit of its flesh; but as such it is "a very remarkable variant" (VI, 136; *VI,* 179), for it is that sensible mass which is sensible for itself; it is an exemplary sensible, a carnal being with two dimensions which but concretizes the spread-out visibility of the visible; the body is a sensing-sensible. We are confronted here with a paradox, although one which, Merleau-Ponty insists, does not pertain to man but to Being itself. (VI, 136; *VI,* 180) Hence he maintains, "because it is evident," that the body is "a being of two leaves, from one side a thing among things and otherwise what sees them and touches them." (VI, 137; *VI,* 180) To speak of two leaves is not however quite correct, as he goes on to say, because it is at *one and the same time* that the body belongs to the order of the "object" and to that of the "subject."

If therefore this is the way things are, it cannot, he insists, be because of a mere "incomprehensible accident." (VI, 137; *VI,* 181) This is not, in other words, a reasonless and groundless fact, a merely *contingent* fact. The flesh "is not contingency." (VI, 146; *VI,* 192) If this is the way things are with the sensing and the sensible, the body and the world, if they are the front side and the back side, the inside and the outside of each other,[17] it is because they call for one another, because each "is an archetype for the other" (VI, 137; *VI*, 181), because they are "total parts" of a single Whole and are like the results of a "segregation" (VI, 136; *VI*, 179) of a single reality, a single "in-itself Sensible." This reality which includes everything else, this, as we might say, sub-phenomenal reality, is, as we now know, what Merleau-Ponty calls the flesh.

After presenting this description of the experience of touching and seeing and after drawing the immediate implications it suggests (on the condition that one has first of all abandoned philosophical prejudices and, above all, the notions of the in itself and the for itself), Merleau-Ponty says that "We have to ask ourselves what exactly we have found with this strange adhesion of the seer and the visible." (VI, 138; *VI*, 183) What Merleau-Ponty has found is, in short, this: the seer and the visible, the bodily subject and the perceived world, are not only references to each other, two dialectical entities, but are the differentiations of *the same* fabric; they are made out of the same material. We should therefore not merely say—along with intentional analysis—that subject and object do not exist independent of each other, that they exist always together and but reflect themselves; for if they exist together and are correlative, this can only be because they are both derivative expressions of a more profound reality which binds them together and which guarantees their cohesion as well as their (relative) opposition. The seer and the visible are the two poles of an in-itself Visible, a Tangible, which properly belongs neither to the body nor to the world as de facto entities. (VI, 139; *VI*, 183) Between the seer and the visible there exists a relation, an "in-between," which is more real than either one, "as upon two mirrors facing one another where two indefinite series of images set in one another arise which belong really to neither of the two surfaces, since each is only the rejoinder of the other, and which therefore form a couple, a couple more real than either of them." (VI, 139; *VI*, 183) There is, as Merleau-Ponty observes, "a fundamental narcissism of all vision"; the visible turns back on itself, is "seduced, captivated, alienated" by itself and *sees itself*. The seeing body sees itself as a seeing-visible, "so that the seer and the visible reciprocate one another and we no longer know which sees and which is seen." This narcissism is thus that of a Visibility or an in-itself Vision, of a Being which is at once both vision and visible. It is the same narcissism that one finds in the painter when he paints himself in the act of painting, seeming to imply thereby that there exists a total or absolute Vision (PriP, 169; *OE,* 34) from which nothing escapes, which comprehends everything, both things and the painter himself. This general Visibility or Sensible is what Merleau-Ponty has called the flesh, and he says that "one knows there is no name in traditional philosophy to designate that." (VI, 139; *VI,* 183)

Indeed, for Merleau-Ponty the flesh is not *matter* nor is it *spirit.* Neither is it nature which is immanent to the spirit nor the spirit present in nature. All of the categories of traditional metaphysics are powerless to describe it, because the flesh is in no wise a *substance,* whether material or spiritual. The flesh is not substance, οὐσία, unless the Greek term οὐσία be rethought not as "substance" but, as Heidegger does for instance, as Presence. Even orthodox phenomenology—it might be added—is unable to think the flesh, because the flesh is neither a noesis nor a noema. It is more immanent to the subject than any noesis and more transcendent than any noema; it is in fact the common source of all noeses and all noemas, the source of the intentional relation itself which precisely for this reason eludes all eidetic intuition. In order to designate this, so to speak, sub-phenomenal reality of the flesh, Merleau-Ponty returns to Greek thought and takes up the old term *"element."*

The flesh is an "element" like the water, air, earth, or fire of which the first Greek philosophers spoke and which for them were not things themselves but ῥιζώματα, the roots of all things. As an "element" the flesh is that which enters into the composition of everything and makes it be that everything is what it is; it thus appears in everything but, for this very reason, never appears in person. The flesh is not any particular, individual thing but a *general thing,* the essence or the style of all things, of all beings. The flesh is like a kind of "incarnate principle"; it does not exist in the here and now but is rather the possibility of all wheres and whens. In short, it is not a fact but the *facticity* of all facts, "what makes the fact be a fact." (VI, 140; *VI,* 184) In a word, the flesh is the *elementary.* And since the flesh is what makes the fact be a fact and the precise fact it is, it is also at the same time what makes there be *meaning.* We thus see why Merleau-Ponty calls the flesh "brute being" and "wild logos." The flesh is precisely the original presence of all beings which are present to us, that which makes there be depth, configurations, and meaning.

The flesh, Merleau-Ponty says, is "the formative medium of the object and the subject." (VI, 147; *VI*, 193) It is our medium and our element just as water is the element of fish. Water, for a fish, is an in-depth universe in which it lives and which allows it to encounter and be present to all other marine beings, but which, precisely because water is for the fish the possibility of all presence, is not itself some-thing which is present. Being the medium of its life, water is what the fish never sees; it is for the fish something which is everywhere and no-where. Similarly, the flesh is that element which unites us to things and which makes it be that the sentient body and the sensed thing are compatible within the same universe; the flesh is the latency and the depth and the possibility of all presence and, for this reason, is never itself present, never itself visible. We can thus see that the flesh is, as Merleau-Ponty says, a "prototype of Being," that it is in fact Being itself: the originating, the elementary, the matrix of all that exists, "a unique Space which separates and reunites, which sustains every co-hesion". (PriP, 187; *OE*, 84) The flesh is Being qua Opening. Under the concept of flesh, therefore, Merleau-Ponty is thinking Being. If he speaks of the "flesh," it is to emphasize the fact that in the very depths of our being, at the roots of our being, we are entirely mixed in with Being; we are gathered up with things into a fabric of Being which is quite literally our own flesh.

Having characterized the flesh as an "element," Merleau-Ponty says, "Such are the extravagant consequences to which we are led when we take seriously, when we question, vision." (VI, 140; *VI*, 184) In this chapter he has only begun to sort out the "scraps of this ontology of the visible" and has only caught "sight of this strange domain to which interrogation, properly so-called, gives access." (VI, 140; *VI*, 185) This domain, however, is unlimited, he says; the flesh is an "ultimate notion" in whose light everything must be under-stood anew. Merleau-Ponty was not of course able to spell out this new ontology of the visible; but here, in this introductory chapter, he touches on two other questions of interest to us: that of *intersub-jectivity* and that of *thought*.

Once one has gotten rid of all the conceptual bric-à-brac of a thought turned in upon itself and, in particular, the opposition between consciousness and objects, the way is open to conceiving intersubjec-tivity anew as being originally an *intercorporeality*. Indeed, if that original consciousness, sensation, is born by segregation, fission, and a return of the Sensible upon itself,[18] why should this miracle—this narcissism of the flesh—not occur in pieces of flesh other than my own? At the level of corporeality there is no "problem of the *alter ego* because it is not *I* who sees, not *he* who sees" (VI, 142; *VI*, 187); there is here only a Sensible in general which sees itself. For Merleau-Ponty, sensing, like Heidegger's Dasein, does not signify a *"me voilà,"* but, as Heidegger says, a being-the-there *(être le-là);*[19] and the there is precisely an opening, a fission, an explosion of Being, of the flesh, such that there is a "vision in general," an "anonymous visibility" (VI, 142; *VI*, 187) which inhabits the other and myself, such that "he and I are like organs of one single intercorporeality." (S, 168; *S,* 213) The self and the other are but two dimensions in "primordial being which comprises them all." (S, 170; *S*, 215)

As Merleau-Ponty recognizes, it is another problem to understand how the carnal subject, the sensing-sensible, can also be a *thinking* subject. He does not however propose in this chapter to elucidate the structure peculiar to thought in the intellectual sense of the term. Here he has his regard trained on a more fundamental question, that precisely of the foundation of thought and of its own possibility. Now the fact which must serve as a basis in all inquiries into the being of thought is that "every thought known to us occurs to a flesh." (VI, 146; *VI*, 191) It is inasmuch as we are carnal subjects that we are also thinking subjects, and if therefore we think it can only be because thought is *one of the possibilities of our being* qua carnal beings. This is to say that thought must be included as a possibility in our carnal relation to the world: "it must be made to appear directly in the infra-structure of vision." (VI, 145; *VI*, 191) The "seeds" of thought properly so-called are already present in sensation. Thought is the self-realization and the self-expression of the flesh, of Being. By a process of sublimation and investment the flesh comes to realize itself in thought. Sensation is itself an originating and not yet thematized consciousness which Merleau-Ponty refers to with the term "there is" *(il y a).* Properly speaking, thought is on the contrary what he calls an "it appears to me that." (VI, 145; *VI*, 190) It would appear that the "there is" signifies the first *apparition* of something, its presence, the emergence of a configuration, a meaning. The "it appears to me that" would then be a consciousness which is not only the mere apprehension or the mere presence of the carnal subject to the world, but the reflective grasp of this "there is," of this original presence; it would be thematized reflection, the thought of seeing and sensing.

We have seen in the *Phenomenology of Perception* how Merleau-Ponty in the last analysis upholds the "conscious" character of bodily life. If consciousness were not already present in one way or in another in the prereflective existence of the incarnate subject, consciousness could never exist at the personal level, because, as he said, a "thing" can never begin to think. This beginning consciousness is what he called the "tacit *cogito.*" For him it was a primitive self-consciousness strictly simultaneous with the consciousness of the world. At the level of the tacit *Cogito* the subject possesses himself only because he has a world, and the world exists for him because he is not hidden from himself. Thus in the perspective of the *Phenomenology* the subject at his most basic level is already a consciousness of himself and is defined by his (dialectical) opposition to the world. The last word, for this form of thought, must obviously be contingency, because what we have here is a fundamental and irreducible (although always dialectical) bifurcation of consciousness and the world. The important thing, therefore, is to recognize that the originating consciousness, the "there is," which Merleau-Ponty speaks of here in *The Visible and the Invisible* is no longer the tacit *Cogito* of the *Phenomenology.*[20]

The "there is," orginating apprehension or apparition, must be understood—and here we are touching on the most important point—not in an "existential" or anthropological sense, as the description of a power that man has as a knowing subject; the "there is," sensation, must on the contrary be thought of as an ontological function, as an "attribute" of Being. The sensing-sensible chiasm which constitutes sensible consciousness is a paradox, Merleau-Ponty says, not of man but of Being. The "there is" thus belongs to Being, to the flesh, and not to man. The essence of man as sensible consciousness is precisely to be the "there is" of Being. It is not to man that Presence, sensible consciousness, belongs; it is, on the contrary, Presence which possesses man.

These are but the inescapable conclusions of the notion of the flesh such as Merleau-Ponty has defined it. There is vision, he said, when a particular sensible turns back on itself and becomes visible for itself. Vision and, in general, sensation have to do with "the fundamental fission or segregation of the sentient and the sensible" (VI, 143; VI, 188), with "the dehiscence of the sensible." (VI, 145; VI, 190) This original form of thought which is sensation stems from the "reversibility" of the flesh; it springs up at the moment when the flesh differentiates itself into sentient and sensible and there is established between the two a Presence, a "there is," which is the work of neither one of them but rather makes them be what they are and is their Being.

Thus the "there is," sensation, is a first configuration or articulation of the flesh and, as such, the apparition of meaning. This structured, articulated presence is precisely what Merleau-Ponty calls "natural light." We are required to think of the reversibility of the flesh as an (ontological) process of illumination *(Lichtung)* when, as Merleau-Ponty demands, we no longer define sensation in terms of "consciousness" but on the contrary "understand it as the return of the visible upon itself, a carnal adherence of the sentient to the sensed and of the sensed to the sentient. For, as overlapping and fission, identity and difference, it brings to birth a ray of natural light that illuminates all flesh and not only my own." (VI, 142; *VI,* 187) Hence the definition of sensation is to be the light of the flesh or of Being; it is the "there is," the fission, and the articulation, the *Lichtung,* of primordial Being, "the miraculous promotion of Being to 'consciousness,' or (as we prefer to say) the segregation of the 'within' and the 'without'." (VI, 118; *VI,* 157) Thus for Merleau-Ponty the subject as a sensing (or sentient)-sensible is not a mere project of the world but is rather the turning back upon itself of Nature, of the Sensible, and, as such, a *natural* light, the illumination of Being. There is, Merleau-Ponty says, "a relation of the visible with itself that traverses me and constitutes me as a seer". (VI, 140; *VI,* 185) The important thing is to recognize that "this coiling over of the visible upon the visible" which constitutes me as a vision is something which I do not form but "which forms me." I am there when the visible folds back on itself, sets up in itself a "hollow," and secretes an *invisible* which is vision. The subject and the object are what they are, vision and visible, and are co-present only in so far as they are the "total parts" of one and the same Being, one and the same Visibility; it is in the light of Being that subject and object maintain themselves, are present to each other, and reflect one another. It is in this invisible of the visible, in vision, that Being itself comes to manifest its own meaning, and thus the seeing subject is taken up in a thrust of Being which is his own being. To be a sensing-sensible is to be the "there," the "there is," of the flesh, of Being.

When, by another crisscrossing and by the same "reversibility that defines the flesh" (VI, 144; *VI,* 189), the sentient body grasps itself as such and as bound in the flesh to other sentient bodies, then "in the patient and silent labor of desire, begins the paradox of expression." (VI, 144; *VI,* 189) Desire, Hegel said, is desire for the desire of another human consciousness, and it is this desire constituting sensible consciousness which gives birth to "those strange movements of the throat and mouth that form the cry and the voice." (VI, 144; *VI,* 190) It is the desire of self which is at the same time the desire of another that makes the carnal subject seize hold of himself so as to present himself to another desire: it is in this desire that expression is born.[21] In accordance with the "fundamental narcissism of all vision" (VI, 139; *VI,* 183), the seeing subject desires to see himself seeing, and it is in another vision that he must be reflected, as in a mirror. And so in order to seduce, fascinate, and captivate this other vision he produces gestures and sounds which are the sublimation of his own flesh. And just as in the turning back of the visible upon itself there is born an invisible which is vision, so also these higher-order visibles—gestures and sounds—give birth, by working on one another, to a higher-order invisible which is thought, such that "between sound and meaning, speech and what it means to say, there is still the relation of reversibility, and no question of priority, since the exchange of words is exactly the differentiation of which the thought is the integral." (VI, 145; *VI,* 190)

The important thing is to realize that the new field of ideality thereby inaugurated is not a break with the visible and silent world that comprises the seen body but "the accomplishment by other means of the will of the *there is,* by sublimation of the *there is* and realization of an invisible that is exactly the reverse of the visible, the power of the visible." (VI, 145; *VI,* 190) This is the case above all with artistic and musical ideas, "sensible" ideas, what Merleau-Ponty calls "the ideality of the horizon" (VI, 152; *VI,* 200); and this form of ideality has no other mission than to say what the sensible itself wants to say. This is thus an ideality which is not alien to the flesh; it is rather an identity which draws out of the visible world (as well as the seeing subject included in it) "its axes, its depth, its dimensions." (VI, 152; *VI,* 199) Like the little musical phrase Proust speaks of, the idea at this level is the sublimated power of the visible, its invisible lining; it is, Merleau-Ponty says, "its own and interior possibility, the Being of this being." (VI, 151; *VI,* 198)

As to "pure" ideas, "ideas of the intelligence," Merleau-Ponty puts off an examination of their way of establishing themselves over and above sensible ideas to another chapter (which was never written).

However we might understand it, though, Merleau-Ponty emphasizes here that it can only be a question of a "surpassing that does not leave its field of origin." (VI, 153; *VI,* 200) In pure ideality it is, he says, as if the flesh of this world emigrated into another, less heavy and more transparent flesh, that of language. However, between language and "pure" thoughts—even those of mathematics or science—we will rediscover, he insists, the same sort of relation as between the visible and the invisible of the carnal world. Language secretes within itself a meaning which cannot be detached from it at all. In operative, triumphant language, that by which one for the first time arrives at ideas—mathematical algorithms included—ideas are but the invisible "other side" of language; they "are that certain divergence, that never-finished differentiation, that openness ever to be reopened between the sign and the sign, as the flesh is, we said, the dehiscence of the seeing into the visible and the visible into the seeing." (VI, 153; *VI,* 201)

Hence for Merleau-Ponty ideas of the intelligence must still be understood in relation to "the same fundamental phenomenon of reversibility" (VI, 155; *VI,* 203) that is at work in the visible. For him the "ultimate truth" is indeed nothing other than this reversibility, which makes it be that "if we were to make completely explicit the architectonics of the human body, its ontological framework,…we would see that the structure of its mute world is such that all the possibilities of language are already given in it." (VI, 155; *VI,* 203) Merleau-Ponty's thought is here an ontology in the full sense of the term, because for him, as the text we have just quoted clearly shows, the reversibility which is the ultimate truth is nothing other than what one could call a *teleology of the flesh*—thought is at one and the same time a latent possibility of the flesh and its highest realization—and the flesh, as a fundamental matrix, is Being itself. In rediscovering wild being, Merleau-Ponty rediscovers a "teleology of the 'natural light'." (VI, 201; *VI,* 255) With Heidegger he could thus have said that Being is incessantly on the way towards thought, and that thought, for its part, brings to a stand and accomplishes in language this explosion of Being. It is Being which expresses itself in man, and language, Merleau-Ponty says, is the "house of Being," the inscription of Being." When Merleau-Ponty says with Valéry that by reason of this reversibility language "is the voice of no one, since it is the very voice of the things, the waves, and the forests" (VI, 155; *VI,* 204), it is impossible not to think of another philosopher for whom language is the language of

Being as the clouds are the clouds of the sky. It is Being which has the absolute priority and which, in vision, in speech, and in thought, ends by manifesting its own meaning.

If then the carnal subject is the "there is" of the flesh or of Being, its own manifestation, philosophical thought would have no other mission than to think the tie which ties the thinking subject to the flesh, to Being, and in the end to conceive of this tie as Being itself. Philosophical interrogation would be a thinking of Being by thinking its own relation to a teleology of Being, of which it is itself the highest revelation and realization, a teleology of Being in which it is comprehended and of which it is the comprehension. In this way philosophy, as Merleau-Ponty says, would be the expression of an ontogenesis of which it is itself a part.

## 2. Philosophical Interrogation

Merleau-Ponty's philosophy thus shows itself, in the author's last writings, to be an *ontology* in the proper sense of the term, that is, a philosophy of Being. It is no longer merely a philosophy (a phenomenology) of the subject of perception or of the perceived world or of perception as the subject's relation to the world; it is infinitely more than that because it is a philosophy of the Being of being in the world. In the place of phenomenological "relativism," which conceives of the being of the subject as a project of the world and of the being of the world as a correlate to the subject's projects, there springs up an ontology which initiates an interrogation into the very Being of this relativity and which attempts to think the "irrelative" outside of which it has in the last analysis no meaning. Thus instead of merely defining the subject and the world as reciprocal references, Merleau-Ponty now maintains that they imply each other and mutually define each other only because they are both *dimensions* and *differentiations* of a primordial Being which includes them both. Each thing is a dimension, and Being is dimensionality itself. (VI, 227; *VI, 280*) Invoking Heidegger, Merleau-Ponty says that there is "a *universal dimensionality* which is Being". (VI, 265; *VI, 319*) This ultimate dimensionality is what he calls the "flesh," so as to insist on the point that Being is not a *principle* or *reality* transcendent to the phenomenological world but precisely that which is constitutive of our being as well as of the world's being. The subject and the world are of the same flesh, and Being is this flesh itself. Being is the *element* which makes it be that the subject is a subject and the world is a world, and which makes it be that they exist one for the other, one "upright" before the other. In opposition to what he said in the *Phenomenology*, Being, not being in the world, is primary.

In *The Visible and the Invisible* Merleau-Ponty thus realizes a philosophical radicalism which was still lacking in the *Phenomenology*. For if formerly he wanted to reject all metaphysical prejudices and in particular that of a transcendent Reason which would be the cause of the intelligibility of our de facto situation and wanted to describe the apparition of the world for us without presupposing anything, it was nonetheless still by a kind of anti-intellectualist prejudice (which was itself of a properly metaphysical nature) that he characterized the apparition of Being for us as a pure *contingency* and as a *gratuitous* event with no intelligible grounding. That was, obviously, a way of approaching the question which called forth in advance a certain kind of answer. It is on the contrary a new point of departure that *The Visible and the Invisible* takes. The de facto situation that philosophy must clarify is no longer conceived of as the unmotivated presence of the world but as, quite simply, the world's *presence*. The starting point of this "new ontology" (VI, 169; *VI*, 222) is: "there is being, there is a world, there is *something*; in the strong sense in which the Greek speaks of τὸ λέγειν, there is cohesion, there is meaning." (VI, 88; *VI*, 121) What is to be understood is this "there is," this orginating Presence, "that λόγος that pronounces itself silently in each sensible thing". (VI, 208; *VI*, 261) In this way, presence is no longer presupposed by being conceived of as brute and irreducible fact, but becomes itself the starting point of the interrogation. It is Presence that philosophy must think by raising the question, What is the "there is"? (VI, 129; *VI*, 171) A reflection on the "there is" or on the presence of the sentient to the sensible and of the sensible to the sentient, on their belonging to one another, leads one to conceive of them as the differentiations, the articulations (λέγειν) of a single fabric; a reflection on the double polarity of sensation ends up in the notion of the flesh (λόγος).

If however Merleau-Ponty glimpsed the realm to be explored, it remained for him to specify the meaning of the philosophy that must undertake this, as he had done for phenomenology conceived of as an exploration of being in the world.[22] How then can one think the flesh? Merleau-Ponty thus begins *The Visible and the Invisible* with a critique of the kinds of thought unsuitable to the goal he has set himself—a working out of a philosophy of the flesh conceived of as latency, dimensionality—and which are incapable of bringing experience to the pure expression of its own meaning.

The three first chapters of the manuscript contain his criticisms of science, "reflexive" philosophy, the philosophy of Being and Nothingness (Sartre), and phenomenology (Husserl). He criticizes science—with moreover an intensity which might surprise us—because the flesh is not an ob-ject outside of consciouness which could be investigated and manipulated with total impartiality, and because science, according to Merleau-Ponty, is by nature an objectivism and a utilitarianism. He criticizes so-called "reflexive" philosophy because the flesh is not a "condition of possibility," a logical a priori, a "that without which" to be deduced, starting from experience. He criticizes Sartrian ontology because the flesh is not Being in itself, and he who inquires into the flesh is not a Nothingness; he is himself a carnal being, he "is of it." And finally he criticizes Husserlian phenomenology because the flesh is not an "essence" which lends itself to an eidetic vision (it cannot be directly present, "in person," to consciousness); it is not the correlate of a transcendental Ego. Since the manuscript of *The Visible and the Invisible* does not include a positive exposition of the way in which Merleau-Ponty understood his new ontology, it is in this latter framework—the critique of phenomenology—that we will situate our remarks. Besides, our central problem is to know what exactly the relation between phenomenology and ontology is in Merleau-Ponty; it is to know how he effects the passage from the one to the other.

In a working note of July 1959 Merleau-Ponty makes a self-criticism which clearly indicates what the transition in his thought from a phenomenology of perception to an ontology of visibility consists in. Speaking of the *Phenomenology of Perception* he says, "The problems posed in *Ph.P.* are insoluble because I start there from the 'consciousness'—'object' distinction." (VI, 200; *VI*, 253) One could not ask for a more judicious summing up. Merleau-Ponty criticizes himself for having considered as self-evident the subject-object relation as he presented it in the *Phenomenology* and for having merely dialecticized these two notions by making them correlates of one another. The *Phenomenology of Perception* was not radical *enough*, because if it rejected all *dualism* of consciousness and the world, as of mind and body, it nevertheless did not call into question the *duality* of consciousness and nature; on the contrary, it took this duality to be a fundamental fact without asking if it really was. What Merleau-Ponty calls into question here at the time of *The Visible and the Invisible* is thus in the last analysis the very notion of *intentionality,* the intentional relation consciousness-world. It is "intentional analysis" itself and the philosophy of consciousness—classical phenomenology—that he criticizes. "The whole Husserlian analysis is blocked by the framework of *acts* which imposes upon it the philosophy of *consciousness.*" (VI, 244; *VI, 297*)

It would be necessary, he says, to return to that nonthematic, *"fungierende"* or *latent* intentionality that Husserl caught a glimpse of without however having sufficiently explored it, and which he in fact could not have explored without a prior and radical revision of his conception of phenomenology; because the notion of a latent intentionality which operated inside, not of consciousness, but of *Being* "is not compatible with 'phenomenology,' that is, with an ontology that obliges whatever is not nothing to *present* itself to the *consciousness* across *Abschattungen* and as deriving from an originating donation which is an *act,* i.e. one *Erlebnis* among others". (VI, 244; *VI, 298*)

For Merleau-Ponty the descent into the "archeology" of the subject and the meditation on the natural reflexivity of the body, wherein it shows itself to be a being with two sides, a sensing-sensible, a sensing thing, calls for a reworking of one's analytical instruments; this archeological investigation changes "our conception of noesis, noema, and intentionality." (S, 165; *S, 208*) The discovery of the flesh calls for nothing less than a "complete reconstruction of philosophy." (VI, 193; *VI, 246*) Owing to this fact philosophy can no longer be intentional analysis, a description of acts of consciousness, a search for *essences.* The eidetic method does not suffice for two reasons.

In the first place, intentional analysis, such as Husserl presented it, presupposes the existence of an *Ego* or a consciousness which dominates with its regard the spectacle which itself exists only insofar as it presents itself to this consciousness.[23] The subject who sees is not however a κοσμοθεωρός, a pure gaze; he is himself a part of the spectacle, he "is of it." What is needed therefore is neither a philosophy of acts of consciousness nor a philosophy of things "in themselves," such as they would be apart from all contact with consciousness,[24] but a philosophy which conceives of consciousness itself as *Offenheit* (VI, 198; *VI,* 252), as the turning back of the sensible on itself as an expression of the flesh, an openness of Being. What is necessary, Merleau-Ponty says, is to "leave the philosophy of *Erlebnisse* and pass to the philosophy of our *Urstiftung*". (VI, 221; *VI,* 275) For a philosophy which conceives of the subject as the "other side" of nature, as its invisible lining, there can be no question of an intuition of essences, because the subject himself is not and can never be a mere intuition, a wide-eyed gaze, as Heidegger would say. He is the upsurge of Being itself, the place where Being becomes sensible for itself.

Philosophy moreover cannot be an intuition, an eidetic insight, because what is present to consciousness is not "essences." Pure essences do not exist. It is significant, Merleau-Ponty remarks, that Husserl never obtained a single eidetic vision that he did not feel obliged to rework afterwards. "Now would be the time," he says, "to reject the myths of inductivity and of the *Wesenschau,* which are transmitted, as points of honor, from generation to generation." (VI, 115–6; *VI,* 155) The orginating is not the essence; the essence is not the *Sein,* Merleau-Ponty says, but the *Sosein.* (VI, 109–115; *VI,* 148–154) The essence is not Being itself, the possible in itself; it cannot be understood and does not exist except as the result of the dehiscence of Being. Essences, as well as facts moreover, are abstractions. What exists are dimensions, areas of virtuality, styles which are all so many ways by which primordial flesh, "undivided" Being, explodes and articulates itself; essences are only the *articuli* of Being. Referring to Heidegger, Merleau-Ponty says that in each case, rather than an essence, there is a certain *Wesen,* on the condition that one understands this term in a verbal sense. (VI, 115; *VI,* 154) An essence is a certain way in which the flesh of the visible articulates itself or actualizes itself in the seeing-visible relationship.

There are therefore no pure essences, an essence always being the general style of many facts, their way of being *(Wesen),* just as there are no absolutely individual facts, each fact being nothing other than a certain instance wherein the undivided and general flesh of the world concretizes itself. There are "operative essences" or fact-dimensions, which as phenomena refer back to a sub-phenomenal Being and which are its dimensions and differentiations. It must be recognized, Merleau-Ponty says, that "the unique Being, the dimensionality to which these moments, these leaves, and these dimensions belong, is beyond the classical essence and existence and renders their relationship comprehensible." (VI, 117; *VI*, 157) In short therefore, in Merleau-Ponty as in Heidegger, "under the concept of 'essence', philosophy thinks Being."[25]

It is thus a wholly new notion of intentionality, of the subject-object relation, that Merleau-Ponty is aiming at. He wants to explore an "intentionality within being." (VI, 244; *VI*, 298) He wants to make of the subject-object relation a *derived* relation which itself occurs within Being and which therefore can be understood only in relation to Being.[26] Beneath the subject and beneath the object is what makes their relation possible and which is the flesh, Being. Intentional analysis, Merleau-Ponty writes in a working note of January 1960, does not see that the intentional threads with which it attempts to compose the phenomenological field "are emanations and idealizations of one fabric, differentiations of the fabric." (VI, 231; *VI*, 284) What is primary is not the phenomenological world, the subject-world, consciousness-noema correlation; it is the single fabric which comprises them, it is Being. It is thus "a Being in transcendence not reduced to the 'perspectives' of 'consciousness'" (VI, 243; *VI*, 297) that Merleau-Ponty is attempting to think. This project calls for a new philosophy because for classical phenomenology being is conceivable only as that which appears to consciousness. To be is to have a meaning, and, in the end, the meaning of beings refers back to a work of constitution on the part of consciousness, an activity of *Sinngebung.* The Husserlian eidetic vision is a creative intuition which constitutes the object in what it is. For Merleau-Ponty, however, Being is not that which appears to consciousness (or even that which exists for a bodily subject), but is the very Presence in which consciousness or the subject is present to the world (and which therefore is not itself a being which is present). Being is the flesh of which the subject-object relation is the articulation. The classical phenomenological method does not suffice because Being, as the ground of all appearance and the possibility of all perception, is not itself what appears and is perceived.

But if Being does not offer itself to consciousness and cannot be "phenomenologically" described, if it is not a phenomenon or a *"Sache"* to which philosophy can return, how can philosophy seize hold of the meaning of Being? Is Merleau-Ponty obliged to abandon phenomenology? In contrast to his assertion in the *Phenomenology of*

*Perception* that phenomenology "rests on itself or, again, provides its own foundation" (PhP, XX–XXI; *PP,* XVI), he says now that "integral, self-contained, or self-supporting phenomenology remains problematic". (S, 178; *S,* 224)

Heidegger's philosophy, his *Seinsdenken,* is one way in which philosophy can overcome phenomenology, intentional analysis, the description of what appears to consciousness, so as to become a thought of Being as the source of all presence and the possibility of all appearance. Merleau-Ponty was well acquainted with this Heideggerian attempt. It is therefore significant that, even though his conception of Being comes closer and closer to Heidegger's, his conception of philosophy and its method does not cease to take its distances from that of the German philosopher. It seems that Merleau-Ponty had the impression that Heidegger was aiming at Being over and above, so to speak, beings and over and above subjectivity.

This is no doubt why he felt closer after all to Husserl in spite even of the the latter's idealism. If *The Visible and the Invisible* seems in general to be a very severe criticism of Husserlian phenomenology, Merleau-Ponty's essay "The Philosopher and His Shadow," written at the same time, shows quite clearly that this criticism of Husserl and of the manifest content of his doctrine is situated in the larger context of an attempt to remain faithful to Husserl's latent thought, to his "unthought thought," such as Merleau-Ponty discerns it "in the margin of some old pages." (S, 160; *S,* 202) This is why the reading of this essay teaches us, not only what Merleau-Ponty thought of Husserlian phenomenology and it latent possibilities, but also and above all what he thought of phenomenology in general. It reveals the new direction Merleau-Ponty's phenomenology was finally to take.

According to Merleau-Ponty, by ceasing to be a philosophy of states or acts of consciousness and its thoughts so as to embrace experience in its entirety, the philosophy of consciousness in the later Husserl "has been sufficiently expanded or transformed to be the match for anything, even for what challenges it." (S, 177; *S,* 224) Whether or not this is true of Husserlian philosophy is of little importance, because what this assertion of Merleau-Ponty's indicates above all is that *for him* phenomenology could become ontology, not by ceasing to be a philosophy of consciousness but by enlarging itself *as such* so as to even include in itself that which resists consciousness, that is, sub-phenomenal Being. The ultimate task of phenomenology, as a philosophy of consciousness, a task by which precisely it can become an ontology, "is to understand its relationship to non-phenomenology." (S, 178; *S*, 225) One might find this reference to non-phenomenology surprising, for in the *Phenomenology of Perception* phenomenology was conceived of as an ultimate inquiry which embraces everything, outside of which there remains nothing to be understood. Merleau-Ponty's ontology is this same phenomenology, only now become conscious of its limit and desirous of thinking the limit as such. In thinking its limit, in taking the limit itself as its theme, phenomenology attains its limit, which is to say—according to the Greek sense of the term in which the limit is not a mere lack but the perfection of something—phenomenology realizes and perfects itself as phenomenology; it becomes an ontology, because the limits of phenomenology as a philosophy of consciousness and what is immanent to it is "the point where it becomes a philosophy of transcendence." (VI, 244; *VI*, 297)

The notion of "non-phenomenology" refers back to the notion of *natural being* that the *Phenomenology of Perception* had invoked, without however making it an explicit theme of phenomenological analysis. What makes for the difference between the *Phenomenology* and Merleau-Ponty's later philosophy is that now this "natural being" of the *Phenomenology,* the being underneath the intentional relation, is no longer a mere curiosity unearthed by intentional analysis, but becomes itself its principal theme, that which is most properly to-be-thought. "What resists phenomenology within us—natural being, the 'barbarous' source Schelling spoke of—cannot remain outside phenomenology and should have its place within it" (S, 178; *S*, 225) The philosophy of consciousness must cease to be a philosophy of what is immanent to consciousness—or to experience in general—so as to think what transcends and to think it, precisely, as an irreducible transcendence, as what can be grasped only in its very transcendence.

Unlike Heidegger, however, who wants to "abandon subjectivity" and leave behind the notions of subject and object and even phenomenology itself, Merleau-Ponty does not want to think a "Being in transcendence not reduced to the 'perspectives' of 'consciousness'" except by means of phenomenology, by pushing phenomenology to its extreme limit, by resolutely taking up a position at the center of subjectivity itself, and by digging down into it as deeply as possible. At the very heart of subjectivity and experience Merleau-Ponty discovers a Being in transcendence not reduced to subjectivity. Since he himself liked to compare philosophy to art, we would compare him as a philosopher to the sculptor Henry Moore, who, when asked how he had hit upon his technique of making statues with holes in them, said that he had come upon it one day when, digging deeply into the stone, he ended up by discovering daylight on the other side. It is precisely these holes in Moore's statues, this space which penetrates them, which makes them be what they are, and yet these holes are nothing in themselves which can be grasped separately. It is by virtue of their holes, the empty spaces they enclose, that Moore's statues have a definite form, but space, openness, does not itself appear except insofar as it is articulated and limited by the stone. This relation between space and stone is more or less—although in a different language—of the same sort as the relation in Merleau-Ponty between Being and consciousness. Just as the manifest meaning of consciousness is understandable only insofar as it is a reference to a latent Being not reduced to consciousness, so also Being is thinkable only through consciousness or subjectivity which articulates and informs it.

Merleau-Ponty's ontology thus works itself out in the form of a philosophy of reflection or consciousness, but one which, precisely as such, attempts to think that which resists consciousness, intentional analysis, phenomenology. In an obvious reference to Heidegger, Merleau-Ponty said in 1956 that the "subjectivity" brought to light by modern philosophy is "one of those ideas which make it impossible for us to return to a time prior to their existence, even and especially if we have moved beyond them." (S, 154; *S,* 194) For Merleau-Ponty, a philosopher like Heidegger "who now regrets Parmenides and would like to give us back our relationships to Being such as they were prior to self-consciousness owes his idea of and taste for primordial ontology to just this self-consciousness." (S, 154; *S,* 194) The whole effort of the late Merleau-Ponty was directed towards overcoming the subjectivism and immanentism of a philosophy of consciousness so as to situate subjectivity in the "field of Being" and so as to think our experience as "Being speaking in us"; but he did not want to do this except by remaining faithful to experience and by rediscovering Being at the very heart of subjectivity. It is, as he said in a working note, an "Intra ontology" (VI, 227; *VI,* 280) that he wanted to work out, an interpretation of experience by means of experience. This is why his thought is as little an ontology in the Heideggerian mode as it is a mere humanism, as Sartre nonetheless wanted to believe.

*"One cannot make a direct ontology,"* Merleau-Ponty writes in a working note of January 1959, underlining the phrase. (VI, 179; *VI,* 233) One can think Being only by means of an "'indirect' method (being in the beings)." Merleau-Ponty gives us to understand that this "indirect" ontology is realizable only as a "negative philosophy"—the expression is his—similar in some ways to a "negative theology." If we want to know what this "negative" philosophy of Merleau-Ponty's would finally have looked like, we should look for a possible mode for it, not on the side of Heidegger's ontology, but perhaps in that discipline completely ignored by Heidegger—Freudian psychoanalysis. Indeed, a direct consequence of the change in Merleau-Ponty's perspective and of his discovery of the flesh—a discovery which forces him to revise completely the "prereflective *cogito*" of the *Phenomenology*— is an increased sympathy for psychoanalysis and, in particular, its notion of the *unconscious.* Asked to write a preface for a book on Freud by Dr. A. Hesnard, president of the *Société française de psychanalyse,* published in 1960, Merleau-Ponty says there that "to the degree that one reads, that one relates to oneself, and the years go by, a kind of evidence for psychoanalysis unexplainably builds up."[27] Invoking in this preface the "unthought thought" of the late Husserl and phenomenology's discovery of the "archeology" of the subject, Merleau-Ponty says that "this phenomenology which descends into its own substration more than ever converges with Freud's investigations."[28] This should not be taken to mean that phenomenology says clearly what psychoanalysis says only confusedly, but rather that they are both turned "towards the same *latency.*" If there is an agreement between the two, Merleau-Ponty says, it is because at its limit phenomenology finds itself obliged to confront its own *"latent content* or its *unconscious."*

Just as for psychoanalysis the unconscious is that which founds consciousness and which consciousness presupposes inasmuch as it is consciousness, but which itself does not enter into consciousness as such and cannot be observed in person, visible only in its "effects" which must be "interpreted" (through, notably, an interpretation of dreams), so also philosophical consciousness recognizes that it stems from the flesh of the world, which is itself neither consciousness nor object but the "element" in which consciousness can be present to itself by being present to the world. Like psychoanalysis, philosophy must interpret that "unconscious" which for it is brute being, the flesh. Philosophy would in this way be a self-criticism on the part of consciousness and the reminding (S, 22; *S*, 30) of wild Being, the Being of the depths and far off places. Since, like the Freudian unconscious, Being is underneath consciousness and its intentional relation to the world and can never for this reason become itself consciousness or an object of consciousness, but since also, like the unconscious of psychoanalysis, Being, even while being this ungraspable Other, is everywhere and alway present, it can be uncovered by the philosopher only indirectly, and its meaning can be read only by a kind of deciphering of experience. Being is the latent content of consciousness which can be uncovered only through its manifest content. It is in this sense that Merleau-Ponty says, in a working note of November 1960, that what must be done is "a psychoanalysis of Nature," for, he says, "it is the flesh, the mother." (VI, 267; *VI*, 321) This is to say that philosophy must interrogate Being, the flesh, or Nature which, as the matrix or foundation of all that exists, is the "mother." Now since the flesh is the matrix or the element, since it is latency, it does not appear "in person" but only in sensible things and sentient subjects. Philosophy can therefore think the meaning of this undivided Being— the flesh—only indirectly, through an *interpretation* of phenomenological experience. Exactly like psychoanalysis, it cannot be a description of its object but must be an interpretation and deciphering of it. What is to be done, in short, is a psychoanalysis of Being, a psychoanalysis which is not "existential" but *"ontological."* (VI, 270; *VI*, 323)

This "negative" philosophy is one which recognizes that it is impossible for consciousness to get out of consciousness so as to coincide with an undivided Being prior to the consciousness-object distinction. The theme of ontology must then be consciousness itself and the impossibility of its forgetting itself as consciousness, so as to obtain a positive intuition of Being as such. This is to say that the theme of philosophy can be none other than what Merleau-Ponty calls the "blindness *(punctum caecum)* of 'consciousness'." (VI, 248; *VI*, 301) Consciousness must think Being as that which it does not see and which it cannot see, as that which itself is neither consciousness nor an object of consciousness, since it is precisely that which makes it be that consciousness is consciousness and that it has before itself a world of objects. Consciousness can think Being only as that which is its own "unconscious," its *punctum caecum*; "as the retina is blind at the point where the fibers that will permit the vision spread out into it" so also there is *that which* consciousness does not see and cannot see because it is "what makes it see." (VI, 248; *VI,* 301) It is thus because it is consciousness that consciousness does not see that which it does not see. What consciousness does not see is what makes it consciousness; it is "its tie to Being, is its corporeity,...is the flesh wherein the *ob*ject is born." Consciousness is always consciousness of something, of an object, and thus it cannot see the unitary fabric, the flesh, from which stem both consciousness and its objects. Consciousness is always taken up in the intentional relation; it is its nature to be intentional, to be directed towards objects; and what it does not see is the flesh which unites it to what it sees and which makes it see. "It is inevitable that consciousness be mystified, inverted, indirect," Merleau-Ponty says; "in principle it sees things *through the other end,* in principle it disregards Being and prefers the object to it." (VI, 248; *VI,* 312) Since it is consciousness's nature to intend objects, it cannot get out of this intentional relation so as to see itself as the other end of a relation which occurs *within Being.* Since it is consciousness's nature to be the consciousness of something, it disregards or is unaware of Being which, by definition, is not something but rather the possibility of there being something present to consciousness, the flesh which upholds the consciousness-object relation. Being is thus that which consciousness does not see and cannot see precisely because it is consciousness. A philosophy of consciousness becomes a philosophy of Being when this philosophy recognizes that it is impossible for it to transcend itself as a philosophy of consciousness, and when it takes this very impossibility for its theme.

Ontology is possible only as phenomenology, as the self-criticism of consciousness and the recognition of its limits, as negative philosophy. What the phenomenological reduction teaches is thus the "incompleteness of the reduction" (VI, 178; *VI,* 232), the impossibility of revealing not the phenomenological field but the ontological field which comprises it, the flesh, Being. This incompleteness of the reduction is not, however, a failure; it "is not an obstacle to the reduction, it is the reduction itself, the rediscovery of vertical being." (VI, 178; *VI,* 232) It is precisely by thinking the impossibility of a total reduction that phenomenology thinks "a Being in transcendence not reduced to the 'perspectives' of 'consciousness'." For such an ontology Being is the invisible background which upholds the intentional relation, the phenomenological world, being in the world, and which thus co-appears with everything appearing to consciousness but never appears in person; Being is like the background of a Gestalt which is not visible in itself, being precisely that latency which gives to figures all their depth and dimensionality, their visibility.

In this way phenomenology ceases to be a positive philosophy, the description of what shows itself to consciousness, to become a *negative philosophy, the thought of that which is always hidden*—in this way it becomes an ontology. Phenomenology becomes an ontology when it recognizes that the dream of a phenomenological *positivism* is indeed over. "All consciousness is consciousness of something or of the world, but this *something, this world,* is no longer, as 'phenomenological positivism' appeared to teach, an object that is what it is, exactly adjusted to acts of consciousness. Consciousness is now 'Heraclitus' soul', and Being, which is around about it rather than in front of it, is an oneiric Being which is by definition hidden."[29]

Phenomenological consciousness thus never sees its flesh, *that which makes* it see and which makes objects be "there" in front of it; but, like the psychoanalyst in regard to the latent content of his dreams, thinks it, and it thinks it as the "originating" (VI, 124; VI, 165) which in its explosion and dehiscence gets differentiated and articulated in the seeing-visible, consciousness-object relation.

We see thereby the way in which the expression "negative philosophy" must be understood. Philosophy's "negativity" does not refer to its "object"—it is not a philosophy of the subject or of Being conceived of as *nothingness*—but rather its "methodology." Merleau-Ponty's ontology is a "negative philosophy" solely in the sense that for it the ultimate criterion of evidence is not, as Husserl insists, that the "object" of philosophical knowledge be present "in person," "in flesh and blood"; it is "negative" because it is not a "phenomenological positivism" which culminates in an eidetic intuition, in a *seeing.* Since Being is precisely the *invisible* of the visible, that which is present in every visible but is not itself a visible, even a hidden one, it cannot be the object of consciousness except "negatively," that is, indirectly. It cannot be *seen* but must be *interpreted,* deciphered; it is thus not *present* and is not graspable except in its *absence.*

Hence with this theme of the blindness of consciousness, its latent content and its unconscious that consciousness must think *as such*, Merleau-Ponty succeeds in discovering a genuine meaning in the notion of a "transcendence in immanence" that he had rejected as a gratuitous and unverifiable hypothesis thirteen years before. (SNS, 96 n; *SNS,* 169 n) For him now Being is nothing other than this transcendence in immanence. Consciousness can think Being or the flesh only as that which resists and hides itself from consciousness, and as latency and transcendence as such. Thus a complete development in his thought has taken place in a little over a decade; and now a thought conscious of its limit and which wants to think its limit as such takes the place of a phenomenology too confident in itself, too "positive," which wanted to found itself and rest on itself and which postulated that beyond the phenomenological field there is nothing to be understood.[30] This philosophy of Being worked out in the form of a negative philosophy does indeed therefore, by its method, resemble a "negative theology," because for such a theology the highest knowledge of God, the ultimate Transcendence, can be obtained only when everything has been done to know what God is and when one thus comes to know that one knows nothing of him; for it is then that one comes to know God, in his very proximity, as the totally other. "The philosopher," Merleau-Ponty writes, "bears along with him his shadow, which is not simply the factual absence of future light." (S, 178; *S,* 225) As the shadow of consciousness and its own latency, Being is the absence of light and what consciousness can never illuminate, since it is the very source of its own light. Consciousness cannot think Being except by thinking its own blindness, what it cannot see because it is that which makes it see. "In the dark night of thought," Merleau-Ponty says, "dwells a glimmering of Being." (S, 15; *S,* 21) In the shadows of consciousness a light shines forth and a wild λόγος comes to light.

We can thus indeed see why Merleau-Ponty's ontology can only be an *indirect* ontology. It is a philosophy of Being as inexhaustible latency and irreducible transcendence, a transcendence, however, grasped in its immanence to consciousness. Nothing could be farther from Merleau-Ponty's reflective method than a direct or objectivistic ontology, one of those great systems of modern philosophy or medieval theology which set out on the same hierarchical plane Being, the world, and man, and which assign to man from a semi-divine point of view his place in the universe. Merleau-Ponty's ontology can be understood only as a radical *phenomenology,* because like all phenomenology it rejects the notion of an in-itself Being[31] of which one could have an intuition or form a representation, or about which one could simply objectively deduce and describe the essential traits and attributes. For Merleau-Ponty philosophy has no access to Being such as it would be in itself, because that kind of Being simply does not exist. Merleau-Ponty's ontology wants to take no other guide than our experience itself; it wants to be an elucidation of experience by means of experience, an attempt to lead experience to the pure expression of its own meaning; and if it discovers in experience signs of a transcendence it is therefore because experience seizes hold of itself as a cipher of transcendence. It would be necessary for a concrete philosophy, Merleau-Ponty says, to "stick close to experience, and yet not limit itself to the empirical but restore to each experience the ontological cipher which marks it internally." (S, 157; *S*, 198)

In one of his most notable but also most enigmatic texts Merleau-Ponty writes, "We are interrogating our experience precisely in order to know how it opens us to what is not ourselves. *This does not even exclude the possibility that we find in our experience a movement toward what could not in any event be present to us in the original and whose irremediable absence would thus count among our originating experiences.*"[32] (VI, 159; *VI*, 211) Being is conceivable only as the "shadow" and the latency of our experience, that which is present to us only by remaining irremediably absent from us. In a working note of May 1960, Merleau-Ponty says that the junction between the touching and the touched—that is, that "in-between" which links up the two "leaves" of the flesh, the sentient and the sensible—takes place in the *untouchable,* that is, in the flesh, in Being. Now this untouchable (this invisible or ungraspable) is not a touchable which would only be de facto inaccessible, just as the unconscious is not merely a preconscious "representation" which could become conscious. "The negative here," Merleau-Ponty says, "is not a *positive that is elsewhere* (a transcendent)——It is a true negative, i.e., an *Unverborgenheit* of the *Verborgenheit,* an *Urpräsentation* of the *Nichturpräsentierbar*". (VI, 254; *VI,* 308) This is a very revealing text, for it shows that Merleau-Ponty still refuses the idea of a "transcendent," that is, something which would have an existence in itself outside of our experience. Being is not a transcendent but rather transcendence; it is "the untouchable of the touch, the invisible of vision, the uncon-

scious of consciousness (its central *punctum caecum,* that blindness
that makes it consciousness". (VI, 254; *VI, 308*) Being is the original
presence of that which could never be present in person; it is the non-
dissimulation of that which is always dissimulated.

Since Being is that which makes it be that consciousness is present to the world and to itself, and since it is thus not itself something present, it must be said that Being hides itself at the same time
that it reveals itself and to the precise degree that it reveals itself.
Thought cannot think Being except as that which withdraws from
consciousness, since it is that which makes consciousness be consciousness and which is the possibility or the latency of all presence: "if
Being is hidden, this is itself a characteristic of Being, and no disclosure will make us comprehend it." (VI, 122; *VI, 162*) Paul Klee's
expression for which Merleau-Ponty showed a certain predilection
expresses well the essence of Being as the latter conceives it (negatively): "I am ungraspable in immanence." It is finally for this reason
that philosophy cannot be an objective knowledge, a rigorous science,
a coincidence and fusion with the object of its knowing. Being is
nothing determinate (it is not a being), and is not before consciousness but around about it; philosophy cannot therefore look for it
elsewhere than everywhere. Since it is thus of the essence of Being
to dissimulate itself in its presence, philosophy cannot be a positive
description and intuition; it must be an interpretation and negative
knowledge.

If it is precisely qua negative philosophy that philosophy thinks
Being, this negative knowledge is therefore not the "unhappy consciousness." (VI, 178; *VI, 232*) In thinking Being as that which hides
itself to the degree that it reveals itself, philosophy, to be sure, thinks
its distance from Being and how Being remains dissimulated to it; but
it also thinks this distance and this dissimulation as precisely an expression of Being, as the very essence of Being. Philosophy in this
way knows that it is not a stranger to Being but is rather its most faithful witness. It must however be admitted that on this question of the
relations between thought and Being Merleau-Ponty's thought is most
ambiguous and difficult to grasp. This, though, is to be expected,
since with this question we touch upon the central core of his ontology
which is itself uncompleted. Let us therefore attempt to force a bit
the philosopher's silence.

Philosophy thinks Being by a kind of archeological analysis, by
turning towards "the night of thought." It is important to understand

that *the meaning of this regressive, archeological movement is entirely progressive, entirely teleological.* The "remembering" of Being is not the opposite of *creation.* Even if Merleau-Ponty had revised for instance his assessment of the Freudian unconscious, he would yet never have admitted that the unconscious acts on consciousness by a kind of causal action, and that the unconscious is something positive in itself which shapes consciousness it its own image. Such a notion would have been for him "neither satisfactory nor even philosophically understandable."[33] Philosophical thought cannot coincide with Being "and rejoin in Being a philosophy that is there ready-made" (VI, 125; *VI,* 166), because as pure latency Being possesses nothing positive and is nothing real. Being is nothing other than the very reality of sensible life and of thought. This means that in the last resort the meaning of Being cannot be other than the thought which thinks it. Thought is not a mere representation or reflection of Being, but is rather its own realization, its highest self-expression. It is necessary to reflect on this last point so as to bring out its meaning and see how it can be said of philosophy that it is the very truth of Being.

For Merleau-Ponty as for Aristotle, the logic of thought is the very logic of Being. This is not due to some kind of "preestablished harmony" between the two, or because thought is an adequation to Being (realism), or because Being is an adequation to thought (idealism), but because thought is itself at the limit the λόγος of Being itself. This has to do with the "double polarity of reflection." (VI, 49; *VI,* 74) Radical reflection is that reflection which grasps itself as given to itself on the basis of bodily life. Now reflection thinks sensible life itself as a dehiscence and explosion of the undivided flesh of the world and as the sensing-sensible articulation or chiasm. In this way thought conceives of and expresses an ontogenesis (a genesis of the flesh), of which in the last analysis it is itself a part. It does not however suffice for thought, for a truly radical reflection, to raise the question, What is Being? and to conceive of it as the dehiscence and articulation of the flesh. At the same time that it aims at the signification "being," it must aim at "the being of the signification and the place of the signification within Being." (VI, 120; *VI,* 160) This is to say that reflection must not forget that the originating meaning of Being (as dehiscence and articulation) that it expresses is a meaning which it itself brings into existence. Reflection expresses the meaning of the silent life of perception; precisely for this reason, however, it is not itself silence, fusion, and coincidence with perception. It is this silence which has been *spoken.* What philosophy "finds in thus returning to the sources, it says. It is itself a human construction". (VI, 102; *VI, 139*)

Thus the speech of reflection, precisely as speech, can be neither identical nor can it form an antinomy with the silence of carnal life, because it is only by means of speech, by means of the transcendence effected by reflection, that the silent life of carnal existence is made manifest. If therefore there is no coincidence of reflection with the unreflected, and if the *return* of reflection to its unreflected constitutes in fact a *promotion* of sensible existence to its meaning, it is because truth itself is not a coincidence or a real adequation but rather transcendence. If truth fully exists only in language which is not a coincidence with but a deliverance of silence, this means that "language is not a mask over Being, but...the most valuable witness to Being". (VI, 126; *VI, 167*)

Why is this so? It can only be because Being is finally *"what requires creation of us* for us to experience it." (VI, 197; *VI, 251*) Thought is faithful to Being only if it remembers that it is not a mere reflection of an already-made truth but, qua human work, the realization of this truth. Reflection must think Being, not as a primordial state of affairs to which it could return, but as a pure appeal to transcendence, to creation. The "originating," Merleau-Ponty says, is not behind us. "The appeal to the originating goes in several directions: the originating breaks up, and philosophy must accompany this breakup, this non-coincidence, this differentiation." (VI, 124; *VI, 165*) In returning to the flesh philosophy discovers a Being which is nothing in itself but rather the explosion, the dehiscence of the sensible, and of which the sensing-sensible chiasm is a first articulation, a brute or wild logos. What it discovers is a *teleology* of the flesh or light. Grasping itself in this way as a prolongation of carnal life and as that which unveils and realizes its meaning, philosophical reflection grasps itself as a prolongation or sublimation of this teleology or this desire of the flesh. Philosophy transmutes the silent logos (λόγος ἐνδιάθετος) of the flesh into a professed logos (λόγος προφορικός); as operative language it is a spontaneous transcendence of the flesh towards the idea, a transcendence which germinates in the very depths of silent experience.

The theme of philosophy must therefore be precisely this speaking speech that it is as militant, conquering philosophy. Philosophy is the transcendence of speech towards thought, of experience towards expression, which knows itself "from within" (VI, 126; *VI*, 168), which knows itself as issuing from a "need to speak" (VI, 126; *VI*, 167), as "called forth by the voices of silence" and as "an effort of articulation which is the Being of every being." (VI, 127; *VI*, 168) Philosophy is a creation, a *Gebilde* (VI, 174; *VI*, 227), a human construction, a transcendence of silence into language. What it must then think is precisely the fact that it is by means of its very creativity that it unveils the source of all creativity, the flesh, Being. And in the last analysis this means that Being itself cannot be something which rests in itself that philosophy represents to itself, but is rather the possibility of and the demand for creation. Thus it is only in appearance that in its creativity philosophy distances itself from its source (Being); for this distancing and transcendence is in fact an understanding and a realization of Being as transcendence itself, as that which impels us to create. Philosophy is thus in its very creativity a "reintegration of Being." (VI, 197; *VI*, 250) As a creation philosophy is, paradoxically, an adequation to Being; it is, qua creation, "the only way to obtain an adequation."[34] Being in this way a creation which knows itself to be such and knows that in its creativity it is a response to that which impels us to create, to Being as the demand for creation, philosophy is "Being speaking within us." (VI, 197; *VI*, 250) It is the λόγος, the meaning of Being itself. Being and thought do not form an antinomy; Being is the possibility of and demand for thought, and thought is the realization of Being. Man, and creative thought—philosophy—in particular, is "a field of Being." (VI, 240; *VI*, 293) It is, Merleau-Ponty says, "being that speaks within us and not we who speak of being." (VI, 194; *VI*, 247) And thus, he says, "things *are said* and *are thought* by a Speech and by a Thought which we do not have but which has us." (S, 19; *S*, 27)

Merleau-Ponty's philosophy has become an ontology since he now recognizes that the "wave of transcendence" that in the *Phenomenology* he saw at work in bodily life and in the speaking subject—this movement of transcendence which is the very definition of man—is nothing other than Being itself. "All verticality comes from vertical Being." (VI, 234; *VI*, 287) We are ourselves the upsurge of Being, the place where Being qua transcendence becomes conscious of itself. At the limit philosophy is nothing other than the taking note of such an ontogenesis. "Hence it is a question," he writes, "whether philosophy as reconquest of brute or wild being can be accomplished by the resources of eloquent language, or whether it would not be necessary for philosophy to use language in a way that takes from it its power of immediate or direct signification in order to equal it with what it wishes all the same to say." (VI, 102; *VI, 139*) Philosophy would need a language which could equal by its symbolic power the generative power of Being. It would need an indirect language which could convert into a proximity the distance between it and what it wished to say, such that reflection, dialectic, mediation, which are of the essence of philosophy and of language, would not be obstacles to a grasping of what is underneath or beyond philosophy and language, but the only means of attaining and thinking it. Language must not be an *intermediary* between thought and silence; it must rather be the *mediation* of the two, the realization of silence as meaning.

The ever-present theme of philosophy is, What is thinking? (S, 14; *S, 20*) Philosophy is thought which interrogates itself, and it is by the term "interrogation" that in his unfinished manuscript Merleau-Ponty finally designates his new ontology. It is in philosophy that "the central question that is ourselves" (VI, 104; *VI, 141*) appears in its naked state, that that desire to know *where* we are and *who* we are achieves the status of a question, an inexhaustible question since no factual answer can satisfy its hunger. Where is the world itself? And why am I myself? (VI, 104; *VI, 141*) In this questioning attitude that all men know and that philosophy does no more than radicalize, man appears to himself as τό δεινότατον, as Sophocles says, the strangest of beings. "The end of a philosophy," Merleau-Ponty says, "is the account of its beginning." (VI, 177; *VI, 231*) Philosophy reaches its end when it rediscovers the fundamental question which silently pronounces itself in the depths of our being and gives it at last a philosophical status. His own being-there is for man the fundamental question. "The philosopher is the man who wakes up and speaks," who realizes that his being is for him the ultimate question, who interrogates himself on the meaning of Being—What is it to be there? What is the *there is*?—and who in raising the question notices that the question is itself unsurpassable, as if it were the fundamental mode of his relation to Being. The interrogative, Merleau-Ponty writes, is "an original manner of aiming at something, as it were a *question-knowing*, which by principle no statement or 'answer' can go beyond and which perhaps therefore is the proper mode of our relationship with Being, as though it were the mute or reticent interlocutor of our questions." (VI, 129;

*VI,* 171) It is in us and through us that Being interrogates itself and thinks itself. We are ourselves the question which Being addresses to itself. Philosophy is the becoming-conscious of this question which is spread out throughout our life. And therefore as a question which interrogates that which leads it to question, philosophical interrogation is "as the ultimate relation to Being and as an ontological organ." (VI, 121; *VI,* 162) Questioning is an unsurpassable philosophical attitude, the form of an ontology which in the last analysis is negative philosophy, the grasping of Being in its very proximity as the ungraspable.

## Conclusion

THAT there is in this way a history of thought which is the very history of Being, that there is a philosophy immanent in the history of philosophy (VI, 188; *VI,* 242), a history wherein truth little by little capitalizes itself (PriP, 9; *Inédit,* 417), without however this history's being a Hegelian finalism but an open and endless history wherein Being unfolds itself in the infinity of its unfathomable latency—these considerations we will have to investigate in the following chapter.

## Chapter V

# The Field of Being

καὶ δή χαὶ τό πάλαι τε χαὶ νῦν
χαὶ ἀεὶ ζητούμενον χαί ἀεὶ
ἀπορούμενον τί τὸ ὄν...
*And indeed the question which was raised*
*of old and is raised now and always, and*
*is always the subject of puzzlement "What*
*is being?"...*

Aristotle, *Metaphysics*, 1028 b

WHAT is most striking in *The Visible and the Invisible* and in his late philosophy is perhaps Merleau-Ponty's obvious desire to begin everything again, to take up a new starting point, the desire not to deny what he had said previously but to take it up and re-express it in a truly fundamental way. τί τὸ ὄν (PriP, 178; *OE*, 60); What is Being? he asks. It is this radical question of philosophy that he raises, and his way of pursuing it is just as radical. Wanting to free himself from all the "bric-à-brac" of conceptualist-intellectualist thought and all philosophical prejudices, Merleau-Ponty will take no other starting point than our actual experience, one wherein we are immediately present to others and to the world; and it is to this experience that he addresses himself, asking of it its secret. (VI, 159; *VI*, 211) The set purpose of interrogating our experience itself is in Merleau-Ponty the explicit rejection of an idealist conception of experience which defines it as that which is *immanent* to consciousness; for it is not excluded, he says, that our experience be a movement towards what could never be present in person in this experience, what would remain irremediably transcendent to us, and whose absence would be for us precisely an originating experience. (VI, 159; *VI,* 211)

Thus it is that Merleau-Ponty completely rejects Husserl's transcendental subjectivity and phenomenological immanentism—and the notion of evidence as *Erfüllung,* the filling of an intentional void—and resolutely takes up a position at the center of natural experience.[1] What he wants to explicate is the experience of the natural man for whom things, the world, and others are not pure noemata exactly proportioned to various intentional attitudes, but realities full of mystery and depth which really exist, according to natural conviction, outside of experience (and which are not merely *ideal* realities immanent in consciousness). It is thus that Merleau-Ponty finally overcomes a Husserlian prejudice which had always been one of the great sources of ambiguity in his own thought, namely, the one according to which to be is to be an object, that is, a correlate to the intentionality of the subject. It is this prejudice which gave rise to the ambiguity—if not the equivocation—in his analysis of the "natural world" in the *Phenomenology* and which lay behind his inability to conceive of a "transcendence in immanence." In *The Visible and the Invisible* it is therefore the idealism of Husserl—of phenomenology—that Merleau-Ponty overcomes; it is here that he begins to pursue a new and untrodden path.

In the perspective of his new ontology Being is no longer what is defined in relation to the subject (bodily projects); it is rather the single source of the subject as well as of the object itself. Merleau-Ponty's ontology rests on a new conception of intentionality (of the subject-object relationship), and in the last analysis is understandable only as an overcoming of the Husserlian ontology.

And it is indeed a matter of an *overcoming* of Husserlian phenomenology and idealist philosophy, for Merleau-Ponty does not fall back on this side of subjectivity and of phenomenology into a "naturalist" or "materialist" ("dialectical" or otherwise) philosophy which, on the contrary, he does not cease to criticize. While, however, he continues to recognize the "undeniability" of self-consciousness, of the *Cogito,* he deliberately overcomes it by thinking subjectivity as itself an expression of Being, derived from and comprised, along with the world, in it. Merleau-Ponty does not attempt to "get out" of subjectivity (this would have no meaning for him); he attempts rather to conceive of subjectivity (perception and thought) as a self-expression or opening of Being. Since therefore for Merleau-Ponty philosophy can think Being only through subjectivity, since it can be ontology only "indirectly," and since philosophy, rather than be an eidetic intuition and a direct vision, must attempt to interpret, to decipher the "ontological ciphers" with which experience is internally marked (S, 157; S, 198), must try to scrutinize the "margins of presence" of experience and to discern its "references" (VI, 159; VI, 211), we will be able to thematize his notion of Being only indirectly as well, by relating it to these other notions: world, meaning, subjectivity, time. What we have to deal with is in a way a "topology of Being," as he says, a search for Being in beings, a "being—which is glimpsed through time's stirrings and always intended by our temporality, perception and our carnal being, but to which there can be no question of our being transported". (S, 156; S, 197)

## I.    Being and the World

FROM the *Phenomenology of Perception* to *The Visible and the Invisible* a certain ambiguity in Merleau-Ponty between the notions of being and world remains undissipated, for it is perhaps philosophically undissolvable. It is basically the ancient problem of the relation between being and phenomenon, being and appearing. In *The Visible and the Invisible* Merleau-Ponty still has nothing to say about being in general, being as such, entirely disassociated from beings, because for him such a notion is but the height of abstraction, the night wherein all cows are black. Being is for him always the Being of beings, and the expression "pure being" remains for him what it was in the *Phenomenology*, a pejorative term. (PhP, XX; PP, XV: VI, 84; VI, 116) Nevertheless, even though he wants to remain close to the concrete and to lived experience, his thought has nonetheless undergone a development. For if formerly he was hardly at all concerned with the question of the being or the ontological status of the world (which in practice he defined merely in reference to the subject), it is now precisely this question which underlies all of *The Visible and the Invisible*. It is "the question concerning the meaning of the world's being." (VI, 96; VI, 131) It could even be said that in regard to this question concerning the meaning of the world's being a veritable "reversal" has taken place in his thought. For if in the *Phenomenology* Merleau-Ponty in effect defined the world as the correlate of the existential-bodily projects of the subject, in *The Visible and the Invisible* the subject is defined in relation to the world of which it is the "self-realization."

Still however we should not say that a pure and simple reversal has taken place, but rather a deepening and overcoming, for the "world" which plays such a large role in his later thought is no longer simply the phenomenal or perceived world of the *Phenomenology*. In its deepest meaning the notion of the world in Merleau-Ponty's later philosophy joins up with that of Nature, whose equivalent one would look for in vain in the *Phenomenology*. It is true that in this work Merleau-Ponty spoke occasionally of "being," which he presented as a kind of "preworld," as an undifferentiated being, and in some way prior to the world properly speaking which, itself, is the correlate (the horizon) of human existence. In reading the *Phenomenology* one is tempted to say that is it the subject's mysterious and ineffable presence to this vague being, this in-itself being, which makes the world in the proper sense of the term, the world of our experience, appear (which constitutes it). All this however was not very specific, and one remained with the impression that Merleau-Ponty was satisfied in this work with, so to speak, merely touching up the Sartrian notions of the in itself and the for itself without really subjecting them to a critical examination. However this may be, the "Being" of *The Visible and the Invisible* has nothing to do with this "being" of the *Phenomenology;* and in this regard it is interesting to note that now not only does Merleau-Ponty very often write the word with a capital letter, as if to underline the originality of the term in his thought, but again he devotes almost an entire chapter in *The Visible and the Invisible* to a very detailed critique of Sartrian ontology, as if he felt the obligation to make quite specific once and for all his position in relation to Sartre's and to underline the distance which separates them, and which does so definitively.

In the new perspective opened up by *The Visible and the Invisible* Being is not to be looked for on the side of the object (Sartre) nor on the side of the subject (Husserl), but there where object and subject encounter each other, in this "in-between." Neither the world (as object, correlate of existence) nor the subject has the ontological priority, but rather Being, which is neither the one nor the other (nor some *other* thing) but rather their common flesh, the single fabric of which they themselves are differentiations. The key notion in

Merleau-Ponty's ontology, the one which underlines its originality, is the *flesh*.

This notion furnishes him with the means of definitively overcoming all notions of being in itself, while at the same time it keeps him from falling back into the transcendental trap, into an immanentist philosophy which thinks that it has eliminated being in itself by merely bracketing it and by defining being as being-for-us. What Merleau-Ponty is looking for "is a dialectical definition of being that can be neither being for itself nor being in itself...that must rediscover the being that lies before the cleavage operated by reflection, about it, on its horizon, not outside of us and not in us, but there where the two movements cross, there where 'there is' something." (VI, 95; *VI, 130*) Again he says, "For us the essential is to know precisely what the being of the world means." Here nothing must be presupposed, "neither the naive idea of being in itself, therefore, nor the correlative idea of a being of representation, of a being for consciousness, of a being for man." (VI, 6; *VI, 21*)

Merleau-Ponty discovers this dialectical definition of being in the notion of the flesh. The flesh is "the formative medium of the object and the subject" (VI, 147; *VI, 193*); it is the "single stuff," as he says in "Eye and Mind," out of which the body and things are made. It is not the world or things which produce the subject, nor is it the subject (even the bodily subject) which constitutes the world; but rather both are strictly "simultaneous" (VI, 250; *VI, 304*) for both stem from the same Being. The sentient body and sensible things, Merleau-Ponty says, are "total parts  of the same Being." (PriP, 162; *OE, 17*) This is to say that there is no antinomy between the subject and the world, as if one had to explain the one in terms of the other (there is no antinomy between a philosophy of transcendental constitution and a philosophy of material causality); subject and object are indissociable partners precisely because they are what they are only insofar as they stem from and are part of the same fabric and are the derived and simultaneous expressions of the same Being, the same Whole.

We can thus see that with the notion of the flesh Merleau-Ponty is attempting to think Being as the absolute source of the subject as well as of the object, as that which is neither noesis nor noema, but the ultimate foundation of phenomenal being in the world, of the intentional and dialectical subject-object (world) relationship. Being or reality, Merleau-Ponty says in effect, is not something *behind* things; it is "their common inner framework," it is *"between them, this side of them."* (VI, 226; *VI,* 280) Being is "the totality above the divergencies" (VI, 228; *VI,* 281)—the references among things, their mutual references back and forth—but it is not for all that "absolute plenitude and absolute positivity." (VI, 52; *VI,* 78) One must on the contrary "reject entirely the idea of the In Itself." (VI, 223; *VI,* 276) Being, the fabric of which things are the articulations or modulations, is not *in front of* the subject but surrounds him and, as Merleau-Ponty says, traverses him, "my vision of Being not forming itself from elsewhere, but from the midst of Being". (VI, 114; *VI,* 154) Being encompasses the object *and* the subject (VI, 202; *VI,* 256); it is their common inner framework and their single source. If Merleau-Ponty speaks of the "flesh" of the world, it is, he specifies, not because the world is sentient, sensible for itself, but because it is absolutely not an ob-ject, a pro-ject of the subject. The flesh of the world "is of the Being-seen," the complement to Being-seeing; and this exchange and this reciprocity between the sensible (the object) and the sentient (the subject) "is finally possible and means something only because *there is* Being" (VI, 250; *VI,* 304), not Being as absolute plenitude but Being which is a process of differentiation. The subject-object, in itself–for itself correspondence takes place neither in the de facto world nor in the subject qua consciousness, but in a "being of promiscuity" (VI, 253; *VI,* 307), a "narcissistic" Being, one of "transitivism." Between the subject and the world there is their common flesh, and this flesh is being itself expressing itself in this relation. Were we to rethink a Heideggerian expression, we could say that for Merleau-Ponty between man and being there is a relation which is Being itself.

Is this to say that Merleau-Ponty was advancing towards a philosophical monism, towards an identification of man with nature? It is impossible to answer this question with a mere yes or no, for the answer depends precisely on how one understands the terms "world" or "nature," and in Merleau-Ponty these terms do not have a single meaning. Let us however briefly recall the important change which has taken place in his thought concerning the relations of the subject to the world, for the meaning of the later Merleau-Ponty's monism is precisely the meaning of this development.

The *Phenomenology,* we said, ends up in an ontological "relativism." In basing himself on the Husserlian notion of intentionality, Merleau-Ponty succeeded in eliminating all *dualism* between the subject and the world (as moreover between consciousness and the body) by conceiving of them as the two dialectical moments, reciprocally defined (as with Husserl's noesis and noema), of a single circular system. The subject is essentially being in the world, a project of the world, and the world is in sum the correlate of the bodily projects of the subject. One cannot be understood except in relation to the other. It is solely within this intentional (dialectical) relationship that the subject and the world have meaning and being, and thus this relationship, this mutual reference, is the final truth. It is evident that the price to be paid for such a reinterpretation of the subject-world relation is the establishment of an unsurpassable *duality*. Subject and world are no longer two independent substances external to one another, but, precisely because they are now defined as two moments of a single dialectical circularity, there exists but an incessant referring back of one to the other. The "circularity" of the *Phenomenology* is thus an unsurpassable dialectical opposition. The concept of "being in the world" expresses this radical duality, and the *Phenomenology* is in this sense the height of relativism. To speak therefore of monism in regard to this work would obviously not have much meaning.

However, in Merleau-Ponty's last writings this is no longer the way things stand. The introduction of the notion of the flesh upsets everything, a notion which comes to replace that of being in the world, the theme of the *Phenomenology*. The flesh, defined in the way we know, is neither subject nor object as such, but their common source or their single ground. It is the "stuff" of which body and things are made. The flesh is the "irrelative" which grounds and internally upholds the two "relativities" of the subject and the world; it is the texture and the source of their co-presence. The flesh is the "undivided Being" of which subject and world are, as such, derived expressions (modulations) and "total parts." One can thus say that Merleau-Ponty's later philosophy is indeed a monism, for since the subject and the world are conceived of as the results of a dehiscence of Being, as Being articulating itself, there is basically only Being.

It is nevertheless necessary to be even more specific, because Merleau-Ponty never ceases insisting in *The Visible and the Invisible* on this point, that "there is no coinciding of the seer with the visible." (VI, 261; *VI,* 314) When for example one hand touches another in the process of touching things, there is never an identity or complete coincidence between the touching hand (the subject) and the touched hand (the object). (VI, 148; *VI,* 194) There is, Merleau-Ponty says, neither identity nor non-identity nor non-coincidence (VI, 264; *VI,* 317), but rather an "identity by principle (always abortive)." (VI, 272; *VI,* 325) Quite simply, there would be neither the visible properly speaking nor vision if between them there did not exist a certain distance, a separation, an irreducibility of the one to the other. But neither would there be either visible or vision if between them there did not exist a certain proximity or relatedness. This relation, this "chiasm," between the sentient and the sensible (subject and object) is what Merleau-Ponty calls "reversibility"; and this term expresses an idea fundamentally different from that intended by the term "circularity" in the *Phenomenology,* for what it means is that, while not coinciding, the sentient and the sensible are tightly and inseparably overlapped onto one another, and that precisely because they are "abstracts from one sole tissue." (VI, 262; *VI,* 315)

Thus at the level of sensorial and conscious experience there is indeed a duality between the sentient and the sensible, but this duality, Merleau-Ponty says, is understandable in the last analysis only in relation to a single, undivided Being. There is at one and the same time distance and proximity between the sensible and the sentient only because these two terms are of the same flesh, are the results of a "fission" of Being. Hence, if one takes the term "world" in the sense of the de facto sensible, as the universe of *sensibilia,* there is certainly no coincidence of identity (monism) between the subject and the world; but if one grants it its deepest meaning, as the fundamental matrix from which emerge by a kind of process of "segregation" the de facto sensible and sentient, then the world or nature is synonymous with Being, and Merleau-Ponty's ontology appears in this case as a monist philosophy, since the (de facto) world and the subject are both derived from Nature, from this single sub- or trans-phenomenal Being. Merleau-Ponty does not therefore *suppress* the subject-world duality in his later philosophy, but he does *overcome* it by conceiving of the intentional relation as a relation occurring within Being (Nature) itself. In order to bring out better the meaning of Merleau-Ponty's ontology, it is therefore important to form a clearer idea of this fundamental notion of Nature.

In the preceding chapter we pointed out the few enigmatic remarks Merleau-Ponty makes on the subject of the "Earth" in his essay on Husserl. To a great extent this essay is in fact a reworking of ideas already presented in his courses at the Collège de France. Starting in 1957 Merleau-Ponty devoted a series of courses to the "Concept of Nature."[2] In them he retraces the history of the idea of Nature since Descartes and attempts to disengage from the meanderings of this history the fundamental sense which little by little comes to light. His goal is precisely to return to the primordial sense of Nature so as to discover the "fundamental" and thereby to set up the bases of a new ontology.[3] Whether or not this program was directly inspired by the Heideggerian project of a recapitulation and an overcoming of the history of "metaphysics," Merleau-Ponty in any event refers to it in *The Visible and the Invisible* in terms identical to those of Heidegger: "A *wiederholung* is necessary: 'destruction' of the objectivistic ontology of the Cartesians. Rediscovery of φύσις..." (VI, 183; *VI*, 237) It is in any event interesting to note that Merleau-Ponty sometimes speaks of the "forgetfulness of the Earth" just as Heidegger, for his part, speaks of *Seinsvergessenheit*. This similarity in language reveals in any case an interest which is genuinely common to the two philosophers, that of overcoming objectivistic thought (materialist or idealist) so as to formulate a new ontology.

It is at the moment when, in this new examination of the concept of Nature, Merleau-Ponty comes to Husserl that one gets the impression that he has at last made contact with the basis of his own thought. And it is above all his original interpretation of the notion of "Earth" in Husserl which shows itself to be the culminating point of his analysis. The Earth, Merleau-Ponty says in interpreting Husserl, is the "ground [*sol*] of experience," "the stock [*souche*] from which objects are engendered."[4] The Earth is in a way prior to all experience and encompasses in advance "all further possibilities of experience." It is, he says, "something initial, a possibility of reality, the cradle, the base, and the ground of all experience." The Earth is therefore not an object confronting the subject, correlative to him, but is rather a "pre-object." It is not contained in space but is rather the possibility of space; "it is not a place in the sense that worldly objects have a place. The Earth is our source [*souche*], our *Urheimat*. It is the root of our spatiality, our common homeland".

In 1960, the last year for which we have the summaries of his courses at the Collége de France, Merleau-Ponty returns to this notion in his course "Husserl at the Limits of Phenomenology."[5] Commenting on Husserl (*Umsturz der Kopernikanischen Lehre...*), he says that in the Copernican view of the universe (as in the Cartesian conception) there are in the world only *Körper,* that is, material objects situated in a Euclidean space (like Descartes' *res extensa*). "Through meditation," Merleau-Ponty says, "we must again learn of a mode of being whose conception he [Copernican man] has lost, the being of the 'ground' *(Boden),* and that of the Earth first of all—the earth where we live, that which is this side of rest and movement, being the ground from which all rest and all movement are separated, which is not made out of *Körper,* being the 'source' from which they are drawn through division, which has no 'place', being that which surrounds all place, which lifts all particular beings out of nothingness, as Noah's Ark preserved the living creatures from the Flood." (TFL, 121–2; *RC,* 168–9) It is precisely this primordial "mode of being" that is *forgotten* ("forgetfulness of the Earth") as we progressively adopt "the Copernican constitution of the world" whereby we leave behind our starting point, forget our terrestrial roots and "come to consider the world as the pure object on an infinite reflection before which there are only interchangeable objects." This forgetfulness of the originating, of the *archē*, reaches its completion in the Cartesian view of the world and in the classical sciences of nature.

To what degree are we dealing here with Merleau-Ponty's own thought? Isn't Merleau-Ponty claiming to be merely interpreting Husserl? It is doubtful however if Husserl, even in his late interest in the question of Nature, ever wanted to look for the "fundamental" elsewhere than in pure, constituting, transcendental subjectivity. And it is true that even if he wants to see Husserl go in a direction other than that of "transcendental idealism," Merleau-Ponty does recognize that this idea of the Earth as the *Ur-arche* and of Nature as the matrix of the subject's relations to things and to others posed "a difficulty for Husserl, who himself was by temperament extremely reflective."[6] Husserlian intentional analysis, Merleau-Ponty recognizes, is a matter "habitually of ascending from the product to the productive thought."

From this point of view, the analysis of Nature would contribute nothing new and would serve only as an occasion for better discerning the thematic activity of constituting consciousness. Merleau-Ponty admits to the likelihood that in this case Husserl's analysis of Nature "would be of a preparatory and provisional character, destined to be relegated to a secondary position. After the reduction," he goes on to say, "phenomenology properly speaking would be concerned with the pure Ego along with his intentional correlates, with the pure Ego as the ultimate subject of all subordinate constitutions. Everything would be constituted and produced by acts of the ultimate phenomenological consciousness, which makes the acts of the natural attitude." But, Merleau-Ponty says, that appears "to be in contradiction" to his own interpretation of Husserl's concept of Nature, since "if everything is correlated to the act of an Ego, we return to transcendental idealism." But did Husserl ever abandon his transcendental idealism? Merleau-Ponty himself admits that "Husserl seems to fall back and say that the deep sphere of primordial intentionalities is engendered by the act of an Ego." It would seem however that he sees here more of a temptation on Husserl's part than a deliberate and conscious option. And this is a temptation in the face of a danger which Merleau-Ponty agrees with Husserl must at all cost be avoided, the "danger of a reinstatement a naturalist philosophy." For Merleau-Ponty as for Husserl Nature can never be a cause "of which we would be the effects." But if Nature, the *Ur-arche,* is not for Merleau-Ponty an in-itself material object nor, moreover, an intentional correlate "engendered by the act of an Ego," what is it?

If one does not take up the Husserlian idealist path, the temptation is indeed great of conceiving of Nature as being wholly external to the immanence of consciousness, as being a pure and simple transcendent, as being a kind of "Ding-an-sich." It is however precisely this alternative of being in itself–being for itself that Merleau-Ponty wants to overcome. It is precisely the alternatives posed by a philosophy of consciousness that Merleau-Ponty wants to overcome; it is precisely the philosophy of consciousness itself that he wants to get rid of. If Nature is not "simply the object, the accessory of consciousness in its tête-à-tête with knowledge," neither is it "the in itself, massive being, pure being." (TFL, 64; *RC,* 94) Nature should rather be conceived of as "primordial being which is not yet subject-being nor object-being". (TFL, 65; *RC,* 95) Again, however, we must not simply conceive of Nature as a mode of being which exists *prior* to the subject-object bifurcation, for that would bring us back to conceiving of Nature as a kind of pre-existant being, and we would once again find ourselves in an objectivistic and substantialistic philosophy.

Merleau-Ponty thinks he can overcome this dilemma by understanding Nature or primordial Being, not as an "elsewhere" of the world of our experiences, but as the internal and proper possibility of this world, as that which makes the carnal world surrounding us what it is. Nature (Being) is not something positive in itself; we can neither really separate Nature (qua Being) from the world (qua being, fact) nor completely identify them. For if we identify them, we end up in a monism, whether materialistic or idealistic; if we separate them we make of Being a *thing* wholly transcendent both to consciousness and the de facto world of which we can know nothing and with which we can have no contact. What Merleau-Ponty needs is therefore a notion of "ontological difference" (VI, 270; *VI,* 324) which precisely can preserve the distinction between Being or Nature and the world without introducing between them a real difference.

He succeeds in conceiving of this "ontological difference" with the help of the notions of *latency, depth, invisibility, dimensionality,* etc. Being, he says, is the world's latency; the relation between the the world and Being is that of the visible and the invisible. (VI, 251; *VI,* 305) Being is the invisible of the visible, but here the invisible is not merely a visible which is absent, a de facto invisible. The relation between Being and the world is in a way like that which exists between the figure and the background of a Gestalt; "every visible...involves a ground which is not visible in the sense the figure is" (VI, 246; *VI,* 300), and which, as ground, could never be a de facto visible. The invisible is the "depth" of the visible and is therefore not behind it, like a hidden visible, an unseen visible, but penetrates it, surrounds it, englobes it. Qua invisible Being is, in a word, the flesh of things, their element, their milieu, their ground, their latency, which is not reducible to them but which transpires and is present only in them; "the proper essence of the visible is to have a lining of invisibility in the strict sense, which it makes present as a certain absence." (PriP, 187; *OE,* 85) As the visible of the invisible (Being), the carnal world (sensible things and the sentient body) is the *Unverborgenheit* of *Verborgenheit,* the "orginating presentation of the unpresentable." (VI, 203; *VI,* 257) If the world is the nondissimulation, the active presence of Being, Being is the ungraspable latency of the world, that which gives it its depth and reality; it is its inaccessible "other side," present however as such.

To speak of the latency or the depth of the world is to speak of "an inexhaustible reserve of being" (VI, 169; *VI,* 223); it is to speak of the *infinite.* The identification of Being and the infinite is a constant theme of philosophy which Merleau-Ponty takes up on his own account. In Leibniz, he observes, the infinite is precisely this "inexhaust-ible reserve of being which is not only this and that but could have been other"; or again in Spinoza, with his notion of unknown attri-butes, it is the character Being has of being "effectively more than we know." (VI, 169; *VI, 223*) What Merleau-Ponty objects to in these two philosophers and in the modern tradition in general is their having made, in spite of everything, the infinite into something positive. It is spoken of as some *thing*; it is referred to as *Unendlichkeit*, as that which has no limits; it is frozen into an in itself or an object. In place of this "congealed infinity" (VI, 169; *VI, 223*), Merleau-Ponty wants to think the "infinity of Being" as an "*operative, militant finitude.*" (VI, 251; *VI, 305*) That Being is infinite does not mean that it is what knows no limits, that it is an immense hidden underside of the world which has only partially revealed itself, but rather that it is the very openness of the world, the fact that the world is open and in the end eludes our grasp. The infinity of Being is the openness or *Offenheit* of the *Umwelt*; it is the fact that the lived world, the *Lebenswelt*, is not an ob-ject, identical to what it is for a consciousness, but is open and, as to its ground, ungraspable.

On the subject of Being and the infinite, however, we find in Merleau-Ponty only a small number of remarks which are all very ambiguous and even extremely vague. It would therefore be hazardous to attempt to explicitate his thought on this subject. At the least we can recognize that all these remarks fall into the framework of his general attempt to conceive of Being as the very Being of the world and not as a hidden in itself, an *Ens realissimum*, of which we would have no direct experience; Merleau-Ponty is attempting to think of Being as the very transcendency of the world, its latency and inex-haustible depth. Behind the notion of the infinite a thought is at work which is looking for its precise expression, a thought which we discover also in the notion of *dimensionality*.

Being is the *Offenheit* of the world; it is also the dimensionality of all dimensions. All things have something pregnant about them, are dimensions; and Being is dimensionality itself. (VI, 217-8, 227; *VI, 271, 280*) All particular things, Merleau-Ponty says, referring to Heidegger, "are integrated into a *universal dimensionality* which is Being". (VI, 236, 265; *VI, 289, 309*) Being is the totality of which each thing is a dimension, a "total part." (VI, 218; *VI, 271*) Spatial dimensions, for example, "are taken...from a single dimensionality, a polymorphous Being, which justifies all without being fully expressed by any." (PriP, 174; *OE,* 48)

It is thus that the notion of Being as dimensionality refers back to the notion of Being as *fecundity* or *pregnancy.* Being is precisely the *matrix* which comprises an infinity of possibilities. It is the "poly-morphism" or the "amorphism" of which each thing is a partial ex-pression (but expressive as such of the totality). We find in Merleau-Ponty a great number of expressions for designating Being as the possibility of every actual thing, encompassing it and encompassed in it, notably these: "pregnancy," "productivity," "fecundity," "latency," "depth," "polymorphism," "pregnancy of possibilities," "polymorphous matrix." The important thing is to remember that Being qua possibility is not "some thing" chronologically prior to the actual world (like Leibniz's infinity), but that it is the very actuality of the world, for only that is actual which includes its own possibility. Being is thus the possibility and the fecundity of the actual world, comprehended in it and comprehending it. In his attempt to think the *archē*, Merleau-Ponty does not want, like Aristotle, to have to choose between the chicken and the egg.

There is, however, a danger in all these expressions, the danger that even if with them one avoids the temptation of really separating Being and the world—while still not confusing them—one could nonetheless be led to conceive of Being as something static. And so to end we must advance yet another step so as to see how, for Merleau-Ponty, "Being holds together only in movement," as he says (S, 22; *S,* 30), how the ultimate meaning of Being is something dynamic, how the essence of Being is to be essence—*Wesen*—on the condition that this word is used in its verbal sense. The world is Being manifest-*ing* itself, and Being is "*Self-manifestation,* disclosure in the process of forming itself." (VI, 91; *VI,* 125) "Every visual something," Merleau-Ponty writes, "as individual as it is, functions also as a dimension, because it gives itself as the result of a dehiscence of Being." (PriP, 187; *OE,* 85) All things are therefore dimensions, because they are like the expressions of a "Being in dehiscence," because they are pre-cisely the *rays (rayonnements)* of Being. And the essence of Being is to be a shining forth *(rayonnement)*, *Erscheinung*, ψαίνεσθαι. The terms with which Merleau-Ponty expresses this dynamic sense of Being here are the following: "pure there is," "advent," "apparition," "shining forth," "phenomenon," "bursting" (*éclatement*), "explosion," "dehiscence," "fission," "upsurge," "gushing," "*wesen.*"

To use a phrase to which he often returns, Being is "pure there is"; but obviously there can be no "there is" if there is not something which is "there," such that to ask the question, What is Being? is to ask not only, "What is the *there is?*" (VI, 129; *VI,* 171), but also, "What is this *there is* of the sensible world, of nature?" (VI, 214; *VI,* 267) It would be as absurd to want to think being "in itself" as it would be to want to see pure light, for although light is not identical with what it illuminates, *there is* no light except in illuminated things. Likewise, Being is nothing in itself but is the "there is" of the world; it is the world appearing, "surging up from polymorphism." (VI, 207; *VI,* 260) Being is nowhere else than in the fact that the world *is,* is present; it is not the world as a fact, but it is that which makes the world be a "fact"; it is the "facticity" of the fact (VI, 140; *VI,* 184), its presence. Being is not something which is positive in itself, but rather "that event by which there is something," "the advent of the positive." (VI, 206; *VI,* 259) The phenomenon (the world) is not a mask covering Being which itself would be an "unknown X" or a "Ding-an-sich," but neither is it identical with Being. It is Being being, so to speak; it is the manifestation and realization of Being, since Being, qua shining forth and generativity, does not realize itself as such except in phenomena. One could therefore say that Being is the very phenomenality of the phenomenon, that which gives it the power of shining forth. The world is the field of Being (and in this right is *open*), the place where Being makes its advent; it is Being adventing, the advent of Being (*il est l'Etre advenant, l'avènement de l'Etre*).

Being is therefore Nature, but this does not permit us for all that to assert that Merleau-Ponty's ontology is a species of naturalist philosophy, since Nature, as he understands it, is not material nature, either opposed to consciousness or including it, but is rather the foundation or the "ground" of that nature. It is in fact the "flesh" of the world, the ultimate source both of the sensible world and the sentient subject. Being is a kind of primordial Sensible, ontologically prior to the sensible properly so-called, which in its dehiscence makes its advent and *is (west)*[7] in the (subject) sensing (thing) sensible chiasm. In a working note of January 1959, Merleau-Ponty says that the "amorphous," "perceptual world"—by which he understands not the de facto world, the world as perceived, but Nature qua "pregnancy of possibilities," destined, so to speak, to perception—"is at bottom Being in Heidegger's sense". (VI, 170; *VI*, 223) He does not explain what he means, and it would be impossible to give a definitive interpretation of this text; it is nonetheless very suggestive. We know for example that Heidegger identifies Being and ψύσις; and it is perhaps indeed to this conception of ψύσις that Merleau-Ponty is referring, since in another note of the month following, just after having said that what is needed is a *"Wiederholung:* 'destruction' of the objectivistic ontology of the Cartesians"—an expression which obviously comes from Heidegger—he speaks of the "rediscovery of ψύσις." (VI, 183; *VI*, 237) Now for Heidegger ψύσις means " self-blossoming emergence," what unfolds itself in opening up; it is "the process of a-rising *(Ent-stehen),* of emerging from the hidden *(das Verborgene),"* and of enduring in this appearing.[8] One finds the same idea in Aristotle when he says that ψύσις means the genesis of that which is in genesis, this meaning being suggested, he says, by the word itself when the "υ" in "ψύσις" is pronounced long. *(Metaphysics,* 1014b17) This is essentially what Being, Nature, is for Merleau-Ponty. Nature is the active presence between the subject and things, and this chiasm, this brute or wild logos is the "result of a dehiscence of Being." In the last resort Being or Nature is therefore the upsurge of this chiasm, the articulating presence between the sentient and the sensible. We can thus see that the notions of Being as ψύσις, or springing forth, and as λόγος, or sentient-sensible chiasm, are strictly interlinked. We will return to this question in the following section.

By way of anticipating what is to follow, we can note here that this dynamic conception of Being as ψύσις, upsurge, shining forth, exploding, etc., opens up the way to a conception of the history of Being, to a kind of *Seinsgeschichte.* (VI, 182; *VI*, 236) For in this perspective all appearing is a becoming; every event is an advent. The "unmotivated upsurge of brute Being" (VI, 211; *VI*, 264) founds a universal history of which thought is in a sense the supreme λόγος or articulation. It is not only the world but also the subject himself who is englobed in Being, who is a field of Being, the event of the advent of Being, cipher of transcendence.


## II.   Being and Logos

AS Heidegger observes, philosophy has always associated being with truth. Merleau-Ponty makes the same association because on this point his thought is also very influenced by Husserlian phenomenology. For Husserl being is always being-for-the-subject; the being of the phenomenon is to be an object for consciousness. This is to say that the being of beings is their meaning; to be is to have meaning. And to speak of meaning is naturally to speak of a *consciousness* for which this meaning exists. In addition, to the degree that Husserl takes up an ever more resolute position in his "transcendental idealism," the meaning which is the being of beings is conceived of as the result of an act of constitution on the part of transcendental subjectivity.[9] Having identified being and meaning, Husserl ends up by positing pure transcendental consciousness as the ultimate foundation of both. How does Merleau-Ponty avoid this radical (transcendental, if one prefers) subjectivization of being?

It must indeed be said that for him the terms "being" and "logos" are practically interchangeable. This is understandable and perhaps even inevitable given his definition of Being as φύσις, as explosion or fission of Nature, of the "Sensible," of undivided being into the sensing-sensible chiasm or articulation (λόγος). The brute or wild Logos he speaks of is Being, Nature itself, inasmuch as in its dehiscence it articulates or differentiates itself into the sensing-sensible chiasm. We are obliged to say that Being or Nature *is (west)* as logos, that the sensing-sensible chiasm is the essence *(Wesen)* of Being, the word essence being taken here in a verbal sense. Being is the "there is" of the world, and the world is "there" only insofar as it is "there" for sensation or vision—for consciousness. Sensation itself, sensible consciousness, is the turning back of the visible on itself, the advent of a seeing-visible. This advent of the sensing-sensible chiasm is the "fragmentation of being," "the advent of the difference," the miraculous promotion of Being to consciousness"; it is the dehiscence, the splitting up of Being; it is Being transforming itself into logos. The terms with which Merleau-Ponty describes Being as shining forth, advent, are also the terms with which he describes the emergence of sensing in the midst of the sensible: "differentiation," "articulation," "structuration," "crystallization," etc.

The fact that all these terms can serve to describe Nature either as explosion or as a mode of being "there," of being present, that is, the fact that these terms can serve at one and the same time as verbs or as substantives (can describe Nature either as *natura naturans* or as *natura naturata,* so to speak) only underlines the double meaning of

Being (Nature)—as process and as meaning (configuration). The emergence of sensation in the midst of the sensible is not the product of a prior Being; it is rather Being manifesting itself and *being.* One could perhaps in a certain sense compare Merleau-Ponty's thought to the idea of the Trinity, where, although the Word proceeds from the Father, he is strictly simultaneous, co-substantial, and co-eternal with him. Similarly, in Merleau-Ponty's ontology, at the beginning is the λόγος, and the λόγος is comprehended within Being, and the λόγος is Being com-prehending itself. The sensing-sensible differentiation (brute logos) is the very definition or logos of Being; it is Being being, Being articulating itself.

If this is how things stand, however, it could be wondered if an ontology such as this, which identifies the meaning of Being with its appearing, with the emergence of sensation in the midst of the sensible, does not end up, as in the case of Husserl, by tying together Being and its presence, Being and consciousness therefore, in short, Being and man. This is a serious question to which, it would appear, an affirmative answer is required. This makes it all the more important to have another look at what, in this case, "man" is, when all is said and done.

For the time being we may note that the question as to what Being might be without man, or before him, does not seem to have much meaning for Merleau-Ponty. He hardly ever even raises the question. In one passage, however, he writes, "If it were possible to abolish in thought all individual consciousness there would remain only a flash [*jaillissement*] of instantaneous being, extinguished no sooner than it has appeared." (TFL, 65; *RC,* 95) As we have already observed, Merleau-Ponty's "new ontology" is not a pure and simple abandonment of phenomenology and a return to realist and objectivistic thought. Even though Merleau-Ponty wants to overcome phenomenology qua philosophy of consciousness, qua ontology which reduces everything to subjectivity (even if it be transcendental), he does not want to do so except from the "inside" of phenomenology; he wants to overcome subjectivity by making of it the necessary starting point.

Now a phenomenological approach to the question of Being must always ground itself on the phenomenal, on what is effectively given, on what is *present:* "we do indeed first have to fix our gaze on what is apparently *given* to us." (VI, 159; *VI,* 211) The consequence of this is that a phenomenological ontology can raise the question of Being only by asking what the Being of beings is, what Being is as the "there is," the presence of the world. From this point of view, the question of knowing what Being is in itself, as such, abstracting from what actually is, quite simply has no meaning at all. To ask what the meaning of Being is is to ask what makes it be that the world exists, is "there," is present. Now for the world to be, to be "there," to be present, it is essential that it be present to consciousness. From a phenomenological point of view, the transcendence of Being can be grasped and thought only in relation to immanence, only in relation to its presence to consciousness. This does not necessarily mean—and herein lies the originality of Merleau-Ponty's philosophy—that the transcendence of Being is constituted in or is founded upon its immanence to consciousness. It is, however, in any event a fact that man exists and that the world is "there" for him; consciousness is indeed an undeniable fact, a fact which conditions for us all other facts. There can, therefore, be no question of pretending that we do not exist so as to then attempt to engender ourselves by some imaginative causal process. The whole question is rather one of knowing what our existence *means.* As a philosophy of Being, metaphysics must be a metaphysics of experience. The question, What is the "there is" of the world? is the question, What is consciousness? or, What is man?

## III.    Being and Man

"ONE of the tests in which philosophy best reveals its essence is its confrontation with Christianity" (S, 140; *S,* 176), Merleau-Ponty wrote in the middle of the 1950s. That seems to be eminently true of his own philosophy, for unlike Husserl's philosophy, for instance, which was formed in an almost exclusively mathematico-logico-psychological context, Merleau-Ponty's thought and the basic positions he takes can finally be understood only in relation to Christianity. It would seem, therefore, that in its confrontation with Christianity Merleau-Ponty's philosophy not only reveals its essence but, even more, finds it. In writing a preface to Christian philosophy for the project "philosophes célèbres," Merleau-Ponty said that there assuredly is a Christian philosophy, just as there is a romantic or a French philosophy, but that it is "incomparably more extensive, since in addition to the two philosophies we have mentioned it contains all that has been thought in the West for twenty centuries." (S, 142; *S,* 179) This amounts to recognizing that Christianity, with its ideas of "history, subjectivity, incarnation," etc., constitutes a fact of history and conditions all of Western thought. But to say this, he also remarks, is not for all that to resolve the question of what Christian philosophy is; for the real problem of Christian philosophy is the relation between philosophy and Christianity understood, not as a historical institution, as "a mental horizon or matrix of culture," but as that which is "effectively lived and practiced in a positive faith." (S, 142; *S,* 179) For Merleau-Ponty, therefore, the real encounter between philosophy and Christianity is "a conflict...within each Christian in the form of the conflict between Christianity 'understood' and Christianity lived, between universality and choice." (S, 142-3; *S,* 180) It is the conflict between reason and faith, between the natural powers of knowledge and the supernatural demands of faith. And it is in this sense that Merleau-Ponty's philosophy can be defined in relation to Christianity.

His philosophy is in a way the expression of his attempt to resolve the internal conflict in that Christian he himself was (a conflict which was perhaps even greater in that he was not, so to speak, born into Catholicism and was baptized at a relatively late date). Even after he left the Church, Christianity, it seems, continued to play the role of interlocutor in the depths of his thought. When one has first of all looked to Christianity for an answer to the questions of existence, it is doubtful that this first engagement should cease to influence in one way or another what one is or thinks afterwards. Even revolt, Merleau-Ponty says, does not quit us of that against which we revolt; on the contrary, it continues to be present to us by becoming the motive and the *raison d'être* of our revolt, "as an act confers a certain quality upon us for ever, even though we may afterwards repudiate it and change our beliefs." (PhP, 393; *PP,* 450) And he says as well, "in every life, one's birth and one's past define categories or basic dimensions which do not impose any particular act but which can be read or found in all." (SNS, 24; *SNS,* 42)

Merleau-Ponty was still a believer and was attempting to work out the meaning of his membership in the Church (even though he was not, it seems, completely orthodox in his practice of Catholicism) when he was a student at the École Normale Supérieure. It was afterwards, on witnessing the internal contradictions of contemporary Christianity, which preaches love for one's fellow man but is uninterested in the material welfare of men, which teaches justice but tem-

porizes with the most reactionary of powers, that he was personally
scandalized, no doubt due to the great demands for purity of faith
that he imposed on himself, and was led to leave the Church and to
denounce it as an institution. "God will not fully have come to the
earth until the Church feels the same obligation toward other men as
it does toward its own ministers, toward the houses of Guernica as
toward its own temples," he said. (SNS, 178; *SNS,* 316) Indeed,
Merleau-Ponty wanted nothing to do with a God posited over and
above the world and at its expense, transcendent and indifferent to
the fate of men. If God exists and if we can speak of him, it is only
insofar as he is *immanent* to this world, only insofar as he assumes its
flesh and makes himself into man. What counts for man is not to believe that his life's conflicts are solved elsewhere, under another sky,
but "to enter body and soul into an enigmatic life, the obscurities of
which cannot be dissipated but can only be concentrated in a few
mysteries where man contemplates the enlarged image of his own condition." If the doctrines of the Incarnation and Original Sin have some
meaning for us, it is, he says, "because they reflect man's contradictions
of body and soul, nobility and wretchedness." (SNS, 175; *SNS,* 310–1)
Similarly, if the word "freedom" has a meaning, it is because man
cannot rediscover in some divine legislation the secret of the universe
and of his life, but must realize himself with the means given to him
by virtue of his earthly condition. To posit a God as an infinite thought
which has already regulated everything is quite simply to deny man;
it is to throw a mask over the fact that *in any event* it is always man
who must make his own decisons. "Whether there is or is not an absolute thought and an absolute evaluation in each practical problem,"
Merleau-Ponty says, "my own opinions, which remain capable of error
no matter how rigorously I examine them, are still my only equipment
for judging." (SNS, 95; *SNS,* 166)

It is not our intention to recall here Merleau-Ponty's changes of
attitude towards Christianity. We are only raising the question because
it seems to help us in understanding the positions he takes up in his
philosophy. The questions of the relation between being and subjectivity, between immanence and transcendence, which are indeed central questions in his phenomenology and in every philosophy of consciousness in general, are better illuminated when they are considered
against the background of Christian thought. One cannot for instance
understand Merleau-Ponty's rejection of the "absolute" in the *Phenomenology* and the other writings of this period and his obstinate

defense of "contingency" except in relation to a certain notion of transcendence current in Christian thought. The fact that in the *Phenomenology* the terms "absolute thought" and "divine thought" are interchangeable and constitute an essential element in his argument against intellectualism shows clearly that Merleau-Ponty's philosophical argument is situated against a backdrop of Christian notions.

Unlike Sartre, who declared himself an atheist for entirely philosophical reasons, it seems very much that Merleau-Ponty's abandonment of Catholicism was due to a crisis of conscience, and that philosophy was not the cause but the reply to this rupture. His subsequent study of Husserl gave him perhaps above all a certain philosophical attitude, a certain way of philosophizing and of regarding experience. In any event, it is striking that the primary demands of the German philosopher are also those that Merleau-Ponty defends the most: philosophy as rigorous knowledge, philosophical radicalism, and the autonomy of philosophy. These are requirements that Merleau-Ponty never abandoned but which, in the course of his philosophical life, changed in meaning. In a certain sense, the development of his thought appears as the attempt to free himself from certain fundamental theses of Husserlian phenomenology while still holding firmly to the same demands that motivated Husserl's enterprise.

In the *Phenomenology* for instance, in wanting to keep philosophy in contact with experience and in wanting to conceive of our actual experience as the absolute source of meaning for us, Merleau-Ponty nevertheless does not escape the idealistic consequences of Husserlian phenomenology. Wanting to eliminate all "reference to an absolute knowledge and an absolute being in relation to which our factual self-evidences, or synthetic truths, are considered inadequate," Merleau-Ponty subscribes without reserve to "the phenomenological conception" and with Husserl defines "being as that which appears, and consciousness as a universal fact." (PhP, 397; *PP*, 455) A step of this sort entails numerous consequences: not only does it safeguard the originality and the intrinsic value of human experience, but, as a matter of fact, it makes of subjectivity the ground of being, which for its part is essentially no longer anything other than the correlate of the subject's intentions. Such a step sets up immanence as the criterion of truth and being and denies all transcendence as such.

If, Merleau-Ponty says, I try to imagine a divine logic, this logic has to figure in my own universe. He therefore draws the conclusion that "My thought, my self-evident truth is not one fact among others, but a value-fact which envelops and conditions every other possible one." (PhP, 398; *PP*, 456) My world, he says, is the only possible world, not because it is necessary being, but because any "other world" I might conceive of would have to be constituted on the basis of this world and "would consequently merely fuse with it." This, it can be seen, is a variation on Berkeley's famous argument that Merleau-Ponty, after Husserl, is taking up on his own account, an argument which asserts that even the most deserted of places has at least one observer, namely, me when I imagine it. One might want to say that this is a rather naive argument which proves that, for it to appear to me, all being must be immanent to my consciousness, but which does not prove that the being of beings is nothing but an intentional correlate immanent to my consciousness. In any event, Merleau-Ponty makes the rather significant remark that what is sometimes "termed Husserl's rationalism is in reality the recognition of subjectivity as an inalienable fact, and of the world to which it is directed as *omnitudo realitatis.*" (PhP, 398 n; *PP*, 456, n) At the time of the *Phenomenology* Merleau-Ponty is quite ready to maintain that the only kind of being of which I can speak is being-for-me. (SNS, 93; *SNS*, 164) It is thus not surprising that at this time he should be led to reject the idea of a "transcendence in immanence." Although Merleau-Ponty refuses to recognize Husserl's transcendental Ego, substituting for it instead the lived body as the first subject of perception, his position basically does not differ in any radical way from Husserl's; for, like Husserl, Merleau-Ponty postulates that the only meaning of being is being-for-the-subject and maintains immanence as the first requirement of philosophical method.[10]

In the preceding chapter we saw how the "idealistic" orientation of the *Phenomenology* displeased Merleau-Ponty and how, in *The Visible and the Invisible,* he reproached himself with having started out with the consciousness-object distinction and with not having rethought in a sufficiently radical way the notion of intentionality.[11] This change in his thought is basically a change in his conception of the relations between being and subjectivity, between transcendence and immanence. A fact of interest is that this change is contemporaneous with a development in his attitude towards Christianity. Indeed, one sees him, in remarks made in the 1950s, returning anew to the notion of a transcendence in immanence, to the notions of philosophical radicalism and autonomy; one sees him sketching out, as it were, the project of what was to be his "negative philosophy" or his "indirect ontology."

What Merleau-Ponty still refuses and what he will always refuse is the Cartesian notion of a *veracitas divina* as the guarantee of philosophical truth, the idea, therefore, that if philosophy effectively uncovers the enigmas and the "unreason" of human existence (such as, for instance, the mysterious union of body and soul) and is a statement of the contingency of being and truth for us, it can nevertheless find a solution to these enigmas in a transcendent reason, in an absolute or divine thought, which it posits over and above the aporias of life. However, it is perhaps by confronting him with Pascal, not Descartes, that one can best grasp the essence of his position. It does indeed appear, as Sartre attests,[12] that the young Merleau-Ponty was very Pascalian in temperament. In any case, the similarity between their conceptions of man is altogether striking. Like Pascal, Merleau-Ponty accentuates to the utmost the finitude and the contingency of existence. For Merleau-Ponty also, the nobility of man resides in his very wretchedness, in his awareness of his own contingency. Just as for Pascal man "is but a reed, the weakest thing in nature"—although, as a thinking reed, he transcends the universe by *knowing* the advantage held over him by the universe, chance, and adversity which dominate him—so also for Merleau-Ponty man "is not a force but a weakness at the heart of being, not a cosmological factor but the place where all cosmological factors, by a mutation which is never finished, change in sense and become history." (IPP, 44; *EP*, 71) As for Pascal, man, suspended between nothingness and infinity, becomes conscious that "the end of things and their principle are for him hopelessly hidden in an impenetrable secret," notes that he desires to find "a firm ground and an ultimate constant base," but discovers that every "foundation cracks and the earth opens to abysses" and that this state which is natural to him is yet most contrary to his inclinations;[13] so also for Merleau-Ponty, man, who is animated by the desire for a "total manifestation," a "presumption on reason's part," a "teleology of consciousness," must nonetheless admit that he can never see the idea face to face (SNS, 25; *SNS*, 44), that the "highest form of reason cohabits with unreason," and must recognize "the background of nonsense against which every universal undertaking is silhouetted and by which it is threatened with failure." (SNS, 4; *SNS*, 9)

This comparison could be carried much further, but what must above all be insisted on is the point where Merleau-Ponty branches off from Pascal and goes his own way. For what Merleau-Ponty cannot accept in the Pascalian view of things is precisely his famous "wager"—the idea that, since reason cannot discover a solid, ultimate foundation, one must by an act of faith wager everything on an ineffable beyond in the patient hope of receiving a light different from that of reason and of which reason can know nothing. For Merleau-Ponty, if in the depths of his being man is open to a transcendence, this transcendence cannot be alien to him but must announce itself in his experience and be an integral part of it. Merleau-Ponty is perhaps being even more faithful than Pascal to the lesson that Pascal draws from the fact that man is but a thinking reed—namely, that all of man's dignity consists in thought and that the essential thing therefore is to think *well*. If to philosophize truly and authentically is to philosophize *radically*, the philosopher can accept nothing that he cannot himself experience qua philosopher. What Merleau-Ponty cannot accept in Pascal is thus his return to mysticism, intuition, and irrational feeling. What finally he cannot accept is the idea of there being "two orders" (S, 143; *S,* 181)—a natural order and a supernatural order, an order of immanence and an order of transcendence, the first being that of reason and natural knowledge, the second that of faith alone.

What in this regard Merleau-Ponty finds interesting in Malebranche is the idea that the relation between philosophy and religion is not one wherein religion transcends and replaces philosophy but one wherein philosophy and religion co-exist simultaneously. Religious vision does not replace philosophical thought at a certain point; philosophy and religion are parallel to each other and reach God by complementary ways because philosophy itself arises from a kind of "natural revelation." Thus even in the natural order itself, according to Malebranche as summarized by Merleau-Ponty, "we are neither our own light to ourselves nor the source of our ideas.... All there can be in us of light and of intentional being comes from our participation in God." (S, 144; *S,* 181) Were one to substitute the word "Being" for that of "God," one would have here Merleau-Ponty's own thought such as one discovers it four years later in "Eye and Mind." In this last essay of his, Merleau-Ponty speaks of "a vision, a seeing...which we do not make, which makes itself in us," and of an "inspiration and expiration of Being, action and passion so slightly discernible that it becomes impossible to distinguish between what sees and what is seen". (PriP,

167; *OE,* 30–2) It is as though Merleau-Ponty had seized hold of this chance to speak of Christian philosophy in order, so to speak, to try out a few ideas which were beginning to take shape in his own mind.[14]

There is yet another thing to note in these remarks on the "two orders" or "two realms," and it is that here Merleau-Ponty speaks of "negative philosophy." (S, 146; *S,* 184) He observes that in taking up Pascal's idea Brunschwieg had expressed the hypothesis of a philosophy which acknowledges its own insufficiency and thereby provides an introduction to Christianity as the ultimate interpretation of man. He links up this idea to the position expressed by Blondel, for whom "philosophy *was* thought realizing that it cannot 'close the gap,' locating and palpating inside and outside of us a reality whose source is not philosophical awareness." (S, 140; *S,* 177) When we recall that for the Merleau-Ponty of the *Phenomenology* philosophy, as radical reflection, is the awareness of its own insufficiency and its inability to complete itself as reflection, we can understand that these remarks on Christian philosophy are not a mere commentary on the history of philosophy, but are for him an occasion to refine his own position. It is therefore significant that if "negative philosophy" is conceived of in this sense—as merely motivating a passage which it itself cannot accomplish and from which it must stand back like Moses before the Promised Land—Merleau-Ponty rejects it. If, he asks, "philosophy is universal and autonomous, how could it leave responsibility for its conclusions to an absolute decision?...how could it help wanting to be a witness to this very passage from universal to particular? How could it possibly dwell in the negative and abandon the positive to a 'wholly other' solicitation?" (S, 146; *S,* 184) Philosophy cannot merely be an interrogation which prepares the way for a massive affirmation lying beyond its competence. If philosophy recognizes its own insufficiency, it can only be because in one way or another it has grasped that which surpasses it. Philosophical interrogation is everything or it is nothing. In any event, it cannot be merely the means of a transcendent end or the emptiness of a certain fullness, the negative of a certain positive. It must itself be the dialectical relation between the two. Hence, because philosophy is an autonomous and radical knowledge or interrogation, there is nothing that can remain outside of it.

Although Merleau-Ponty does not pursue this idea of a "negative philosophy" here, this text on Christianity appears to be no less full of significance as regards the meaning and the development of his own thought. In spite of the apparently rather specialized character of the subject in question—Christian philosophy—this text stands out as a turning point in the development of his philosophy, constituting for him an occasion to reconsider a question which concerns, not merely the relation between reason and faith, but also phenomenology itself as such, the question of the relations between immanence and transcendence, being and subjectivity. In the last analysis the question is this: While not abandoning subjectivity, to what degree can a philosophy of consciousness, of subjectivity, overcome itself so as to think a Being of transcendence not reduced to subjectivity? This question expresses the meaning and the effort of Merleau-Ponty's later philosophy which we must now attempt to make more precise.

As regards the relations between Being and man, we could perhaps find an introduction to Merleau-Ponty's later thought and grasp its originality in regard to what precedes it by taking as an example his way of conceiving of the birth of the subject. It is perhaps in regard to this question that one can best realize the deepening which has occurred in his philosophy. In the *Phenomenology* Merleau-Ponty says that the ultimate foundation of rationality is the subject's (bodily) presence to the world. Now when one looks for the origin and the ground of this presence, one comes back in the end to the event of the individual's birth. From a phenomenological point of view the subject's birth is what is truly fundamental and irreducible; it is the *Urarchē*. In the *Phenomenology* however (PhP, 406-7; PP, 465-6), Merleau-Ponty conceives of the individual's birth, certainly not as an event like all other events—since it is in fact that event which founds all others and which thus provides for a history (it is, he said, an advent or a transcendental event)—but as a wholly gratuitous and thoroughly incomprehensible event in regard to everything else. Once the individual is born, he will not fail to be a meaningful existence which gives to the world "a new layer of meaning." With the subject's birth the world is, as it were, dedicated to reason; a "teleology" of meaning is instituted. Merleau-Ponty thus posits birth as an absolute *origin* of meaning. He does not, however, seek to clarify the event of birth itself; on the contrary, he posits it as a kind of absolute zero point, as the completely gratuitous irruption of the subject, of meaning, in the world. This is to say that his way of conceiving of birth here only underlines all the more the fundamental opposition between the subject and the world, the incomprehensibility, and the unsurpassable contingency of this relationship.

Indeed, Merleau-Ponty is faced with the following dilemma: either he maintains that the subject's birth is a true *origin* of meaning and the first instance of the radical contingency of our situation vis-à-vis the world—and in this case he is obliged (or so he thinks) to deny all ideas of causality and all attempts at explanation—or else he admits the possibility of a kind of necessity behind the event of birth and makes it into an understandable event—but in this case he returns (or so he thinks) to causalistic thought (whether the cause here is God or the material world) and does away with the contingency of existence. In other words, either birth is a contingent event, and in this case there is no absolute, or there is an absolute somewhere, and in this case contingency no longer exists. It is however a fact that there is contingency in existence—theologians themselves admit it—therefore, Merleau-Ponty concludes, there can be no absolute. What precisely he objects to in theology is that it "recognizes the contingency of human existence only to derive it from a necessary Being, that is, to do away with it." (IPP, 44; *EP,* 72) If, however, one effectively makes of contingency the last word, and if one refuses to admit that subjectivity is derived from something else, maintaining instead that it comes into the world from, as it were, nowhere, one is coming dangerously close to the Sartrian notion of subjectivity as *nothingness.* That the alternative which Merleau-Ponty is setting up in the *Phenomenology* is not the only one and that there is as a matter of fact a third way he himself will see later. This third way he will attempt to follow up under the title of ontology.

Indeed, in his last writings everything has changed. In short, Merleau-Ponty says here that, if the subject finds himself present to the world and a project of the world, it is not due to a gratuitous and wholly incomprehensible (because it is itself the foundation of all rationality) event; it is, rather, the result of an explosion of Being. A human body is there, he says, when the undivided flesh of the sensible differentiates itself and articulates itself in the sensing-sensible chiasm. A natural light is thereby engendered that will not cease to shine "until some accident of the body will undo *what no accident would have sufficed to do.*" (PriP, 164; *OE,* 21; emphasis ours) The subject's birth is therefore not an *accident,* an absolutely gratuitous and contingent fact, an incomprehensible chance event; it is rather *the coming to light of Being itself.* If Merleau-Ponty always insisted on the point of man's being a natural light, this notion receives a new and deepened meaning in his later philosophy; for if man is effectively a light in nature, he is so because he is the illumination of Being (Nature) itself. If man finds himself face to face with the world, this state is not pure contingency nor does it result because he is produced by the world, but rather because both he and the world are together derived from a single Being which englobes and upholds them. It is, Merleau-Ponty says, in a "being of promiscuity," a "polymorphous being," that "is found the reservoir whence proceeds this new absolute life. All verticality comes from vertical Being." (VI, 234; *VI,* 287) The subject is "there" because he is the self-realization of Being itself.

What is to be noted here is that Merleau-Ponty overcomes phenomenology and the point of view of subjectivity so as to recognize as the ultimate foundation a Being of transcendence that is not reduced to subjectivity, and he does so without having any recourse to a "leap" of the Heideggerian sort towards an ineffable beyond; in other words, he does so without any abandonment of subjectivity.

Indeed, as modern philosophy has recognized, subjectivity is an altogether original and irreducible fact. There can therefore be no question of *explaining* it, as if it were a secondary realm of being, as if it were something passive, an effect produced by something else. On the contrary, subjectivity is what is presupposed by all explanations; it is a necessary starting point, because, if we conceive of subjectivity as a secondary effect or as a product (of, for instance, divine causality), it is still we who do so, and this proves that subjectivity is indeed an irreducible and always presupposed fact. Does this mean that the only genuinely possible philosophy is a philosophy of consciousness, a transcendental philosophy of pure immanence which posits subjectivity as the ground of being, of everything which can be and can be thought? Merleau-Ponty does not think so. In a working note of November 1959 he says that if philosophy has spoken of our activity, it has, in comparison, never spoken "of the passivity of our activity." (VI, 221; *VI,* 273) It is, he admits, a fact that we always think and that we cannot not think. But the fact of thinking, of being conscious, is not, truly speaking, an *activity* on our part. I think, I am a stream of consciousness; but it is nonetheless not I who *makes it be* that I think. I am not, he says, the author of my consciousness; "it is not I who makes myself think any more than it is I who makes my heart beat." And from this he draws the conclusion that it is necessary to "leave the philosophy of *Erlebnisse* and pass to the philosophy of our *Urstiftung*". (VI, 221; *VI,* 275)

Consciousness is indeed undeniable, but it is not and cannot be *causa sui* in regard to itself, its own origin, and its own foundation, its *Urstiftung*. It is in thinking its genesis that consciousness realizes that it cannot grasp itself, cannot "close the gap," that it cannot return beneath itself so as to ground itself. And thus consciousness cannot coincide with its genesis and cannot assist at its own birth. As Pascal said of man, "the end of things and their origin are hopelessly hidden from him in an impenetrable secret." A philosophy of consciousness— phenomenology—can be overcome only by a philosophy which, from within consciousness (one can obviously never get outside of consciousness), takes as its theme the limits of consciousness. One can think a Being not reduced to consciousness only through consciousness, as that which makes consciousness consciousness, as that which dissimulates itself from consciousness by the very fact that it is consciousness.

Confronted with this dilemma—"how to be resigned to consciousness? how to challenge consciousness?"—Merleau-Ponty replies, "to be surmounted by the idea of consciousness as *Offenheit*." (VI, 198; VI, 252) There can be no question of conceiving of a Being which would be the cause of itself, a *Selbsterscheinung*, an auto-apparition (VI, 191; VI, 244-5), because consciousness or the "for itself" has an "uncontestable character." Rather, in recognizing the "derived" character of subjectivity, it is necessary to think of it as "the culmination of separation (*écart*) in *differentiation*," that is, as the end result or the expression of the segregation or the dehiscence of Being (the flesh) in the sensing-sensible differentiation or chiasm. In this way consciousness would be an *opening* in Being; it would be Being opening itself up. The presence to oneself, which is the definition of consciousness, would be the very *presence* which is instituted in the Sensible when it differentiates itself and secretes an "inside" which is sensation. The advent of consciousness is the "advent of difference" that is, the surging up of the sensing-sensible differentiation. The "for itself," as phenomenology has recognized, has nothing in itself about it, but is wholly intentional, a project of the world. It is indeed, therefore, a kind of *nothingness*. However, Merleau-Ponty locates this "nothingness" in the very heart of Being. It is Being itself which contains its nothingness, which differentiates itself into the "in itself" (the sensible) and the "for itself" (the sentient). "If indeed *being* is not only being," Hyppolite says in commenting on Hegel, "if it contains the possibility of a *knowledge* of being, the possibility of the *question* about being, it is because it is its negation."[15] Similarly, Merleau-Ponty says that the sensible world–sentient body dialectical relation "is finally possible and means something only because *there is* Being, not Being in itself, identical to itself, in the night, but the Being that also contains its negation". (VI, 250-1; *VI, 304*) The negation of Being is not a *nichtiges Nichts* (VI, 196, 201; *VI,* 249, 254) opposed to it as to a "hard core"; rather, being itself is its own negation. For Merleau-Ponty the "negative" is the sensing-sensible difference or differentiation "that is instituted by the flesh, by its dehiscence". (VI, 263; *VI,* 316) For him "the negative, nothingness, is the doubled-up, the two leaves of my body, the inside and the outside articulated over one another."[16] The negative is the *Offenheit,* the opening within Being; it is that originating presence or that "inaugural there is" which is sensible consciousness. "It is," Merleau-Ponty says, "the Cartesian idealization applied to the mind as to things (Husserl) that has persuaded us that we were a flux of individual *Erlebnisse*, whereas *we are a field of Being*." (VI, 240; *VI,* 293; emphasis ours)

Merleau-Ponty's ontology is thus not an "objective philosophy" (VI, 169, *VI,* 223) because it refuses to consider Being and subjectivity as two real entities between which there could be causal relations and thus an ontological subordination. It is, on the contrary, an "indirect ontology" which conceives of Being in beings and notably in that being which is man. It is, as we have seen, a "negative philosophy" which does not attempt to think Being except as the presupposed but ungraspable ground of subjectivity. Just as a negative theology might be said to be one which recognizes that original sin, that distance or that rent *(fissure)* between man and God, is at the root of the desire to know and return to God but at the same time necessarily makes this attempt impossible (here below), since if original sin were suppressed our existence as carnal beings would be likewise, so also a "negative philosophy" such as Merleau-Ponty's could be said to be one which recognizes that the "fission" of Being which produces subjectivity is also that which inevitably makes it be that the subject cannot turn back and coincide with a "pure" or "undivided Being." If subjectivity can be understood only in relation to Being, but if, on the other hand, Being expresses itself only in subjectivity through a fission, an explosion, or a differentiation which is in a way its own negation, then the relation between man and Being in Merleau-Ponty recalls Hegel's *Aufheben:* the advent of subjectivity qua advent of a *Seinsverständnis*, qua emergence of presence, of the "there is" or of consciousness, is a *negation* of Being whereby Being realizes itself, a negation of Being which is "the miraculous promotion of Being to 'consciousness'." (VI, 118; *VI,* 158)

Still, it remains that the relation between Being and subjectivity is a *dialectical* relation through and through. Subjectivity may be derived from Being, which itself holds in this way the "absolute primacy," but Being is conceivable only through and always in relation to subjectivity. This is the reason why one can speak of a "negative philosophy" in Merleau-Ponty: Being is thinkable only indirectly, as the absence or ungraspable latency behind all presence; it is thinkable only in relation to subjectivity, which is the expression of its own "negation." "This being—which is glimpsed through time's stirrings and always intended by our temporality, perception, and our carnal being," Merleau-Ponty writes, "but to which there can be no question of our being transported because to abolish its distance would be to take away its consistency of being—this being 'of distances' as Heidegger will put it, which is always offered to our transcendence, is the dialectical idea of being as defined in the *Parmenides*—beyond the empirical multiplicity of existent things and as a matter of principle intended through them, because separated from them it would be only lightning flash or darkness." (S, 156; *S,* 197) If man is a natural light, an illumination in Being, Being without man could only be "the night wherein all cows are black."

It is thus entirely as though in Merleau-Ponty Being needs man in order to *truly* be, such that man is the "there is," the presence, the *truth,* the very λόγος of Being. We find yet again in Merleau-Ponty's remarks on theological questions something like the outline of his own thought. It is a fact that he was always intrigued by the notion of a God "underneath" us, a God incarnated in the flesh of the world. He said that the Christian God "is not simply a principle of which we are the consequence, a will whose instruments we are, or even a model of which human values are only the reflection. There is a sort of impotence of God without us, and Christ attests that God would not be fully God without becoming fully man." (S, 71; *S,* 88) What interests him is the idea of a God not above but beneath us, and this leads him to say that "transcendence no longer hangs over man: he becomes, strangely, its privileged bearer." In his inaugural lesson at the Collège de France, Merleau-Ponty speaks at length of God in Bergson's philosophy. "There is in Bergsonian theology," he says, "as perhaps in every theology since Christianity, an ambiguity thanks to which we never know if it is God who sustains men in their human being or if it is the inverse, since in order to know his existence it is necessary to pass through ours, and this is not an optional detour." (IPP, 26; *EP,* 44)

It seems to us that this interest which Merleau-Ponty manifested throughout the whole of his life for the question concerning the relations between God and the world, God and man, is not merely a peripheral curiosity in his philosophy, but must rather be considered as belonging to and as revealing it essence. For at bottom it is not merely a theological question, but is first of all and most properly a philosophical one. Again it is the question as to the relations between transcendence and immanence, Being and subjectivity, which constitutes the central problematic in phenomenology and which especially interests Merleau-Ponty. In this way it is difficult to disassociate the "God" he speaks of from the "Being" of his late philosophy; whether he speaks of God or of Being, the question he is raising comes down in the end to the same thing, because it is that of subjectivity and what transcends it. What indeed, he insists on above all is that, as we have just seen, transcendence does not hang over man; rather, man is its "privileged bearer." He says in *In Praise of Philosophy* that with respect to a God conceived of as a transcendent force, our life of men would be insignificant, without any real importance; but with respect a "God who is on the side of men corresponds, on the contrary, a forward-looking history which is an experience searching for its accomplishment." (IPP, 26; *EP,* 44–5) If Being is underneath man and only expresses itself in him, human history then possesses an ontological significance because it is the history of the becoming of Being itself. This is to say, therefore, that the truth or the meaning of Being is always something to be realized and constitutes the task or the vocation of man himself. We must now follow up this last point if we want to get to the bottom of the question of the relations between Being and man.

"How a truth can be the work of men, set out at the very heart of existence, by the very mediation of existence, and yet surpass this existence.... This problem is not resolved in any clear way by Hegel.... It is the problem raised today in existentialism as well as in Marxism as in Christianity." This problem, which Hyppolite encounters in his reading of Hegel,[17] is also the one found in Merleau-Ponty. It could even be said that the whole of his later philosophy is, when all is said and done, the attempt to resolve this problem. What is in question is to know how, out of man's presence to the world, a truth or a meaning (a λόγος) is born which is, by this very fact, inseparable from man and his presence to the world, but which for all that does not have a merely "anthropological" significance but is rather the truth of a Being which possesses man; it is the question of knowing how man is the realization and the expression of a truth which is the truth of Being itself.

The notion of the flesh is the key to the problem of truth or meaning in Merleau-Ponty. He discerns two orders or two levels of meaning which are those of perceptual (or natural) meaning and intellectual (or cultural) meaning, the latter grounding itself on the former, on the carnal relation of man to the world. The important thing, therefore, is to understand correctly what is for Merleau-Ponty man's perceptual or carnal presence to the world.

The notion of meaning obviously refers back to that of consciousness; meaning does not exist except in relation to a consciousness (either actual or possible); to speak of the meaning of the world is to speak of what exists for a consciousness. What is sensible consciousness therefore? We recognize here the same problematic as that worked out in *The Structure of Behavior*. However, the originality of *The Visible and the Invisible* resides above all in the radically new way in which Merleau-Ponty conceives of sensible consciousness through his use of the notion of the flesh. This is the foundation of his entire ontology; it allows him to say in the end that it is not we who perceive or think, but Being which sees itself and thinks itself in us.

In Merleau-Ponty "this reform of 'consciousness'" (VI, 239; *VI*, 292) carries along with it a complete rejection of all psychologistic "bric-à-brac." He does not want to interrogate consciousness with the help of notions such as "act," "concept," "perception," "nature," "form," "image," "*Erlebenisse*," etc., because all these notions belong to the point of view which Merleau-Ponty is, precisely, seeking to overcome. For instance, he does not want to speak of *Erlebnesse* because this would mean adopting from the outset a quasi-psychologistic point of view (and this is, moreover, what he criticizes Husserl for); it would amount to presupposing that we know only our own experiences. If ever one cuts consciousness off from the world, one will in the end be able to win back the world for consciousness only by idealizing it and by defining being as that which appears to us, as being-for-us. Unlike Husserl, Merleau-Ponty does not want to untie the psychologistic knot; in one stroke he cuts this Gordian knot and rejects the problem in it totality; he does not even so much as consider it but proposes instead a wholly new way of conceiving of consciousness.

"States of consciousness" and "acts of consciousness" and all the rest of positivistic "bric-à-brac," Merleau-Ponty says, are *"differentiations* of one sole and *massive* adhesion to Being which is the flesh". (VI, 270; *VI,* 324) Perceptual consciousness is not something which exists "in relation to" the world but is, rather, its own flesh. Consciousness and the world are a single Totality. Sensible consciousness is the world's "other side," the inside of its outside; sensation is "the return of the visible upon itself, a carnal adherence of the sentient to the sensed and of the sensed to the sentient." (VI, 142; *VI,* 187) Sensible consciousness is the invisible of the visible; it is the visible which turns back upon itself, doubles itself up, and secrets an "inside." "It must not be imagined," Merleau-Ponty says, "that I add to the visible perfectly defined as in Itself a non-visible....One has to understand that it is visibility itself that involves a non-visibility." (VI, 247; *VI,* 300) No break exists between sensation and the sensible; it is not *me* as a subject opposed to the world who sees; it is the very visible which sees itself. "I" am there precisely when the flesh of the world prepares in itself a "hollow," an "interior"; qua sensible consciousness "I" am this *body* which sees itself and which is thereby open to all the rest of the sensible. It must therefore be said that, as a presence to the world and as the "there is," the appearing and presence of the world, sensible consciousness is the world itself as it *opens up,* or, more precisely, that consciousness is the result of the dehiscence and the opening up of Being into the sensing-sensible chiasm.

Perceptual meaning, what Merleau-Ponty calls λόγος ἐνδιάθετος or "perceptual openness to the world" (VI, 212; *VI,* 266), is therefore to be understood, not as the work of "consciousness," but as the result of the dehiscence of Being. In and through sensible consciousness, in and through the emergence of perceptual meaning, it is Being itself which comes to manifest its own meaning, this meaning being the articulation or configuration that Being assumes in exploding, in differentiating itself. Obviously the sense of the perceived world is its appearance to the subject, its being-for-the-subject; but this presence of the world to the subject is not something made by the subject. The world appears to him and he is present to the world only because *there is* Being, Being which explodes and differentiates itself in the sensing-sensible articulation. "For Sartre," Merleau-Ponty says, "it is always *I* who forms depth, who hollows it out, who does everything, and who closes from within my prison in upon myself." (VI, 237; *VI*, 290–1) For Merleau-Ponty, on the contrary, it is not the subject who *makes* vision be; he *is* his vision, and vision is the result of the doubling up of the flesh, of Being, into seeing-visible; he is Being expressing itself. "The *visible,*" Merleau-Ponty writes in a note of March 1961, "has to be described as something that is realized through man, but which is nowise anthropology" (VI, 274; *VI,* 328)[18]

The perceived world has meaning only in man, through perception, but perception is not a "function" on man's part, an activity of *Sinngebung* coming from him; it is Being acceding to its own meaning. Subjectivity is assuredly a fact and even a value-fact, but it is nevertheless not a creative *fiat* which comes into the world from nowhere and confers upon it its form and meaning.[19] Both the fact that "we" perceive and the fact that the world is "there" for us are understandable only as the result of a dehiscence and an articulation of Being into sentient subject and sensible thing. "Vision," Merleau-Ponty writes, "is not a certain mode of thought or presence to self; it is the means given me for being absent from myself, for *being present at the fission of Being from the inside*—the fission at whose termination, and not before, I come back to myself." (PriP, 186; *OE,* 81; emphasis ours)

If, however, as Merleau-Ponty says, it is not *I* who perceives, one might want to ask, Who is it then who perceives? To do so would, however, be to misconstrue the sense of his entire effort and to speak from a point of view which, precisely, Merleau-Ponty wants to overcome. He does not deny that it is the subject who perceives, and he does not say without more ado that it is Being which *perceives itself.* The subject is not a mere occasion or instrument in the service of a transcendent Thought. For Merleau-Ponty it is indeed the subject, the *I,* who perceives; but precisely because he wants to redefine subjectivity he prefers to avoid the expression "I perceive," since it inevitably leads one into conceiving of perception as an *act* or *state of consciousness* of a subject closed in upon himself and in some way op-posed to the world and ontologically distinct from being which is perceived. The expression draws along with it the Cartesian notion of subjectivity that one discovers, Merleau-Ponty says, even in Husserl.

"We will get out of the difficulty only by renouncing the bifurcation of 'consciousness of' and the object". (VI, 141; *VI,* 186) What Merleau-Ponty is renouncing here is effectively the Husserlian notion of intentionality. On the contrary, if, as he says, "one starts from the visible and the vision, the sensible and the sensing, one acquires a wholly new idea of 'subjectivity'." (VI, 269; *VI,* 322) Then there is indeed a subject who perceives, but this subject is not merely in front of the world, a view upon the world; he is of the "same stuff" as the world, he is part of the same flesh, and he is a "fragment" of the world's flesh which has become sensible for itself and, in this way, sensitive to the rest of the sensible world. Since the subject of perception is not a transcendental Ego which is unaware of itself as such, Merleau-Ponty says that it is *no one,* that it is *anonymous.* This notion which we have already noted in the *Phenomenology* finally finds in his later writings a properly ontological significance. Let us attempt to seize hold of it.

If for Merleau-Ponty there is no problem of the alter ego at the level of perception, it is "because it is not *I* who sees, not *he* who sees, because an anonymous visibility inhabits both of us, a vision in general,"—"in virtue of that primordial property that belongs to the flesh,... being an individual, of being also a dimension and a universal." (VI, 142; *VI,* 187–8) For the time being let us leave the meaning of the last phrase just quoted in suspense. In a working note Merleau-Ponty says that "In reality there is neither me nor the other as positive, positive subjectivities." These are, he says, "two opennesses, two stages where something will take place." The I and the other together belong to "the stage of Being." (VI, 263; *VI,* 317) On this point Merleau-Ponty's thought is remarkably close to Heidegger's. The latter has said that for him "Da-sein" does not so much mean "me voilà!" (Here I am!) as it does "être-le-là" (to-be-the-there), and *le-là* (the-there) is precisely ἀλήθεια—non-dissimulation *(Unverborgenheit),* openness.[20] Likewise for Merleau-Ponty, perception, rather than being a "me voilà!" or the *act* of a subject, is an openness in Being or the flesh, and the "something" which happens on this "stage," "that which" takes place in this openness, is Being itself; or, again, this opening that is subjectivity is Being opening itself up, exploding; it is the advent of perception, of the "there is," of meaning, of a λόγος which is the λόγος of Being itself.

Merleau-Ponty sometimes calls sensible consciousness or sensation—the fact that the carnal subject can see precisely because he can see himself, is a sensible which is sensible for itself—a *narcissism*. Perception comes from a "fundamental narcissism" of the flesh, of Being. It is as if Being wanted to accede to "consciousness," wanted to see itself, and could only do so by means of a kind of inner negation, a differentiation, or a doubling up into the seeing-visible couple. It is precisely this "ontological" narcissism, this "metamorphosis," this "promiscuity" of the seeing and the visible "which defines our flesh" (PriP, 169; *OE*, 34) our subjectivity.[21] If the I and the other are inhabited by an "anonymous visibility," if they both participate in "a single Vision" (S, 15; *S*, 22), it is because they are both so many "Narcissus" (VI, 141; *VI*, 185), because they are born in the same way, from the same flesh. They are anonymous and are "no one," because in both of them an absolutely general or universal (anonymous, therefore) phenomenon takes place when a "fragment" of the world's flesh turns back on itself, is captivated, alienated by itself, and sees itself. The perceiving subject is anonymous because, like all other subjects, he stems from a universal and undifferentiated flesh. At the basis of every subject there is the flesh, "this anonymity innate to Myself." (VI, 139; *VI*, 183)

Instead of "narcissism" one could also speak of *individuation*. One does not come across this term in Merleau-Ponty, but it seems to us to sum up his thought rather well. It serves in any event to bring out the meaning of the phrase we left in suspense, the one where he says that if an anonymous visibility inhabits the I and the other, it is "in virtue of that primordial property that belongs to the flesh...being an individual, of being also a dimension and a universal." One could then say that the advent of the subject, the individual, comes about by means of a process of individuation through which "undivided" Being, the undivided and general flesh of the Sensible, is crystallized, concretized, doubles back on itself, and forms in a "fragment" of the flesh a "hollow," an "inside," or an "invisible side" which is sensation. The subject is precisely the individual, and this individual is the result of an individuation of the universal flesh of the world—which makes it be that the carnal subject, being an "individual," is also a dimension and a universal. In regard to the bases of their being, the I and the other are anonymous, general, and universal, because as individuals they stem precisely from the same general sensible: "our glances," Merleau-Ponty says, "are not 'acts of consciousness'...but openings of our flesh which are immediately filled by the universal flesh of the world." (S, 16; S, 23) This does not mean that there is no difference or distinction between the I and the other; "there does not exist," Merleau-Ponty says, "some huge animal whose organs our bodies would be, as, for each of our bodies, our hands, our eyes are the organs." (VI, 142; VI, 187)[22] The I and the other are indeed individuals in the proper sense of the term; they are, however, both alike and are open to each other (are in a relation of *Einfühlung*) because they are individuals only insofar as they derive from the same generality or universality of the flesh, of primordial Being.[23] The relations between man and Being are the same as those between the individual and the generality from which he stems, of which he is a crystallization or a concretion; the carnal subject is a certain "modulation" (among others) of a "polymorphous" or "amorphous" Being.

There exists thereby the possibility of an intersubjectivity, because the subject himself is not a consciousness closed in on itself, contemplating his ideally immanent noemata, but an opening onto or in Being. All subjectivities are so many openings "in the same field" (S, 15; S, 23), are specific configurations of the same flesh. Thus for Merleau-Ponty "everything rests upon the insurpassable richness, the miraculous *multiplication* of the sensible." (S, 16; S, 23; emphasis ours) The *Urstiftung,* the ultimate foundation, is the Sensible, Being, the Infinite, which *is* a process of inner negation through which it becomes in the form of so many "consciousnesses of," so many subjects. All subjectivities originate in a "primordial generality" (S, 174; S, 220), in an anonymous Sensible in which they exist as "differentiations" or negativities." "'Negativities'," Merleau-Ponty writes, "also count in the sensible world, which is decidedly the universal one." (S, 172; S, 217) Being is the universal, the Earth, "pregnancy of possibilities," "polymorphous matrix"; it is the flesh, the "mother" (VI, 267; VI, 321) from which individuals are born, "where individuals are formed through differentiation."

Therefore, between Being, the diffuse and primordial generality, and the subject, the articulated individual, there is a strictly dialectical relationship. If it is in "the return of the visible upon itself, a carnal adherence of the sentiment to the sensed and of the sensed to the sentient" that there is born "a ray of natural light" (VI, 142; *VI,* 187), "a flash of meaning" (S, 175; *S,* 221), then, on the one hand, "pure," "undivided" Being is but an abyss of night and unintelligibility so long as it is not differentiated so as to form individuals, subjectivities, and, on the other hand, subjectivity itself is neither a "positive" nor a pure nothingness, a *nichtiges Nichts,* but rather a negation internal to Being, its own realization, advent, and *Gelichtetheit.* With Merleau-Ponty the question concerning Being—his *Seinsfrage*—is the question concerning the Being of the world, the "there is" of the world, its presence; and in the last analysis this presence, this "there is" of the world, is nothing other than subjectivity itself, for subjectivity is a sensing-sensible, the doubling back of the sensible on itself and its *presence* to itself. It is finally for this reason that, for Merleau-Ponty, to speak of Being without man (abstracting from subjectivity), Being "outside" of beings, has no meaning. This is not because Being is dependent upon the subject and is constituted by him, but because subjectivity is the presence, the illumination, the "there is" of Being itself. Hence it must be said that Being without man has no meaning precisely because man, as the presence of Being, is the very meaning—the logos—of Being. What Merleau-Ponty calls savage or brute logos is indeed the sensing-sensible chiasm; it is subjectivity conceived of as the articulation of the dehiscence of Being. That sensing-sensible which is the body is a "universal measurant." (VI, 260; *VI,* 313) For Merleau-Ponty it is this *reversibility* between the sentient and the sensible "which is the ultimate truth." (VI, 155; *VI,* 204)

When Merleau-Ponty speaks in this way of a "reversibility which is the ultimate truth," it is hard not to think of Heraclitus' dialectic. And as a matter of fact, the similarity—at least in appearance—between Merleau-Ponty's ontology and mythopoeic and cosmogonical thought in general is quite remarkable. In Greek mythology the common *mother* of the gods and men is Γῆ, the Earth. For Merleau-Ponty the originating is also the Earth, the mother; and his "polymorphous," "undivided Being" has a strange resemblance to the original chaos of the cosmogonical myths which is the one and the many, ἐν καὶ πᾶν. As it is written in a text which itself rests on a long mythological tradition extending beyond the memory of men, "In the beginning...the earth was without form, and void; and darkness was upon the face of the deep." The moment of "creation" or of the emergence of the world is, more often than not, conceived of as a process of differentiation or segregation through which this undivided being breaks up inside of itself and divides into two (for example, the separation of day from night, the division of "the waters which were under the firmament from the waters which were above the firmament," the separation of the earth from the waters). This moment is moreover (as in the *Book of Genesis* or Hesiod's *Theogony*) conceived of as the advent of light ("And God said, Let there be light...and God divided the light from the darkness"). One could also describe it in Merleau-Ponty's own language as "the miraculous promotion of Being to 'consciousness,' or the segregation of the 'within' and the 'without'." (VI, 118; *VI,* 157)

In the Ionian schoc., at the dawn of philosophy, the search for the originating or the principle of all things becomes the search for the ἀρχή, a term used for the first time, according to Simplicius, by Anaximander. For the latter the ἀρχή, the ground of all phenomenal and determinate existence, cannot itself be determinate, cannot be a direct object of experience, but must be looked for, so to speak, underneath experience. Anaximander calls this ἀρχή τὸ ἄπειρον, the infinite. In itself it is nothing determinate (ἀόριστος), has never had a beginning (ἀθάνατος καὶ ἀγήρως), is inexhaustible and indestructible. Just as Merleau-Ponty says that the "fragmentation of being," the "advent of the difference," takes place on the ground of polymorphous Being, "on the ground of the ὁμοῦ ἦν πάντα"[24] (VI, 217; *VI,* 270), so also for Anaximander the genesis of the world and of things takes place through a process of "segregation" within the original "stuff" (*Urstoff*) which is ἐν καὶ πᾶν, the one and the many. In Anaximenes, for example, Anaximander's successor, the genesis of things takes place by condensation or rarefaction of the primordial element; fire, water, air, and earth represent so many degrees of condensation. According to Aristotle's testimony (*Physics,* I, 4, 187a20), certain pre-Socratics "assert that the contraries are contained in the one and emerge from it by segregation, for example Anaximander and also all those who assert that 'what is' is one and many". However, Anaximander had seen that if the ἀρχή, the ἄπειρον (the Infinite), is to differentiate itself, it must contain within itself something like a principle of difference; while being undifferentiated and indeterminate, it must include incipient oppositions within itself.

Here one thinks of Merleau-Ponty, who places the negative within Being. But whereas Anaximander and all the other Ionians seem to have considered the ἀρχή or the principle of the world as a point situated in a far-off past and the world's origin as a process accomplished once and for all (or as a process which periodically repeats itself in a cyclic fashion, going each time from a beginning to an end); and whereas for Anaximander the Infinite, the Originating, appears as a kind of support underlying the world; for Heraclitus, the ἀρχή is not a kind of substance underneath things, but is rather their very essence, and it is nothing other than process. For Heraclitus, Being has nothing static about it; it is not a primitive state of affairs or the ground of the world's becoming, but is rather this becoming itself. The ἀρχή is not differentiated so as to produce the phenomenal world; it is rather this very differentiation—πόλεμος, as Heraclitus says. There is nothing stable, everything is in a constant flux and battle (πόλεμος); each thing is but the momentary articulation of the perpetual differentiation (Heraclitus calls πόλεμος the father of all things). This, however, is not chaos, for in these incessant changes and reversals there is a harmony (ἁρμονιή), an order (δίχη), or a meaning (λόγος). The ultimate truth of things for Heraclitus is these constant developments in accordance with their hidden λόγος or δίχη, just as for Merleau-Ponty the ultimate truth is "reversibility." And just as for Merleau-Ponty the philosophy which thinks Being as both principle *and* process is not a theory of *evolution* but a "cosmology of the visible" where there is no question "of origins, nor limits, nor of a series of events going to a first cause, but one sole explosion of Being which is forever" (VI, 265; VI, 318), in a similar way Heraclitus' thought is not a *cosmogony* like that of his predecessors, but a *cosmology* where the question is not so much to discover a temporal beginning of the world and trace its development up to the present as it is to unveil its actual or present essence, an essence which is a process without beginning or end. "This world," Heraclitus writes, "which is the same for all, no god, no man has made it, but it was always, is now and is forever an eternally living fire," a perpetual effort at articulation (πόλεμος).

We have no intention of *explaining* Merleau-Ponty's philosophy with these references to pre-Socratic thought, but it seems to us that the mere fact of invoking them immediately gives to his ontology a richness and a depth which, to our knowledge, have hitherto gone unnoticed. That Merleau-Ponty should have found in the thought of the pre-Socratics a certain inspiration, or, at the very least, a support for his own thought, is more than likely; the similarity between his terminology and theirs is too great and too constant for it to be a mere accident. One might also wonder if this knowledge of the pre-Socratics did not go hand in hand with his reading of the second Heidegger in the 1950s and even if it was not one of its consequences. However, if one can disentangle certain influences and can detect in his own thought the far-off presence of Anaximander's ἀρχή and Heraclitus' πόλεμος, it must also be said that this *arche* and this dialectic take on in his case a new meaning in contact with the Christian notions of subjectivity and history. We will return to the question of history in the following section, but in order to prepare the way for this we need to continue our examination of subjectivity in Merleau-Ponty so as to see how thought, in the proper sense of the term, is instituted over and above sensible consciousness, over and above the brute logos, and how in the relation between Being and thought there is realized a Logos which is not only sensible but also cultural, an "infinite" Logos, as he says.

That for Merleau-Ponty there is no rupture between sensible consciousness and intellectual consciousness, between perceptual meaning and cultural meaning, is something we know from the preceding chapter. We summed up there the way Merleau-Ponty handles this subject in *The Visible and the Invisible.* Thus we want here only to recall the nature of the relation between thought and Being—the latter being conceived of as a kind of upsurge from below which makes its advent, which articulates itself, first of all in the sensing-sensible chiasm (λόγος), in sensible consciousness—in order to bring out more clearly the significance of this relation. Merleau-Ponty was never interested in intellectual thought for its own sake. When he does consider it, it is always from the point of view of its foundation or origin. It is likely that in *The Visible and the Invisible* he would have analyzed thought *sensu stricto* at greater length and would have given more consideration to its specificity in regard to sensible consciousness if his work had not been interrupted by death. Nonetheless, it is equally apparent that what interested him the most was always the place of thought in our existence as carnal subjects, rather than thought for its own sake. This is what we must now examine here, keeping always in mind the notion that sensible consciousness is itself the presence, the "there is," of the flesh or Being.

It is evident from Merleau-Ponty's very terminology that thought and the truth proper to it not only are grounded on sensible consciousness and perceptual meaning but are, so to speak, their *direct contin-*

*uation.* The logos of perception, the "perceptual opening to the world," is what he calls λόγος ἐνδιάθετος, while the intellectual logos, the "opening to a cultural world," is what he calls λόγος προρορίχος, *professed logos.* What is proper to thought is thus that in one way or another it unveils, makes explicit, delivers up, or liberates (lets-be) the immediate meaning of our life as carnal subjects and transforms it into an open, available meaning, into a meaning which is not only lived but which is reflected upon and conscious of itself. Intellectual consciousness is thus not a conferrer but a liberator of meaning. In place of the Husserlian notion of constitution, Merleau-Ponty substitutes the notion of *sublimation.* (e.g., VI, 155; *VI, 203*) What is proper to the professed logos is that its "inner structure sublimates our carnal relation to the world." "Pure" ideality is not "without flesh"; it is in fact a *reinvestment* of our flesh, a transfiguration or a generalization of the immediate meaning of our life into a quasi-eternal meaning, into a motif which allows us to understand how and why we are what we are and how what we do has universal and intersubjective ramifications; it is expressive not only of our own particular condition but of the human condition in its entirety.

Without doubt, it is in his reflections on painting that Merleau-Ponty has best set forth his thought on what concerns the relation between natural and symbolic expression and the ontological significance of this relation. Let us take as our sole examples the two essays which mark the beginning and the end of his philosophical life—"Cézanne's Doubt" and "Eye and Mind."

In the former, Merleau-Ponty says that what the painter attempts to reveal and express is our perceptual relation to the world, the "circular" or dialectical relation between the perceiving subject and the perceived world such as it was defined in the *Phenomenology.* What is proper to the painter is that he takes this relation as his theme, reveals and re-expresses it through symbolic means. Hence the meaning of the act of painting (the meaning of symbolic expression) is precisely the meaning of perception (the perceiving subject–perceived world "structure"), which by means of painting is "made manifest."

The important difference between this essay and "Eye and Mind" lies in the way Merleau-Ponty conceives of the perceptual logos itself. The perceiving subject and the perceived world are no longer merely in a relationship of "circularity" but of "reversibility" because they are both differentiations of a *single* flesh, a *single* Being. The logos of perception is thereby the logos of Being itself, that is, the seeing-visible configuration or articulation assumed by Being as dehiscence or fission. The act of symbolic expression thus has a deeper significance, because if what is proper to symbolic expression is that it makes the perceptual logos manifest and delivers up the "voices of silence," and if this logos or this silent speech is the very logos of Being, if it is Being coming to presence and articulating itself, then it must be said that symbolic or creative expression but "continues an effort of articulation which is the Being of every being." (VI, 127; *VI*, 168) In the painter's work, "it is, therefore, mute Being which itself comes to show forth its own meaning." (PriP, 188; *OE*, 87) "The painter's vision," Merleau-Ponty says, "is a continued birth." (PriP, 168; *OE*, 32) The vision of the painter, like the thought of the thinker, expresses and gives an added impetus to the genesis of the visible, which, itself, is an advent (explosion) of Being. This is why Merleau-Ponty says that language is the house of Being (VI, 214; *VI*, 267), the inscription of Being (VI, 197; *VI*, 251), that "it is being that speaks within us and not we who speak of being." (VI, 194; *VI*, 247) This does not mean that man is a mere occasion for Being to manifest itself, the instrument of an overriding transcendence; man is himself the realization (of the transcendence) of Being, that instance without which Being would not fully be.

This conception of subjectivity in the proper sense of the term (personal, intellectual subjectivity) that we see taking shape in Merleau-Ponty's last writings recalls certain themes of Heideggerian ontology. For the German thinker, what constitutes the "humanity" of man is that he has for being (vocation) to be the "guardian of Being"; he takes up and "manages" the irruption of Being. Taking his inspiration from Heraclitus as well, Heidegger says that Being is πόλεμος, *Auseinandersetzung* or differentiation, and that the λόγος or meaning realized in this differentiation "is then sustained by the creators, poets, thinkers, statesmen."[25] Likewise, Merleau-Ponty writes, "Man and society are not exactly outside of nature and the biological; they distinguish themselves from them by bringing nature's 'stakes' together and risking them all together." (S, 125; *S*, 157) Merleau-Ponty says here that what distinguishes or characterizes man in his humanity (in regard to nature) is that he *brings together*—one thinks of the Greek word, λέγειν—the primitive articulations (λόγος brut) or the "stakes" of nature so as to advance them even further. Man is thus "the privileged bearer" of transcendence (Being); in him is realized a Logos which is in no way his property. (VI, 274; *VI,* 328) This is why Merleau-Ponty says with Valéry that language "is the voice of no one, since it is the very voice of things, waves, and forests." (VI, 155; *VI,* 204) Man exists and subjectivity is indeed undeniable, but man is not his own foundation or the constituting source of Being. As Merleau-Ponty said in regard to the artist, it is rather man who is born in Being by a sort of concentration or coming-to-itself of Being. (cf. PriP, 181; *OE,* 69) "Henceforth," he says, "the irrelative is not nature in itself, nor the system of absolute consciousness' apprehensions, nor man either, but that 'teleology'…that jointing and framing of Being which is being realized through man." (S, 181; *S,* 228)

In this way we finally arrive at the notion of Being as *teleology* or *transcendence.* If, for instance, symbolic expression—thought—is an activity of sublimation, there must be something which is sublimated. Now what is sublimated is Being. If, following Merleau-Ponty's custom, we were to borrow metaphors from psychoanalysis, we could say that Being, as the "unconscious of consciousness," is a kind of Eros, a kind of reservoir of power indeterminate in itself ("pregnancy of possibilities"), which (like, precisely, the Freudian unconscious) is eternal and "indestructible" (VI, 267; *VI,* 321), whose upsurge gives birth to consciousness. The relations between this derived consciousness and the "instinctual" Being from which it emerges are afterwards those of sublimation and reinvestment; all of consciousness' energy comes to it from below, and consciousness merely gives new forms or figures to this polymorphous power. Thus there is neither determination on the part of Being nor constitution on the part of consciousness (subjectivity); Being is but an indeterminate, polymorphous power (like Freud's infantile "libido"), and consciousness is but the articulation and reappropriation of the "unmotivated upsurge of brute Being." Consciousness emerges from Being and is like a first determination or articulation of this unlimited power; and, once consciousness is there, it takes in hand and manages this constant irruption of Being. By means of symbolic and creative expression it sets off again the genesis of Being, reinvests the brute power of Being in cultural figures or articulations; it is then in and through man that Being fulfills itself and realizes itself as logos. The law of Being is the very law of thought, of consciousness; it is Being which is itself the "teleology" of consciousness, which imposes on consciousness the "task" of becoming conscious.

It will perhaps be recalled how in our chapter on language, in beginning to sort out the "scraps" of Merleau-Ponty's ontology, we roughly distinguished three key elements: the Logos, man, and Being. We have just now seen what exactly in the last analysis the relation is between these three notions in Merleau-Ponty. If we take man as subjectivity, consciousness, or thought, and Being as upsurge of Nature, we see that in Merleau-Ponty the notions of what could be called φύσις, λόγος, and νοεῖν mutually imply each other and are strictly interdependent. The unmotivated upsurge of Being (φύσις), of a polymorphous or amorphous Being, is first crystallized or articulated in the sensing-sensible chiasm (λόγος); this differentiation or explosion of Being and this doubling up of the flesh into sensing and sensible constitute the definition (λόγος) of the human body, of sensible consciousness. What is proper to man as intellectual consciousness (νοεῖν) is that he then transcends himself as a merely sensible consciousness, grasps, gathers together (λέγειν), and expresses what he is, thereby transforming the sensible or ἐνδιάθετος logos which he is and which is the logos, the configuration assumed by Being in its explosion into a cultural or προϑορικός logos. Since, however, the transcendence incarnate in symbolic expression is a transcendence which it does not constitute but rather sublimates, it must be said that in and through human consciousness (νοεῖν) it is Being (φύσις) which comes to manifest its own meaning (λόγος)—that is, that symbolic expression, in grasping itself as a transcendence, grasps that it is part of an upsurge of Being, an "ontogenesis," whose meaning is revealed and realized by it itself. If Being is a wave of transcendence, and if thought is a transcendence which is aware of itself as such, then thought is the realization of the very meaning Being. As Merleau-Ponty says, "we are a field of Being" (VI, 240; VI, 293); "every human enterprise is...a cipher of transcendence" (VI, 208; VI, 262); "the action of thinking is caught up in the thrust [poussée] of being." (S, 14; S, 21) Being is that which in us "wishes, speaks, and finally thinks." (VI, 176; VI, 230)

We thus see clarified in the light of his last writings the notion of a "movement" or "wave" of transcendence by which, in the Phenomenology, Merleau-Ponty defined man. As was pointed out in the preceding chapter, what characterizes the deepening of Merleau-Ponty's phenomenology into an ontology is that he now says that this wave of transcendence is Being itself. When Merleau-Ponty said in the Phenom-

*enology* that man is a "miracle" because he has no explanation but is at bottom a movement of transcendence in relation to the world, he left us in the dark as to the ground of man's relation to the world. Although Merleau-Ponty refused to go any farther and was content with pointing out the "miraculous" and "mysterious" character of human existence, his position called for a follow-up. He could have defined man, like Sartre, as a *nichtiges Nichts* who comes into the world from nowhere, or he could have adopted a resolutely transcendentalist position and characterized man as a constituting consciousness à la Husserl. In the end Merleau-Ponty chose to follow neither one of these two ways. On the contrary, he ends up by maintaining that, if the expressivity which is natural to man appears nonetheless as a miracle, it is precisely because as an event man is the very advent of Being. The human phenomenon is a miracle because in him and through him everything that is becomes meaningful, because in him and through him Being makes itself into logos. Man is a miracle because in him alone the genesis of Being itself becomes visible and is accomplished.

Thus if, like Heraclitus' ἀρχη, the "originating," the "fundamental," is for Merleau-Ponty not a being, a substance underneath Nature, but rather the very upsurge of Nature, its explosion or dehiscence and its differentiation into the sensing-sensible chiasm (logos), if for Merleau-Ponty as for Heraclitus Being is not the foundation or substrate of Nature but Nature itself as process, there is nevertheless in Merleau-Ponty's dialectic something which is not to be found in Heraclitus— the notion of a "teleology." Being is not only a process, a differentiation (πόλεμος), but also a becoming—not, as it were, a static becoming as in Heraclitus, a mere, eternal repetition in accordance with a fixed λόγος but a vertical becoming, an opening up in the full sense of the word where something is realized which did not exist before, where it is the Logos of Being itself which becomes. When Merleau-Ponty speaks of the "teleology" of Being, it is to indicate that the upsurge of Being is an upsurge from below which directs itself to the above. Taking over an expression of Heidegger's, he says, "the so-called *Grund* is *Abgrund*. But the abyss one thus discovers is not such *by lack of ground,* it is upsurge of a *Hoheit* which holds from above". (VI, 250; VI, 303) Being is not a ground or a substrate, but an abyss, an inexhaustible and unfathomable source of transcendence. To this infinite *archē* there must therefore correspond an infinite telos, an eternal teleological history, a teleology which paradoxically is without a telos, without an end. We will return to this question of Being and Time in the following section, and with it we will conclude this study.

To round off this reflection on the relations between Being and man in Merleau-Ponty, we might attempt to point out the originality of his position by contrasting it with those of his two closest contemporaries—Heidegger and Sartre.

It is a fact—upon which almost all commentators are agreed—that Merleau-Ponty became more and more interested in Heideggerian thought, in the thought of the later Heidegger. But even though this fact is practically undeniable, there is nevertheless an important lack of unanimity as to its significance.[26] We maintain for our part that Merleau-Ponty did draw nearer to the thought of the second Heidegger and that his notion of Being in some ways resembles that of the German thinker. If, however, we can say that Merleau-Ponty went towards Heidegger, we must also say that he did not go in the same direction as Heidegger. Indeed, if Merleau-Ponty says with Heidegger that what is first is not man but Being, if he thereby gives the primacy to Being and maintains that man is not understandable except in relation to Being, if he says that our experience is Being speaking in us, it is also true that for Merleau-Ponty Being needs man in order to truly be. For Merleau-Ponty the relation between Being and man is not a relation wherein Being freely gives itself to thought in order that thought may think it. The upsurge of Being in man is not a free gift or a grace (Huld, Gunst) on Being's part. And thinking (Denken) is not a "thanking" (Danken) for Being's generosity; it is the very realization of Being. The authentic philosophical attitude is therefore not a "releasement" or "resignation" (Gelassenheit) of thought before Being, but that of a free and active creation wherein thought joins up with Being only by realizing itself as human thought. What therefore characterizes Merleau-Ponty's opposition to Heidegger is ultimately Merleau-Ponty's insistence on the special and irreducible value of subjectivity.

From this it emerges that Merleau-Ponty would reject the Heideggerian notion of a "leap." Philosophical thinking is not a leap towards an ineffable beyond; it is an interrogation which remains close to experience, it is experience turning back on itself, it is, as he says, "the perceptual faith questioning itself about itself." (VI, 103; VI, 139) If at the limit philosophy thinks a "transcendence," this is not by passing to another order; it is a transcendence grasped in immanence.

Thought's attitude towards Being is therefore not that of an emptiness waiting to be filled. If the reflecting subject can recognize that he does not constitute Being but is himself derived from Being, it is not because he has transcended himself as subjectivity but because he has himself discovered something like an abyss at the bottom of his being, an "innate anonymity" in himself; it is because he has himself an original experience of Being as that which cannot be present to him "in person," as that which is present to him by remaining irremediably absent, as, precisely, an abyss at the bottom of his being.

It goes without saying that if, because of his insistence on subjectivity, Merleau-Ponty is in opposition to Heidegger, his way of conceiving of subjectivity separates him also from Sartre. Against Heidegger, Merleau-Ponty says that man is the center of all reference and that nothing can be understood without him. But if this is so, it is because man is the very opening of Being, its *presence.* Merleau-Ponty thus completely rejects the Sartrian thesis which maintains that "we are on a level where there are only men,"[27] saying instead that "we are a field of Being." What upset Sartre in the late Merleau-Ponty were these more and more numerous references to Being, and Sartre said that "it is annoying that today a man can write that the absolute is not man."[28] If Merleau-Ponty's remarks are "annoying" for Sartre, it is for a good reason: they express, precisely, an unequivocal rejection of the Sartrian conception of man. What Merleau-Ponty refuses is Sartre's philosophical atheism which, in proclaiming the death of God, puts at once man in his place and makes man into the absolute. For Merleau-Ponty, on the contrary, man is not the last word, is not his own ground, but is, at the bottom of his being, an opening onto Being and a cipher of transcendence. If what man does has a meaning, it is not because he has the absolute freedom to do and to be what he wants, but rather because he is in the field of Being, a field whence come and wherein are inscribed all of his initiatives.

Thus, while holding on to his constant insistence on the irreducible value of subjectivity, Merleau-Ponty recognizes in his late philosophy the primacy of Being; while holding on to his demand regarding immanence, he recognizes a transcendence. If, as there is some question, there was a reconciliation at the end of his life between Merleau-Ponty and the Church, this reconciliation would have occurred without any abandonment of what he was himself able to acknowledge as a philosopher. It would have occurred in complete fidelity to his demands for philosophical autonomy and radicalism. What Merleau-Ponty said two years before his death about Bergson before *his* death would have a personal significance, as is so often the case in Merleau-Ponty's habitually indirect language: "what for my part strikes me is the tranquility with which Bergson, at the very moment he is giving his personal assent and moral adherence to Catholicism, sticks to his method in philosophy." (S, 191; *S,* 241)

## IV.   Being and Time

WHAT Merleau-Ponty was always looking for is a dialectical conception of history which would take account, at one and the same time, of its *logic* and its *contingency*. What he wanted was a theory which recognizes and safeguards the liberty and initiative of men, but which also recognizes a kind of order or inner meaning in history and in this way rules out chaos. It is for him an indisputable fact that it is men who are responsible for history and who *make* it; but it is equally a fact that there is an inner meaning to history which is not due merely to the free choices of individuals. Or, as he says in *Signs,* "Everywhere there are meanings, dimensions, and forms in excess of what each 'consciousness' could have produced; and yet it is men who speak and think and see." (S, 20; *S,* 28) What interests us in the comings and goings of Merleau-Ponty's reflections on history is how the notion of Being or the flesh, as it is worked out in his late philosophy, finally succeeds in providing the means of satisfying these two requirements: necessity and contingency.

In his courses at the Sorbonne which were given from 1949 on, Merleau-Ponty returns quite often to the notion of history. In them he attempts to clarify his own position in relation to the "two important attitudes of philosophy regarding history": the "causal" one which only sees in history a succession of events without any intimate relation to each other, and the "teleological" or "providential" one (*BP,* 216, 259) which conceives of history as the mere unfolding or explicitation of rational projects, as directed by intentions constituted either in a human mind or in a transcendent Reason. He rejects the first conception because it makes history the gratuitous result of mere contingency (chance encounters) and thereby ignores the inner and proper meaning of history; and he similarly rejects the second because, if it is indeed capable of thinking a logic in history, it nevertheless ignores contingency and makes of historical becoming an unavoidable fatality. In reflecting on the Marxist conception of history, he sees there on the contrary "a search for *logic* in history which is not unaware of *factual contingency."* (*BP,* 216) According to this third way—which is perhaps more properly Merleau-Ponty's own conception rather than that of the Marxists—all notions of "historical destiny" are only so many "retrospective rationalizations." It is only after the event, he says, that we can say that things happened as they "should have." On the spur of the moment, on the contrary, everything depends on what the individual will do, and this is not at all determined in advance. Taking over an expression from Lenin, Merleau-Ponty says that the individual is the "midwife" of history; it is by means of individuals that what in things was only a possibility or a probability is either realized and finally sees the light of day (like, for instance, the Russian revolution), or is "aborted" and the current of history is driven back and directed in another direction unsuspected up until then. This means that the future is always motivated but is never determined. Thus according to this conception history is "neither an *ex nihilo* creation nor the mere reflection of the pre-existing situation." (*BP.* 217) The notion which Merleau-Ponty finally proposes as the ground of history and as that which can account for both its logic and its contingency is the *notion of situation.* (*BP,* 217)

It is in the light of this notion that he attempts to understand why what we do is not determined in advance and yet always has a greater meaning than that of our merely personal and conscious projects. In the *Phenomenology* for instance (PhP, 171, 173, 442, 447; *PP,* 199, 202, 505, 511) he describes the coming to revolutionary awareness as the *response* to a given, lived situation. The actual being of the world of men is such that it calls forth in them a responsive awareness but does not dictate any particular awareness. The existential, lived situation is thus the foundation of historical becoming. The situation is a meaning in the process of becoming, and history is the result of the way individuals respond to their collective and concrete situation by taking it up in their existential projects. On the level of individual history or psychogenesis, for example, the individual's development must be understood in relation to the structures of his bodily existence. This is not because sexuality exerts a causal influence on the formation of the personality, but rather because personality is to be considered as the result of attitudes the individual chooses to adopt in regard to his psychosomatic situation. "What the body will contribute [to the individual's development]," Merleau-Ponty says, "is a confused, blind drive which alone is incapable of arriving at the new state, the demand for a certain overcoming." (*BP,* 217) Thus, whether it be a question of collective history or of personal development, it must be said that even though it is individuals who are responsible for their history, it is nevertheless not they who make it be *that there is* a history. The ground of history is not the person's will but his pregiven *situation,* which is to be conceived of in the last analysis as a *demand for overcoming,* a *wave of transcendence.* The individual's will is only a way of responding and giving a precise form to this confused and blind thrust.

In his essay of 1953 on language and painting Merleau-Ponty says that we would have the greatest likelihood of recovering the true sense of history if we were to model it after the example of the arts and language. (S, 73; *S,* 91) We have seen in previous chapters how, in seeking to understand the development of language or the history of painting, Merleau-Ponty conceives their foundation to be, on the one hand, the "need" or the "instinct" of expression and communication and, on the other hand, the "natural" expressivity of the lived body. There is a logic to history because in each case the acts of individuals are like responses to a deep down demand which is identical in them all, inasmuch as it stems from the generality of bodily existence. In all of his writings up towards the end of the 1950s where he considers the question, Merleau-Ponty posits as the ground of history the notion of existential (bodily) situation. The last word, the "ultimate fact," for him is, as he said in the *Phenomenology,* "that productivity which is man's deepest essence". (PhP, 196; *PP,* 229) Looking always for what is fundamental, Merleau-Ponty, the phenomenologist, took therefore the final step of pointing to, as an ultimate fact, a mysterious power of transcendence and natural expressivity without explanation or name. He thought he could guarantee the possibility of a logic in history which respects its contingency by linking up historical becoming to the structures of bodily existence; but since he maintains that man's existential presence to the world is an incomprehensible and wholly contingent fact, it is hard to see how he could defend himself against the accusation that in the final resort he lets contingency override logic. His "existential" phenomenology seems here to lack coherence and seems incapable of justifying the notion of a logic of history or a "teleology" of consciousness.

However, this criticism we are addressing to Merleau-Ponty's phenomenology is in the end not all that different from the one he formulates himself when he recognizes the necessity for an ontological clarification of the results of his phenomenology. In his last philosophy Merleau-Ponty indeed recognizes that the notion of situation with which he had attempted to think history is not, as a matter of fact, an ultimate notion. It is then that he asks himself how the existential situation itself must be understood, how it is that one must understand man's ex-sistential relation to the world—the fact that in regard to the world and merely biological existence man is essentially a movement of transcendence. How must one understand that "teleology" which characterizes man and which makes it be that he continually transcends himself, thereby instituting a history? If the motive force of history is a "natural" movement of transcendence, and if this transcendence, this confused impetus, is the very definition of human being in the world, it is not sufficient for a philosophy seeking the "fundamental" merely to point out this fact and to take it as a mysterious and unjustifiable presupposition. It must, on the contrary, ask what it means—"then the question is: what is this ferment?" (VI, 202; *VI*, 255)

It is perhaps in "Eye and Mind" that Merleau-Ponty went the farthest in his search for the "fundamental" (PriP, 161; *OE*, 15), for that dimension of his existence which allows man always to transcend himself and to share in this way in a universal life which is that of all humanity. Now, as we have already seen, in this essay he does not present man's exploding presence to the world as an ultimate fact, but rather as a derived fact. Human being in the world includes within it a ferment of transcendence because, precisely, it is the expression or result of a primordial Being which, itself, is nothing but transcendence, upsurge, explosion. Man's presence to the world (the existential situation) is to be understood as Being coming to presence (as Being articulating itself in the sensing-sensible structure). Bodily or carnal existence is nothing other than a first articulation assumed by Being in its exploding, and it is thus a power of natural expression because it is Being itself expressing and articulating itself (the definition of the flesh, of man, is the definition, the logos, of Being itself). If it can be said that *temporality* is subjectivity itself qua continuous advent of

Being, it must be said that *historicity* is personal subjectivity qua reappropriation, sublimation, and reinvestment in symbols and institutions of this same upsurge of Being. What characterizes history is that it represents and is the accumulation of the transformations man effects on his existential situation; it is like the sedimentation and gathering together (λόγος) of man's attempts to understand himself in his carnal relation to the world and others and to transform into an open and available meaning the indigenous meaning of his natural existence. Now, since the meaning of natural, carnal existence is the meaning of Being itself in its exploding and its advent in the sensing-sensible articulation (brute or wild logos), it must be said that in and through symbolic expression "it is mute Being which comes to manifest its own meaning," that man's (cultural) history is the history of Being itself, that the becoming of history is the very becoming of Being. Let us take philosophy as an example.

In a working note Merleau-Ponty says that there is "an absolute, a philosophy, which is immanent in the history of philosophy, and which nonetheless is not a reabsorption of all the philosophies into one sole philosophy, nor eclecticism and skepticism either." (VI, 188; VI, 242) The history of philosophy is identity in difference. To be sure, every philosophy has its own proper reality or personality and is not reducible to a moment in a huge impersonal philosophy which would be the synthesis of them all, as for instance Hegelianism claimed to be. It is also true, however, that this diversity is understandable only in regard to something which is identical for them all. Now, the identical, the absolute, the One, is Being. There exists, Merleau-Ponty writes, a "spread staggered out in depth" between the various philosophies: "they nevertheless refer to one another, it is nevertheless a question of the same Being." (VI, 186; VI, 239)

In what sense is it a question of the same Being? If for Merleau-Ponty all philosophies are part of one and the same "vertical history" (VI, 199; VI, 253), if for him as for Heidegger all philosophies say in a sense the same thing, it is not inasmuch as they are so many *systems* of thought, so many collections of theses and propositions, but is rather because "in their integrality" they are a *question* (VI, 200; VI, 253), because they are located in one and the same "*interrogative* ensemble." (VI, 187; VI, 241) The history of the various philosophies is one single and unique history of philosophy itself, for all the philosophies are only so many ways of responding to that "central question that is ourselves." (VI, 104; *VI,* 141) What tomorrow's philosophers will learn from Leibniz and Spinoza, Merleau-Ponty says, is how, through the notions of "monad," "conatus," "substance," "attribute," etc., these philosophers "thought to tame the Sphinx," and what will characterize tomorrow's philosophers will be their "less figurative and more abrupt fashion" of responding "to the many riddles" proposed by this same sphinx. (S, 158; *S,* 200) The problems of philosophy are all "within the problem of Being." (VI, 198; *VI,* 251) It is Being which is the "sphinx"; it calls forth our questioning, for it is that which seeks to understand itself, that which, in its exploding, is an effort at articulation, this articulation coming about first of all in the sensing-sensible chiasm. "Coming after the world, after nature, after life, after thought, and finding them constituted before it, philosophy indeed questions this antecedent being and questions itself concerning its own relationship with it." (VI, 123; *VI,* 164) Thus, what for Merleau-Ponty defines philosophy is, as we saw in the preceding chapter, that it is essentially an *interrogation;* it does no more than elevate to a supreme degree that question which we are in our being, that attempt to seize hold of ourselves, to gather ourselves together, and to com-prehend ourselves. Now, since this perpetual movement of transcendence which constitutes us and makes it be that we are always in search of ourselves and are a question for ourselves is Being itself as a wave of transcendence "speaking in us," it must be said that in its questioning philosophy but continues "an attempt at articulation which is the Being of every being". All the various philosophies basically say the same thing, because in them all it is the same Being which is expressing itself and is in pursuit of itself. The history of philosophy is thus the history of Being. "Being holds together only in movement," and philosophy, Merleau-Ponty says in an expression which reminds one of Heidegger, "is a reminding of this being." (S, 22; *S,* 30) This is why he says that in its questioning philosophy is "as the ultimate relation to Being and as an ontological organ." (VI, 121; *VI,* 162)

As an aid to understanding the relation between different philosophies and how this relation is as an "ontological organ," the very voice of silence, of Being, Merleau-Ponty offers the example of perception. There is, he says, a *perceptual* relation between the philosophies; we can understand their kinship if we make "of philosophy a perception, and of the history of philosophy a perception of history." (VI, 188; *VI,* 242) He does not, however, develop this idea suggested in various working notes (VI, 186, 188, 198; *VI,* 239, 240, 242, 251), and its meaning remains rather obscure. But with the help of the notion of the "individuation" of the flesh which we sketched out in the preceding section, we can at least form an approximate idea of its general significance.

Indeed, Merleau-Ponty says that we must "apply here the very conception of perceptual being and *Offenheit*". (VI, 186; *VI,* 240) A relation of *Einfühlung* exists between the philosophies as between the perceptions of different subjects because, no more than is the case with perception, to understand philosophically "is not to constitute in intellectual immanence,...to comprehend is to apprehend by coexistence". (VI, 188; *VI,* 242) As we have seen, perception is always the perception of a particular subject, but it is not for all that an act which is "immanent" to a "consciousness." On the contrary, perception attests to the subject's fundamental generality, for it is a function not of "consciousness" but of the flesh, of Being. Perception, the "there is," sensible consciousness, is precisely an *Offenheit* in Being, a crystallization of the world's undivided flesh into a sensing-sensible. All perceiving subjects are so many "Narcissus" who are born together alongside each other in the same flesh through a "fundamental narcissism" of Being itself. They are so many openings in the same field, so many instances where the general flesh, Being, individualizes and expresses itself. An "intercorporeality" exists between perceiving subjects, and they are open to each other because they are all of the same flesh, are all dimensions of the same Being, because it is the same Being which expresses itself in them all.

*Mutatis mutandis,* the same situation prevails among the different philosophies. There is an internal relation between them, an absolute in their difference, because they all speak of the same thing, of our relation to being (to the world), and this relation is Being itself speaking in us. It is the same Being which is questioning itself in all the philosophies. So when Merleau-Ponty says that there is *one* philosophy immanent to the history of philosophy, he does not mean that there is one philosophy which contains all the others but that "philosophy as a whole is at certain moments in each philosophy." (S, 128; *S,* 161) Like sentient subjects, philosophies are "total parts" of a single Whole; they all stem from that "attempt at articulation which is the Being of all beings".

This idea of a "perceptual" relation between philosophies must not, however, be allowed to conceal from us the important difference which exists between perception and philosophy (and symbolic expression in general). This is the difference between *time* and *history*. That opening in Being which is the bodily subject is a fragile and transitory opening which exists only once and closes up forever on the individual's death. The sensing-sensible logos is a momentary articulation of Being, a logos always new and always the same. What is proper to philosophy and symbolic expression in its entirety is that it takes up this wave of transcendence which springs up in the carnal opening and reinvests it in cultural figures, which, as it were, become sedimented in a cultural opening and become a kind of acquisition, belonging henceforth not only to a particular individual's horizon but to that of all possible individuals. Hence by means of symbolic expression is instituted a new kind of universality which is not merely an anonymous and amorphous generality underneath individuals, but which is this same generality transformed by the subjectivity which emerges from it into a "figurative" universality, into a cultural universe where the logos of Being is no longer always identical to itself in its eternal difference, but turns back on itself and becomes more and more rich and fruitful. "There is a history of thought," Merleau-Ponty writes, "i.e., the succession of the works of the spirit (no matter how many detours we see in it) is really a single experience which develops of itself and in whose development, so to speak, truth capitalizes itself." (PriP, 9; *Inédit*, 407) If bodily subjectivity is Being occurring in the form of time, symbolic expression is Being occurring in the form of history.

Even if this conception of history succeeds in justifying the notion of a logic of history and a "teleology" of consciousness, this vertical or cumulative history must nevertheless not be thought of as if it proceeded, so to speak, in a straight line, as if each work constituted a moment which would then be surpassed by the next work, such that one would end up with a complete totalization wherein Being would be made completely manifest. Merleau-Ponty's vertical history is not Hegel's teleological history. Although the cultural logos, in the course of the history of expression, becomes more and more rich, for him no great work of the past is ever surpassed and can never be reduced to a paragraph in some great final system.

A great philosophy of the past can never be simply overcome nor can its truth be delimited and integrated into another, larger truth, so that one would end up with a philosophy which contains in its "total" truth all the "partial" truths of the past. This is not possible because for Merleau-Ponty one can never even be certain as to what is and is not "contained" in any given philosophy. For him "a philosophy, like a work of art, is an object that can arouse more thoughts than those that are 'contained' in it". (VI, 199; *VI*, 253) Taking over an idea of Heidegger's, he says that in every philosophy there is an "unthought thought" *(impensé–Ungedachte)* (S, 160; *S*, 202), a wealth of latent meaning which is proper to it but which was never exploited by the philosopher in question and which is finally incumbent upon *us* to think. Thus he says that a philosophy preserves its meaning outside of its historical context, and that for this reason it "even *has* meaning only outside of that context." (VI, 199; *VI*, 253) Since, therefore, the truth of a philosophy lies also in its unthought thought, in the thought which it calls forth from us, one can never definitively delimit this truth, for there always exists the possibility of reappropriations other than our own. Merleau-Ponty sums this up by saying that past works are *classics*. The truth of a classic—Marx's work for instance—is a "second-order truth," that is, the work is not true in the sense the author thought it to be; it is true rather in the sense that over and beyond its peculiarities and limits it continues to instruct us and stimulate us to think, opening up horizons and directions of thought which without it would remain closed to us. What is proper to the classics, Merleau-Ponty says, is that "no one takes them literally, and yet new facts are never absolutely outside their province but call forth new echoes from them and reveal new lustres in them." (S, 11; *S*, 16–17)

We can see in this way what *progress* in vertical or cultural history amounts to. A cultural "acquisition" is not something which is possessed, which can be catalogued and then overcome; it is rather that which lives always and always gives rise to new thoughts, that which is always presupposed and is *present* in all future developments. If, as Merleau-Ponty says in his last meditation on painting, no work is ever realized, this is not because "some fate holds us back; it is, rather, because the very first painting in some sense went to the farthest reach of the future." "If," he also writes at the end of this last writing published in his lifetime, "creations are not an acquisition or a possession, it is not only that, like all things, they pass away; it is also that they have almost all their life still before them." (PriP, 190; *OE*, 92–3)

Thus, even though Merleau-Ponty recognizes a vertical history, a cumulative becoming of Being, he rejects any kind of Hegelian or Marxist notion of an end of history. For him there is no evolution or historical progress, as if history were headed towards a determined or determinable end and each cultural work had its hierarchical place in this great unfolding. For him no philosophy, no work, ever replaces any other; rather they are all contemporaries and are "total parts" of a single great experience which goes on indefinitely. The history of culture or of "transcendental man" (PriP, 10; *Inédit*, 408) is the "teleological" history of an upsurge of Being "which holds from above" (VI, 250; *VI*, 303); but this above is not a ceiling and a limit—it is an *infinite* Logos or Telos. This is why the word "teleology" "is written and thought about in parentheses". (S, 181; *S*, 228) There is a "teleology" of Being because the upsurge of Being is not a Heraclitean flow which is eternally the same, but is rather an experience wherein the meaning of this advent becomes more and more rich and "capitalizes itself"; there is, however, no teleology of Being if this is taken to mean that this progressive realization of Being could one day reach a preordained end.

The "telos" of history is an infinite telos, just as the *archē*, the fundamental, is an infinite *archē*. Primordial Being is an inexhaustible source of transcendence. Infinity here is not Hegel's infinity, because for the latter the ground of history is a Being, a Subject, an In Itself which is unaware of itself. This is why for Hegel there can be an end of history when Being finally becomes For Itself when in the beginning it was only as an In Itself. For Merleau-Ponty this is a "frozen" or false infinity, in opposition to which he conceives of an "operant" or "militant" infinity. His infinite and "indestructible" (VI, 267; *VI*, 321) *archē* is a Being which is nothing but explosion and unmotivated upsurge. For him therefore there is no question of any *finalism*, because the advent of the sentient body, of the wild logos, is not a "positive production" but rather the result of an (unmotivated) dehiscence of Being. (VI, 265; *VI*, 319) The advent of man and culture is not the reflection of an in-itself Being; it is rather Being in the making, in the process of realizing itself. And there is no specificable end to this advent of Being since it is not the exteriorization of a hidden interior, but a pure transcendence. In a way, Being is nothing but *natura naturans;* it is nothing in itself, being rather Nature itself coming to presence. Since therefore Being is nothing but upsurge, the most proper characteristic of Being is that *it never fully is*. For Merleau-Ponty there is no reality underlying the world which would be the bearer of its becoming which could exhaustively unveil itself in this becoming;

there is no "question of origins, nor limits, nor of a series of events going to a first cause, but one sole explosion of Being which is forever." (VI, 265; *VI,* 318) Being is therefore that which in its progressive revelation remains always and irremediably dissimulated. Merleau-Ponty's ontology is a philosophy of Being conceived of as "that which never fully is" (PriP, 190; *OE,* 92) as that which in its presence and immanence remains always and necessarily absent and ungraspable.

Thus for Merleau-Ponty there is a logic in history since history is the "inscription of Being," but this logic does not override man and does not do away with contingency and human freedom. It is man in his freedom and creativity who makes history and is responsible for it by letting Being be; but since in the last analysis the "vague thrust" which man transforms into history does not have its origin in him but comes from Being and is Being expressing itself in him, human action always has a richer meaning than that one which each "consciousness" thinks it puts or discerns in it. There is a second-order value of truth (S, 78, 11; *S,* 97, 17) to history which is not due to "mere" subjectivity. Thus, if Merleau-Ponty's philosophy is not a quietism before an overpowering force or transcendence, neither is it a form of Promethean humanism. Unlike Sartre, Merleau-Ponty does not believe that "without any support or help, man is at each moment condemned to invent man," that "there is no other universe than a human universe, the universe of human subjectivity."[29] On the contrary, he thinks that man does not invent anything—and most certainly does not invent himself—but transforms and transfigures everything because, precisely, he does not exist on a level where there are only men, but inhabits rather the field of Being. There is always another dimensionality to what we are and what we do because we are borne along in our being by Being. This is why in the end Merleau-Ponty recognized the possibility and perhaps even the need for *hope.*[30] (S, 23; *S,* 32) To conclude, one could say of him what he himself said of Bergson: "Everything happens, according to Bergson, as if man encountered at the roots of his constituted being a generosity which is not a compromise with the adversity of the world and which is on his side against it" (IPP, 25; *EP,* 43)

## Conclusion

SUCH are in short the overall lines of a philosophy of Being in the nascent state which emerge from a reading of the ambiguous and unfinished work of Maurice Merleau-Ponty. We should not perhaps seek to discover in this ontology which comes to us in "scraps" overly precise ideas and certainly not definitive answers to well-delimited problems. "Philosophy," Merleau-Ponty himself says, "does not raise questions and does not provide answers that would little by little fill in the blanks." (VI, 105; *VI*, 142) The questions of philosophy are not questions of knowledge which aim at an absolute knowledge or a rigorous science, but rather questions wherein philosophy is a question for itself, wherein its most proper and radical problematic is itself; they are therefore questions which turn back on themselves as questions, unsurpassable questions, therefore, which by that very fact bear witness to the irreducibility of the philosophical wonder before the "there is" of the world and our presence to it and to others. It is in man, who is an opening in Being, that the question about Being arises; it is therefore in man that Being makes its advent or puts itself into question. Now since man or subjectivity is unsurpassable, the question that he is in his being is also, such that our ultimate relation to Being is that of an interminable questioning, and the presence of Being to us is that of an enigma or a mystery where Being reveals itself only in dissimulating itself. There is no answer to the question, What is Being? τί τὸ ὄν, as if Being was or could be a direct object of our experience or an immediate given of consciousness. The question Merleau-Ponty raises is in the last analysis that same eternal question which, as Aristotle said more than two thousand years ago, was raised of old and is raised now and always and is always the subject of our puzzlement. Merleau-Ponty's ontology is in this way the realization of Being as that which is eternally sought after and is eternally the subject of our wonder, a transcendence which is eternally ungraspable in its immanence.

# Concerning Merleau-Ponty: Two Readings of His Work[1]

## 1. ON TH. F. GERAETS' INTERPRETATION OF MERLEAU-PONTY, by G.B. Madison

IN publishing three years ago his admirable study[2] of the work of the young Merleau-Ponty, Professor Geraets has rendered an important service to the philosophical public and to the growing number of those interested in the insightful work of Merleau-Ponty, "the greatest of French phenomenologists," as Paul Ricoeur remarked. This book is a model of historical research and constitutes the most important and most detailed of the studies of this period in the thought of the French philosopher.

Geraets' book can be recommended for many reasons, but its major interest stems from the fact that it presents us with a detailed and continuing analysis of the philosopher's search for an appropriate *method*. The book's title itself clearly emphasizes Geraets' interest in this question of methodology. His principal concern is to show us how

Merleau-Ponty finally came to the conception of philosophy which was afterwards to be tried out in the *Phenomenology of Perception.* As Geraets shows, from its beginning the deep motivation in Merleau-Ponty's thought was of an "existentialist" sort. Merleau-Ponty embodied the old tradition of French moral philosophy, and, as Sartre says, the young Merleau-Ponty was very Pascalian in temperament. However, Merleau-Ponty wanted to pursue an academic career. This meant that he had to come to terms with the philosophy of the schools. There was, on the one side, criticist, neo-Kantian philosophy, and, on the other, traditional realism. However, neither the one nor the other seemed to him to be capable of rendering justice to recent discoveries in the areas of physiology and psychology in which he had begun to be interested (see Merleau-Ponty's text "La nature de la perception," included as an appendix in Geraets' book). What Merleau-Ponty needed was therefore a means of escaping the two classical alternatives of intellectualism and objectivism, of idealism and realism. He needed a methodology which would allow him to realize his existentialist interests but which at the same time would be more than a mere personal reflection of the Marcelian sort—that is, a conceptual apparatus which, precisely, would allow him, not to skirt the then dominant philosophies, but to enter into a full-fledged debate with them and finally to refute them. In short, what Merleau-Ponty was looking for was a "third way" between idealism and realism, between criticist philosophy and objectivist science (see for instance the text quoted on pp. 36–7 of Geraets' book). Merleau-Ponty, Geraets tells us, was caught in this ambiguous methodological situation up until 1939. This Geraets calls Merleau-Ponty's "hesitation": he wanted "neither to renounce all transcendental philosophy nor to definitively take up the point of view of transcendental constituting consciousness". (p. 2) Merleau-Ponty wanted to adopt fully neither the point of view of the outside onlooker in vigor in the science nor idealism's idea of a sovereign and constituting transcendental consciousness. In short, Merleau-Ponty wanted to maintain the transcendental tradition in philosophy, while at the same time rejecting its idealist aspects which for him were unacceptable. How was Merleau-Ponty able to overcome this "hesitation"?

Geraets' thesis, which is developed in the last chapter of his book—a chapter which constitutes a good study of the young Merleau-Ponty's relation to Husserl—consists in situating the moment when

Merleau-Ponty was able "to accomplish this decisive step" (p. 134) in the beginning of 1939, following a deepened understanding of the work of the later Husserl. What would have led him to pass "an important threshold" (p. 134) would have been his discovery of a kind of "philosophy of existence" in Husserl himself. This is to say that this development would have come about after *The Structure of Behavior,* a work which was finished in 1938. According to Geraets, *The Structure of Behavior* is a "difficult book" (pp. 31–2, 39), for the author's attitude is here ambiguous, and in the course of the book a "change in method" takes place which "is not clearly recognized by the author himself". (p. 39) The change in method to which Geraets refers is the passage from a consideration of perception as seen from the outside to an elucidation of perception as lived from the inside—in short, the passage to the transcendental point of view. However, in *The Structure of Behavior* Merleau-Ponty does not succeed in distinguishing clearly between the transcendental point of view and idealism or criticism *tout court,* which he still refuses to take on. This is to say that here Merleau-Ponty's position is rather ambiguous. As Geraets says, "it seems that before 1939 Merleau-Ponty did not see how it would be possible to develop a transcendental philosophy if one gives up the idea of a universal constituting consciousness." (p. 130) If therefore in *The Structure of Behavior,* as Geraets says, "phenomenology and transcendental idealism are...actually looked upon as the same kind of philosophy" (p. 90), the important change which occurred in 1939 would have consisted in the fact that Merleau-Ponty was able—or at least thought he was able—to dissociate the two. What would have suggested this possibility to Merleau-Ponty would have been his discovery in Husserl himself—that is, in a philosopher who passed for an idealist—of the "existential" notions of the *Lebenswelt,* the life-world, and operative intentionality. I shall return to this point in a moment, for it will furnish me with a starting point for my critique; but for the time being I must admit that Geraets' thesis is very plausible on the whole and that his argument is convincing. What gives it weight is that there is an incontestable difference between *The Structure of Behavior* and the *Phenomenology of Perception.* The latter is not a mere prolongation of the former, but takes up the analysis of perception at a different, higher level. This is to say that there is a break between the two books, and one can accordingly suppose along with Geraets that something important happened in the author's mind between the two; the most probable hypothesis is that the cause of this change was his deepened reading of Husserl.

In addition to spelling out in this way the nature of the change in Merleau-Ponty, Geraets tells us that the fundamental attitude which made its appearance in 1939 "presides over the whole of his future work and makes it understandable". (p. 3) Merleau-Ponty's reading of Husserl would have allowed him to "find the fundamental philosophical attitude which he will keep for the rest of his life". (p. 171) It is precisely in regard to this assertion that I would like to question Professor Geraets. For it seems to me that there was a change in Merleau-Ponty even more important than the one so admirably analyzed by Geraets, and that this change is the one which intervened between the *Phenomenology of Perception* and *The Visible and the Invisible*—such that the philosophical attitude taken up by Merleau-Ponty in 1939 is precisely not the one "which he will keep for the rest of his life." In other words, Professor Geraets attempts to show us how Merleau-Ponty succeeded in 1939 in navigating between the Scylla and the Charybdis of idealism and realism. Although Merleau-Ponty did attempt this passage then, I am not so sure that he did not rather strand himself on the rocks. In order to give some weight to this objection, I must try to indicate what I consider to be a radical insufficiency in the position which was gained in 1939 and which was expressed in the *Phenomenology of Perception*.

In my opinion, the trouble with the *Phenomenology of Perception* stems precisely from the relation that Merleau-Ponty maintains in regard to Husserl. This relation is the most ambiguous one possible. Whereas Merleau-Ponty thought he discerned an "existential philosophy" in Husserl, all the evidence indicates that Husserl never gave up his desire to raise philosophy to the level of an absolute science. If, however, Husserl maintained the notion of philosophy as science, he also necessarily maintained the concepts which flow from this, in particular the notion of transcendental, constituting consciousness. This amounts to saying that Husserl's philosophy remained up until its end a philosophy of consciousness and thoroughgoing idealism. There never was in Husserl himself what, nevertheless, Merleau-Ponty calls "the existentialism of the last period." To speak of "existentialism" in connection with Husserl is, in my opinion, to speak of a pure fiction (or else it amounts to doing philosophy rather than the history of philosophy). I do not mean to say that Merleau-Ponty completely misunderstood Husserlian philosophy (the text quoted of on p. 58 of Geraets' study indicates the contrary by demonstrating Merleau-Ponty's recognition of Husserl's basically idealist character), but only that he did not want or could not believe that Husserl was nothing more than the idealist he was. If he had thought so, he would no doubt not have been able to find in Husserl the help and encouragement he needed to continue in his attempt to overcome idealism from the inside. It is, moreover, highly significant that to a great extent, as Geraets shows, Merleau-Ponty read Husserl through the eyes of Fink. Fink's attempt to "existentialize" Husserl without, however, breaking out of the framework of Husserlian thought must have been highly attractive to Merleau-Ponty. It is, however, precisely this attempt to bend Husserlian transcendental idealism to fit the demands of an existentialist thought that I find impossible.

It is of course true that one can find in the later Husserl certain "existential" notions, such as that of the *Lebenswelt*, but Merleau-Ponty's error was to think that one can properly develop the notions within transcendental thought, within idealistic intentional phenomenology. Merleau-Ponty attempted to work out a compromise between Husserl's intention-constitutional analysis and existential philosophy. This compromise is not tenable, and to attempt it is to condemn oneself to a philosophy of ambiguity, even more, to a bad, *ambiguous philosophy*.[3] Wanting therefore to preserve traditional transcendental philosophy while at the same time dissociating if from idealism, Merleau-Ponty seeks to provide a new definition of the transcendental. For him, the "true transcendental" is no longer the constituting transcendental Ego, but is instead the bodily subject or, more precisely, perceptual, prereflective, *lived experience*. However, to speak like Merleau-Ponty of a concrete, factual a priori cannot have much philosophical meaning when everything is said and done (that is within the rationalist tradition to which he nonetheless continues to adhere), and the impossible mixture of transcendentalism and empiricism makes him vulnerable to criticism coming from genuine transcendentalists[4] as well as authentic empiricists.[5] Merleau-Ponty rejects the outside point of view for that of the inside (cf. p. 186 in Geraets)—this in accordance with traditional transcendental philosophy—but his originality in regard to the tradition consists in his attempt to "deintellectualize" this inside; the true transcendental is not intellectual consciousness but perceptual consciousness, lived experience. All of this, if I may be allowed to express myself in this way, is a palace revolution, a revolution *within* idealism, which for this very reason does not succeed in calling into question idealism as such. What Merleau-Ponty did not see in 1939 and in the forties is that *the mere substitution of a philosophy of experience for a philosophy of consciousness changes nothing in regard to the basic structures of this philosophy.* Merleau-Ponty's philosophy of lived experience operates with all the presuppositions of a philosophy of consciousness; the same idealistic presuppositions are still at work. The world, for instance, is still "subjectivized" or "relativized," and being is still defined as being-for-a-subject, even if now this subject is the lived body and no longer the transcendental Ego. Cartesian dualism continues to have free reign in the *Phenomenology of Perception.* One of the most pertinent criticisms addressed to Merleau-Ponty at the time was, in my opinion, that of Jean Beaufret who said that, as far as he was concerned, Merleau-Ponty had not been radical *enough*, for the whole question is to know if a fully realized phenomenology does not require abandoning the idealistic vocabulary still retained in the *Phenomenology of Perception.* Neither in 1939 nor in the *Phenomenology* did Merleau-Ponty genuinely succeed in getting out of the idealistic tradition.

In a recent text Michel Henry makes the following remarks which for my part I would apply to the philosophy of existence, the "existential transcendentalism" of the *Phenomenology of Perception*:

Insofar as meaning, all possible meaning in general, is constituted by a consciousness, the question as to the meaning of existence moves in a circle as soon as what is thought under the term existence is in reality nothing other than consciousness. It is of course true that in its project the philosophy of existence defined itself in opposition to the classical philosophy of consciousness, but it can be doubted if it was able to follow through with such a project. This is what becomes evident when we see that the original ontological structure of existence defined as transcendence and intentionality does precisely no more than take over the structure of consciousness itself, traditionally understood as a relation to an object, as representation.[6]

This vicious circle of the philosophy of consciousness referred to by Michel Henry is, I maintain, what Merleau-Ponty became fully conscious of towards the end of his life and what he then wanted to come to terms with. The following text bears witness to this: "The problems posed in *Ph.P* are insoluble because I start there from the 'consciousness'-'object' distinction." (VI, 200; *VI*, 253) As this attempt by Merleau-Ponty to escape once and for all from idealism constitutes the central subject of my book, I will not go into the details here; in what follows and to finish, I would like only to take a look at Merleau-Ponty's itinerary from a contemporary point of view so as to raise the question of its present relevance.

Professor Geraets says that in *The Structure of Behavior* Merleau-Ponty had not yet succeeded in reconciling or overcoming in a resolute way the realism-idealism alternative. One can therefore say that this book fails in what it attempts. Now, for my part, I would say that the *Phenomenology of Perception* fails also, this time on a higher level. When, however, the *Phenomenology* fails, it is transcendental philosophy itself which is called into question. Geraets says that "since Kant one can no longer conceive of a philosophy, worthy of the name, which would no longer be transcendental" (p. 87), but it seems to me that it is precisely about this assumption that Merleau-Ponty began to have doubts towards the middle of the fifties. When one resolutely attempts to escape from idealism, one is in reality beginning to take one's distances from traditional philosophy, and it is the latter which begins to be suspicious. This is to say that one then begins to have questions about the very possibility of philosophy. The philosophical enterprise itself is called into question. "Our state of non-philosophy——Never has the crisis been so radical" (VI, 165; *VI*, 219), Merleau-Ponty wrote in 1959, twenty years after the "decisive step" of 1939. In any event, what had come to an end for Merleau-Ponty was intentional phenomenology, whether in an idealistic *or* in an existentialist form. It was in a situation of distress that he then found himself, forced up against the necessity of tracing out a new path in an unknown country, beyond the tradition.

In a recent work, G. Granel writes in regard to Husserlian phenomenology, "it is possible and it is even certain that this philosophy too will come to an end, and even that it already has come to an end; its attempt to survive as a philosophical school either had produced Epigones or else has led to the ritual killing of the Father, which Merleau-Ponty was in the process of committing, piously and pitilessly, and which would be something over and done with if he had not himself died" ...[7] Just as Merleau-Ponty's first "decisive step," about which Professor Geraets speaks to us, was effectuated thanks to Merleau-Ponty's reading of Husserl, so also I would say that the second decisive step that *The Visible and the Invisible* begins to bring about was due to his reading of the later Heidegger. As Granel remarks, "... the slow ascension of Merleau-Ponty in and towards thought had brought him to a 'place' strangely close to that of Heidegger."[8] We must, however, be clear about the later Merleau-Ponty's relationship with Heidegger just as we must be, moreover, about his relationship with Husserl.

For me it is an indisputable fact that at the end Merleau-Ponty had clearly distanced himself from Husserl and from the tradition itself, but this does not mean that he had become "Heideggerian." On the contrary, what can be of interest to us in the final and unfinished work of Merleau-Ponty is that one finds here an attempt to overcome traditional philosophy in general and Husserlian phenomenology in particular, one which does not for all that fall into the "mystical" excesses which abound in the later Heidegger. If Heidegger shows us a road leading beyond traditional philosophy, beyond idealism, Merleau-Ponty indicates another one to us, an "alternative route" which is perhaps more passable and more promising than Heidegger's, a road which, unlike Heidegger's, is not a *Holzweg*—that is, it is *not* a road leading nowhere. Indeed, while in his reaction against the tradition Heidegger appears to reject all concern for *method* (an obsession, he would say, of the tradition and an instance of its subjectivism) and quite simply gives up all attempts to validate and justify his remarks, Merleau-Ponty, *faithful still in this to Husserl* and traditional philosophy, tries to *justify* his overcoming of the tradition. In this regard it is significant that whereas Heidegger abandons the term "philosophy," Merleau-Ponty holds on to it and speaks of a "new philosophy" to be worked out. (TFL, 102; *RC*, 144) Merleau-Ponty wanted to overcome the dogmatism of traditional philosophy and of Husserlianism which reduces Being to what can be known about it, but he was opposed to the idea that the thinker of Being is condemned to an eloquent silence or to oracular poetry. Merleau-Ponty's critique of Heidegger centers around this question of method. In his eyes Heidegger condemns us to silence, for he is looking for "a direct expression of the fundamental" and thereby ignores "the mirrors of Being." (TFL, 112; *RC*, 156) Contrary to Heidegger, Merleau-Ponty was preoccupied with our access to Being, its insertion in phenomenal, lived experience, questions of method and of the language appropriate to a philosophy of Being. Merleau-Ponty's thought always remained a "philosophy," for it remained conscious of its *human* character and resisted the temptation of Heideggerian hubris which transforms the thought of the thinker into the thought of Being and makes language into the language of Being in the mode of the *genitivus subjectivus*. For Merleau-Ponty, it is not language which speaks; it is rather man, even though in this human activity it is finally Being which expresses itself.[9]

Merleau-Ponty was finally able to overcome philosophical dogmatism as well as ontological muteness by conceiving of philosophy as a *human interrogation*. In his late work what he inquires into is the very meaning of philosophical inquiry, and he does so in a resolute and methodical way. Thirteen years after his death, this itinerary which loses itself in the night has lost nothing of its relevance and its power of teaching and inspiring us in our current distress. Fashions pass, but the thing, the very thing that provokes us to think—that remains.

## 2. MERLEAU-PONTY ACCORDING TO MADISON,
by Th. F. Geraets

IT was the intention of Gary Brent Madison to disclose—in an interpretive reappropriation rather than a presentation or a commentary—the fundamental intention or the deep meaning of the philosophy of Maurice Merleau-Ponty. (pp. xxx–xxxii)[10] His study is chronological in its presentation (p. xxviii), but regressive in its methodological aim: what is involved in an "ontological" reading of Merleau-Ponty's work. (pp. xiii, xxxi) The structure of the book is quite simple: the author shows how the passage from the "positive" phenomenology of the first two works (chap. 1) to the "negative" ontology of the last writings (chap. 5) came about; by interpreting what at different times Merleau-Ponty wrote about painting (chap. 2), language (chap. 3), and philosophy (chap. 4).

The significance of the passage to ontology is described in the following terms: "a radical *calling into question*," the setting up of "a wholly new starting point," "a *total taking up again* of the *Phenomenology [of Perception]*, transposing it in its entirety into a wholly other field where alone the theses of this first important book receive their true and ultimate significance." (p. 167–8) It is not a question of "a refutation or an abandonment" (ibid.), but of a realization, by phenomenology, of its limits—which are those of a "philosophy of consciousness and what is immanent to it." (p. 190) This realization takes place "within consciousness (one can obviously never get outside of consciousness)" (p. 233); but "by thinking its own blindness" (p. 195) consciousness thinks Being and "phenomenological positivism" is transformed into "negative ontology." (p. 195) It must be recognized that this passage and this transformation—even if the interpreter refuses to see here a refutation or a renouncement (pp. 204, 167–8)—do indeed contain for him an element of negation. What is denied is the claim of Merleau-Ponty's "first philosophy" to ground itself and to rest on itself qua positive phenomenology. (pp. 196, 190) What is denied is the affirmation of our bodily communication with the world "as a brute fact without any intelligible foundation," (p. 169) as a "contingent" (p. xxviii, passim), "ultimate" (pp. 51, 118), "irrational" (p. 92) fact, a product of chance (pp. 67–68)

This thesis about contingency would be founded on "a fundamental and irreducible (although always dialectical) bifurcation of consciousness and the world." (p. 179) What therefore will be called into question is "the very notion of *intentionality*, the intentional relation consciousness-world" (p. 186), the intentional relation qua correlativity. (pp. 27, 30, 32, 33, 169, 185) The intentional analysis of acts (pp. 170, 186, 188, 191) will be replaced by the description of a "wholly new" intentionality which "occurs within Being" (p. 188): "We can see thereby how the notion of intentionality presented in the *Phenomenology* has been radically transformed." (p. 185, n. 17) "It is thus that Merleau-Ponty finally overcomes a Husserlian prejudice which had always been one of the great sources of ambiguity in his own thought, namely, the one according to which to be is to be an object, that is, a correlate to the intentionality of the subject. (p. 205)

To be sure, from the *Phenomenology of Perception* on, Merleau-Ponty "refused the notion of a constituting transcendental Ego," but this refusal seems to condemn him to "an incessant coming and going" between the lived body and the world "without ever arriving at the ultimate source of this dialectical relation," at what "*justifies*" the necessary concordance between these two terms. (p. 333, n. 11) It is precisely when Merleau-Ponty discovers the source or the ground of these two "relativities" ("consciousness" or the lived body and the "object" or the perceived world) in Being that he passes from a phenomenology which seemed self-sufficient to him to an ontology. (ibid.)

"No longer does he conceive the basic origin of truth or meaning to be the dialectical and gratuitous relation of the subject to the world, and the theme of his thought is no longer 'being in the world' but rather 'Being'." (p. 328, n. 12) (See p. 327, n. 12 for a complete description of the development of Merleau-Ponty's thought in three periods.) This interpretation raises questions concerning three areas: Merleau-Ponty's "first philosophy," his interpretation of Husserl in the early, middle, and late works, and the notion of Being in the last writings.

As to the "first philosophy"—in order to determine to what degree it is a question of a phenomenology which could still be classified as a "philosophy of consciousness," it would be necessary to:

a.  examine thoroughly the distinction between "consciousness" and "experience";
b.  measure the divergence between the intentionality of acts, with which intentional analysis is concerned, and operative intentionality, which Merleau-Ponty privileges from the *Phenomenology of Perception* on;
c.  bring out the meaning and the limits of the correlativity between the perceiving and the perceived;
d.  determine in exactly what sense the often affirmed contingency indicates the negation of a grounding.

It seems to me that Madison has not completely escaped one of the dangers inherent in a regressive analysis, that of seeing the "first philosophy" too much as a "lack" of what constitutes the substance of the last philosophy and thereby overaccentuating the contrast between the two.

To be sure, Merleau-Ponty himself criticizes his first works, the *Phenomenology of Perception* in particular: "The problems posed in *Ph.P* are insoluble because I start there from the 'consciousness'-'object' distinction." (VI, 200; *VI*, 253) "The problems that remain after this first description: they are due to the fact that in part I retained the philosophy of 'consciousness' ". (VI, 183; *VI*, 237) We should not, however, exclude the possibility that this criticism is somewhat exaggerated and that—as in the case of his criticism of the tacit *Cogito*—we should say, with Tilliette, that "Merleau-Ponty slanders himslef retrospectively."[11] In any event, we should ask ourselves *exactly how* the distinction 'consciousness'-'object' served as a starting point, and in what sense Merleau-Ponty could be said to have *in part* held on to the philosophy of consciousness.

In my opinion, a single answer must be given to the two questions at the same time: the philosophical language of the *Phenomenology of Perception* is that of a philosophy of consciousness. All of this linguistic *system* is articulated around the radical distinction 'consciousness'-'object', but the *use* Merleau-Ponty makes of this language aims precisely at calling into question the distinction itself. The in-between (*entre-deux*) that Merleau-Ponty wants to bring out can therefore be expressed only indirectly, mainly through negations; and this is why it is perhaps not possible to grasp the meaning of Merleau-Ponty's first two works by withdrawing them from "the double polemic that exhausts a good part of Merleau-Ponty's energy".[12] This "first description" (VI, 183; *VI*, 237) had to remain inadequate, for the "part" of the philosophy of consciousness that Merleau-Ponty there retained is a "total part": its language or, in the terminology of Eric Weil, its "category."[13] This is not negligible, above all for a philosophy which insists so much on the unity of thought and speech, but this should not make us forget that it is through the distortion (*décentration*), the coherent deformation of Husserlian language, that the signifying intention of Merleau-Ponty's discourse reveals itself. (Cf. S, 115; *S*, 144) It is thus that it reveals itself to us, his readers, as well as to the author himself. (Cf. S, 92; *S*, 115) "What we *mean* is not before us, outside all speech, as sheer signification. It is only the excess of what we live over what has already been said." (S, 83; *S*, 104) What I have called Merleau-Ponty's "fundamental philosophical attitude"[14] is precisely this excess of the lived-through; it is the signifying intention which *expresses itself* in a rather indirect fashion in the *Phenomenology of Perception*, in a more direct fashion in the last writings.

Let us return to the four points we raised in connection with the "first philosophy":

a. The distinction between "consciousness" and "experience."

It is clear that, for Merleau-Ponty, the term "consciousness" tends to retain an aspect of exteriority, expressed most clearly by the idea of the outside spectator. The term "experience," on the contrary, expresses well "the communication of a finite subject with an opaque being from which it emerges but to which it remains committed." (PhP, 219; *PP*, 253) There therefore exists—besides the interiorization of the point of view in relation to the external point of view which dominates *The Structure of Behavior*—what Madison calls a "deintellectualization" of this interior. (Cf. above p. 271) One however has the right to ask if such a displacement of the transcendental instance to the interior of the subject is truly all that Merleau-Ponty means to express.

The "true transcendental" is not perceptual *consciousness*, the perceiving *subject*, the lived body—it is "that ambiguous life in which the forms of transcendence have their *Ursprung*". (PhP, 365; *PP*, 418) To be sure, Merleau-Ponty still speaks of "transcendental subjectivity," in order to say that it is "an intersubjectivity" (PhP, 361; *PP*, 415); but the true transcendental, rather than being identifiable with a subject of whatever sort, is life itself, the transcendental field, the very origin of the subject-object opposition. The latter—the lived body and the perceived world—are essentially the poles of this field, grounded in it, emerging from it. Thus, "interiority" is no longer that of traditional transcendental philosophy, even "deintellectualized," but is *the interiority of the subject himself*, whatever he be, *to experience or life.*[15] In this sense, it is not a question of a "mere substitution of a philosophy of experience for a philosophy of consciousness" which would leave the basic structures of the latter intact. (Cf. above p. 272) It is already true that "the transcendental, being a resolute overcoming of the *mens sive anima* and the psychological, *goes beyond subjectivity* in the sense of counter-transcendence and immanence." (VI, 172; *VI*, 226)

b. It is in the same sense that, according to me, we should properly interpret the privilege Merleau-Ponty accords, from the *Phenomenology of Perception* on, to operative intentionality. Madison asserts that in *The Visible and the Invisible* Merleau-Ponty introduces "a wholly new notion of intentionality": an "intentionality within being." (VI, 244; *VI*, 298) (Cf. p. 188) But let us quote the context in which this new notion is found: "The whole Husserlian analysis is blocked by the framework of *acts* which imposes upon it the philosophy of *consciousness*. It is necessary to take up again and develop the *fungierende* or *latent* intentionality which is the intentionality within being. That is not compatible with 'phenomenology,' that is, with an ontology that obliges whatever is not nothing to *present* itself to *consciousness* across *Abschattungen* and as deriving from an originating donation which is an *act*, i.e., one *Erlebnis* among others....It is necessary to take as primary, not consciousness and its *Ablaufspanomen* with its distinct intentional threads, but the vortex which this *Ablaufsphano-men* schematizes, the spatializing-temporalizing vortex (which is flesh and not consciousness facing a noema". (VI, 244; *VI*, 298) Already in the *Phenomenology of Perception* Merleau-Ponty asserted, in referring to Fink's article which appeared in the *Revue internationale de philo-sophie* (Jan., 1939), that "beneath the 'intentionality of the act', which is the thetic consciousness of an object..., we must recognize an 'operative' intentionality which makes the former possible, and which is what Heidegger terms transcendence." (PhP, 418; *PP*, 478) Indeed, he says elsewhere, "Husserl's originality lies beyond the notion of intentionality; it is to be found in the elaboration of this notion and in the discovery, beneath the intentionality of representations, of a deeper intentionality, which others have called existence." (PhP, 121, n. 5; *PP*, 141, n. 4)

I therefore do not think that Michel Henry is right in saying that "the original ontological structure of existence defined as transcendence and intentionality does precisely no more than take over the structure of consciousness itself, traditionally understood as a relation to an object, as representation." (text quoted by Madison p. 272) Obviously, in Merleau-Ponty it is a question of a deintellectualization which is also a critique of the privilege traditionally accorded to representational consciousness. The question raised above returns: Does this critique not entail, does it not imply, a "desubjectivization" of the transcendental?

To be sure, Merleau-Ponty asserts that "I am a field, I am an experience" (PhP, 406; *PP*, 465), but does that mean that the transcendental field, that experience or life are but "me," contained in the immanence of a perceptual idealism? In reading the *Phenomenology of Perception* we have rather the impression that it is already the world, the phenomenological world, comprising the phenomenon of "non-human nature," that is the true encompassing. My life is mine— and it is not mine, for I am "given to myself." (PhP, 360; *PP*, 413) Merleau-Ponty speaks of this encompassing world in one of the rare spots in the *Phenomenology of Perception* where the term is used without having the pejorative sense of "objective" being: "The world remains the same world throughout my life, because it is that permanent being within which I make all corrections to my knowledge, a world which in its unity remains unaffected by those corrections....

from the very start I am in communication with one being, and one only, a vast individual from which my own experiences are taken". (PhP, 327-8; *PP*, 378; cf. PhP, 68-9; *PP*, 82-3)

c. In reflecting on this communicative relationship, we are confronted with the necessity of extricating the meaning and the limits of the correlativity between the (perceiving) subject and the (perceived) world. This correlativity is originally located on the natural or prepersonal level: "The natural world is the horizon of all horizons, the style of all possible styles, which guarantees for my experiences a given, not a willed, unity underlying all the disruptions of my personal and historical life. Its counterpart within me is the given, general and prepersonal existence of my sensory functions in which we have discovered the definition of the body." (PhP, 330; *PP*, 381) According to Madison, this correlativity would in the last analysis not be a communion between ontologically equal partners: in this "correlativity" it would finally be the world which is the "correlate." Merleau-Ponty, Madison says, "makes of subjectivity the ground of being, which for its part is essentially no longer anything other than the correlate of the subject's intentions. Such a step sets up immanence as the criterion of truth and being and denies all transcendence as such." (p. 225) Does this mean that all birth of meaning takes place in an essentially centrifugal movement?

To be sure, Merleau-Ponty says that operative intentionality "produces the natural and antepredicative unity of the world and of our life" (PhP, XVIII; *PP*, XIII), and even that "I am the absolute source, my existence does not stem from my antecedents, from my physical and social environment; instead it moves out towards them and sustains them, for I alone bring into being for myself (and therefore into being in the only sense that the word can have for me) the tradition which I elect to carry on, or the horizon whose distance from me would be abolished—since that distance is not one of its properties—if I were not there to scan it with my gaze." (PhP, IX; *PP*, III; quoted on p. 332, n. 10) But what can one prove by this quotation? Does it express *all* of Merleau-Ponty's thought on the subject? Is it not essential to recognize that it is to be found in a passage which wants to show that "scientific points of view, according to which my existence is a moment of the world's, are always both naive and at the same time dishonest..."? (PhP, IX; *PP*, III) Must we not take such assertions to be part of the "polemic," the group of expressions, which are sometimes hyperbolical, which Merleau-Ponty lays out so as to affirm the impossibility of according to realism the negation of the reflective point of view and to idealism the negation of the objective point of view? If it is true that there is a "subjectivization" of the world in Merleau-Ponty, it is in my opinion *equally* true that there is a "mundanization" of the subject. (cf. PhP, 407; *PP*, 467; quoted on p. 46) Never is the subject alone conceived of as a final transcendental instance.

d. This leads us to the question of contingency and the negation of an ultimate grounding. What is the meaning of the radical contingency which Merleau-Ponty speaks of so often in his first works, and is this contingency denied or overcome in his "last philosophy" by an affirmation of another ultimate ground?

Let us begin by studying two texts in *The Visible and the Invisible* which Madison relies on (p. 174) to demonstrate the negation of contingency, but from which he quotes only the words we shall italicize. Merleau-Ponty says, "our body is a being of two leaves, from one side a thing among things and otherwise what sees them and touches them;...and its double belongingness to the order of the 'object' and to the order of the 'subject' reveals to us quite unexpected relations between the two orders. It cannot be by *incomprehensible accident* that the body has this double reference; it teaches us that each calls for the other." (VI, 137; *VI*, 180–1) What is ruled out here is a purely external or, so to speak, arbitrary relationship. The relationship is internal to each of the two references, each of the two orders: each is essentially ordained to the other. Do we not rediscover here what in the *Phenomenology of Perception* Merleau-Ponty calls the original pact between the perceiving body and the perceived world? This same structure is expressed in another location, in the context of another negation of contingency: "This concentration of the visibles about one of them...this magical relation, this pact between them and me according to which I lend them my body in order that they inscribe upon it and give me their resemblance, this fold, this central cavity of the visible which is my vision, these two mirror arrangements of the seeing and the visible, the touching and the touched, form a close-bound system that I count on....*The flesh* (of the world or my own) *is not contingency*, chaos, but a texture that returns to itself and conforms to itself." (VI, 146; *VI*, 192) The contingency ruled out here is again that of an arbitrary, chaotic relationship, without genuine structure.

But is there not after all an essential difference between these texts and those of the *Phenomenology of Perception* which deal with the original pact? Does not the unity of the carnal fabric win out here in relation to the duality of the terms it includes? This is the question of the correlativity of the perceiving subject and the perceived world which comes back here, but the answer that Madison appears now to give to it seems to be different from the one given above.

Indeed, it must be asked how the brute, contingent fact which is the ground of rationality (in the *Phenomenology of Perception*) is to be understood. In a single sentence, Madison gives three descriptions of it—which are not necessarily equivalent: "the presence of the world, the subject-world structure, being in the world." (p. 67) The following questions thus arise:

Is it the case that in the *Phenomenology of Perception* the only foundation, the genuinely ultimate one, is being in the world, bodily existence, the "deintellectualized" subject? It seems that the answer would have to be affirmative to the degree that, with Madison, one interprets the *Phenomenology of Perception* as leaving intact the basic structures of *idealism*. (Cf. p. 293 and above p. 272) This is not my opinion.

Is it the case, on the other hand, that the two terms of the relationship of presence are really *two ultimate foundations*, standing in a dialectical relation without a single source which would justify it? This is what Madison asserts when he says that the thesis concerning contingency is founded on "a fundamental and irreducible (although always dialectical) bifurcation of consciousness and the world." (p. 179) There would thus be a double ultimate foundation, an unsurpassable duality. (p. 209, 186) This interpretation seems to us difficult to uphold. To be sure, Merleau-Ponty speaks in terms of consciousness and world, of subject and object, but while insisting always on their intrinsic and essential relationship—criticizing idealism and realism—so as to bring out an "in-between" which is itself the ultimate, sole foundation. In *The Visible and the Invisible* he writes, "We know: hands do not suffice for touch—but to decide for this reason alone that our hands do not touch, and to relegate them to the world of objects or of instruments, would be, in acquiescing to the bifurcation of subject and object, to forego in advance the understanding of the sensible and to deprive ourselves of its lights." (VI, 137; *VI*, 180) Did he not already know that at the time when he finished the writing of the *Phenomenology of Perception*? Can one not read here that "the analysis of time...discloses subject and object as two abstract 'moments' of a unique structure which is *presence*"? (PhP, 430; *PP*, 492)

The fundamental fact is not "being in the world" interpreted in an idealistic sense nor "the subject-object structure" interpreted in the sense of an absolutely irreducible bifurcation, it is being in the world understood as not only a deintellectualized subject but a subject standing before his existence itself, at its "suturation" onto the "primordial world" (PhP, 350; *PP*, 402); it is the existence-world structure understood as an essential articulation of the true transcendental which is life or experience. (v.s.) It is also "the presence of the world," a presence of which in one instance Madison says that it is not the subject which constitutes it (p. 67), while elsewhere he asserts that "it is I who bring *presence* into being." (p. 332, n. 10)

In what concerns contingency it seems to us that when—in passing rapidly over the equivalence of presence and time—he concludes with the thesis that "truth or rationality is but 'the accident of time,' " that "everything comes down to the 'fundamental accident which made us appear and will make us disappear.'" (p. 68) Madison tends to hold onto "the usual notion of necessity and contingency," a notion which for Merleau-Ponty it was a question of revising. (PhP, 170–1; *PP*, 199) Is it not significant that Merleau-Ponty says that "ontological contingency" is "that of the world itself"? (PhP, 398; *PP*, 456) And is the difference between the *Phenomenology of Perception* and *The Visible and the Invisible* all that great in what concerns contingency, when Merleau-Ponty speaks, in the *Phenomenology*, of "the unmotivated upsurge of the world" (PhP, XIV; *PP*, VIII) and, in *The Visible and the Invisible*, of "the unmotivated upsurge of brute Being"? (VI, 211; *VI*, 264; quoted by Madison, p. 330, n. 32, and 219)

We hope to have the occasion later or elsewhere to study Merleau-Ponty's interpretation of Husserl as it is viewed by Madison, as well as his interpretation of the notion of Being in the last writings.[16] However, we wish to state that Madison's book has forced us to reconsider problems that we thought we had already sufficiently studied.


## REPLY TO TH. F. GERAETS, by G.B. Madison

As Geraets indicates, I proposed in my book to carry out an "interpretive reappropriation" rather than a "presentation" or a "commentary" of Merleau-Ponty's work. This amounts to saying that my study is not "historical" in the habitual sense of the term, an attempt to show how Merleau-Ponty's work came into being over the course of years. I did not wish to project myself into the past and relive Merleau-Ponty's philosophy as he himself lived it, but wanted to examine it from a contemporary point of view. My interest was therefore more of a critical nature than a documentary or historical one. This is why I did not want to limit myself solely to the interpretation which Merleau-Ponty himself made of his work. That would have amounted to taking the author's *intentions* as the sole and adequate indication of the meaning and the worth of what he *actually realized*. Now I believe that there often exists a discrepancy between what one believes one is doing and what one is really doing, that the self-understanding one has of oneself is often misleading, and that, in a word, good intentions do not necessarily make for good works. What therefore interested me was not so much the conscious aim of Merleau-Ponty in the *Phenomenology of Perception* such as he himself lived and understood it as it was the question of this work's adequation to the reality of things. And what I thought I discovered was that the *Phenomenology* is inadequate, the reason being that Merleau-Ponty had not yet there broken sufficiently with the philosophy of consciousness, with traditional idealism.

This is the thesis which seems to constitute a point of disagreement between Geraets and me. Geraets tends rather to say that the *Phenomenology* already accomplishes a decisive step in the overcoming of the philosophy of consciousness. Perhaps, however, this difference is more apparent than real and has to do with our ways of approaching Merleau-Ponty rather than with what we find there. In addition to this question concerning the "first philosophy," Geraets points out two other areas where there appears to be a difference in interpretation between us: Merleau-Ponty's attitude in regard to Husserl, and the notion of Being in the last writings. As in the time allotted I cannot respond to each of these points in detail, I am going to try to treat all three together, but in an oblique way, by taking as my theme the question of philosophical language. Perhaps in this way I will be able not only to respond to the substance of Geraets' remarks but also better clarify the significance of our divergences and perhaps even dissipate certain possible misunderstandings.

One thing which Merleau-Ponty has taught us is that there is a strict and indissoluble relation between thought and speech. Language is not the mere vehicle of an autonomous thought. Even if in some ways thought may transcend its expression, it is by means of expression that this transcendence is made possible. This consequently means that the meaning of what one says cannot remain indifferent to the way in which one says it, or, to say it another way, that the expressions and the words one uses determine to a great extent the significance of what one says, whatever might be in other respects one's intended meaning. Thus it is, for instance, that a critique of technology which wants to be radical and which yet employs only technological terms and concepts would fail as a critique and would continue to play the game of technology. It is precisely for this reason that I maintain that the *Phenomenology of Perception* fails in its attempt to overcome intellectualism and that what in the last analysis it teaches is a bad amiguity. I am in complete agreement with Geraets when he maintains that the true aim of Merleau-Ponty in the *Phenomenology* is to break with the traditional categories of idealism. The only difference is that I consider that Merleau-Ponty did not succeed in this attempt due to the key-concepts he uses, such as the Husserlian notion of intentionality which is finally the expression of an idealistic philosophy. It is because of this that I speak of a bad ambiguity, for in the *Phenomenology* the author's intention and the real meaning of the work do not coincide. Perhaps the difference between Geraets and me stems to a large extent from the fact that Geraets is ready to give more consideration to the author's intentions than I am, the work itself being of more interest to me than the author.

To be sure, Geraets is ready to allow that the *language* of the *Phenomenology* is effectively "idealistic": "the *philosophical language* of the *Phenomenology of Perception* is that of a philosophy of consciousness. All of this linguistic system is articulated around the radical distinction 'consciousness'-'object' ". Only he adds, "...but the use Merleau-Ponty makes of this language aims precisely at calling into question the distinction itself." This however, does not prevent it from being the case that because of its idealistic conceptuality the project of the *Phenomenology*—and it is Geraets who is speaking—"had to remain inadequate." Thus the difference between us seems to be that Geraets wants to speak of inadequacy, whereas I prefer to speak quite simply of a failure. But Geraets himself adds, "this is not negligible, above all for a philosophy which insists on the unity of thought and speech".

When it is a question of a thinker as fertile as Merleau-Ponty, there does indeed exist a margin of freedom which allows different interpreters to accentuate different things. Since Geraets considers that "since Kant one can no longer conceive of a philosophy, worthy of the name, which would no longer be transcendental," he attempts to show how Merleau-Ponty brought about a *new* transcendental philosophy freed from the prejudices of a philosophy of consciousness. But since for my part I consider that transcendental philosophy, philosophy of consciousness, and idealism are all strictly interrelated and that a philosophy of experience such as the *Phenomenology of Perception* presents operates with the same basic presuppositions of a more traditional philosophy of consciousness, I can, in the last analysis, only see the *Phenomenology* as a failure. The book is a failure, for what Merleau-Ponty seems to want to say there simply cannot be said in the language and with the conceptuality to which he has recourse and which are those of the tradition. As Granel has observed, "it remains to be seen if words are only words that one can dress up with such and such a meaning, as little girls think they are changing dolls in changing their dresses; or if words are always the words of a certain language, invested with the meaning which invests itself in them and to which they implacably reduce all significations that one claims to give them from the outside." (*Le sens du temps et de la perception chez E. Husserl*, p. 106.)

It is therefore all the more significant that when in *The Visible and the Invisible* Merleau-Ponty attempts to work out "a new starting point," he also attempts, and explicitly so, to break with the terminology of traditional philosophy. When he says that philosophy "must recommence everything" (VI, 130; *VI*, 172), he means to say that one must break with the traditional concepts—such as subject, object, existence, essence—and form "new instruments" both linguistical and conceptual. He writes, "...we do not allow ourselves to introduce into our description concepts issued from reflection, whether psychological or transcendental....we must, at the beginning, eschew notions such as 'acts of consciousness', 'states of consciousness', 'matter', 'form', and even 'image' and 'perception'." (VI, 157–8; *VI*, 209) This should suffice to show that the late Merleau-Ponty was fully aware of the difficulties of language and wanted then to overcome them. What, moreover, is of the greatest interest to us today in Merleau-Ponty's final work is the way in which he raises the question of philosophical discourse. In reality it is the whole question of the status of philosophical discourse that comes to occupy a central position when he writes, "hence it is a question whether philosophy as reconquest of brute or wild being can be accomplished by the resources of eloquent language, or whether it would not be necessary for philosophy to use language in a way that takes from it its power of immediate or direct signification in order to equal it with what it wishes all the same to say." (VI, 102-3; *VI*, 139)

However, and I repeat, the new starting point of the late Merleau-Ponty is not a Heideggerian *Kehre*, a mere break or rupture with the tradition (and one may even ask if Heidegger is as radical as he thinks he is). Unlike Heidegger, it is in starting from consciousness, subjectivity, Husserl, and the tradition that Merleau-Ponty pursues his inquiry, and in a radical manner. This is to say that Merleau-Ponty never wanted simply to abandon Husserl; he wanted to overcome transcendental philosophy, but, so to speak, *from the inside*. I can therefore fully accept Geraets' remarks when he says that "it is through the distortion, the coherent deformation of Husserlian language that the signifying intention of Merleau-Ponty's discourse reveals itself." Only I would add that this deformation ends up by breaking the framework of the transcendentalism and immanentism (the reduction of all being to consciousness, to experience) which stem from it. A phenomenology which resolutely thinks its limits has already overcome classical phenomenology, and perhaps even the tradition.

All this leads us to the notion of Being in the last writings. I shall however limit myself to the following remarks. The term "Being" is the most traditional of terms—and also the most *equivocal*. It is true that Merleau-Ponty uses it in his late work, but he also employs another term—the *flesh*—and as he says, "one knows there is no name in traditional philosophy to designate that." (VI, 139; *VI*, 183) It is this "Being" which is not reducible to being-in-the-world—that is, to the subject-world relation, to "experience"—which allows Merleau-Ponty to overcome *contingency*. But this overcoming of contingency is not a return to *necessity*, for "Being" here is neither a supreme and necessary being (*ens causa sui, ens realissimum*) nor a transcendental logical principle (a "that without which" nothing is thinkable). It has neither logical nor ontic reality; it is therefore not so much a *ground* as an abyss, an unfathomable and inexhaustible source of *transcendence*. This "Being" which escapes from the order of essence escapes at the same time from the conceptual couple contingency-necessity (whereas a rationalist like Husserl conceives of the first term of this couple as being subordinated to the second, the young Merleau-Ponty, being an antirationalist, was content with merely inverting the priority). Beyond all essence, it is also, in the last analysis, beyond language and can be grasped only indirectly, in the interstices of the speech of men.


## 4. RESPONSE TO G.B. MADISON, by Th. F. Geraets

I am surprised to see Madison declare that his study of Merleau-Ponty "is not 'historical' in the habitual sense of the term". Is not to want "to intercept and follow the genesis of Merleau-Ponty's ontology" (p. xxviii) to want to engage in the work of a historian? Indeed, I do not think that when he labels his work an "interpretive reappropriation," Madison understands this in the sense wherein Heidegger's book on Kant can be called this. The meaning the term takes in Madison's case seems closer to what one normally calls "historical," even if it is above all a question of the internal history of the work rather than of external factors which influenced his development.

Madison is right in insisting on the necessity of not restricting himself to the explicit interpretation Merleau-Ponty himself gives to his work, to his intentions expressed in a programmatic way. One must study what the author "actually realized," that is, what he succeeded in expressing. In my opinion, what Merleau-Ponty actually expressed in the *Phenomenology of Perception* constitutes a genuine overcoming of traditional transcendental philosophy. However, in breaking with the traditional presupposition of the subject and in beginning in this way to develop a new philosophy, he still insisted on calling it transcendental. It is not in my own name that I wrote that "since Kant one can no longer conceive of a philosophy, worthy of the name, which would no longer be transcendental." (my book, p. 87) This is what Merleau-Ponty thought in writing *The Structure of Behavior* (ibid., n. 46), and what, in a new sense which began to assert itself in the *Phenomenology of Perception*, he maintained up to the end. (Cf. VI, 172; *VI*, 226; cf. above p. 273)

I in no way mean to oppose intention and actual expression, in the sense that I would be more interested by the author's intentions than by his work itself. But it seems to me that the real meaning of the *Phenomenology* already includes the anti-idealistic intention: the distortion of Husserlian language—a distortion which Madison admits— is such that it already breaks "the framework of transcendentalism and immanentism," and it brings out a new notion of experience which is not the result of a mere deintellectualization of consciousness.

Can it be said that "this deformation ends up by calling everything into question"? We should distinguish between the aspects of Husserlian thought which Merleau-Ponty actually did call into question and others from which he drew his inspiration up to the end. And it would be necessary to determine the moment of this calling into question. To do this is impossible within the framework of a brief discussion. Let us return, nonetheless, to the notion of intentionality for a moment. Either Madison's thesis that this "Husserlian notion...is in the last analysis the expression of an idealistic philosophy" is valid for all intentionality—and in this case the late Merleau-Ponty is still an idealist—or else it does not apply to operative intentionality—and then the Merleau-Ponty of the *Phenomenology* is no longer an idealist.

That the overcoming of traditional transcendental philosophy first takes place (and, to a certain degree, up until the end) by means of a speech which subverts (*décentre*) Husserlian language—does that authorize us to speak of a failure? It seems to me that it is a real step in the right direction, calling for future explicitations, but one which is much more than a mere declaration of intention. I do not think that one can oppose, to the degree that Madison seems to do so, what Merleau-Ponty thought he was doing and what he really did.

# M erleau - Ponty and the Counter - Tradition[1]

This history of Western thought, Heidegger tells us, takes place within the unity of a coherent and well-defined tradition. It may be that on this score he is largely right. However that may be, Heidegger's work itself becomes intelligible when it is viewed in the light of this tradition of which it speaks. Heidegger's work, it can then be said, is the attempt to overcome the Western tradition so as to institute a "new beginning" by returning, over and beyond the tradition, to its first beginning, that is, to the thought of the pre-Socratics, the thought of Parmenides and Heraclitus in particular. This tradition which Heidegger believes he has detected is what he calls the history of metaphysics. In its Heideggerian meaning, metaphysics is that mode of thought which defines being as presence. Metaphysics thus defined has its origins in Plato (according to Heidegger) and reaches its culmination in modern idealism or subjectivism where being is reduced to its presence to consciousness, a subjectivism of which contemporary science and technology—where being is reduced to what is knowable in view of technical mastery—are but the ultimate logical consequences. Metaphysics culminates in nihilism.

It is difficult not to agree with Heidegger when he asserts that the history of western thought possesses an inner unity, for there does indeed exist a Tradition in which are reunited almost all of the great thinkers of the West ("great" here meaning "famous," "dominant," "recognized," "respected," etc.). There exists an orthodoxy of philosophical thought. Unlike Heidegger, however, I would prefer to give to this tradition the name Rationalism. The history of philosophy—in its main outlines—is none other than the history of rationalist thought.

That thought is rationalist which postulates or presupposes that between thought and reality, between man and the universe, there exists a kind of natural affinity. The universe is in fact not a chaos but a *cosmos*, that is, a Totality, a Great Whole which is well structured and which, consequently, is intelligible (chaos being by definition unintelligible). Human reason is part of the Totality (or of Nature, to speak like Spinoza); human reason is thus co-natural with the Reason with regulates things or is immanent in them. According to the Hegelian formula, all that is rational is real and all that is real is rational. It is because of this equivalence between the real and the rational that there can be a *science* of reality, of being. All those forms of thought, ancient or modern, are rationalist which seek to discover and to say what reality is, exactly. The legitimation of rationalism is its basic belief in a noumenal and intelligible reality (intelligible at least in principle in itself if not for us), in the existence of a *cosmos*. Its motivation, however, is other. It is the Promethean desire—a desire more often than not unadmitted—on the part of man to overcome the contingencies of existence and achieve a knowledge—a science—of the reality, so as to become master of his own destiny.

It is therefore evident that just like "metaphysics," in the Heideggerian sense, rationalism culminates in modern technology and in the nihilism which flows from it. But when one defines the Tradition in the way I have just done another thing becomes evident, an important thing that Heidegger's analysis obscures. This is that the Tradition does not begin with Plato (even though he was, so to speak, its first great consolidator). The rationalist Tradition begins precisely with those to whom Heidegger proposes to return so as to overcome the Tradition: the pre-Socratics! A moment's reflection is indeed sufficient to realize that all the cosmologists of the Ionian school—those referred to as the first philosophers (Thales, Anaximander, Anaximenes)—were rationalists in the sense in which I use this term, for they were attempting to discover the true nature of things, and this by means of theoretical reason (by postulating theoretical or metaphysical entities capable of "explaining" phenomenal reality). And it is also evident that the first great rationalist was none other than Parmenides, he who preached the existence of a transphenomenal reality, intelligible and accessible to reason alone. In Parmenides one finds, in an operative state, a conceptuality—Plato's merit was to have thematized it—which has become the cornerstone of the Tradition in its entirety, a conceptuality (or *Begrifflichkeit*, as Heidegger would say) which expresses itself in conceptual oppositions and dichotomies, such as the opposition between knowledge (or science) and opinion, between reality and appearance, between fact and value, etc.

When one defines the tradition in this way still another thing becomes apparent, the most important thing of all. Ever since the Tradition has existed, there has existed what could be called a Counter-tradition which is defined by its reaction and opposition to the Tradition. If the Tradition begins with the Ionian school in general and with Parmenides in particular, the Counter-tradition has its origins in what is called—wrongly, moreover—the Socratic revolution. Wrongly, I say, since the revolution or revolt so referred to was the work of the sophists and rhetoricians, men like Protagoras and Gorgias. What characterizes the Counter-tradition is its refusal, constantly reiterated over the course of time, of the claims and pretensions of rationalism or, to use one of Merleau-Ponty's expressions, its refusal of the "presumption on the part of reason." The entire history of philosophy can indeed be considered to be constituted by two movements: there is the dominant current of rationalism and, within this current, a countercurrent which attempts to bring man back to a more just appreciation of his powers and limits.

This way of viewing the history of philosophy as being made up of two currents is not new. In the Prologue to his *Lives of the Philosophers*, Diogenes Laertius wrote, "philosophers may be divided into dogmatists and skeptics."[2] Those Diogenes refers to as skeptics I would also call counter-traditionalists. Thus, to mention only a few of the more important counter-traditionalists: Protagoras and Gorgias, who protested against the rationalist dogmatism of Parmenides and the cosmologists; Isocrates, who was opposed to the rationalism of Plato; Sextus Empiricus, who criticized all the dogmatists up until then, the Stoics in particular; Montaigne, who mounted an offensive against the rationalism of the Renaissance from which modern science was to emerge; Pascal, who was opposed to Cartesian rationalism; Kierkegaard, who attacked Hegel's rationalist pretensions; Nietzsche, who fought against more than two thousand years of rationalist orthodoxy. In general, the Counter-tradition includes three abiding traits: humanism, skepticism, and, since the Christian era, fideism.

That, within the Tradition and in opposition to it, there exists a Counter-tradition is something Heidegger seems unaware of. His conception of the history of philosophy tends indeed to be rather monolithic, for him the entire history of thought since Plato is but the history of "metaphysics." This fact becomes important when we want to appreciate the significance of Merleau-Ponty's philosophical project in relation to that of Heidegger. For, exactly like Heidegger, Merleau-Ponty believed he discerned the existence of a Tradition which he wanted to overturn or overcome. If, however, Merleau-Ponty was to a large extent in agreement with Heidegger on this score, he still remained rather skeptical towards the Heideggerian idea that the problems confronting modern thought can be resolved by reversing the current of thought and rehabilitating a mode of thought which presided over the origin of our tradition.

For my part, I believe—and this is the thesis I wish to put forward here—that this distrust, this skepticism even, of Merleau-Ponty's towards Heidegger's project stems from the fact that Merleau-Ponty was himself a part of the Counter-tradition. A word of explanation is called for, however. To say that Merleau-Ponty was a part of the Counter-tradition is not to say that he was fully *conscious* of belonging to this tradition (or even that he was fully conscious of the existence of such a tradition). But the task of the historian is not merely to repeat what has happened or what people have said; it is rather to understand it. And to understand something always amounts to envisaging it from a certain angle, seeing it in a certain context; it amounts to *interpreting* it. One interprets a thought when, on the one hand, one presents it in such a way as to reveal an inner unity in it, when one reveals the unique arrangement of ideas which—according to the interpreter—constitute the very *essence* of this thought. And one interprets it when, on the other hand, one situates it thus envisaged in a larger context. This is to say that understanding always involves an exercise of our freedom; indeed everything depends on the point of view we *choose* to adopt.[3] There can be, consequently, no interpretation which would be final or which would be the only "correct" one. Certain interpretations, however, are better—that is, more fruitful—than others, because they better succeed in disengaging a thought's essence (its inner coherence) and in revealing relations between this thought and others, since they succeed in situating it in a better-defined context. Now I believe that Merleau-Ponty's work becomes eminently intelligible or understandable when one sees in Merleau-Ponty a philosopher of the Counter-tradition. There is, indeed, a certain constellation or, as Lévi-Strauss would say, a certain "arrangement" of concepts, ideas, and attitudes which serve to define the Tradition and which allow the interpreter to situate a given thinker in it when he discovers in him a certain number of key concepts which figure in this ideal constellation. Similarly, there is a certain complex of ideas which serve to define the Counter-tradition. What I maintain is that Merleau-Ponty's key concepts, as uncovered by interpretation, are of the same order as those of the Counter-tradition. This is what I propose to show.

## II.

In regard to the two other "greats" of the phenomenological movement—Husserl and Heidegger—Merleau-Ponty's position in this movement is unique. And what makes it unique is also what makes of Merleau-Ponty a counter-traditionalist. This will become evident by examining both his originality and his differences as far as Husserl and Heidegger are concerned in regard to two areas (which will tend to overlap): the idea of science and rationality, on the one hand, and the role of the phenomenological reduction and philosophical "methodology," on the other. That Merleau-Ponty is a counter-traditionalist will finally be confirmed by an examination of his political philosophy.

1) The Counter-tradition is, by definition, antirationalist (it is essentially a reaction *against, counter to* the Tradition). It rejects the idea of a "pre-established harmony" (to speak like Leibniz) between reason and reality and the idea which stems from this, the idea that man can attain to a science of the real—that is, a true knowledge of what reality is in itself (the Counter-tradition does not even know what this formula could possibly mean). The Counter-tradition is not

for all that "anti-science" and does not have for its goal the suppression of science (or technology). It simply attempts to remind us of the thoroughly human character of what presents itself—with a great deal of presumptuousness, it must be said—as an "objective" knowledge of things as they are in themselves (this is what Merleau-Ponty called "objective thought"). This is to say that the true Counter-tradition is not, in any way, an irrationalism. Far from it. What characterizes a properly counter-traditionalist thinker is that he appeals to reason precisely so as to point out, by its means, the limits of reason. One is reminded, for instance, of Sextus Empiricus who employed all the techniques of rational argumentation in order to refute the rationalists. One is reminded also of Pascal, himself a skeptic in regard to the pretensions of reason, who said, "the last step of reason is to recognize that there is an infinity of things which surpass it; it is only feeble if it does not go so far as to recognize that....There is nothing more in conformity with reason than this disavowal of reason."[4] (We should not forget that Pascal, the critic of science and of the "spirit of geometry," had himself been a famous scientist and mathematical genius.)

In the last analysis, the *rational* critique of reason has for its goal, not the denial of reason, but rather an enlargement of it; its goal is to enlarge our idea of what makes a discourse or a belief a *rational* discourse or belief. Rationality cannot be reduced to the rules of formal logic or the procedures of those modes of knowledge called "scientific." Any discourse is rational if it enables men to better understand one another and to better coexist.

By his own expressed intentions, Husserl is situated at the very heart of the Tradition. Throughout his entire philosophical life he dreamed of only one thing: establishing philosophy as a science, as, as he said, a serious, rigorous, apodictic science. For him phenomenology was to have been "a method...to establish...a kind of super-rationalism which transcends the old rationalism as inadequate and yet vindicates its inmost objectives."[5] Now it is well known that it was precisely on this point that Merleau-Ponty distanced himself the most from Husserl.

For Merleau-Ponty there can never be an absolute, apodictic knowledge of the world or of man. Speaking of Montaigne, he said what he himself thought: "there cannot in all good conscience be any question of solving the human problem; there can only be a question of describing man as problematic." (S, 202; S, 255) Philosophy for Merleau-Ponty is not a science; it is, on the contrary, the keen aware-

ness of the invincible uncertainties of existence. If he rejects rationalism, the reason is this: "If a universal constituting consciousness were
possible, the opacity of the fact would disappear." (PhP, 61; *PP*, 74)
But for Merleau-Ponty, as for the existentialists in general, the experience of the *opacity* of our existence is a primordial fact that no philosophy can allow itself to forget. If it can be said that the world and
reason are mysterious, it must also be said that "their mystery defines
them: there can be no question of dispelling it by some 'solution', it is
on the hither side of all solutions." (PhP, XX; *PP*, XVI; see also PhP,
333; *PP*, 384) With this insistence on the *opacity of the fact* and the
*mystery of the world* Merleau-Ponty joins up with Heidegger's fundamental attitude in *Sein und Zeit*.[6]

If, however, Merleau-Ponty was in agreement with Heidegger on
this point, his *way* of criticizing the Tradition set him from Heidegger.
Whereas after *Sein und Zeit* Heidegger progressively abandoned all
concern for rational argument in the philosophical sense of the word,
all concern for logic and dialectics, even abandoning the very term
philosophy, Merleau-Ponty remained faithful to Husserl and to the
Tradition by wanting to *rationally* justify his refusal of rationalism.
Contrary to Heidegger, Merleau-Ponty—who was just as opposed to
modern subjectivism as Heidegger—never desired for all that simply
to abandon "subjectivity" and philosophical rationality. It was with
Heidegger in mind that he had written, "...the thought of subjectivity
[*la pensée du subjectif*] is one of these solids that philosophy will
have to digest. Or let us say that once 'infected' by certain ways of
thinking, philosophy can no longer annul them but must cure itself
of them by inventing better ones. The same philosopher who now
regrets Parmenides and would like to give us back our relationships to
Being such as they were prior to self-consciousness owes his idea of
and taste for primordial ontology to just this self-consciousness. There
are some ideas which make it impossible for us to return to a time
prior to their existence, even and especially if we have moved beyond
them, and subjectivity is one of them." (S, 154; *S*, 194)

Thus, whereas Husserl merely continued on with the Tradition,
and whereas Heidegger, in refusing it, placed himself squarely outside
it, Merleau-Ponty attempted to criticize it, so to speak, *from within*.
This is what makes him a counter-traditionalist.

Unlike Husserl, who never managed to take seriously all the un-
reasonableness and absurdity of life,[7] Merleau-Ponty, like Heidegger,
did his best to underline it, by drawing our attention to the non-sense

which surrounds all human enterprises and threatens them with failure. This did not, however, serve as an occasion for him to plead for a "leap," a "resolute" choice which would be irrational, without criteria. Merleau-Ponty was not an irrationalist, a mystic, or a philosopher of the absurd. What he wanted was, on the contrary, to enlarge reason itself: "The experience of unreason cannot simply be forgotten: we must form a new idea of reason." (SNS, 3; *SNS*, 8) Because Merleau-Ponty wanted to redefine reason rather than abandon it and pass beyond, he did not see any antinomy between existential thought and science. "Philosophical self-consciousness," the consciousness of contingency, he said, "does not make science's effort at objectification futile." (SNS, 97; *SNS*, 170) All thinking, Merleau-Ponty recognizes— and here he is *very* far from Heidegger—"is inevitably objectification." The only difference is that existential thought knows that objectification cannot surpass itself and afford us access to a more fundamental level of being. and its task in relation to science is to recall it to its origins: the fumbling and uncertain dialogue pursued by men.

Merleau-Ponty was not against rationality; he wanted neither to reject it nor, like Heidegger, to transcend it towards "a *Logos* whose essence logic and dialectics, which stem from metaphysics, are never able to experience."[8] This is so because for Merleau-Ponty, unlike Heidegger, when it comes to confronting life's problems, we have no resource other than reason. What is called the "natural light" *is* the light of reason.[9] What Merleau-Ponty refuses is, therefore, what could be called Heidegger's mysticism, his recourse to a Logos which would not be human reason but the very logos of Being itself. Here Merleau-Ponty remains in agreement with Husserl and with the great tradition of rational philosophy. He does not believe that the Tradition overestimates reason; he thinks rather that it forms an inadequate and even false idea of it.

Traditionally, one says that reason is a faculty of man, a component part of his being, whereby he is able to discover the true nature of things. And one naturally postulates also that that there is a reason or a rationality in the things themselves, this being the "essence" of things which it is the function of human reason to represent to itself. Between man and the universe there exists a natural relation which is reason. This is the rationalist conception of reason which I described at the beginning of this article. It is also—it should be noted—the conception of reason to be found in Husserl. For him, it must be said—

"provided we speak reasonably"—that there is an essential correlation between "that which truly or really is" and "that which is rationally demonstrable," between reality and reason; it is "rational consciousness which lays out this reality within itself.[10] The only difference between Husserl and a more classic rationalism is that for Husserl it is consciousness which constitutes the intelligible structure of reality and not reality which determines consciousness.

However, Merleau-Ponty accepts rationalism neither in its realist version nor in its idealist version. For him reason is neither a "faculty" of man nor an objective trait of Nature. Reason or rationality refer rather to a certain possible mode of interhuman relationships, a certain mode of men's behavior. It is habitually said that a thought or an action is rational (or moral) if one can apply to it "the principal of universalizability" (which could be expressed, in a Kantian fashion, thus: an idea [or an action whose maxim] is not capable of being universalized shows itself thereby to be irrational [or immoral]). The following text enables us to see the nonrationalist way in which Merleau-Ponty interprets this principle: "The universality of knowledge is no longer guaranteed in each of us by that stronghold of absolute consciousness in which the Kantian 'I think'—linked, as it was, to a certain spatio-temporal perspective—is assured *a priori* of being identical to every other possible 'I think'. The germ of universality or the 'natural light' without which there could be no knowledge is to be found ahead of us, in the thing where our perception places us, in the dialogue into which our experience of other people throws us by means of a movement not all of whose sources are known to us." (SNS, 93; *SNS*, 163)

When Merleau-Ponty says that it is in dialogue that the germ of universality is to be found, he is rejecting the rationalist idea that an idea is rational only if it can be generalized without limit and possess a uniform (univocal) value in all situations, thereby making contact with some kind of absolute. Men are rational not because what they say and do has a transcendent guarantee, but simply because of the fact that, in spite of all the differences which set them apart, they can still, if they make the effort, communicate with and understand one another. Rationality has no other foundation than the uncertain communication among men whereby they succeed in working out mutual agreements: "It remains just as hard to reach agreement with myself and with others, and for all my belief that it is in principle always attainable, I have no other reason to affirm this principle than my experience of certain concordances, so that in the end whatever solidity there is in my belief in the absolute is nothing but my experience of agreement with myself and others." (SNS, 95; *SNS*, 166) The foundation of truth or rationality, Merleau-Ponty continues, is in this "progressive experience," this "experience of agreement with myself and others." The universality of thought, he says elsewhere, is always "presumptive"; it "is never the universality of a pure concept which would be identical for every mind. It is rather the call which a situated thought addresses to other thoughts, equally situated, and each one responds to the call with its own resources." (PriP, 8; *Inédit,* 406)

Rationality, it could be said in taking over an expression from Merleau-Ponty, is the art of "taking the risk of communicating" (*communiquer dans le risque*). (PriP, 9; *Inédit,* 407) It has absolutely no guarantee in being and depends solely on the *good will* of men.[11] Reason is a power not of discovering the "truth" but of "going further" in what is called the search for truth; it is what maintains that great, always interrupted and always rebegun discourse which we call Culture. It is also what thereby makes it be that there is "a history of humanity or, more simply, *a* humanity. In other words, granting all the periods of stagnation and retreat, human relations are able to grow to change their avatars into lessons, to pick out the truth of their past in the present, to eliminate certain mysteries which render them opaque and thereby make themselves more translucent." (PriP, 9; *Inédit*, 107) For Merleau-Ponty, "our life is essentially universal," but he insists, and rightly so, that "this methodological rationalism is not to be confused with a dogmatic rationalism which eliminates historical contingency in advance by supposing a 'World Spirit' (Hegel) behind the course of events." (PriP, 10; *Inédit*, 408)

In attacking in this way all idealizations and all reifications of reason, Merleau-Ponty is in the tradition of Isocrates and other rhetoricians who rejected Plato's attempt to found "appearances" on a transcendent reality and who sought to bring reason back down to the peaceful and dialogal coexistence of men who live in the realm of "opinion."

2) The most important notion in phenomenology, considered as a method, is that of the phenomenological reduction. It is the way Merleau-Ponty conceived of the reduction which makes him a counter-

traditionalist. For it must be said that the reduction or epoche is a methodological invention of the Counter-tradition. The epoche was indeed the strategy whereby Pyrrhonian skepticism sought to overcome the dogmatic attitude. According to Sextus Empiricus, dogmatism essentially consists in the positing of "metaphysical entities," transcendent realities, in order, precisely, to make our lived experience intelligible, in order, therefore, to "explain" it—that is, in order to arrive at a *science* of experience. All of these realities are, however, unverifiable, precisely because they transcend our experience which alone is the realm of true evidence. As in Husserlian phenomenology, the Pyrrhonian epoche is the commitment to remain close to experience; it is the suspension of judgment in regard to, the suspension of belief in, everything which presents itself in our experience; it is the reduction of the transcendent to the immanent (to speak like Husserl). By means of the epoche or the inhibition of belief, skeptics, Diogenes Laertius says, "hold to phenomena alone." The skeptic's only criterion is what appears: " 'We admit the apparent fact,' say they, 'without admitting that it really is what it appears to be.' ...We merely object to accepting the unknown substance behind phenomena."[12] This is to say that the skeptic suspends his belief (it is Sextus speaking) in "the non-evident objects of scientific inquiry."[13] He does not make "any positive assertion regarding the external realities," that is, those realities which are supposed to be the nonappearing causes of what, in experience, appears.[14] Since, by means of the epoche, skepticism "holds to phenomena alone," it is in the most proper sense of the word a phenomenology.

And just as in Husserlian phenomenology, the skeptical epoche is in no way a *doubt* (it has absolutely nothing to do with Descartes' systematic doubt). If the skeptic does not affirm realities transcendent to experience, neither does he deny them.[15] Doubt is still part of the natural attitude, Husserl rightly says, and it is precisely the natural attitude, naive belief, "dogmatic rashness," as Sextus says, that skepticism seeks to overcome. The ultimate goal of the skeptical epoche is to free us from the Promethean desire to master the uncertainties of life by finding a *fundamentum inconcussum* on which one could erect a science of reality or, as Pascal would say, "solid ground and an ultimate sure foundation whereon to build a tower reaching to the Infinite."[16] Skepticism attempts to demonstrate the impossibility of a science of reality. This recognition of the limits of knowledge is the means for arriving at *wisdom* or what Sextus calls *ataraxia*, quietude or peace of mind.

Now although Husserl's phenomenological reduction is, in itself, exactly of the same sort as the antidogmatic epoche of the skeptics and is something altogether different from the Cartesian doubt, the curious, even weird, fact is that Husserl attempts to use the epoche so as to realize Descartes' goal, the goal of all rationalists: achieving a science of reality. Merleau-Ponty's originality is that, without knowing it,[17] he reconfers on the epoche its true role and goal: demonstrating the *impossibility* of such a science. "The most important lesson which the reduction teaches us," he wrote in the preface to the *Phenomenology of Perception*, "is the impossibility of a complete reduction." (PhP, XIV; *PP*, VIII) By this he meant that the reduction does not afford us access to a sphere of apodictic evidence on which we could erect an absolute science (as it is supposed to do for Husserl), but rather reveals to us reflection's dependence "on an unreflective life which is its initial situation, unchanging, given once and for all." (PhP, XIV; *PP*, IX) Far from discovering reasons for everything which is, the reduction in Merleau-Ponty's case teaches us rather "the unmotivated upsurge of the world." (PhP, XIV; *PP*, VIII)

This, therefore, amounts to saying that by means of the reduction we experience the *failure* of a total reflection, the failure of our attempt to make ourselves transparent to ourselves; we experience the *opacity* of our being. Even towards the end of his life, in a working note of February 1959, Merleau-Ponty still spoke of the "incompleteness of the reduction." (VI, 178; *VI*, 232) This incompleteness is not, however, as a rationalist might think, "an obstacle to the reduction, it is the reduction itself, the rediscovery of vertical being."

This reference to vertical being brings us back once more to the Merleau-Ponty–Heidegger relationship. As a number of interpreters have pointed out, the notion of being in the late Merleau-Ponty is very close to the one found in the late Heidegger. For both of these philosophers being is to be defined above all by its *absence* from consciousness (that is, both of them disown the "metaphysics of presence" still to be found in Husserl). His way of conceiving of being as that which could never under any circumstances be immanent (present) to consciousness distances Merleau-Ponty from Husserl and allies him with Heidegger. A very important difference, however, distinguishes

Merleau-Ponty and Heidegger in this context, and this difference once again demonstrates Merleau-Ponty's membership in the Counter-tradition.

Heidegger, in his attempt to think that being which is more than a mere object for consciousness, rejects the Tradition, which he accuses of subjectivism, and passes beyond, into a kind of philosophical no-man's-land. Merleau-Ponty does not do so. Like the other counter-traditionalists, he seeks to correct the Tradition from within, utilizing the same rational methods as the Tradition. Indeed, for Merleau-Ponty, as we have seen, the self-consciousness and subjectivity which Heidegger unmercifully rejects is one of those "ideas which make it impossible for us to return to a time prior to their existence, even and especially if we have moved beyond them". (S, 154; *S*, 194) For Merleau-Ponty, the thought of subjectivity "is one of these solids that philosophy will have to digest." Merleau-Ponty wanted just as much as Heidegger to overcome modern subjectivism, but his way of doing so— or of attempting to do so—was altogether different from Heidegger's. He did not regurgitate subjectivity but attempted rather to digest it. That is, to get rid of subjectivism he used the same method which engendered it in its modern form: the transcendental method. Up until its end, Merleau-Ponty's philosophy remained a transcendental philosophy, a philosophy of experience.

Like Heidegger, Merleau-Ponty in his late work was interested in being (which he often wrote with a capital); but, unlike Heidegger, he did not think being *as such* could be the object of philosophical reflection. He thought that Heidegger was condemning the rational man to silence (and to condemn the rational man to silence is precisely to take "reason" away from him) precisely because he was looking for "a direct expression of the fundamental" and was thereby unaware of "the mirrors of Being." (TFL, 112; *RC*, 156) Unlike Heidegger (the later Heidegger, that is, not the author of *Sein und Zeit*), who wanted to "think Being without regard to its being grounded in terms of beings," who wanted to "think Being without beings,"[18] Merleau-Ponty did not want to pursue fundamental ontology except "through contact with beings" (TFL, 112; *RC*, 156); what he was attempting to formulate was an "intra-ontology." "*One cannot make a direct ontology*," he insisted. "My 'indirect' method (being in beings) is alone conformed with being." (VI, 179; *VI*, 233) In opposition to Heidegger, therefore, who wanted to "abandon subjectivity" and leave behind him the notions of subject and object and even phenomenology, Merleau-Ponty did not want to think "a Being in transcendence not reduced to the 'perspectives' of 'consciousness' " (VI, 243; *VI*, 297) except by means of phenomenology, by pushing phenomenology to its extreme limit, by resolutely taking up a position at the center of subjectivity itself and by digging down into it as deeply as possible.[19] Like Husserl, therefore, Merleau-Ponty attempted to hold himself rigorously close to experience and refused to accept anything whatever which did not present itself in this experience; but, as in the case of the skeptics, this was in the last analysis in order to better discern the *limits* of experience, of consciousness, and of the method of transcendental reflection.[20]

This is why Merleau-Ponty's philosophy is also, like that of Protagoras, Isocrates, Sextus, and Montaigne, but unlike that of Heidegger—as, moreover, that of Husserl—a *humanism*. Heidegger rejects "humanism" (in the traditional sense, that is, as that form of thought which is concerned with the *humanitas* of human beings) because, according to him, it is part of "metaphysics" and, consequently, is unmindful of "Being";[21] and the only thing which matters for Heidegger is not man as such but Being, man being without value except inasmuch as he places himself in the service of Being (so that Being may be) and makes himself its "shepherd."[22] Similarly, Husserl dissolves man into his transcendental essence, into a transcendental Ego which is the absolute itself.

Nevertheless, Merleau-Ponty's humanism was not the dogmatic, rationalist humanism of Marx or Sartre, a humanism which suppresses the absolute only so as to immediately put man in its place. For Merleau-Ponty, as for Protagoras, man is, as he says, "universal measure"—not in the sense that man is the constituting source of everything which can be and can be thought (which would indeed be a total subjectivism), but only in the sense (which is, moreover, the sense intended, in my opinion, by Protagoras) that man is the indispensable reference point for all that which exists for him. It is only by thinking being in relation to man that it is possible to understand what being truly is: something which encompasses us and which transcends us and is absolutely not reducible to whatever idea we might form of it. No more than Pascal, Merleau-Ponty did not believe that man, proud master of the universe that he takes himself to be, is sufficient unto himself or that he is the last word; but with Pascal he could have said, "If man studied himself the first, he would see how impossible it is to pass beyond."[23]

This is moreover a constant theme in French philosophy which, for its part, is the one which has best perpetuated the Counter-tradition since the Middle Ages. It was a disciple of Montaigne and a *Christian* Pyrrhonian of the sixteenth century, Pierre Charron, who said, "the true science and the true study of man is man."[24] Merleau-Ponty could have said the same thing—and with the same intentions. For Merleau-Ponty's humanism is not a "Promethean humanism." (IPP, 43; *EP*, 70) Man, he said, "is not a force but a weakness at the heart of being, not a cosmological factor but the place where all cosmological factors, by a mutation which is never finished, change in sense and become history."[25] Since Merleau-Ponty believes that "one explains nothing by man" (IPP, 44; *EP*, 71), his humanism is antirationalist, counter-traditionalist. It rests on "an awareness of contingency" and is "the methodical refusal of explanations, because they destroy the mixture we are made of and make us incomprehensible to ourselves." (S, 241; *S*, 305–6) This humanism could be described in the following words of Charron: "It is to maintain modesty and recognize in good faith the human condition full of ignorance, weakness, uncertainty."[26]

This is why, unlike Sartre's and Marx's atheistic humanism, but just like the Christian humanism of Erasmus, Montaigne, and Charron, Merleau-Ponty's humanism is not opposed to religion,[27] that is, to recognizing a dimension of being which surpasses man and which could be called the sacred. Only—like any Christian humanism moreover—Merleau-Ponty wants nothing to do with a God posited at man's expense and jealous of his freedom.[28] Merleau-Ponty's humanism is perfectly compatible with a recognition of a "hidden god" (VI, 211; *VI*, 264), a *deus absconditus*, and the recognition of such "an endless abyss, without bottom and without sides" is, according to Charron, the premise of "the true religion."[29]

Merleau-Ponty is a counter-traditionalist by reason of his skepticism, his humanism, and his antirationalist conception of reason. He is also one, as we shall now see, by reason of the position he defends in political matters.

3) In the two preceding sections we have seen in regard to *theoretical* questions,—concerning, in short, the nature and limits of human reason—how Merleau-Ponty's philosophical position joins up with that of the Counter-tradition. We must now see how, in what has

to do with *practical reason*, that is, politics, Merleau-Ponty's thought is just as counter-traditionalist. It is counter-traditionalist not only by its content (as we shall see) but also by its form, that is, by the very fact that for Merleau-Ponty theoretical (epistemological, metaphysical) questions are strictly inseparable from practical (moral, political) questions, those having to do with the life of men—by the fact, therefore, that for him there is an "identity of practice and theory." (AD, 230; *AD*, 310) For one of the most important characteristics of the Counter-tradition is the importance it places on moral philosophy; indeed, for it speculative, theoretical reason must always be subordinated to practical reason. For it the true is always a modality of the good; what is good for living takes precedence over and in fact determines what is true for thinking. Like the Pyrrhonians, the Cynics (Antisthenes, for instance) divided philosophy into three parts—logic, physics, ethics—and subordinated the first two to the last. This value accorded to moral philosophy stems from the importance the Counter-tradition attaches to the *freedom* of the individual (see for instance in this regard Erasmus, *De libero arbitrio*). Here, quite naturally, moral concerns join up with political ones, with questions concerning the collective life of men.

(We might note in passing that the priority accorded by Merleau-Ponty to practice and his interest in politics serves once again to distinguish him from Husserl. For, in a properly rationalist spirit, Husserl made a radical bifurcation between culture, wisdom, or *Weltanschauungsphilosophie*, on the one hand, and [philosophical] science, on the other, and did not hesitate to fully subordinate the former to the latter.[30] We should therefore not be surprised by Husserl's total lack of interest in politics nor by the fact that, plunged into the barbarian decadence of Nazi Germany and fully conscious of the crisis that our Western civilization was then undergoing, he had nothing better to propose to humanity than the ancient rationalist and Platonic idea of Science which alone, he asserted, can make mankind "blessed".[31])

In the work of a great thinker everything holds together. Such a thought has, to take up one of Merleau-Ponty's expressions, its *style* (cf. PhP, 327; *PP*, 378), which means that all the ideas which, together, make up this philosophy are coherent; and they are coherent because they all stem from a certain ideal structure or a certain deep motivation. The thesis I wish to defend in this article is that the deep structure of Merleau-Ponty's thought is of the same sort as that to be found in the thought of the counter-traditionalists. A counter-traditionalist thinker can be recognized by the fact that, at one and the same time, he is a skeptic and a humanist, and, having grasped the structure of his thought, one can legitimately expect that—when he turns to politics—his position, if it is coherent with the rest of his thought, will be that of *liberalism*.[32]

Now a reflection on Merleau-Ponty's political thought serves to justify this thesis. Indeed, Merleau-Ponty is a skeptic and a humanist— and he is also a liberal thinker. What is, however, above all interesting in his case is that at the beginning his political thought is not coherent with the rest of his thought, with his skepticism and his humanism. In its maturation, though, it is precisely this incoherence that it manages to eliminate. The change in his ideas on politics is thus particularly significant, for it is a development by which, to speak like Nietzsche, he becomes more himself—and more thoroughly counter-traditionalist. For what we see here is an unequivocal rejection on his part of Marxist and revolutionary dogmatism and ideology in favor of liberal thought.

Let us first look at what the young Merleau-Ponty had to say. In *Humanism and Terror* ("An Essay on the Communist Problem"), published in 1947, he reflected on the Moscow trials and attempted, if not to justify them, at least to "understand" the mentality behind them. Above all and in contrast to the defenders of the West, he kept himself from condemning the Soviet regime because of the terror and violence it practiced. For, he said, this violence is there not institutionalized and is only a means—a regrettable one, no doubt, but a means nonetheless—for bringing into being a society which in the long run would be more humanistic than our present-day Western ones.[33] To condemn the U.S.S.R. would thus be to play into the hands of the propagandists of the capitalist system, one which is fundamentally inhuman. "A regime which is nominally liberal can be oppressive in reality. A regime which acknowledges its violence *might* have in it more genuine humanity." (HT, XV: *HT*, X) *"Might"* (it is Merleau-Ponty's own emphasis) is the key word. Here Merleau-Ponty makes an excuse for violence—if it is in the service of humanism. His criticism of the liberal regimes of the West is, in this essay, altogether of the Marxist sort. Taking over the Marxist distinction between "formal liberties" and "real freedom," he says that the former count for nothing if society lacks the latter; he denounces "the liberal mystification" and calls for a criticism of "the liberty-idol, the one inscribed on a flag or in a

Constitution, which legitimates the classical means of police and military oppression—and this in the name of an effective or real freedom which spreads through the lives of everyone, from the Vietnamese or Palestinian peasant to the Western intellectual." (HT, XXIV; *HT*, XIX)

Merleau-Ponty does not deny that violence flourishes in Russia, but he does say that at least the Soviet regime is not, like the liberal democracies of the West, hypocritical. Unlike these, the U.S.S.R. does not dissimulate its violence behind the facade of an official humanism, thereby sanctioning "the classical means of police and military oppression." "Within the U.S.S.R.," he writes, "violence and deception have official status while humanity is to be found in daily life. On the contrary, in the [liberal] democracies the principles are humane but deception and violence rule daily life."[34]

Thus, if in *Humanism and Terror* Merleau-Ponty leans towards the U.S.S.R., still he does not accord it his complete moral approval. His position is a sort of "Yes, but..." Here he is in agreement with Marxist *theory*, only worrying about what this theory has become *in practice*. And where he shows reticence towards the Soviet regime is precisely where he joins up with the Counter-tradition, namely in what concerns his humanism. What at the time he wanted to do was "to recall Marxists to their humanist inspiration, to remind the [liberal] democracies of their fundamental hypocrisy." (HT, 179; *HT*, 196)

One can detect in *Humanism and Terror* a kind of *hesitation* on Merleau-Ponty's part,[35] a hesitation in at least two respects: between, on the one hand, an unequivocal condemnation of violence—such as it appears in the Moscow Trials and in the Stalinist repression—and a guarded acceptance of violence—if it serves to bring about a genuine humanism. And between, on the other hand—and this second hesitation is linked to the first—communism and anticommunism. "The Marxist critique of capitalism is still valid," Merleau-Ponty insists here, but he does admit at the same time that "the Revolution has come to a halt: it maintains and aggravates the dictatorial apparatus while renouncing the revolutionary liberty of the proletariat in the Soviets and its Party and abandoning the human appropriation of the state." It is therefore in this way that Merleau-Ponty expresses his "hesitation": "It is impossible to be an anti-communist and it is not possible to be a communist." (HT, XXI; *HT*, XVII) This is a position which in *Adventures of the Dialectic,* written about six years later, he called " a Marxist wait-and-see attitude." (AD, 228; *AD*, 307) And it is this hesitation and this Marxist wait-and-see attitude which, in this second book of his on politics, he was to abandon. The ambiguity in his attitude towards Marxism in *Humanism and Terror* was what he was to overcome.[36]

For it must indeed be admitted that *Humanism and Terror* is an ambiguous work. Although Merleau-Ponty's intention seems to have been that of finding a middle road between communism and anticommunism and of rescuing what he took to be Marx's true humanism (it was naturally the young Marx he appealed to) from "communist orthodoxy," it is impossible simply to accuse both those who took this work to be a justification of the Trials and the Stalinist state of having completely misunderstood it.[37] Speaking in Marxist terms, it could even be said that in spite of his "subjective" intentions, "objectively" Merleau-Ponty is here playing into the hands of communism. This, moreover, is something he himself was later to recognize: "Marxist wait-and-see became communist action." (AD, 229; *AD*, 308)

What in particular Merleau-Ponty did not see in *Humanism and Terror* was that the notion of the "objective crime" or "enemy" is the height of dogmatism. As is known, it is this notion which within Marxism justifies the practice exemplified by the Moscow Trials; and it is one which cannot but scandalize a non-Marxist and a liberal above all, for it justifies the condemnation of people who are innocent from the point of view of the liberal conception of justice that is, who to their knowledge have never betrayed their country in either words or deeds but who, however, when accused of having done so end up by denouncing themselves.[38] The notion of the objective enemy ("enemy of the revolution") is the height of dogmatism, since it presupposes that there is a Law of history and that this Law can be discerned by certain men (this is the function of the Party), such that whoever, by what he thinks or merely by what he unknowingly does, impedes the objective movement of history from realizing itself is "guilty" before history and merits being punished by "those-in-the-know." This is what makes it be that, in practice, this dogmatism cannot but give rise to a dehumanizing terror and, for instance, to concentration camps.[39]

It is precisely Merleau-Ponty's *humanism* and his *skepticism* (his antidogmatism)—the two principle traits linking him to the Countertradition—which, in *Adventures of the Dialectic*, were to lead him to reject his "Marxist wait-and-see attitude."

What in this book Merleau-Ponty rejects is precisely the idea that a regime which abolishes the so-called "formal" liberties, liberty in the liberal sense of the word, and which "acknowledges its violence *might* have in it more genuine humanity." This is to say that Merleau-Ponty here rejects the essential elements of Marxism; he rejects revolutionary ideology and reaffirms his solidarity with the liberal tradition of the West. In *Adventures of the Dialectic* he defends those same liberal institutions which he had denounced in *Humanism and Terror* as so many mystifications. He says here that "the revolution which would recreate history is infinitely distant" (AD, 220; *AD*, 296), and he speaks of the "fiction of proletarian power, of direct democracy, and of the withering-away of the State." (AD, 222; *AD*, 299) Against the notion of the dictatorship of the proletariat, which he rejects, he defends, in the name of a non-communist left, "parliamentary and democratic action," for, he says "Parliament is the only known institution that guarantees a minimum of opposition and of truth." (AD, 226; *AD*, 304) The fact of the matter is that in the West people have the liberty (a "formal" liberty!) to criticize the existing regime in the name of justice, whereas this possibility does not even exist in a communist regime.[40] For him, therefore, the essential thing is "to keep a hand on both ends of the chain, on the social problem and on liberty" (AD, 227; *AD*, 305)—and by liberty Merleau-Ponty understands here liberty in the liberal sense of the word, those "formal" liberties denounced by the Marxists as "bourgeois."[41]

In an interview published in *L'Express* in 1958, Merleau-Ponty returns to this theme and develops it further. Speaking of the current French crisis, he says that "if there is a solution to our problems it is a liberal one". (S, 348; *S*, 433) Coming back to the question of Parliament he says, in a more general way, "The problem is to find institutions which implant this practice of freedom in our customs." (S, 349; *S*, 434) And by institutions there is no doubt that Merleau-Ponty means liberal institutions. For the Merleau-Ponty who has resolved the ambiguity in his thought and has come to perceive, in politics, the "identity of practice and theory," the humanist ideal must not serve in practice to justify violence and terror, and the search for justice must not dispense with freedom in the liberal sense of the word. Marxist theory cannot be true, even as a theory, if it gives rise to an illiberal practice. "So we already know that a worthwhile society will not be less but more free than our own."[42] And his hope, as he expresses it in the very last lines of *Adventures of the Dialectic*, was to "inspire a few—or many—to bear their freedom, not to exchange it at a loss; for it is not only their own thing, their secret, their pleasure, their salvation—it involves everyone else." (AD, 233; *AD*, 313) In the end, for Merleau-Ponty a genuine humanism will also always be a liberalism.

It is important for us to note also that Merleau-Ponty's liberal humanism goes along with his skepticism (just as Camus' did with his). In *Adventures of the Dialectic* he discovers that the inhumanity of the Soviet regime is not merely a falling off of Marxism and an infidelity towards it—as he had formerly thought—but is in fact foreshadowed in the dogmatic nature of this thought. He concludes that the premises of the "degeneration" of the revolution and Soviet society are to be looked for not only in Bolshevism but in Marx himself.[43] What is at question in the failure of Soviet communism, he says, is Marx's philosophy. (AD, 91; *AD*, 124) What Merleau-Ponty objects to the most is Marx's realism, that is, the fact that he "placed the dialectic in things themselves." (AD, 89; *AD*, 122) Marx thereby justified in advance all sorts of repression: "For if the revolution is in things, how can one hesitate to brush aside, by any means, oppositions which are only apparent?" (AD, 85; *AD*, 116) If one believes (and this is what dogmatism is) that history has a meaning and one moreover which can be discerned by men, then one can expect that men will get impatient and will attempt "to bring history by iron and fire to express its meaning." (AD, 86; *AD*, 117) "Dogmatic rashness" (as Sextus says) goes along with intolerance and man's inhumanity towards man.

For Merleau-Ponty, as for the great skeptics of the Counter-tradition, the dialectic is not in the things themselves; it exists only between men, residing in their differences of *opinion* as to what constitutes the true and the good. What is proper to dogmatism is that it always confuses our ideas with reality; the dogmatist attempts to triumph over the opinions of others by a direct appeal to Nature or History or Providence, that is, the Absolute—which always has for its consequence the breaking off of the dialogue between men, one which is always groping at best. Merleau-Ponty had always rejected the "thought of the absolute" in general, and when he came to do so in political matters he became a liberal thinker and fully joined up with the Counter-tradition. By his humanism, his skepticism, and his liberalism he makes us think of Protagoras who, at the beginning of the Counter-tradition, denounced the pretensions of the dogmatists so as to guarantee respect for others, and who believed that only the free exchange of opinions by means of rational and peaceful persuasion could make of a society both a just and a free one. As for the other counter-traditionalists, so also for Merleau-Ponty philosophy, conceived of as the reasoned exchange of opinions (and not of "knowledge"), has a role to play in social life: to make it be that the relations between men be ones not of force or violence but of persuasion, that is, to insure that the freedom and dignity of men be recognized and respected.

Unlike Husserl, Merleau-Ponty was a *skeptic* and an *antirationalist,* but, unlike Heidegger, he was a *humanist* who believed in the virtues of reasoned and reasonable discourse (if it is true, as I believe, that Heidegger's adherence to National-Socialism was not a *consequence* of his philosophy, it is just as true that one does not find in his philosophy anything which would prevent someone from subscribing to it). In my opinion, it is this originality of his position which accounts also for its worth. For, unlike Husserl, his example shows that it is perhaps possible to rationally contest rationalism and the tyranny of science and technology which flows from it without, like Heidegger, disowning the control of reason and of the reasoned opinion of men of good will, the moderation and tolerance without which there can be no freedom and which make up the essence of civilization.

otes

## Translator's Preface

1. I have developed this point further in my article, "Eine Kritik an Hirschs Begriff der 'Richtigkeit' " in H.-G. Gadamer and G. Boehm, eds., *Die Hermeneutik und die Wissenschaften* (Frankfurt: Suhrkamp Verlag, 1978), pp. 393–425.

2. This general principle underlies my discussion with Th. F. Geraets in Appendix I of this book, "Concerning Merleau-Ponty: Two Readings of His Work"; I argue there that Merleau-Ponty's use of a Husserlian-idealistic vocabulary in the *Phenomenology of Perception* significantly affects the meaning of the work and makes it, in fact, much more idealistic in its philosophical implications than Merleau-Ponty himself would have desired.

## Chapter I

1. "The theory of form is aware of the consequences which a purely structural conception entails and seeks to expand into a philosophy of form which would be substituted for the philosophy of substances. It has never pushed this work of philosophical analysis very far. This is because 'form' can be fully understood and all the implications of this notion brought out only in a philosophy which would be liberated from the realist

postulates which are those of every psychology." (SB, 132; SC, 142-3) "Instead of wondering what sort of being can belong to form...it is placed among the number of events of nature; it is used like a cause or a real thing; and to this very extent one is no longer thinking according to 'form.' " (SB, 136-7; SC, 147)

2.    When we come to the human order of behavior properly speaking, there will be a third kind of form to consider: "symbolic" forms.

3.    "We will say that there is form whenever the properties of a system are modified by every change brought about in a single one of its parts and, on the contrary, are conserved when they all change while maintaining the same relationship among themselves. These definitions are applicable to nerve phenomena since, as we have just seen, each part of a reaction cannot be related to a partial condition, and since there is reciprocal action and internal connection among the afferent excitations on the one hand, the motor influxes on the other, and finally between both of these systems." (SB, 47; SC, 50)

4.    "To be sure, psychoanalysis insists on the importance of the past, and of childhood in particular, but the relation between the earlier and what follows is *a relation of integration, of part to whole*.... No given from our past continues to play its role without being taken up and modified by the rest of our life.

"Everything happens as if the givens of our childhood were themes used by us. We confer a meaning on these givens. The beginnings of life do not constitute a fatality; all of the possibilities remain. Childhood is but a starting point....What the adult inherits is the preponderance of such and such a dimension, such and such an order of problems, such and such difficulties: how the individual will resolve them is another matter; this is not determined." (*BP*, 315)

5.    "At first glance 'the unconscious' evokes the realm of a dynamics of impulses whose results alone would presumably be given to us. And yet the unconscious which chooses what aspect of us will be admitted to official existence, which avoids the thoughts or situation we are resisting, and which is therefore not *un-knowing* but rather an unacknowledged and unformulated knowing that we do not want to assume." (S, 229; S, 291)

6.    "We have rejected Freud's causal categories and replaced his energetic metaphors with structural metaphors." (SB, 220; SC, 237)

7.    "Mind is not a specific difference which would be added to vital or psychological being in order to constitute a man. Man is not a rational animal. The appearance of reason and mind does not leave intact a sphere of self-enclosed instincts in man....Man can never be an animal: his life is always more or less integrated than that of an animal." (SB, 181; SC, 196)

8.    "But if the alleged instincts of man do not exist *apart* from the mental dialectic, correlatively, this dialectic is not conceivable outside of the concrete situations in which it is embodied. One does not act with mind alone." (SB, 181; SC, 196)

9.    The problem of the relations between the objective and the subjective will persist throughout all of Merleau-Ponty's work. It could indeed be said that it is the problem which was always at the center of preoccupations, a problem which he successively approached from different sides and which he never ceased attempting to clarify, such that his entire work constitutes a prolonged and continuous meditation on this question.

10.    "We were concerned [in *The Structure of Behavior*] with gaining an understanding of the relationships between consciousness and nature, between the interior and the exterior....the whole question is ultimately one of understanding what, in ourselves and in the world, is the relation between *sense* and *non-sense*. Is the element of sense or mean-

ing which is evident in the world produced and carried forward by the assemblage or convergence of independent facts or, on the other hand, is it merely the expression of an absolute reason?" (PhP, 428; *PP*, 489–90)

11.  "…what Gestalt psychology lacks is a set of new categories; it has admitted the principle, and applied it to a few individual cases, but without realizing that a complete reform of understanding is called for if we are to translate phenomena accurately, and that to this end the objective thinking of classical logic and philosophy will have to be questioned, the categories of the world suspended, the alleged self-evidence of realism placed in doubt, in the Cartesian sense, and a true 'phenomenological reduction' undertaken." (PhP, 49; *PP*, 60)

12.  Our reading of the *Phenomenology* will thus not be a summary of this book; we will take note only of what will have direct repercussions on Merleau-Ponty's ontological thought and which thereby anticipates this ontology as its own fulfillment.

13.  The characteristic of interiority, as we say, in the relationship of the perceiving subject to the perceived world is very clearly visible in the following text where Merleau-Ponty speaks of *movement*: "What makes part of the field count as an object in motion, and another as the background, is the way in which we establish our relations with them by the act of looking. The stone flies through the air. What do these words mean, other than that our gaze, lodged and anchored in the garden, is attracted by the stone and, so to speak, drags at its anchors. *The relation between the moving object and its background passes through our body.*" (PhP, 278; *PP*, 322; emphasis ours)

14.  "The primordial principle of Husserl's philosophy—even though it is more often than not implicitly presupposed rather than explicitly expressed—is this, that *to be is to have a meaning*; true being is 'being for' a subject." "According to the phenomenological attitude, the existence of reality is an existence within consciousness, and reality is determined by a mode of consciousness called experience—that is real which is an actual or possible object of experience. It is experience qua evidence that delivers up a reality, because it delivers up the meaning which defines a reality. All being is being-for-the-subject, and every mode of being is defined by a mode of being-for-the-subject that is, by a mode of consciousness." Q. Lauer, *Phénoménologie de Husserl* (Paris: Presses Universitaires de France, 1955), pp. 4 and 266, n. 2.

15.  " 'Presence within the world' may at first sight appear to be a rather ingenious way of replacing the *ego cogito* by a neutral datum which finally bridges the gap between the subject and the object that epistemology had not been able to fill. But does it really do so? Isn't the price of such an assertion, if we do not want to be dogmatic, a grading down of our concept of the world from something which exists, whether or not we are in contact with it, to something which is nothing apart from our being inserted in it? As such the world becomes what Merleau-Ponty himself has called at times an 'inter-world'….We still have to answer the question of what will be left of 'the world' once we disrupt our contact with it. Simply to assert our presence within the world seems to be an attempt to cut the Gordian knot instead of untangling it. Is Merleau-Ponty's sword even strong enough to do it?" H. Spiegelberg, *The Phenomenological Movement* (The Hague: Martinus Nijhoff, 1960), vol. 11, pp. 551–2.

16.  But this is exactly what the case is for Husserl in his *Cartesian Meditations*. The quotation from St. Augustine with which he ends the work is very revealing in this regard: *Noli foras ire, in te redi, in interiore homine habitat veritas.* We all know Merleau-Ponty's rejoinder. Referring to this sentence himself he writes: "Truth does not 'inhabit' only 'the inner man,' or more accurately, there is no inner man." Man is not "a source of intrinsic truth, but a subject destined to be in the world." (PhP, XI; *PP*, V) And elsewhere in the *Phenomenology* he says: "internal experience, which is indeed incommu-

nicable, but incommunicable because meaningless." (PhP, 276; PP, 319) Is it really meaningless? This is, it must be admitted, a very strong statement that Merleau-Ponty will have the occasion, not to disown certainly, but to nuance nevertheless.

17.    "It is through my body that I understand other people, just as it is through my body that I perceive 'things.' " (PhP, 186; PP, 216)

18.    As an expression of affection, the kiss was unknown to the natives of Easter Island, for instance, before contact with Europeans.

19.    "It will be objected that I might have nails, ears, or lungs of some other kind which would involve no change in my existence. But then my nails, ears, and lungs taken separately have no existence. It is science which has accustomed us to regard the body as a collection of parts, and also the experience of its disintegration at death. But the fact is that a decomposed body is no longer a body. When I restore my ears, nails, and lungs to my living body, they no longer appear in the light of contingent details. They are not indifferent to the idea that others form of me, contributing as they do to my physiognomy or my general bearing, and it is not impossible that science may tomorrow express in the form of objective correlations precisely how necessary it was that I should have that kind of ears, nails, and lungs, and whether, moreover, I was destined to be dexterous or clumsy, placid or highly strung, intelligent or stupid, in short whether I was destined to be myself." (PhP, 431; PP, 493)

20.    At least in the case of "authentic speech which formulates for the first time." (PhP, 178; PP, 207)

21.    Antoine de Saint-Exupéry, Terres des hommes (Paris: Gallimard, 1939), p. 174. This sentence almost seems to be an echo to the following sentence of Merleau-Ponty: "Consciousness holds itself responsible for everything, and takes everything upon itself, but it has nothing of its own and makes its life in the world." (PhP, 452-3; PP, 516)

22.    He does not himself often use the term, but, as the following sentence shows, neither is it foreign to him: "That being the case, and since consciousness takes root [s'enracine] in being and time by taking up a situation, how are we then to describe it?" (PhP, 424; PP, 485) See also PriP, 3; Inédit, 402; "I have tried, first of all, to re-establish the roots [l'enracinement] of the mind in its body and in its world".

23.    Alain, Spinoza, collection "Idées"    (Paris: Gallimard, 1965), p. 45.

24.    We have not thought it necessary to comment on this analysis.

25.    See for instance: PhP, 166; PP, 193; SNS, 53: SNS, 96; CAL, 102: BP, 259; PriP, 83: SHP, 43; S, 232: S, 294; S, 235: S, 298.

26.    Max Scheler, The Nature of Sympathy (London: Routledge and Kegan Paul, 1954), p. 253.

27.    "The holders of atomism have had to admit to the evidence that their science is but a link in the infinite chain of dialogues between man and nature and that it can no longer simply speak of an 'in itself' nature. The sciences of nature always presuppose man, and, as Bohr has said, we must realize that we are not spectators but actors in the theatre of life." W. Heisenberg, La Nature dans la physique contemporaine, Collection "Idées" (Paris: Gallimard, 1962), pp. 18-9.

28.    See for instance Proust, Du côté de chez Swann (Paris: Gallimard, 1954), Vol. II, pp. 172-3: "Thereby Vinteuil's phrase had, like such-and-such a theme from Tristan, for example, which also represents for us a certain sentimental acquisition, espoused our mortal condition, taken on something human which was rather touching. Its fate was tied to the future, to the reality of our soul of which it was one of the most intimate, most differentiated ornaments." (emphasis ours) Also: "It was his work itself which, by impregnating the rare minds capable of understanding it, will make them

grow and multiply....What is called posterity is the posterity of the work. It is necessary that the work...itself create its posterity....this time yet to come, the true perspective of materpieces". *A la recherche du temps perdu (A l'ombre des jeunes filles en fleurs)* (Paris: Gallimard, Pléiade edition, 1954), vol. I, pp. 531–2.

29.  PhP, 400; *PP*, 458. See also PhP, 359; *PP*, 453 where Merleau-Ponty indicates the text of Husserl from which he borrows the term. It is for him an expression which in his later works will take on considerable importance. See for instance S, 96: *S*, 120; VI, 91: *VI*, 125.

30.  We thus see that in a certain sense the question of time imposes on reflection its most radical task. Reflection does not seize hold of itself if it does not take account of the fact that subjectivity is temporality. The fact that I exist in time, that is, that *I was born*, that I am not my own origin, poses for reflection a problem of the first magnitude. This is why we shall reserve a discussion of the question of time for Chapter IV which will deal with philosophical reflection.

31.  "The world is that reality of which the necessary and the possible are merely provinces." (PhP, 398; *PP*, 456)

32.  See Merleau-Ponty's preface to *L'Œuvre de Freud* by A. Hesnard (Paris: Payot, 1960), p. 8.

33.  "...there is not a single human act or passion which does not testify to man's humanity. There is not a single love which is simply a bodily mechanism and which—even and most of all when it attaches itself insanely to its object—does not prove our ability to put ourselves to the test, our power of absolute self-dedication, our metaphysical significance." (SNS, 74; *SNS*, 129)

34.  Hegel, *La Phénoménologie de l'esprit*, trans. by J. Hyppolite (Paris: Aubier, 1939), vol. I, p. 71.

## Chapter II

1.  "Cézanne's Doubt" in SNS, 9–25.

2.  "When I see the bright green of one of Cézanne's vases, it does not make me *think* of pottery, it presents it to me. The pottery is there, with its thin, smooth outer surface and its porous inside, in the particular way in which the green varies in shade." (PhP, 330; *PP*, 380)

3.  J. Hyppolite, *Etudes sur Marx et Hegel* (Paris: Marcel Rivière, 1965), p. 176.

4.  "The artist according to Cézanne or Balzac is not satisfied to be a cultured animal but assimilates the culture down to its very foundations and gives it a new structure: he speaks as the first man spoke and paints as if no one had ever painted before. What he expresses cannot, therefore, be the translation of a clearly defined thought, since such clear thoughts are those which have already been uttered by ourselves or by others." (SNS, 18–9; *SNS*, 32) In the preface to *Sense and Non-Sense* Merleau-Ponty writes (SNS, 3; *SNS*, 8): "the meaning of the work for the artist or for the public cannot be stated except by the work itself: neither the thought which created it nor the thought which receives it is completely its own master."

   Alain, with whose work Merleau-Ponty was familiar, had already said: "The supreme law of human invention is that one invents only by working." "If the power of executing something did not far exceed the power of thinking or dreaming, there would be no artists at all." "Ideas come to [the painter] to the degree that he acts; it would even be more exact to say that ideas come to him afterwards, just as they do to his spectator, and that he is also a spectator of his work as it is being born. It is this which is peculiar to the artist." "...the notion of a model which pre-exists like a phantom and is merely translated by the actual making of the work is itself imaginary." "Painting is the immediate expression of feelings by colored forms; and just as the feeling which is thus drawn together in its transparency is not expressible by means of speech, so also the painter cannot forsee anything; he simply tries to translate with affirmative strength that expression which sometimes is grasped in the gaze, around the forehead and the temples, and on the edge of the lips". *Système des beaux-arts* (Paris: Gallimard, 1926), pp. 33, 34, 41, 246.

5.    M. Eliade, *Le sacré et le profane*, collection "Idées"   (Paris: Gallimard, 1965), p. 179.

6.    By introducing the term "history" into our reading of this essay and by placing it side by side with that of "universality," implying thereby that there is a universal Logos which is the recuperation of generality and particularity, that there is "one truth" wherein all these individual and disparate experiences "would be integrated" (AD, 199; AD, 269), we are aware that we are anticipating the reading to follow. But is not this anticipation in some sense present in the text itself, as the quotation immediately to follow seems to indicate?

7.    It must be added, however, that if esthetic expression makes an appeal to "a reason which would be able to encompass its own origins" and if the painter turns "towards the idea or the project of an infinite Logos," this encompassment, this comprehension is never complete; the infinite Logos remains always an *infinite* Logos, and thus for an absolute painter like Cézanne there is only one emotion possible: "the feeling of strangeness—and only one lyricism—that of existence continually rebegun." (SNS, 18; SNS, 30) The painter lives in fascination, "Eye and Mind" will say, and he lives in it always, "unless, as it has more than once, a mysterious fatigue intervenes". (S, 53; S, 66) If, therefore, as Merleau-Ponty observes, Cézanne thought himself impotent, it was "because he was not omnipotent." (SNS, 19; SNS, 33) The artist is never at the center of his life, "nine days out of ten all he sees around him is the wretchedness of his empirical life and of his unsuccessful attempts, the leftovers of an unknown party. ...We never see our ideas or our freedom face to face." (SNS, 25; SNS, 43-4) "Life is terrifying," Cézanne used to say.

The recuperation of being in the world brought about by reflective or transcendental expression is therefore never absolute. The logos of the phenomenal world is never completely saved. "No one is saved and no one is totally lost." (PhP, 171; PP, 199) Art will never exhaust the "insurpassable richness of the sensible." And, as we shall see in Chapter IV, even that *radical inflection* which is philosophy—whose itenerary in the case of Merleau-Ponty strongly resembles in certain ways a Phenomenology of Mind, that description of "man's efforts to reappropriate himself" (SNS, 65; SNS, 113)—does not manage to consummate itself in an *absolute knowledge*.

8.    "Indirect Language and the Voices of Silence" in S, 39-83.

9.    See S, 75; S, 94. Each of the three sections of our own analysis will correspond to one of these problems. Thus the first section deals primarily with the notion of *expression*, the second is devoted above all to that of *perception*, and the third is concerned with that of *history*.

10.   P. Klee, *Théorie de l'art moderne* (Geneva: Editions Gonthier, 1964), pp. 55, 32.

11.   The quotation is cited by S. Ullmann in *Problèmes et méthodes de la linguistique* by W. von Wartburg (Paris: Presses Universitiares de France, 1963), pp. 218-9, and the second by A. Maurois, *A la recherche de Marcel Proust* (Paris: Hachette, 1949), p. 194.

12.   It will be recalled that in the preceding chapter, in the section entitled, "Being in the World as Rootedness", we considered this question by analyzing what for Merleau-

Ponty constitutes the ground of certainty and evidence, and that we were then able to conclude that, in its origin, truth (rationality) is inseparable from our being in the world. If Merleau-Ponty takes up a theme here which he has already examined, it is because this essay, unlike the *Phenomenology*, is going to rigorously tie up the notion of truth with that of *history*, which is to say that it is going to sketch out the elements of an *ontology*.

13. In searching for the ground of the act of painting, its "spontaneous source," that by which the unity in the history of painting can be understood, Merleau-Ponty returns to perceptual life. He discovers in it what could be called a *teleology of reason*: it is from his perceptual life that the painter receives his *vocation* to paint; it is his perceptual life which sets for him his *task*. It is this single task in terms of which the world is "to be painted," one which is imposed on all painters, which makes it be that they all belong to the same history, that they all participate in a single attempt at expression and are thereby united in "an indefinite future." (It is thus again a question of what "Cézanne's Doubt" called "the idea or the project of an infinite Logos.") What is most important in this essay is thus Merleau-Ponty's recognition of the existence of such a vocation to paint, of the essence of painting as a task, of the teleological nature of expression. However, it will only be in "Eye and Mind" that Merleau-Ponty will not limit himself to merely acknowledging the existence of such a teleology but will ask himself what it signifies and how it is possible.

14. The expression "advent," as Merleau-Ponty notes, is that of Paul Ricoeur.

15. "If it is characteristic of the human gesture to signify beyond its simple existence in fact, to inaugurate a meaning, it follows that every gesture is *comparable* to every other. They all arise from a single syntax. Each is a beginning (and a continuation) which, insofar as it is not walled up in its singularity and finished once and for all like an event, points to a continuation or recommencements. Its value exceeds its simple presence, and in this respect it is allied or accomplished in advance to all other efforts of expression." (S, 68; S, 85)

16. The English language translator of this work has failed to reproduce in his text the sentence just quoted ("The field...").

17. Henry Read, the famous English critic, writes: "If we have regard only for that quality we call 'sensibility', which would throughout history seem to be the essential element in art, ...then no progress whatsoever is discernible between the cave drawings of the paleolithic period and the drawings of Raphael or Picasso." *The Philosophy of Modern Art* (London: Faber and Faber, n.d.), p. 19.

18. A reflection on painting thus demands that thinking engage in a double movement. Reflection, on the one hand, considers itself to be the search for a phenomenal, covered-over logos, which comes to light and expresses itself through the different ways in which it is taken up—this is the *archeological* side of the movement. But, on the other hand, reflection grasps itself as the active transcendence of this phenomenal logos. By revealing it, it brings about, in regard to this logos, a metamorphosis which transforms it into an open and available meaning; reflection is thus itself the coming to light of this invisible, hidden logos. Reflection thus does not appear as a mere effort to return to and coincide with the original silence but as the attempt to speak out this silence; it is therefore *teleological*, and it is such in its very archeology.

Expression is a *recuperation* (of a hidden, phenomenal meaning which coincides with being in the world), but it is such only by being an *interpretation* (the painter makes his natural perception undergo a "coherent deformation"). One could say, therefore, that expression is *creative* or *transcendental*. The difficulty lies in *thinking* these two sides or moments together, but the subtlety such an effort calls for—and which, moreover, we are merely alluding to here—must not obscure its extreme importance for a proper understanding of Merleau-Ponty's thought.

These remarks are, in fact, indispensable if we wish to fully grasp the exact meaning of the expression "advent" which we see at the very center of Merleau-Ponty's analysis. Expression is not a mere event but rather constitutes an advent, because it has a dual nature (because it is archeological-teleological). Expression is at one and the same time the recuperation of a phenomenal logos, of an operant and latent meaning (the "voices of silence"), and the institution of a universal logos, a professed and accessible meaning. Through his interpretive work, man transforms the still scattered and diffuse meaning of his mute encounter with the world into a precise meaning. The truth which in this way makes its appearance is not an event, however, a metaphysical in-itself, for it does not exist as truth, as universal logos, before man discovers and expresses it. Truth is an advent, which is to say that it is the very *generality* of bodily existence which has been *transformed* into *universality*, into a spoken or otherwise offered up meaning, and in this way it founds a history. Truth is thus not created by expression; it calls for expression, "historical inscribing," perhaps, but it does so only because we are its bearers. In the last analysis, advents exist only within events. Expression is thus a recuperation only by being creative, and truth is like life itself such as Kierkegaard viewed it. "What the philosophers say," Kierkegaard writes, "is quite correct: life can be understood only through a turning backwards. But one tends to forget another truth: that it is lived forwards." The turning backwards effected by reflection must not hide from us the fact that the truth discovered in this way is a truth which is brought into being by reflection itself. Klee's expression, which we have already quoted, finds its full meaning in this context: "Art does not reproduce the visible; it makes visible." The fact that man paints is thus not the mark of his subjection to some kind of power outside of him (the Spirit of Painting of idealism or empiricism's objective world); it is precisely the measure of his triumph over the world and of his transcendence in being. The phenomenon of expression attests that man is not a mere event in nature, that he not merely is but rather makes himself, and that in making himself he renews the face of the earth, that he thus institutes a History which includes him and which insures the truth of his life. Man, like the truth, is an advent.

19.   In the text Merleau-Ponty immediately adds: "Perhaps this expectation will always be in some way disappointed."

20.   "Eye and Mind" trans by C. Dallery in PriP. This essay first appeared in *Art de France*, 1 (Jan. 1961), pp. 187–208, and was afterwards reprinted in *Les Temps modernes*, special issue 184–5, pp. 193–227, before being published separately by Editions Gallimard in 1964.

21.   Sartre, "Merleau-Ponty," *Situations IV* (Paris: Gallimard, 1964), p. 282.

22.   This is to say that the meaning of this writing does not only lie in what it says. It is not contained solely in what the author explicitly says, but also it does not simply lie elsewhere. It lies in the back-and-forth between the propositions, in that unsaid around which they all turn and which appears only at the intersection of all the propositions. Meaning (*sens*) here is to be taken literally: rather than a coincidence and identification with itself, it is a direction and a movement. This is to say also that one must look elsewhere in order to discover the full meaning of "Eye and Mind." In order to grasp it as fully as possible, it is necessary to place "Eye and Mind" side by side with the preface to *Signs*, *The Visible and the Invisible*, and other writings of the later Merleau-Ponty. The central aim of his "later" philosophy, which speaks always of Being and of the flesh, would then appear in the way all these writings give articulation to each other, in

the fruitful silence which animates them all. The meaning of "Eye and Mind," like that of *The Visible and the Invisible*, is in the last analysis the "unthought thought" (*l'impensé*) of Merleau-Ponty. It is we, Merleau-Ponty's readers, who must think this unspoken meaning. In this chapter we will do no more than begin this effort.

23.   Klee, *Théorie de l'art moderne*, p. 28.

24.   If Merleau-Ponty sees a valid element in the theory of certain surrealists and, in this case, in the statements of Max Ernst, he remains no less hostile to this interpretation of the expressive operation as a whole. It was thus that he wrote, thinking no doubt of the notion of "automatic writing": "But breaking or burning up language did not suffice to write the *Illuminations*." (S, 56; S, 71)

25.   We can thus see how the notion proposed by "Cézanne's Doubt" and "Indirect Language and the Voices of Silence" that what the painter expresses is his commerce with the world is here much more highly accented, such that, alongside the relatively weak words of "commerce" and "circularity," a new term, *"flesh,"* makes its appearance.

26.   One does not see a picture in its own right any more than one sees the words on the page of a novel: "It is more accurate to say that I see according to it, or with it, than that I *see it*." (PriP, 164; *OE*, 23)

27.   This is to say, therefore, that pictorial reflection attempts to reveal the structure of this "there is" (*il y a*). How is it that things are "there"? What painting aims at is the release of this covered-over or wild logos.

28.   What, therefore, the painter expresses is the system seeing-visible (*voyant-visible*): "Once this strange system of exchanges is given, we find before us all the problems of painting." (PriP, 146; *OE*, 21) The situation which he takes up is the dialogue between vision and the visible, the circularity between the two moments—the flesh—of that unique phenomenon which is visibility: "Painting celebrates no other enigma but that of visibility." (PriP, 166; *OE*, 26) The painter sees to grasp and release "a logos of lines, of lighting, of colors, of reliefs, of masses" (PriP, 182; *OE*, 71), to gather together this diffuse Whole. But just as the logos of the perceived world is not the world as it is "in itself" or a principle beyond it, but is, precisely, the subject's presence to the world, so the painter, by expressing this logos, expresses himself as the "other side" of the world, that is, what he expresses is precisely this relation; he brings to expression the internal and underground commerce of the visible and the seeing. By setting it up on a canvas, the painter expresses the body's commerce with the world, the circularity or dialogue or flesh of vision and the visible, the phenomenon of visibility.

   Painting is in this way an act of reflection, for the painter, by celebrating the phenomenon of visibility, by taking visibility itself as a theme, has ceased to merely live in the visible. On the contrary, he attempts to become conscious of what for the most part is only lived; existence here turns back on itself in order to express itself. "Art," as G. Bachelard says, "is thus a doubling up [*redoublement*] of life." Painting reveals a mode of experience which is different from everyday experience, or, to be more exact, what it reveals is precisely this experience which is ordinarily hidden from itself. In our daily commerce with the world, it appears as meaningful, as a harmonious synthesis which speaks the language of colors and forms, and this meaning of the world is the meaning of our life in the world; it is nothing other than the system seeing-visible. What makes the painter a painter is his astonishment in the face of this phenomenon, and, instead of simply living through it, he attempts to express it. The painter questions himself as to the phenomenon of visibility, and the question he raises in his own way is that of the very visibility of the visible (just as the metaphysician raises the question of the being of beings). Or, inversely, what he attempts to express is vision as operative intentionality. Thus for the painter the phenomenon is itself a phenomenon, and the order of pictorial expression belongs to a transcendental order of expressive experience.

29. Klee, *Théorie de l'art moderne*, p. 59.

30. A continued birth...Painters often have the impression that their painter's vision was already born or sketched out in the visible itself and that they merely perfect this coming-to-itself of the visible. An artists's remarks as reported by Merleau-Ponty attest to this feeling: "In a forest, I have felt many times over that it was not I who looked at the forest. Some days I felt that the trees were looking at me, were speaking to me." (PriP, 167; *OE*, 31) This feeling is also attested to by the fondness of painters for putting in their pictures mirrors and pictures of pictures. In "The Marriage" by Van Eyck, for example, the spectacle is concentrated in a mirror which sees everything which is going on in the picture; a prehuman gaze here gathers the visible together and is like the announcement or "the symbol of that of the painter." (PriP, 167; *OE*, 32) Often, too, one sees painters painting themselves in the process of painting, "adding to what *they* saw then, what *things* saw of them. It is as if they were claiming that there is a total or absolute vision, outside of which there is nothing and which closes itself over them." (PriP, 169; *OE*, 34) A Vision which doubles back on itself and perfects itself in the vision of the painter...In these strange cases where the painter paints himself in the process of painting or where he puts in his picture a picture of the picture, it is as if pictorial expression were the realization of a kind of *absolute*. In any event, they reflect the "narcissistic" structure of Being itself.

31. Klee, *Théorie de l'art moderne*, p. 57.

32. It is still necessary to articulate this mute advent, and therein lies the vocation of the painter, the philosopher, in short of all transcendental, creative expression.

33. "The difficulty has no other origin than a surreptitious and obstinate appeal to the notion of a real-nature-in-itself, to which we are supposed to progressively equal ourselves, truth finally being attained the day when things as they are in themselves will have completely been changed into a mental translation which will deliver them over to us as if we were them." A. de Waelhens, "Merleau-Ponty, philosophe de la peinture," *Revue de métaphysique et de morale*, 4 (Oct.–Dec. 1962), p. 449.

34. See also PhP, 391; *PP*, 448: "What remains true is that in speech, to a greater extent than in music or painting, thought seems able to detach itself from its material instruments and acquire an eternal value."

35. "Heraclitus' writing casts light for us as no broken statues can, because its significance is deposited and concentrated in it in another way than theirs is in them, and because nothing equals the ductility of speech." (S, 80; *S*, 101)

## Chapter III

1. In his writings subsequent to the *Phenomenology*, where Merleau-Ponty speaks explicitly of Saussure, we find, moreover, an interpretation of the Swiss linguist which is, in many ways, quite curious. For, contrary to what Merleau-Ponty says, speech is never the focal point for Saussure. When Merleau-Ponty says that "Saussure's linguistics legitimates, in the study of language...the perspective of the speaking subject who lives in his language (and who may in some cases change it)", it may be that he is confusing the thought of Pos and of Wartburg (who, moreover, he quotes in his article) with that of Saussure (cf. SNS, 87; *SNS*, 152). For Saussure himself "the activity of the speaking subject must be clarified in a collection of disciplines which have a place in linguistics only through their relation to language [*la langue*]" (as opposed to speech, *la parole*) (Saussure, *Cours de linguistique générale* [Paris: Payot, 1964], p. 37). Saussure recog-

nizes that there is a strict "interdependence" between language, conceived of as a system, and the "act of speech," but for him this interdependence "does not prevent them from being two absolutely distinct things". (*Cours*, pp. 37–8) He says that one *could* undertake a "linguistics of speech," but that if one does so, "one must not confuse it with linguistics in the proper sense of the term, that for which language is the sole object". (*Cours*, pp. 38–9) Similarly, Merleau-Ponty betrays a strange understanding of Saussure when he speaks of a "synchronic linguistics of *speech* and a diachronic linguistics of *language*" in Saussure (S, 86; *S*, 107; emphasis ours), because, *for Saussure*, the distinction here is not between speech and language but between two different linguistics of *language itself*. When Merleau-Ponty says that in Saussure this distinction—such as *he* characterizes it—is that of "language as object of thought and language as mind" (S, 86; *S*, 107), it is more the thought of Pos than of Saussure that Merleau-Ponty is summing up. It has been said that Merleau-Ponty's interpretation of Husserl is more philosophical than historical. However it be with regard to Husserl, this is certainly the case with regard to Saussure.

However, as concerns linguistics in general, the fact remains that for Merleau-Ponty a philosophy of language must necessarily take account of the discoveries of linguistics: "Since linguistics is the most rigorous existing examination of language as an institution, one cannot conceive of a philosophy of language which is not obliged to collect and articulate on the basis of its own truths those truths that the linguist has established." (CAL, 82; *BP*, 252)

2. J.P. Sartre, *Qu'est-ce que la littérature?*, collection "Idées" (Paris; Gallimard, 1964), p. 17.

3. "In this predialectical moment of his thought, Sartre is indeed tempted by dualism; if nature and consciousness are irreducibly opposed to each other as in itself and for itself, language, far from being, as we shall attempt to show, nature and consciousness at the same time, the place where an agreement between man and the world is reached, is driven into two extreme situations: either, as in prose, it is a tool of a consciousness which in using it at once transcends its nature towards its meaning and loses itself in its meaning; or else, as in poetry, it is an object in front of a consciousness which is aware of its nature only in order to be surprised by it, and it loses its meaning. Sartre thus hardens the opposition between prose and poetry. ....As a matter of fact, it seems to me that words, like things, can be things and signs at the same time, things which make a sign to us, which carry in themselves their meaning and which propose it to us without our having to imagine it. If Sartre draws back from this idea, it is perhaps because he is always preoccupied with preserving the freedom of a consciousness which remains a giver of meaning....consciousness retains the initiative and, so to speak, a high hand in regard to language." Mikel Dufrenne, *Le Poétique* (Paris: Presses Universitaires de France, 1963), pp. 38–9.

4. "It is because the sign is diacritical from the outset, because it is composed and organized in terms of itself, that it has an interior and ends up laying claim to a meaning." (S, 41; *S*, 51)

5. "...Language is a system of signs which have meaning only in relation to one another, and each of which has its own usage [*valeur d'emploi*] throughout the whole language". (IPP, 55; *EP*, 88)

6. "I express when, utilizing all these already speaking instruments, I make them say something they have never said. We begin reading a philosopher by giving the words he makes use of their 'common' meaning; and little by little, through what is at first an imperceptible reversal, his speech comes to dominate his language, and it is his use of words which ends up assigning them a new and characteristic signification. At this mo-

ment he has made himself understood and his signification has come to dwell in me. We say that a thought is expressed when the converging words intending it are numerous and eloquent enough to designate it unequivocally for me, its author, or for others, and in such a manner that we all have the experience of its presence in the flesh in speech." (S, 91; S, 113) Commenting on Hegel, Jean Hyppolite writes: "[The Self] espouses that language which appeared to be an alienation of self and now makes it say what it had never said with words which nonetheless existed in the past....We read a philosopher and we first give to his words their habitual meaning; little by little the context forces us into imperceptible changes, and the use he makes of them ends up by conferring on them a new signification proper to him, and which is yet universal since we understand it." *Logique et existence* (Paris: Presses Universitaires de France, 1961), p. 57. Should we see here, in this text which was finalized in 1952, an allusion to Merleau-Ponty's text which we have just quoted and which, for its part, was presented to a philosophical congress in 1951? Hyppolite himself quotes Merleau-Ponty on page 29 of his book.

7. It is not our intention to correct Merleau-Ponty or to find contradictions in him, for if he insists—in the *Phenomenology* above all—on the simultaneity of thought and speech, these passages have meaning in the last analysis only in the context of others where he speaks of a meaning-intention which precedes and animates speech. It is precisely the relation between the meaning-intention and the actual speech which incarnates and realizes it which we must bring to a clearer focus.

8. Thus, as if to nuance his polemic against "inner" life, Merleau-Ponty writes: "Language certainly has an inside, but this is not a self-subsistent and self-conscious thought." (PhP, 193; PP, 225)

9. "Visual contents are taken up, utilized and sublimated to the level of thought by a symbolical power which transcends them, but it is on the basis of sight that this power can be constituted." (PhP, 127; PP, 147)

10. "It seems to me that knowledge and the communication with others which it presupposes not only are original formations with respect to the perceptual life but also they preserve and continue our perceptual life even while transforming it. Knowledge and communication sublimate rather than suppress our incarnation, and the characteristic operation of the mind is in the movement by which we recapture our corporeal existence and use it to symbolize instead of merely to coexist." (PriP, 7; Inédit, 405)

11. Quoted by Wartburg in *Problèmes et méthodes de la linguistique*, p. 184.

12. Ibid., p. 216.

13. "For example, certain forms of expression having become decadent by the sole fact that they have been used and have lost their 'expressiveness', we shall show how the gaps or zones of weakness thus created elicit from speaking subjects who want to communicate a recovery and a utilization, in terms of a new principle, of linguisitic débris left by the system in process of regression. It is in this way that a new means of expression is conceived of in a language, and a persistent logic runs through the effects of wear and tear upon the language and its volubility itself. It is in this way that the French system of expression, based upon the preposition, was substituted for the Latin system, which was based upon declension and inflectional changes." (S, 87; S, 108)

14. "How can one understand this generalized meaning which works in historical forms and in the whole of history, which is not the thought of any one *cogito* but which solicits them all?" (IPP, 54; EP, 85)

15. Wartburg, *Problèmes et méthodes de la linguistique*, p. 217.

16. "And we would undoubtedly recover the concept of history in the true sense of the term if we were to get used to modeling it after the example of the arts and language." (S, 73; S, 91)

17. In raising the example of Proust, we are not proposing to undertake, in whatever manner, either a literary or critical study of his work or an examination of the author's personal psychology; we want only to invoke the *project* of Proust as a novelist who sets out in search of time past. It is this project alone which interests us here, what Proust called his "work" and which, as a task to be accomplished, constituted for him the meaning of his life. The work which interests us is thus not that which has such and such literary merits; it is more and it is less than that; it is the work as such, the work as the global project which Proust assigned himself and which was for him the goal of his life. Rather than various writings and rather than the details of the author's life, what interests us is the very relation existing between a *life* which secretes in itself a work and a *work* which is the realization and the recuperation of a life—it is the teleology of a life which transforms itself into a work. We thus propose to sketch out a hermeneutics of Proust's work, to analyze it phenomenologically or eidetically in order to draw out the *eidos* which might have something to teach us about the more general relation between life and the reflective consciousness of life, between lived existence and reflected existence, in short, between existence and truth.

18. In what follows, we shall be quoting, in our own translation, from the three volume edition of *A la recherche du temps perdu*, published by Editions Gallimard in its "Pléiade" collection, citing first volume number and then page.

19. This text could be set next to the following text of Hegel which Merleau-Ponty quotes in *The Structure of Behavior*: "the moments which the mind seems to have behind it are also borne in its present depths." (SB, 207; *SC*, 224)

20. J. Hyppolite, *Etudes sur Marx et Hegel*, p. 180. In *The Structure of Behavior* Merleau-Ponty writes: "And finally, death is not *deprived of meaning*, since the contingency of the lived is a perpetual menace for the eternal significations in which it is believed to be completely expressed. It will be necessary to assure oneself that the experience of eternity is not the unconsciousness of death, that it is not on this side but beyond; similarly, moreover, it will be necessary to distinguish the love of life from the attachment to biological existence. The sacrifice of life will be philosophically impossible; it will be a question only of 'staking' one's life, which is a deeper way of living." (SB, 223–4; *SC*, 240)

21. "It is not man as a biological species which is in question, but rather, at the very heart of life, the emergence of a being who becomes conscious of this life which is the condition of his emergence and who, in this becoming conscious, creates, as it were, a new dimension of being, engenders a history, and in this history makes and discovers a rational truth." Hyppolite, *Etudes sur Marx et Hegel*, p. 174.

22. Ibid., p. 176.

23. "There is truly a reversal when one passes from the sensible world, in which we are caught, to a world of expression, where we seek to capture significations and make them available, although this reversal and the 'retrograde movement' of truth are solicited by a perceptual anticipation. Properly speaking, the expression which language makes possible takes up and amplifies another expression which is revealed in the 'archeology' of the perceived world." (TFL, 4; *RC*, 12)

24. *Etudes sur Marx et Hegel*, p. 176.

25. Ibid., p. 188.

26. Ibid., p. 26.

27. "Thus truth and the whole are there from the start—but as a task to be accomplished, and thus not yet there." (S, 128; *S*, 161)

28. "...The spirit makes use of the world, time, speech, and history in a single movement and animates them with a meaning which is never used up. It would be the function of philosophy, then, to record this passage of meaning". (IPP, 9; *EP*, 18)

29.    "...human language...thus becomes the Logos of lived experience, the very Logos of Being, its universal revelation, as one could say. To utter Being appears as the very task of man, the proper meaning of consciousness which thereby becomes the universal self-consciousness of Being. It is this universal self-consciousness of Being, this saying of Being, which perfectly defines Hegel's Logic; it is in the proper sense of the term the rigorous poem of Being, unveiling itself by and through man, the manifestation of the universal self-consciousness in the individual self-consciousness of the philosopher, the idea appearing in human judgment and which is not merely its more or less arbitrary or subjective product, as one might say....Naive consciousness is Being itself from which it begins to distinguish itself in order to say it; universal self-consciousness, absolute knowledge, is Being itself which says itself, means itself, because this reflection which appears in consciousness as a subject-object duality appears in Being which appears to itself and makes itself into Meaning, comprehends itself in making itself....It is not man who does philosophy, but it is, across man, philosophy which does itself, and the philosophy of philosophy is the becoming-conscious of such an ideal genesis, an attempt to set up metaphysics as the Logic of philosophy." Hyppolite, *Etudes sur Marx et Hegel*, pp. 188–95. If in his later philosophy Merleau-Ponty prefers to invoke the examples of Husserl and Heidegger, it would still appear that in a sense his problematic is none other than that of Hegel as here interpreted by Hyppolite.

## Chapter IV

1.    "...Those who reject this or that in Descartes do so only in terms of reasons which owe a lot to Descartes." (S, 11; *S*, 17)

2.    "...In the last resort, the significance of the *cogito* lies not in revealing a universal constituting force or in reducing perception to intellection, but in establishing the *fact* of reflection which both pierces and sustains the opacity of perception....But even if we grant that existence, individuality, 'facticity' are on the horizon of Cartesian thought, there remains the question whether it has thematized them. Now we must recognize that it could have done so only by transforming itself radically....The Cartesian solution is therefore not to accept as a guarantee of itself human thought in its factual reality, but to base it on a thought which possesses itself absolutely. The connection between essence and existence is not found in experience, but in the idea of the infinite. It is, then, true in the last resort that analytical reflection entirely rests on a dogmatic idea of being, and that in this sense it is not a fully realized act of self-discovery." (PhP, 43–4; *PP*, 53–5)

3.    "...It would be necessary to show that in no case can consciousness entirely cease to be what it is in perception, that is, a fact, and that it cannot take full possession of its operations. The recognition of phenomena, then, implies a theory of reflection and a new *cogito*." (PhP, 50; *PP*, 62)

4.    Hegel, *La phénoméologie de l'esprit*, trans. by J. Hyppolite (Paris: Aubier, 1939), vol. I, p. 176.

5.    In *The Visible and the Invisible* Merleau-Ponty will write: "The search for conditions of possibility is in principle posterior to an actual experience, and from this it follows that even if subsequently one determines rigorously the *sine qua non* of that experience, it can never be washed of the original stain of having been discovered *post festum* nor ever become what positively grounds that experience." (VI, 45; *VI*, 69)

6.    Hegel, *La phénoménologie de l'esprit*, vol. I, p. 8.

7.    IPP, 20; *EP*, 35; Merleau-Ponty is here quoting from Bergson; cf. Bergson, *Evolution créatrice* (Paris: Presses Universitaires de France, 1966), p. 293.

8.  In *The Visible and the Invisible* Merleau-Ponty says: "The remarks we made concerning reflection were nowise intended to disqualify it for the profit of the unreflected or the immediate (which we know only through reflection). It is a question not of putting the perceptual faith in the place of reflection, but on the contrary of taking into account the total situation, which involves reference from the one to the other. What is given is not a massive and opaque world, or a universe of adequate thought; it is a reflection which turns back over the density of the world in order to clarify it, but which, coming second, reflects back to it only its own light." (VI, 35; *VI*, 57)

9.  "The lived is certainly lived by me, nor am I ignorant of the feelings which I repress, and in this sense there is no unconscious. But I can experience more things than I represent to myself, and my being is not reducible to what expressly appears to me concerning myself. That which is merely lived is ambivalent." (PhP, 296; *PP*, 343) "Thus, the pretended unconsciousness of the complex is reduced to the ambivalence of immediate consciousness." (SB, 179; *SC*, 193)

10. Hegel, *La phénoménologie de l'esprit*, vol. I, p. 176.

11. "The world and reason are not problematical. We may say, if we wish, that they are mysterious, but their mystery defines them: there can be no question of dispelling it by some 'solution,' it is on the hither side of all solutions." (PhP, XX; *PP*, XVI)

12. In general, one could divide Merleau-Ponty's philosophical life into three periods. There is first of all that of his two doctoral theses (*The Structure of Behavior* and the *Phenomenology of Perception*). Here Merleau-Ponty is searching for the "originating", "that through which everything else can be and can be thought"; it is here, as we have said, that he is looking for a radical starting point. He finds this ground in the unreflected life of perception, in being in the world conceived of as an existential or bodily project of the world and a blind adherence to the world. The discovery of the lived body as being neither the idea of a constituting consciousness nor a material thing but as a spontaneous source of meaning calls in return for a new conception of intelligence, of the *cogito*—because what is meaningful in our bodily life is no longer the work of intelligence but is a meaningful mode of being prior to it and which it itself presupposes qua intelligence—and, consequently, a new idea of philosophy, which can only be phenomenology (or existentialism). Philosophy has no other mission than that of revealing the meaningful structures of our de facto condition and of taking note of the contingent and unintelligible origin of reason. In delimiting in this way the essence of experience and of philosophy, the *Phenomenology of Perception* functions, in short, as a kind of Prolegommena to Any Future Metaphysics.

    Then, in the numerous essays written between 1945 and the middle of the 1950's, Merleau-Ponty seeks to apply the conclusions of the *Phenomenology of Perception* to various areas of experience—to art, language, and politics, notably. In contrast to the *Phenomenology*, what he is undertaking here is thus not a search for the roots of existence but, so to speak, a horizontal investigation, an effort at interpreting various orders of experience and at realizing a kind of philosophical synthesis and a "metaphysics" (PriP, 11; *Inédit*, 409) in the light of the "fundamental" already unearthed by the *Phenomenology*. The "further studies which I have undertaken since 1945," he wrote in 1952, "...will definitively fix the philosophical significance of my earlier works [*The Structure of Behavior* and the *Phenomenology*] while they, in turn, determine the route and the method of these later studies." (PriP, 6; *Inédit*, 404)

    Towards the end of the 1950's, however, Merleau-Ponty comes to realize—above all through his meditations on the meaning of history—the insufficiency of the perspective set out by the *Phenomenology* and, consequently, of the need to take up again and deepen the results of his first important book. We thus have here a return to an *in depth* study of experience and an attempt to overcome the concepts of the *Phenomenology* so as to realize the ultimate meaning of existence (since it is the "originating", the "fundamental", that Merleau-Ponty was looking for, it would be a great mistake to present him as being primarily and principally a philosopher of the "social world"). No longer does he conceive the basic origin of truth or meaning to be the dialectical and gratuitous relation of the subject to the world, and the theme of this thought is no longer "being in the world" but rather "Being." Merleau-Ponty had only just begun this new and last period in his philosophical life when he so unexpectedly died on May 3, 1961.

13.   Sartre, *Situations IV* (Paris: Gallimard, 1964), p. 266.

14.   Merleau-Ponty's phenomenology becomes an ontology when, at the end of his life, he returns to the question of *natural being* and that of *transcendence* by which he had defined bodily existence in the *Phenomenology of Perception*, resolved now to explore them to the bottom. The later Merleau-Ponty's last word will not be contingency, because the ultimate foundation of rationality will no longer be the dialectical relation (bodily) subject–(perceived) world, but this relation will itself be conceived of as a derivative reality which rests on and stems from an "undivided Being" which is "prior" to the subject-world distinction or bifurcation. Likewise, the transcendence which constitutes human existence will, in the author's last works, no longer be conceived of as a brute and irrational fact but precisely as the expression, the self-manifestation (in a way) of Being. In this way Merleau-Ponty will come to situate the phenomenological field in the field of Being and conceive of man's transcendence and creativity as Being speaking in him. We shall return to these matters in the remainder of this chapter as well as in the chapter following.

15.   This text of Merleau-Ponty has a profound Heideggerian resonance, as much by his use of the expression "in-between" as by the meaning of his thought here. In his "Letter on Humanism," Heidegger says for instance: "Man is never this-worldly and of the world as a 'subject,' whether this 'subject' be understood as 'I' or as 'We.' He is also not essentially a subject who is also always in reference to an object, so that his essence lies in the subject-object relation. Man is rather in his essence ex-sistent in the openness of Being; this Open alone clears the 'between' [*Zwischen, entre-deux*] within which the 'relation' between subject and object can 'be.' " "Letter on Humanism" in W. Barrett and H. Aiken, eds., *Philosophy in the Twentieth Century* (New York: Random House, 1962), vol. III, p. 293.

16.   In this essay as in the *Phenomenology*, Merleau-Ponty recognizes that the natural expressivity of the body is indeed a mystery and a miracle, but (as we saw in Chapter II) he thinks he has said everything by saying that this miracle is self-supporting, that it is natural to us: "There is no doubt that this miracle, whose strangeness the word *man* should not hide from us, is a very great one. But we can at least recognize that this miracle is natural to us, that it begins with our incarnate life, and that there is no reason to look for its explanation in some Spirit of the World which allegedly operates within us but without us". (S, 66; S, 82) The creativity and transcendence already present in bodily existence may be "natural" to us, but if such is the case, must we not reconsider what exactly our "nature" is and can be if it includes within itself such a great miracle? It is this redefinition of man (qua seeing subject) that Merleau-Ponty undertakes in "Eye and Mind"; if vision is something miraculous, he says here, it is because it comes to us from Being and is the expression of our participation in Being. If man is more than a natural species, it is due to his relation to Being, a relation which defines him and which is his very nature.

17.   "One can say that we perceive the things themselves, that we are the world that thinks itself—or that the world is at the heart of our flesh. In any case, once a body-world

relationship is recognized, there is a ramification of my body and a ramification of the world and a correspondence between its inside and my outside, between my inside and its outside." (VI, 136; *VI*, 179) If there is an intentional relation between the body and the world, it is because the two are the differentiations of a single reality. We can see thereby how the notion of intentionality presented in the *Phenomenology* has been radically transformed.

18. When Merleau-Ponty writes "Sensible" with a capital, it is to differentiate it from "sensible," without a capital, the latter signifying those "things" which are the "objects" of sensing. The Sensible is thus not that which is sensed, but the unique and sub-phenomenal fabric of which sensing and the sensible are both differentiations. The Sensible is, in a word, the flesh.

19. Heidegger, *Lettre sur l'humanisme* (Paris: Aubier, 1964), pp. 183–5.

20. "The Cogito of Descartes (reflection) is an operation on significations, a statement of relations between them (and the significations themselves sedimented in acts of expression). It therefore presupposes a prereflective contact of self with self (the non-thetic consciousness [of] self Sartre) or a tacit cogito (being close by oneself)—this is how I reasoned in *Ph.P.*
    "Is this correct? What I call the tacit cogito is impossible." (VI, 170–1; *VI*, 224)

21. "This new reversibility and the emergence of the flesh as expression are the point of insertion of speaking and thinking in the world of silence." (VI, 144–5; *VI*, 190) "Vision sketches out what is accomplished by desire when it pushes two 'thoughts' out toward that line of fire between them, that blazing surface where they seek a fulfillment which will be identically the same for the two of them, as the sensible world is for everyone. Speech, as we said, would interrupt this fascination. It would not suppress it; it would put it off, carrying it on forward. For speech takes flight from where it rolls in the wave of speechless communication....To make of language a means or a code for thought is to break it. When we do so we prohibit ourselves from understanding the depth to which words sound within us—from understanding that we have a need, a passion, for speaking....Language can vary and amplify intercorporeal communication as much as we wish; it has the same spring and style as the latter. In language too, that which was secret must become public and almost *visible*....Thus things *are said* and *are thought* [*se trouvent dites et se trouvent pensées*] by a Speech and by a Thought which we do not have but which has us." (S, 17–9; *S*, 24–7)

22. "It is necessary then on the way to form the theory of this 'reflection' that I practice." (VI, 177; *VI*, 231)

23. "The intentional analytic tacitly assumes a place of absolute contemplation *from which* the intentional explicitation is made, and which could embrace present, past, and even openness toward the future". (VI, 243; *VI*, 297)

24. Merleau-Ponty's return to ontology is not a return to realism, of whatever sort that might be. Merleau-Ponty never abandoned the fundamental requirement of phenomenology which is to refuse to consider consciousness or, in general, experience as a mere segment of the world, as existing alongside things in themselves, whether they be knowable in themselves or not. For Merleau-Ponty's ontology, as for phenomenology in general, the absolutely in-itself does not exist. This means that one cannot take the notion of Being in the later Merleau-Ponty to belong to the objective order. Being transcends the subject-object distinction just as it transcends the consciousness-noema distinction; it is the unique "soil" which sustains all cohesion and all opposition between subject and object. Being is nothing which exists, being precisely the spontaneous source of all that exists. Merleau-Ponty's ontology is an attempt to overcome all realism, as well as all objectivism and all subjectivism. In a working note of February 1959 he writes: "A *wiederholung* is necessary: 'destruction' of the objectivist ontology

of the Cartesians". (VI, 183; VI, 237) This is because for him "what is at stake [is] Being".

25.    Heidegger, De l'essence de la vérité, trans. by A. de Waelhens and W. Biemel (Louvain: E. Nauwelaerts, 1948), p. 104.

26.    It is a revelation of his own thought that Merleau-Ponty gives us when he attempts to make explicit the "unthought thought" of Husserl: "From Ideen II on Husserl's reflections escape this tête-à-tête between pure subject and pure things. They look deeper down for the fundamental. Saying that Husserl's thought goes in another direction tells us little. His thought does not disregard the ideal correlation of subject and object; it very deliberately goes beyond it, since it presents it as relatively founded, true derivatively as a constitutive result it is committed to justifying in its proper time and place." (S, 163; S, 206) One could in fact trace the development of Merleau-Ponty's thought by bringing to light the development in his interpretation of Husserl.

27.    Merleau-Ponty himself clearly indicates that a change in attitude towards psychoanalysis has taken place in him when he writes that "a perhaps more mature philosophy and also the growth of Freudian investigations...would make us today express in another way the relations of phenomenology and psychoanalysis itself—and in the end would make us less indulgent for our first essays [The Structure of Behavior and the Phenomenology of Perception] than Dr. Hesnard is willing to be." Preface to L'Œuvre de Freud by A. Hesnard (Paris: Payot, 1960), p. 8. An English translation of this text under the title, "Phenomenology and Psychoanalysis: Preface to Hesnard's L'Œuvre de Freud," can be found in The Essential Writings of Merleau-Ponty, ed. by A. Fisher (New York: Harcourt, Brace and World, 1969), pp. 81-7.

28.    Preface to Hesnard, L'OEuvre de Freud, p. 8.

29.    Ibid.

30.    What Merleau-Ponty says of philosophy in 1969 applies to his philosophy in 1943: "...philosophy finds its surest evidence at the moment of inception". (S, 3; S, 7)

31.    "...It is precisely a question of rejecting entirely the idea of the In Itself". (VI, 223; VI, 276)

32.    Should this be taken to mean that in his later philosophy Merleau-Ponty was moving towards a philosophical recognition of God, as certain commentators have thought, citing as proof or at least as an indication the text we have just reproduced? This is quite possible, but we should also add that it is not at all certain. In the last resort Merleau-Ponty's work offers no indication which would allow us to affirm it. Even if we knew more about the author's personal life, this would not help us to settle the question, since it concerns not Merleau-Ponty's personal attitude but his philosophy. And one thing which is certain is that on the question of God the philosopher is silent. At the most what one can say is that Merleau-Ponty's new ontology, by recognizing a transcendence in immanence, does not exclude the existence of a God who is not reducible to this world. Thus in the light of The Visible and the Invisible the sentence Merleau-Ponty wrote in 1947 could take on a new meaning: "A God who would not be simply for us but for Himself, could, on the contrary, be sought by metaphysics only behind consciousness, beyond our ideas, as the anonymous force which sustains each of our thoughts and experiences." (SNS, 96; SNS, 168) There is no place in Merleau-Ponty's ontology for an Ens realissimum, for a God conceived of as a kind of super-being, but there is a deep agreement in it with the notion of a "hidden god" (VI, 221; VI, 264) who would not be unrelated to "the unmotivated upsurge of brute Being." With the recognition of the "absolute priority of Being," Merleau-Ponty's philosophy, contrary to Sartre's opinion, can no longer be considered to be a mere humanism. For Merleau-Ponty man is not the final truth, and one can in no way claim that his philos-

ophy is a kind of atheism. But this new ontology is not a kind of theist philosophy either. In a working note written only a few weeks before his death, Merleau-Ponty says that he would have to work out his new ontology "without any compromise with *humanism*, nor moreover with *naturalism*, nor finally with *theology*." (VI, 274; *VI*, 328) He wanted precisely to reject thinking "according to this cleavage: God, man, creatures." Merleau-Ponty's ontology is neither a humanism, nor a naturalism, nor a theologism, but a philosophy of experience which follows no other guide than our experience, even if this would be "a movement toward what could not in any event be present to us in the original and whose irremediable absence would thus count among our originating experiences." Merleau-Ponty does not posit the existence of God, just as he does not posit a prior conception of man. His philosophy is an open philosophy, an "interrogation," which seeks only to explicitate our experience as it is given. If it moves towards God, this is a "hidden god," the only attainable by a "negative philosophy." Concerning religion he had moreover said already in 1947: "As an interrogation, it is justified on the condition that it remain answerless." (S, 203; *S*, 257)

33. Preface to Hesnard, *L'Œuvre de Freud*, p. 9.
34. "...Art and philosophy *together* are precisely not arbitrary fabrications in the universe of the 'spiritual' (of 'culture'), but contact with Being precisely as creations." (VI, 197; *VI*, 251)

## Chapter V

1. "We do not have to choose between a philosophy that installs itself in the world itself or in the other and a philosophy that installs itself 'in us,' between a philosophy that takes our experience 'from within' and a philosophy, if such be possible, that would judge it from without, in the name of logical criteria, for example: these alternatives are not imperative, since perhaps the self and the non-self are like the obverse and the reverse and since perhaps our own experience *is* this turning round that installs us far indeed from 'ourselves,' in the other, in the things. Like the natural man, we situate ourselves in ourselves *and* in the things, in ourselves *and* in the other, at the point where, by a sort of *chiasm*, we become the others and we become world. Philosophy ...abides at the point where the passage from the self into the world and into the other is effected, at the crossing of the avenues." (VI, 159-60; *VI*, 212) In attempting to spell out here his "method" and what he understands by "experience," what Merleau-Ponty refuses at the outset is the notion that phenomenology must limit itself to what is "immanent" to "consciousness." Since it is precisely the phenomenological (Husserlian) problematic that Merleau-Ponty refuses, we must not confuse the experience of the "natural man" of which he speaks with Husserl's "natural attitude" which, far from being natural, is already a philosophical (empiricist) interpretation of experience. It could be said that what Merleau-Ponty wants is precisely to bracket the starting point and the presuppositions of Husserlian phenomenology so as to have another look at what exactly the true relations between immanence and transcendence might be. In a working note he writes: "...a sufficient reduction leads beyond the alleged transcendental 'immanence' ". (VI, 172; *VI*, 226)

2. As the outlines and notes in *The Visible and the Invisible* clearly indicate, the question of Nature was also to occupy an important place in this last work.

3. "It is the aim of an inquiry such as we have pursued here on the ontology of nature to sustain through contact with beings and the exploration of the regions of Being the same attention to the fundamental that remains the privilege and the task of philosophy." (TFL, 112; *RC*, 156)

4.   "Husserl et la notion de Nature," *Revue de métaphysique et de morale* (July–Sept., 1965), p. 264. This article is a reconstruction by Xavier Tilliette of courses given by Merleau-Ponty at the Collège de France on March 14 and 25, 1957.

5.   The title of this course is itself very interesting and highly indicative of Merleau-Ponty's position which is itself at this time "at the limits of phenomenology."

6.   "Husserl et la notion de Nature," p. 268. Quotations in the following paragraph are all from p. 268 of this work.

7.   Merleau-Ponty is here using the term *este* (infinitive: *ester*) rather than *est* ("is") as an equivalent to Heidegger's term *west* ("is," from the infinitive of the old verb *wesen* which Heidegger reads etymologically as meaning "to be"). R. Manheim, the English-language translator of Heidegger's *Introduction to Metaphysics* (New Haven: Yale University Press, 1959), avoids having to give an English equivalent of *west* by completely rephrasing the sentence in question (cf. p. 102).

8.   Heidegger, *Introduction to Metaphysics*, pp. 14–5. On p. 101 Heidegger says (I am altering somewhat the English translation): " 'Being' means 'appearing.' Appearing is not something accidental that sometimes happens to being. Being is [*west*] as appearing."

9.   "Husserl's idealism ties up being with the transcendentally reduced consciousness....for Husserl 'being' exists only for consciousness, and...actually 'being' is nothing apart from the meaning which it receives by the bestowing acts of this consciousness." H. Spiegelberg, *The Phenomenological Movement* (The Hague: Martinus Nijhoff, 1960), vol. I, p. 143.

10.   See SNS, 93; SNS, 164: "This double sense of the *cogito* is the basic fact of metaphysics: I am sure that there is being—on the condition that I do not seek another sort of being than being-for-me." Merleau-Ponty also says (PhP, IX; PP, III): "I am the absolute source, my existence does not stem from my antecedents, from my physical and social environment; instead it moves out towards them and sustains them, for I alone bring into being for myself (and therefore into being in the only sense that the word can have for me) the tradition which I elect to carry on, or the horizon whose distance from me would be abolished—since that distance is not one of its properties—if I were not there to scan it with my gaze." In view of these texts and others of a similar sort (there is no lack of them), A. Dondeyne seems to us to be justified when he speaks of an "idealism of meaning" in Merleau-Ponty; he says for example: "To identify philosophy, a transcendental and basic mode of thought, with phenomenological description is possible only if one begins by setting up the phenomenon, that is to say being-for-us, as the supreme transcendental. The reduction of the whole of philosophy to phenomenology is an implicit acceptance of a more or less idealist interpretation of things, since one is claiming that 'to-be-for-man' is the *only* meaning that the word 'being' can have for us." *Contemporary European Thought and Christian Faith* (Pittsburgh: Duquesne University Press, 1963), p. 112. One could also say with Jean Beaufret (see Chapter 4 above) that the trouble with the *Phenomenology of Perception* is that it is not radical *enough* and that it is still too much dominated by Husserl's idealistic influence. In his later philosophy Merleau-Ponty will not say, as he does in the text just quoted, that I am the absolute source of my existence or that it is *I* who *bring into being* for myself everything that exists for me, that it is I who bring *presence* into being. In the *Phenomenology* Merleau-Ponty says that subject and object are "two abstract 'moments' of a unique structure which is *presence*." (PhP, 430; PP, 492) This notion of "presence" or "field of presence" (*Präsensfeld*) is one he borrows from Husserl (*Zeitbewusstsein*, pp. 32–35). Now in *The Visible and the Invisible* Merleau-Ponty says that Husserl's "error" is to have considered the *Präsensfeld* "as without thickness, as immanent consciousness." (VI, 173; VI, 227) As Claude Lefort observes, the reference here in *The*

*Visible and the Invisible* differs from those in the *Phenomenology* (PhP, 265, 415, 423, 430; PP, 307, 475, 483-4, 492) in that one does not yet find in the *Phenomenology* any criticism of Husserl. What is to be noted is that this criticism that Merleau-Ponty makes of Husserl in *The Visible and the Invisible* is at the same time a *self-criticism*. It is also the case for him in the *Phenomenology* that the field of presence is in the last resort "as without thickness, as immanent consciousness." He says for instance in this book that "all absence is merely the obverse of a presence" (PhP, 364; PP, 418)—which amounts to making presence (to the subject) the very definition of the world and of things, to defining the world and things solely in relation to the subject. Similarly, Merleau-Ponty's definition of the world as "horizon" comes down to making the subject the point of reference and the sine qua non of the world, since there would be no horizon "if I were not there to scan it with my gaze." Merleau-Ponty will not be successful in thinking a "transcendence in immanence" except by overcoming the "immanentism" of phenomenology, its idealism, and its subjectivism, except by recognizing the possibility of an *absence* or *latency* which is not merely the obverse of a presence. In his later philosophy Merleau-Ponty thinks Being not as mere presence but as that which, in its presence, announces itself to be the ground of this presence or its own possibility and which is itself irremediably absent. In a course at the Collège de France given in 1956 he says: "The *Phenomenology of Perception* overestimated the plenitude of the perceived which is present in person, of the *Dingwahrnehmung*, but in overaccenting this aspect it impoverished the other. It is necessary to reinstate the allusive, the lacunary character of perceived which is not a repletion of our sensation. The thing is far from being exhausted in our contact with it. *The thing is presence but also it is absence*." (Text quoted by X. Tilliette in "Maurice Merleau-Ponty ou la mesure de l'homme," *Philosophes contemporains* [Paris: Desclée de Brouwer, 1962], p. 59, emphasis ours.) This amounts to recognizing that the thing is not merely the correlate of our existence and is there before us only because it is drawn from an inexhaustible, *latent* ground (which is therefore not presentable) which encompasses even ourselves. X. Tilliette makes the following remark: "We have just heard Merleau-Ponty reintroduce, in a kind of retraction, the moment of latency, negativity, that on his own admission he had blurred in his thesis [the *Phenomenology*]." (Ibid, 62)

11.  The problem is basically that the *intentional* relation in Husserl is a relation of *constitution*. For Husserl the noesis-noema parallelism is not the last word; in the last resort the noema must serve as a transcendental index or clue referring back to an activity of *Sinngebung* or meaning-giving constitution on the part of a transcendental Ego which produces precisely the noesis-noema correspondence. Merleau-Ponty accepts in Husserl the basic phenomenological notion of a rigorous correspondence between "consciousness" and its "objects," but, having refused the notion of a constituting transcendental Ego, he is left, so to speak, with what is in fact a truncated phenomenology, since in the last analysis he has nothing to *justify* this necessary concordance. The ultimate subject for Merleau-Ponty is the lived body, but although it is the body which makes the world be for me as it is, the body itself can be understood only in relation to the world. One therefore remains in an incessant coming and going between one term of the relation and the other without ever arriving at the ultimate source of this dialectical relation. What therefore makes for an ambiguity in Merleau-Ponty's phenomenology is that he holds on to a basically idealistic interpretation of experience—the only meaning of being is its being for me—while refusing to accept the "logical" consequence of such a conception which is that of a "transcendental idealism." Hence what signals the passage from phenomenology to ontology in Merleau-Ponty is his realization that, like Husserl, he must find an "irrelative" as the source or foundation of these two "relativi-

ties"—"consciousness" (lived body) and "object" (perceived world)—but what definitively frees him from the Husserlian way and from all transcendental idealism is that he finds this "irrelative" not in a transcendental Ego but in Being.

12. Sartre, "Merleau-Ponty," *Situations IV* (Paris: Gallimard, 1964), p. 190.

13. Pascal, *Pensées,* 72 (Brunschvig edition).

14. It is in any event significant that Merleau-Ponty ends this discussion with the following warning: "It goes without saying that these lines commit their signer alone, and not the Christian collaborators who have so kindly agreed to give him their assistance. It would be a poor recognition of their aid to create the slightest ambiguity between their feelings and his. Nor does he give these lines as an introduction to their thought. They are more in the nature of reflections and questions he is writing in the margin of their texts in order to submit them to them." (S, 146; S, 184–5)

15. J. Hyppolite, *Genèse et structure de la Phénoménologie de l'Esprit* (Paris: Aubier, 1946), vol. I, p. 89, n. 2.

16. "The only 'place' where the negative would really be is the fold, the application of the inside and the outside to one another, the turning point." (VI, 264; *VI*, 317)

17. J. Hyppolite, *Etudes sur Marx et Hegel,* p. 187.

18. "This is not anthropologism: by studying the 2 leaves we ought to find the structure of being." (VI, 264; *VI*, 317)

19. "...we must understand that the *sensible world* is this perceptual logic, this system of equivalencies, and not a pile of spatio-temporal individuals. And this logic is neither *produced* by our psychophysical constitution, nor produced by our categorial equipment, but lifted from a *world* whose inner framework our categories, our constitution, our 'subjectivity' render explicit." (VI, 247–8; *VI*, 301)

20. Heidegger, *Lettre sur l'humanisme* (Paris: Aubier, 1964), p. 184. We are quoting from Heidegger's original letter to Jean Beaufret which is appended to the French translation of Heidegger's *Über den Humanismus*; the expressions given above in French are likewise in French in Heidegger's letter.

21. It is to this notion of a "narcissism" or a "promiscuity" of Being that one must relate Merleau-Ponty's fascination for the phenomenon of the *mirror* and the reflected image which is present in his work ever since the *Phenomenology* but which takes on a special meaning in his later writings. In "Eye and Mind," for instance, he says that it is no accident that so often in Dutch painting (among others) there is a mirror in the picture which concentrates and amplifies it. "The mirror appears," he says, "because I am seeing-visible, because there is a reflexivity of the sensible; the mirror translates and reproduces that reflexivity." (PriP, 168; *OE*, 33) The phenomenon of the mirror is a narcissistic phenomenon (cf. VI, 256; *VI*, 309); it re-expresses the "narcissism" of Being which is fission and doubling up into the seeing-visible couple. "Artists have often mused upon mirrors because beneath this 'mechanical trick,' they recognized... the metamorphosis of seeing and seen which defines both our flesh and the painters vocation." (PriP, 168–9; *OE*, 34)

22. "We cannot legitimately consider ourselves instruments of a soul of the world, group, or couple. Rather, we must conceive of a primordial We [*On*] that has its own authenticity and furthermore never ceases but continues to uphold the greatest passions of our adult life and to be experienced anew in each of our perceptions." (S, 175; S, 221)

23. The key to the notion of intersubjectivity (qua intercorporeality) is therefore this notion of the flesh as polymorphous generality which concretizes itself so as to form individuals. See for instance VI, 140; *VI*, 185: "If we can show that the flesh is an ultimate notion, that it is not the union or compound of two substances, but thinkable by itself, if there is a relation of the visible with itself that traverses me and constitutes

me as seer, this circle which I do not form, which forms me, this coiling over of the visible upon the visible, can traverse, animate other bodies as well as my own. And if I was able to understand how this wave arises within me, how the visible which is yonder is simultaneously my landscape, I can understand a fortiori that elsewhere it also closes over upon itself and that there are other landscapes besides my own. If it lets itself be captivated by one of its fragments, the principle of captation is established, the field open for other Narcissus, for an 'intercorporeality.' "

24. There can be no doubt that his expression, ὁμοῦ ἦν παντα ("All things were together"), which Merleau-Ponty introduces without any explanation in a working note is a reference to the pre-Socratics. It is precisely the expression which Aristotle attributes to them (cf. *Physics*, I, 4; 187a30).

25. Heidegger, *Introduction to Metaphysics*, p. 62.

26. Sartre says for instance: "It has been claimed that he came closer to Heidegger. This is hardly doubtful, but it must be properly understood." Sartre remarks that if after the death of his mother Merleau-Ponty "found the occasion to reread Heidegger," this, as he maintains, was "so as to better understand him, not to undergo his influence; their paths crossed, and that is all." *Situations IV*, p. 275.

27. Sartre, *L'Existentialisme est un humanisme* (Paris: Nagel, 1964), p. 36.

28. Sartre, *Situations IV*, p. 276.

29. Sartre, *L'Existentialisme est un humanisme*, pp. 38, 93.

30. Some people, however, believe they can detect a despondency in the later Merleau-Ponty, and they recall these lines which were written only a few months before his death: "To another life which ends too soon, I apply the standard of hope. To mine, which is perpetuated, the severe rule of death." (S, 27; S, 37) Can one therefore speak of a feeling on Merleau-Ponty's part of having failed? It is true that at the end of his life more than ever Merleau-Ponty did not believe in an imminent resolution of the conflicts of history, and this is one of the reasons why he lost all sympathy for communism. Our history, he said, is "a fall for whoever believed that history, like a fan, is going to fold in upon itself." (S, 35; S, 47) And it is also true that Merleau-Ponty was very much preoccupied with the idea of *death* after the death of his mother (see in this regard Sartre's very interesting article, "Merleau-Ponty" in *Situations IV*; Sartre relates how after the death of his mother Merleau-Ponty said one day to Simone de Beauvoir: "I am more than half dead.") The awareness of death, however, need not necessarily mean despair. On the contrary, the awareness of death can be the occasion for learning another kind of hope. Not that, to be sure, of the ardent revolutionary who believes in the inevitable victory of his cause, who believes that the establishment of a new humanity will soon bring history to its end, but the more nuanced hope of he who, having, as a consequence of having lived, lost his illusions, still experiences the hushed presence, on this side of deception and all passion, of that which properly speaking is unnameable, that which is present to us and supports us in its very absence, as immanent to us as our own life but as ungraspable as our birth and our death, that which is there as the ἀρχή and the τέλος of all presence, beneath and beyond death, the presence of "Σιγή the abyss." (VI, 179; VI, 233)

## Appendix I

1. Originally published under the title, "Autour de Merleau-Ponty: Deux lectures de son oeuvre," in *Philosophiques*, II, 1 (April 1975) the following is the record of a discussion between Theordore F. Geraets and G.B. Madison of their respective interpreta-

tions of Merleau-Ponty. The discussion took place at the annual meeting of the Canadian Philosophical Association in Toronto in 1974.

2.    Theordore F. Geraets, *Vers une nouvelle philosophie transcendantale. La genèse de la philosophie de M. Merleau-Ponty jusqu'à la Phénoménologie de la Perception* (The Hague: Martinus Nijhoff, 1971).

3.    Like Kierkegaard in relation to Hegel, in his reaction against Husserl's transcendental idealism Merleau-Ponty only succeeds in the *Phenomenology of Perception* in working out a philosophy of the *unhappy consciousness*. Now such a philosophy does not represent a break with idealism, for it continues to share its basic presuppositions (and this is the reason why in its reaction against idealistic optimism it is preoccupied with the *unhappiness* of consciousness.

4.    See for instance the book of Joseph Moreau, *L'horizon des esprits*: Essai critique sur la Phénoménologie de la perception (Paris: Presses Universitaires de France, 1968), as well as my article, "The Ambiguous Philosophy of Merleau-Ponty," *Philosophical Studies* (Ireland), XXII (1974), pp. 63-77.

5.    See for instance the book of Jean Piaget, *Sagesse et illusions de la Philosophie* (Paris: Presses Universitaires de France, 1968). In addition, the philosophical position of *The Structure of Behavior* and the *Phenomenology of Perception* does not seem to me to be capable of serving as a basis for a genuine mediation between the objective sciences of man and philosophy or of being able to instigate it; see my articles, "Le postulat d'objectivité dans la science et la philosophie du sujet," *Philosophiques*, I, 1 (April 1974), pp. 107-139 and "Ricoeur et la non-philosophie," *Laval théologique et philosophique*, XXIX, 3, (Oct. 1973), pp. 227-241.

6.    Michel Henry, "Phénoménologie de la conscience, Phénoménologie de la vie," in G.B. Madison, ed., *Sens et existence* (Paris: Editions du Seuil, 1975), p. 138.

7.    G. Granel, *Le sens du temps et de la perception chez E. Husserl* (Paris: Gallimard, 1968), p. 103. The text continues thus: "...if he had not himself died (but this time not of an essential death, on the contrary of a 'factitious' death, which makes a hole for us around which we are deprived of our own thought, which was in the process of coming to us through him, and which we perhaps will not have the force to make come to us by ourselves alone, and in any event never under that aspect)."

8.    Ibid., p. 114.

9.    Heidegger writes: "...die Sprache kein Werk des Menschen ist: die Sprache spricht. Der Mensch spricht nur, indem er der Sprache entspricht. Diese Sätze sind nicht die Ausgeburt einer phantastischen 'Mystik.'" "Einige Hinweise auf Hauptgeischtspunkte für das theologische Gespräch über 'Das Problem eines nichtobjektiveirenden Denkens und Sprechens in der heutigen Theologie," in *Les Archives de Philosophie* (1969), p. 404. One would nevertheless like to have more than mere assurances: one would like to know exactly why and how such remarks do not pertain to a fantastical mysticism.

10.    The page numbers cited here refer to the present English translation of *The Phenomenology of Merleau-Ponty*—Trans.

11.    X. Tilliette, *Merleau-Ponty ou la mesure de'homme* (Paris: Seghers, 1970), p. 91. (The reader will find a review by Tilliette of Madison's *La phénoménologie de Merleau-Ponty* in *Etudes* [July 1974] —Trans.

12.    P. Ricoeur, in his foreword to Madison's book, p. xiii.

13.    E. Weil, *Logique de la philosophie* (Paris: Vrin, 1950), p. 71 ff.

14.    *Vers une nouvelle philosophie transcendentale*, p. 171.

15.    This capital point is clearly expressed in my book, in a passage (p. 186) to which Madison refers (cf. above p. 271) but without bringing out the true meaning.

16.    Geraets subsequently published, in French, a lengthy review of *La Phénoménologie de Merleau-Ponty* in *Dialogue*, XIV, 3 (1975), pp. 517-525.—Trans.

## Appendix II

1. This article was presented, in a first version, to the Congress of the Canadian Philosophical Association, held in Fredericton in May 1977. I wish to thank my colleagues, the professors Dennis O'Connor and José Huertas-Jourda for their observations as well as the Canada Council which generously subsidized my research work in 1976-1977. "Merleau-Ponty et la Contre-Tradition" was originally published in *Dialogue*, XVII, 3 (1978), pp. 456-479.

2. Diogenes Laertius, *Vitae Philosophorum*, I, 16.

3. Merleau-Ponty himself said, speaking of Cartesian philosophy: "The history of philosophy can never be the simple transcription of what the philosophers have said or written....As a matter of fact, as soon as one approaches two texts and opposes to them a third, one begins to interpret and to distinguish what is really proper to the thought of Descartes, let us say, and, on the contrary, what is only accidental. Thus in Cartesianism, as it is defined by the texts, one begins to see an intention that the historian has taken the initiative in singling out, and this choice evidently depends on his own way of encountering the problems of philosophy. The history of philosophy cannot be separated from philosophy." (PriP, 46; SHP, 4)

4. Pascal, *Pensées*, 267, 272 (Brunschvicg edition).

5. In a letter to Lévy-Bruhl of March 11, 1935; cited by H. Spiegelberg, *The Phenomenological Movement* (The Hague: Martinus Nijhoff, 1960), vol. I, p. 84.

6. See for example, *Sein und Zeit*, sec. 29.

7. See my article, "Phenomenology and Existentialism: Husserl and the End of Idealism," in F. Elliston and P. McCormick, *Husserl: Expositions and Appraisals* (Notre Dame, Ind.: Notre Dame University Press, 1977); in this article I speak at greater length of Husserl's philosophical project and attempt to point out the important differences which separate it from those of the "existentialists."

8. Heidegger, *The Question of Being*, trans. by W. Kluback and J. Wilde (London: Vision Press, 1958), p. 79.

9. Speaking of this natural light, Merleau-Ponty says: "...the totality of beings known by the name of men and defined by the commonly known physical characteristics also have in common a natural light or opening to being which makes cultural acquisitions communicable to all men and to them alone." (S, 289-90; S, 314) The notion of natural light in Merleau-Ponty goes along with these others: communication, culture, rationality, universality.

10. Husserl, *Ideas*, trans. by W.R.B. Gibson (New York: Collier Books, 1962), pp. 350, 349.

11. When this good will is lacking, rationality itself, that is, the appeal to universality, is transformed into an instrument of oppression: "As a matter of fact, if I believe that I can rejoin the absolute principle of all thought and all evaluation on the basis of evidence, then I have the right to withdraw my judgments from the control of others on the condition that I have my consciousness for myself; my judgments take on a sacred character; in particular—in the realm of the practical—I have at my disposal a plan of escape in which my actions become transfigured: the suffering I create turns into happiness, ruse becomes reason, and I piously cause my adversaries to perish." (SNS, 95; SNS, 166-7)

12. Diogenes Laertius, *Vitae Philosophorum*, IX, 104-7.

13. Sextus Empiricus, *Phrrhoniarum hypotoposeon*, I, 13.

14. Ibid., I, 15.

15. Cf. Ibid., I, 192-3, 201.

16. Pascal, *Pensées*, 72 (Brunschvieg edition).

17.   I indeed say, without knowing it. For although Merleau-Ponty's position has many important affinities with those of the skeptics, it appears that he never had the occasion to free himself from the usual and altogether trivial idea people have of skepticism, namely as a position which maintains that "one can know nothing"—which perhaps describes what is called Academic skepticism but which has absolutely nothing to do with Pyrrhonian skepticism.

18.   Heidegger, *On Time and Being*, trans. by J. Stambaugh (New York: Harper and Row, 1972), p. 2.

19.   I am taking over this sentence from my study, *The Phenomenology of Merleau-Ponty*, to which I refer my reader for a more detailed consideration of Merleau-Ponty's "indirect ontology."

20.   Merleau-Ponty writes: "It is to our experience that we address ourselves....But the choice of this instance does not close the field of possible responses; we are not implicating in *'our experience'* any reference to an *ego* or to a certain type of intellectual relation with being, such as the Spinozist *'experiri.'* We are interrogating our experience precisely in order to know how it opens us to what is not ourselves. *This does not even exclude the possibility that we find in our experience a movement toward what could not in any event be present to us in the original and whose irremediable absence would thus count among our originating experiences.* But, if only in order to see these margins of presence, to discern these references, to put them to the test, or to interrogate them, we do indeed first have to fix our gaze on what is apparently *given* to us." (VI, 159; *VI*, 211)

21.   See Heidegger, "Letter on Humanism," in W. Barrett and H. Aiken, eds., *Philosophy in the Twentieth Century: An Anthology* (New York: Random House, 1962), vol. III, p. 276.

22.   Heidegger writes: "Man is rather 'cast' by Being itself into the truth of Being, in order that he, ex-sisting thus, may guard the truth of Being; in order that in the light of Being, beings as beings may appear as what they are." (Ibid., p. 281) "Thus, what matters in the determination of the humanity of man as ex-sistence is not that man is the essential, but that Being is the essential as the dimension of the ecstatic of ex-sistence." (Ibid., p. 283) Heidegger attempts to justify this *Ontogism* (in constrast to a "humanism") by saying that it makes of man something more noble than a mere "man": "Humanism is opposed because it does not set the *humanitas* of man high enough." (Ibid., p. 281)

23.   Pascal, *Pensées*, 72 (Brunschvieg edition).

24.   Pierre Charron, *De la sagesse* (Paris: 1824), vol. I, p. 2.

25.   IPP, 44; *EP*, 71. One is inclined to see here an echo to the famous text of Pascal on man, the thinking reed (*Pensées*, 347).

26.   *De la sagesse*, vol. II, p. 264.

27.   "Today a humanism does not oppose religion with an explanation of the world." (S, 241; *S*, 305)

28.   Merleau-Ponty writes: "With respect to God who is force, our existence was a failure and the world a decadence which we could not heal except by returning here below. To the God who is on the side of men corresponds, on the contrary, a forward-looking history which is an experience searching for its accomplishment." (IPP, 26; *EP*, 44–5) "...The Christian God wants nothing to do with a vertical relation of subordination. He is not simply a principle of which we are the consequence, a will whose instruments we are, or even a model of which human values are only the reflection. There is a sort of impotence of God without us, and Christ attests that God would not be fully God without becoming fully man." (S, 71; *S*, 88)

29. "Sur la cognoissance de Dieu," in *De la sagesse*, vol. II, pp. 340, 348. (Here one can see the relations between humanism, skepticism, and fideism.)

30. See Husserl, "Philosophy as A Rigorous Science," in *Phenomenology and the Crisis of Philosophy* (New York: Harper Torchbooks, 1965), p. 129 ff.

31. See Husserl, *The Crisis of European Sciences and Transcendental Phenomenology*, trans. by D. Carr (Evanston: Northwestern University Press, 1970), p. 341.

32. This is to say that humanism, skepticism, and liberalism are part of the same structure of thought; indeed, no genuine liberalism can exist without skepticism. The liberal author, F. Hayek, remarks in this regard: "The liberal differs from the conservative in his willingness to face this ignorance and to admit how little we know, without claiming the authority of supernatural sources of knowledge where his reason fails him. It has to be admitted that in some respects the liberal is fundamentally a skeptic...it seems to require a certain degree of diffidence to let others seek their happiness in their own fashion and to adhere consistently to that tolerance which is an essential characteristic of liberalism." "Why I Am Not a Conservative," in *The Constitution of Liberty* (South Bend, Ind.: Gateway Editions, 1972), p. 416.

33. "Thus the essential task of Marxism is to find a violence which recedes with the approach of man's future." (HT, XVIII; *HT*, XIV)

34. HT, 180; *HT*, 197. As regards the difference between the West and communism, "it is only a matter of the different uses of violence. Communism should be thought about and discussed as an attempt to solve the human problem and not be treated as an occasion for heated argument. It is a definite merit of Marxism and an advance in Western thought to have learned to confront ideas with the social functions they claim to articulate, to compare our perspective with others, and to relate our ethics to our politics. Any defense of the West which forgets these truths is a mystification." (HT, 177; *HT*, 191)

35. A "hesitation" in the sense in which Th. Geraets speaks of a hesitation on Merleau-Ponty's part in *The Structure of Behavior* where he wanted "neither to renounce all transcendental philosophy nor to definitively take up the point of view of transcendental, constituting consciousness." See Geraets, *Vers une nouvelle philosophie transcendentale*, p. 2.

36. Just as in his later philosophy in general he overcomes the "bad ambiguity" of the *Phenomenology of Perception*; see my book, *The Phenomenology of Merleau-Ponty*, p. 72.

37. Camus was one of these (the same Camus who, in the very first lines of *L'homme révolté* wrote: "There are crimes of passion and crimes of logic. The penal code distinguishes, rather conveniently, between them in tersm of premeditation. We are now in a time of premeditation and the perfect crime. Our criminals are no longer unarmed children who can invoke love as an excuse. They are, on the contrary, adults, and their alibi is irrefutable: philosophy can serve every purpose, even that of changing murderers into judges."), as Sartre tells us (see his article, "Merleau-Ponty," reprinted in *Situations IV*, p. 215). Merleau-Ponty's preoccupation with Marxism and his attempt to interpret it in a non-dogmatic, non-deterministic (non-orthodox) sense is already apparent in the *Phenomenology of Perception* where, in the chapter on "The Body in its Sexual Being," he subjects historical determinism to a severe criticism (PhP, 171-3; *PP*, 199-202), and in the chapter on Freedom where he speaks of class consciousness and the gaining of revolutionary awareness (PhP, 442-8; *PP*, 505-11). It is precisely this attempt on his part to "humanize" Marxism that he was going to abandon; Merleau-Ponty's Marxism was indeed something which was constantly diminishing (in his article Sartre remarks: "...I had the feeling that, before 1939, he had been closer to Marxism than he ever was afterwards" [*Situations IV*, p. 204], and he viewed *Humanism and Terror* as an impor-

tant stage in the way which led Merleau-Ponty ever further from Marxism).

38.    Merleau-Ponty attempts to "understand" this phenomenon in the second chapter of Part One of *Humanism and Terror*; see especially HT, 34–5; *HT*, 36–7.

39.    For an excellent analysis of the notion of the "objective enemy," see Hannah Arendt, *The Origins of Totalitarianism* (New York: Harcourt, Brace, Jovanovich, 1973), p. 423 ff.

40.    "We are calling for an effort of enlightenment which appears to us impossible for reasons of principle under a communist regime and possible in the noncommunist world." (AD, 227; *AD*, 306)

41.    I am using the word "liberal" in the traditional, European, and specifically Tocquevillian sense of the term, which has precious little to do with the Twentieth Century North American use of the term. It is perhaps worthwhile nothing that in his rejection of Marxism, Merleau-Ponty's attitude is identical with that of Camus, who in 1957 stated: "But without freedom, no socialism either, except the socialism of the gallows." (*Resistance, Rebellion, and Death* [New York: A. Knopf, 1969], p. 171). And, just as after the publication of Camus' systematic critique of Marxist mystification in *L'homme révolté* in 1951 Sartre instigated a vicious tirade against Camus, so also after the publication of *Adventures of the Dialectic* Sartre commissioned his friend Simone de Beauvoir, to publish a scathing attack on Merleau-Ponty.

42.    S, 322; *S*, 401. In this article Merleau-Ponty defends universal suffrage against direct democracy and the dictatorship of the proletariat; he says: "Even though they might be right as rain, those who 'know' cannot put their lights (which are, moreover, flickering ones) in the place of this consentment or refusal. The majority is not always right, but in the long run no one can be right in opposition to it; and if someone evades the test indefinitely, it means that he is wrong. Here we touch rock-bottom. Not that the majority is oracular, but because it is the only check."

43.    See AD, 85 ff; *AD*, 115 ff.

# Index